# IMPLEMENTATION PRACTICE & SCIENCE

Dean L. Fixsen, Karen A. Blase, Melissa K. Van Dyke

Published by: The Active Implementation Research Network

The Active Implementation Research Network is a non-profit organization. The AIRN Active Implementation Research Network™ is a learning organization established to advance implementation practice, research, and policy and to support the development of implementation science as a field and as a profession (https://www.activeimplementation.org).

Contact the publisher at info@activeimplementation.org.

Cover design: Julie Bedford, Jules Creative, LLC

First edition published June 2019

ISBN 978-1-0723655-2-5

Please cite as:

Fixsen, D. L., Blase, K. A., & Van Dyke, M. K. (2019). Implementation practice & science. Chapel Hill, NC: Active Implementation Research Network.

# Acknowledgements

We grew up professionally in the shadow of visionary leaders who taught us to pursue worthy goals and follow the data to overcome obstacles that may impede benefitting others. Montrose Wolf and colleagues created Applied Behavior Analysis, a new approach to understanding human behavior and conducting research to directly benefit recipients and society. Richard Schiefelbusch created the Bureau of Child Research, and Frances Horowitz established a new academic department. Together they taught a staid university how to support messy applied research and education. Saleem Shah at the National Institute of Mental Health led the way toward developing a new way to fund mission-driven research and promote collaboration among potential competitors. William Miller created Motivational Interviewing and established collaborative groups to support implementation capacity to extend its reach in human services. Their creativity and effectiveness were, and still are, inspirational. They demonstrated through their actions what Buckminster Fuller told us all: "You never change things by fighting against the existing reality. To change something, build a new model that makes the old model obsolete."

The information in this book reflects decades of developments in science and human services. The content is influenced by colleagues who do the work of implementation and scaling and evaluate the results and show us what is possible. We are especially indebted to Sonja Schoenwald and Keller Strother and the multisystemic therapy (MST) program; Rob Horner and George Sugai and the Positive Behavioral Interventions and Supports (PBIS) program; Terje Ogden and colleagues at the Norwegian Center for Child Behavioral Development; and Caryn Ward, Kathleen Ryan Jackson, and state-based colleagues who develop implementation capacity and evaluate the results in complex state education systems at the State Implementation and Scaling up of Evidence-based Programs (SISEP) Center. These dedicated professionals and friends have graciously shared their experiences with us for several decades, and we have benefitted greatly from their "bleeding edge" development of knowledge.

Our thanks to Deborah Price-Ellingstad, Jennifer Coffey, Larry Wexler, and Ruth Ryder for their visionary leadership in the U.S. Department of Education Office of Special Education Programs. They provided an opportunity to make implementation predictions, test those predictions in practice, and persistently engage in improvement methods in state education systems until intended outcomes were produced. The learning from this ongoing experience has rapidly advanced practice-based knowledge concerning the role of implementation capacity development in system change. Their ability to apply implementation principles to move a federal agency from compliance to implementation-informed support for improved education outcomes is to be admired.

We want to thank our colleagues who contributed directly to this book.

Amanda Fixsen (Invest in Kids) contributed new information for nearly every chapter in this book through syntheses of implementation frameworks, leading thinking on scaling in human services, and doing the work of implementation and scaling in state systems.

Monisa Aijaz (University of North Carolina at Chapel Hill) reviewed and revised versions of various chapters, clarified concepts and content, and tightened the language used to describe implementation and scaling.

Marie-Therese Schultes (University of Vienna) reviewed the literature and provided an overview of theory and the philosophy of science that informs the content of the chapter on science and implementation.

Hana Haidar (Oxford University) and Sarah Pinkelman (Utah State University) made editorial and professional contributions to the chapter on scaling.

Jonathan Green taught us about instructional design and communication strategies for dissemination of information and did the final formatting to prepare this book for publication.

Rosemarie Kitchin did meticulous and timely copy editing and greatly improved the "final" version of the manuscript.

We thank Claire Burns, Fiona Mitchell, and Eleanor McClorey for their commitment to the application of implementation science and the full and effective use of implementation practice, as well as their professional courage to do whatever it takes to deliver socially significant outcomes for the children and families of Scotland.

We thank Herbert Peterson and Joumana Haidar and the WHO Collaborating Center for Research Evidence for Sexual and Reproductive Health for their enthusiastic support for developing implementation and scaling capacity generally and in the global health community. Their concern for underserved populations provides inspiration for learning more and doing more to produce benefits for all.

Finally, we thank the thousands of people who have participated enthusiastically in our many missteps and eventual successes over the past several decades. Their dedication to "making things better" for recipients of human services is beyond question, and their contributions to the content of this book are beyond measure. Thank you!

# Table of Contents

Chapter 1: Introduction ...................................................................1

Chapter 2: Science and Implementation ........................................ 9

Chapter 3: Definitions.....................................................................19

Chapter 4: Getting Started in Practice......................................... 27

Chapter 5: Strong Variables ......................................................... 53

Chapter 6: Usable Innovations ..................................................... 69

Chapter 7: Implementation Stages ...............................................81

Chapter 8: Implementation Drivers Overview............................. 109

Chapter 9: Implementation Competency Drivers ....................... 121

Chapter 10: Role Play and Behavior Rehearsal...........................163

Chapter 11: Implementation Organization Drivers.....................169

Chapter 12: Implementation Leadership Drivers ........................187

Chapter 13: Improvement Cycles................................................. 201

Chapter 14: Implementation Teams ............................................ 227

Chapter 15: Systemic Change....................................................... 255

Chapter 16: Scaling Implementation Capacity and Innovation Outcomes .................. 281

Chapter 17: A Future for Implementation ................................... 329

References .................................................................................... 333

# Chapter 1: Introduction

To implement is to use. Implementation practice, policy, and science are concerned with the use of innovations in situations where they can add value. It is a truism that people cannot benefit from innovations they do not experience. That is, if innovations are not used as intended, they cannot produce intended results. This fact is the basis for implementation practice and science. The purpose of implementation is to assure the full and effective use of innovations in practice, that is, their use with fidelity and socially significant outcomes. Whatever facilitates or impedes the full and effective use of innovations in practice is the subject matter for implementation practice, policy, and science.

*Populations benefit when effective innovations are supported by effective implementation in enabling contexts that facilitate their use on a socially significant scale.*

Fundamentally, implementation is synonymous with change. To consider the use of innovations is to admit that the current state of affairs (the status quo) is not what it should be. If it is true that each system is perfectly (if unwittingly) designed to produce its current outcomes, then the use of innovations to produce new and improved outcomes requires changes in behavior. Practitioners, managers, directors, funders, regulators, and so on need to learn new ways of doing their work in support of innovations. Implementation must be done well to achieve improved system outcomes.

Implementation is designed to improve socially significant outcomes. It is not enough to do something well one time or even a few times. A few people may benefit from interesting experiments, but not whole populations, and not society. As represented in the Formula for Success (Figure 1), populations benefit when effective innovations are supported by effective implementation in enabling contexts that facilitate use on a socially significant scale.

## Formula For Success

| Effective Innovations | ✗ | Effective Implementation | ✗ | Enabling Contexts | = | Socially Significant Outcomes |
|---|---|---|---|---|---|---|

Figure 1. The Formula for Success.  Fixsen, Naoom, Blase, Friedman, and Wallace (2008, July)

As a factor in producing socially significant outcomes, implementation must be done on purpose And, effective implementation methods must be teachable, learnable, doable, and assessable in practice so that scalable units can be replicated and expanded and improved. Scalable units include effective innovations and effective implementation.  Scaling up innovations to benefit whole populations requires scaling up implementation capacity.  This requires organization and policy contexts that enable effective implementation supports for effective innovations.

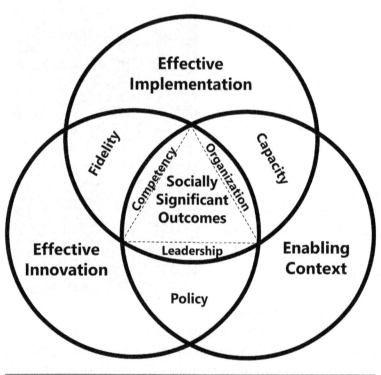

Figure 2. Relationships among factors in the Formula for Success interacting to produce socially significant outcomes

Effective implementation is the missing link in human service systems. It is the reason for the lack of progress in education, social services, and prevention of debilitating and costly diseases where effective innovations have been available and policies have been encouraging, but implementation supports have been weak or missing. Without attention to effective innovations, effective implementation, and enabling contexts socially significant outcomes cannot be produced on purpose and wellbeing will continue to churn around a mediocre mean.

Note that the practice and science of implementation is a separate sphere of influence in the Formula for

2

Success (Figure 2). Like a serum and a syringe, doing more research on syringes will not produce a better serum, and neither one will be useful without adequate system supports for medical organizations to assure the availability of qualified providers and adequate supplies of materials. In the Formula for Success, each factor is important and has an independent basis in practice and science. Nevertheless, they need to be orchestrated and integrated so they will work together to produce intended population benefits.

Implementation is an endlessly fascinating topic. Like any science, every solution simply exposes the next set of problems to solve. If, after years of work, Y is established as the solution to problem Z, then inquiry moves to defining the X conditions necessary for doing Y on purpose so lots of Z problems can be solved. The independent variable in a previous iteration becomes the dependent variable in the next iteration. After a particularly thorny implementation issue finally is resolved, it's like the universe pats us on the head and says, "That's nice, now try this!" For implementation practitioners, researchers, and policy makers, frustration and dissatisfaction are an inescapable part of their work and an inexhaustible source of motivation to do better next time. Winston Churchill might have been describing the history of implementation when he said, "Success is the ability to go from one failure to another with no loss of enthusiasm."

The goal of implementation is the full and effective use of innovations in practice. In this sense, it is mission driven. In the mission-driven mode, barriers are not just to be studied and lamented. Barriers are to be overcome, not once but routinely as implementation supports for an innovation are expanded to encompass an entire national or global effort. Implementation supports must be developed and expanded as the need for an innovation is expanded.

The successful global effort to eradicate smallpox (Fenner, Henderson, Arita, JeZek, & Ladnyi, 1988; Foege, 2011) is a lesson in overcoming barriers. In retrospect, it provides many examples of implementation best practices: for example, use of a Transformation Zone to develop the surveillance and containment program as a Usable Innovation; develop and replicate Implementation Teams to support the use of the surveillance and containment program in region after region in one country after another; assess fidelity of the use of the intervention and implementation methods; use a Decision Support Data System for prompt and effective action planning; and use of Practice-Policy Communication Cycles to direct federal and global action. All of these are recognized as best practices from a modern viewpoint (Fixsen, Blase, Metz, & Van Dyke, 2015; Fixsen, Naoom, Blase, Friedman, & Wallace, 2005) and are described in this book.

Implementation is an important component of the evidence-based movement that has permeated all social sciences and human services. There is great appeal to the idea that governments and service agencies funded by governments should make use of innovations demonstrated to be effective (Haskins & Baron, 2011). Why invest in using what does not work when effective alternatives (evidence-based innovations) are available for use? In their quest for social impact, governments and service agencies are learning to value what is required to support the use of effective innovations. Why leave outcomes to chance when effective alternatives (purposeful implementation supports) are available to realize intended outcomes? There is great appeal to the idea of improving social impact by using Implementation Science to purposefully initiate, manage, and support changes in practices, service organizations, and large systems (Glennan Jr., Bodilly, Galegher, & Kerr, 2004; Kessler & Glasgow, 2011; Perl, 2011).

Given the slow development of implementation as a science, the importance of implementation factors has been slow to be recognized and acted upon. After large investments to achieve national goals in human services did not result in the intended socially significant outcomes, policy makers were among the first to call attention to the need for implementation supports for public policy (Chase, 1979; Pressman & Wildavsky, 1973; Rittel & Webber, 1973; Van Meter & Van Horn, 1975). Only recently has Implementation Science advanced far enough to provide a useful response to these issues. While this is just beginning, it is easy to see where it will lead: more purposeful, more data-based, and more effective implementation practices in human services.

The use of implementation practices on purpose is important for producing breakthroughs in how human services are developed and supported. Kenneth Arrow (1962) won the Nobel Prize for developing information economics. Arrow observed that knowledge-based resources *increase* with use. In contrast, atom-based resources are *depleted* with use. The rapid expansion of digital technologies to support knowledge sharing is testament to the accuracy of Arrow's predictions. Purposeful use of implementation knowledge and best practices likely will lead to a vastly improved knowledge base as implementation practices are used on purpose; their results are studied; the improved practices are used on purpose the next time; and the process is repeated. As implementation knowledge-based resources increase with use, socially significant improvements in health, education, and social wellbeing can be expected in the next few decades.

The development of implementation practice and science in general continues to be multi-disciplinary. The science used to develop innovations is not the same as the science used to develop implementation. And, each is different from the science of organization and system change. With *contributions from* a variety of fields, implementation is now a discipline unto itself. Implementation Science is transdisciplinary, and now makes *contributions to* the many disciplines it borrowed from *en route* to this point of independence. In part because of the profusion of influences on the development of implementation, the field has vestiges of those influences that contribute to confusion. A major impediment to rapid advancements in Implementation Science is the lack of commonly defined concepts, descriptions, and terms. Whereas there is significant alignment in implementation concepts across frameworks, descriptions and terms vary. To progress as a field will require all contributors to manage the desire to hold on to that which is most familiar or one's own niche. This includes the authors of this book.

Like any science, the science of implementation will advance when there are common concepts, common language, and common measures that promote communication within and across disciplines. As we approach the commonalities that enable communication, then advances in science can be crowdsourced with readily understood information leading to the next predictions that can be tested in practice anywhere in the world.

## Active Implementation Frameworks

The implementation knowledge base has been organized in major reviews of the diffusion and dissemination literature (Greenhalgh, Robert, MacFarlane, Bate, & Kyriakidou, 2004), implementation research literature (Fixsen, Naoom, et al., 2005), and policy implementation literature (Saetren, 2005). Two reviews (Meyers, Durlak, & Wandersman, 2012; Tabak, Khoong, Chambers, & Brownson, 2012) have documented 32 different implementation frameworks. The fact that only five frameworks appeared on two lists published in the same year is testament to the confused and fragmented status of "implementation" as an emerging professional discipline and field of study.

The Active Implementation Frameworks have been developed to reduce the clutter and improve the focus on variables that seem to matter when attempting to use innovations in practice. The Active Implementation Frameworks are a product of the past few decades of doing the work of implementation, examining and synthesizing the literature related to implementation, and working with policy and system leaders. The Active Implementation Frameworks are:

# Active Implementation Frameworks

**Usable Innovations**

**Implementation Stages**

**Implementation Drivers**

**Implementation Teams**

**Improvement Cycles**

**Systemic Change**

The Active Implementation Frameworks in this format did not exist ten years ago, and it is expected that continued developments coming from evaluations of practice and research will produce substantially improved versions ten years from now. The Active Implementation Frameworks are based on:

1. The experience of groups doing and evaluating the work of implementation and the accompanying organization and system change over the past five decades (e.g. Bond, Becker, & Drake, 2011; Drake, Goldman, et al., 2001; Fixsen, Blase, Metz, & Van Dyke, 2013; Fixsen, Blase, Timbers, & Wolf, 2001; Fixsen, Phillips, & Wolf, 1978; Glennan Jr. et al., 2004; Havelock & Havelock, 1973; Nord & Tucker, 1987; Omimo et al., 2018; Schoenwald, Sheidow, & Letourneau, 2004; Schoenwald, Sheidow, Letourneau, & Liao, 2003; Vernez, Karam, Mariano, & DeMartini, 2006),

2. Qualitative analyses of information collected systematically from groups of experienced evidence-based program developers and users (Blase & Fixsen, 2003; Blase, Fixsen, Naoom, & Wallace, 2005; Blase, Naoom, Wallace, & Fixsen, 2005b; Fixsen, Blase, Naoom, & Haines, 2005; Fixsen, Blase, Naoom, & Wallace, 2006a, 2006b; Fixsen et al., 2001; Fixsen, Naoom, et al., 2005; Naoom, Blase, & Fixsen, 2006),

3. Comprehensive reviews of the diffusion, dissemination, and implementation evaluation literatures (Brownson, Colditz, & Proctor, 2012; Fixsen, Naoom, et al., 2005; Greenhalgh et al., 2004; Meyers et al., 2012; Tabak et al., 2012), and

4. The use of current versions of the Active Implementation Frameworks in practice. As the first users of new ideas and methods the practice-based evidence provides firsthand experience with the outcomes (did the ideas work or not?). The reality test keeps the Active Implementation Frameworks grounded in methods and measures that are usable and useful in practice (Fixsen & Blase, 2018; Fixsen et al., 2013).

Descriptions of practice and research related to each of the Active Implementation Frameworks are the subjects for a chapter. We will explain each component of the frameworks and how each component interacts with the other components to produce socially significant outcomes. We document relevant research literature for many components. We present concepts and provide operational advice to link concepts to front-line practice. Examples from the experiences of colleagues and others serve to reinforce key points throughout the text.

The Active Implementation Frameworks are an example of bottom-up development (Pülzl & Treib, 2006; Sabatier, 1986), where the experience of doing the work is examined, and the process of doing the work is improved with discernable outcomes in practice (Fixsen & Blase, 2018). Reality is a severe disciplinarian. Good ideas, concepts, approaches, methods, and tools generated by a variety of people over the decades have been used in practice; only the effective, efficient, and repeatable examples have survived the severe tests of usability and effectiveness in practice.

While the history of implementation dates to an earlier time (Saetren, 2005, 2014), the Great Society programs that began in the U.S. in the 1960s mark the beginning of implementation as a self-conscious set of activities and outcomes. The book on *Implementation* by Pressman and Wildavsky (1973) anticipates the developments in the field with its complete title *Implementation: How Great Expectations in Washington are Dashed in Oakland: or, Why It's Amazing that Federal Programs Work at All, This Being a Saga of the Economic Development Administration as Told by Two Sympathetic Observers Who Seek to Build Morals on a Foundation of Ruined Hopes*. The 1960s were a time of declarations of lofty goals and investments in great change in the U.S. Some goals like sending astronauts to the moon and returning them safely, and completing half of the intended 41,000 mile "National System of Interstate and Defense Highways" in ten years were realized in that decade (Dicht, 2009; McNichol, 2006). Other goals–to eliminate poverty; to provide disadvantaged children with a head start in education and follow through in grades K-3; to create jobs for all; and to redevelop healthy urban centers (the subject of the book on *Implementation*)–were not so successful then (Rossi & Wright, 1984; Watkins, 1995). These goals remain challenges today.

The authors of this book did not set out to develop implementation frameworks. We were attempting to understand how to replicate and scale effective innovations, and that still is our goal. Since the 1970s Dean Fixsen and Karen Blase have reviewed practices, read the literature, and accumulated increasingly long lists of "things that apparently matter" when success is achieved. Since 2004 the authors have tried to make sense of the lists by sorting the things that apparently matter under conceptual headings. The frameworks emerged as these conceptual labels were organized into groupings. The long lists remained and became ways to operationalize (put into practice) the conceptual labels. As new experience and new data became available, they either fit the concept labels and frameworks, or the frameworks were changed to include the new findings. For example, the Installation Stage of implementation emerged from experience. Experience taught us and our colleagues that promises made during the Exploration Stage were not always realized during the Initial Implementation Stage. Once this became clear as a general problem, the Installation Stage was established as part of the Implementation Stages framework to discriminate the activities required to establish or acquire the resources required to do the work.

Today, implementation practice has established implementation independent variables worthy of study. The implementation supports that produce full and effective use of effective innovations are now well-established and are being replicated every day in practice. These efforts produce implementation independent variables that can be manipulated, measured, and studied. Some examples of long-term practice-based implementation studies include Assertive Community Treatment (Bond & Salyers, 2004; Teague, Bond, & Drake, 1998; Test, 2010), Multisystemic Therapy (Brunk, Chapman, & Schoenwald, 2014; Henggeler, Pickrel, & Brondino, 1999; Schoenwald et al., 2004), Parent Management Training Oregon (Forgatch, Patterson, & DeGarmo, 2005; Ogden, Forgatch, Askeland, Patterson, & Bullock, 2005; Tommeraas & Ogden, 2016), Motivational Interviewing (W. R. Miller & Mount, 2001; W. R. Miller, Yahne, Moyers, Martinez, & Pirritano, 2004), Positive Behavior Interventions and Support (Horner et al., 2004; McIntosh, Mercer, Nese, & Ghemraoui, 2016; Sugai, Sprague, Horner, & Walker, 2000), and the Teaching-Family Model (Blase, Fixsen, & Phillips, 1984; Fixsen & Blase, 2018; Fixsen et al., 2001; Phillips, Phillips, Fixsen, & Wolf, 1971). The Brookings Institution (2018) refers to exemplars like these as "real-time scaling labs" where knowledge is generated by systematically examining proactive and replicated practice.

The purpose of this book is to sum up the past century of development of implementation practice, science, and policy, and to prepare a path for more rapid development in the future. Implementation practice, science, and policy are mission driven. The mission is to assure that children, families, individuals, villages, communities, and society benefit from effective innovations used as intended in practice.

In practice, implementation is complex and interactive. Chaos theory, complexity theory, principles related to cybernetics and complex adaptive systems, and other views of complex and interactive phenomena help set the foundations for understanding and describing implementation. On the other hand, words on pages are linear, and ideas are presented one at a time—a poor fit with the topic. Yet, that is what we have to offer in the ensuing chapters. To reflect the interactive nature of Implementation Science and practice, similar content and data will be presented at different places in the book to highlight different aspects of an integrated approach to implementation.

# Chapter 2: Science and Implementation

While Implementation Science has been developing for some time (Saetren, 2005), in the last few decades it has begun to develop rapidly. For example, on December 15, 2018, a Google Scholar search for "implementation research" yielded 80,600 returns, 23% of them since 2014. A search for "implementation science" produced 46,100 returns with 40% of them since 2014. Rapid development can be attributed to recognition of the role of implementation in closing the science-to-service gap: the gap between substantial investments in developing effective innovations and the continuing need for significant improvements in health, education, and social services (Bryk, 2016; Kessler & Glasgow, 2011; Perl, 2011).

Given the increasing attention to Implementation Science, the purpose of this chapter is to explore Implementation Science as a science. The idea of science, and the use of the scientific method to test predictions and hypotheses to advance science, are discussed in the practical contexts faced by implementation scientists.

*Implementation science is a science to the extent that 1) predictions are made and 2) those predictions are tested in practice using the scientific method.*

## What is science?

The Merriam-Webster dictionary (https://www.merriam-webster.com/) defines *science* as the "system of knowledge covering general truths or the operation of general laws especially as obtained and tested through scientific method." The *scientific method* is defined as "principles and procedures for the systematic pursuit of knowledge involving the recognition and formulation of a problem, the collection of data through observation and experiment, and the formulation and testing of hypotheses." In his book *The Invention of Science*, Wootton (2015, p. 393) says, "What makes it science is not that it provides an explanation but that it provides reliable predictions." Wootton points to the mission-driven nature of science by noting that "One must always proceed from wonder to no wonder; that is, one should continue one's investigation until that which we thought strange no longer seems strange to us." (Wootton, 2015, p 299, citing the Dutch philosopher and scientist Isaac Beeckman, 1626).

## What is Implementation Science?

The Merriam-Webster dictionary defines *implement* as "to equip" and as a "device used in the performance of a task." After decades of study, Blase, Van Dyke, Fixsen, and Bailey (2012) define *Implementation Science* as "the study of factors that influence the full and effective use of innovations in practice. The goal of Implementation Science is not to answer factual questions about what is, but to determine what is required (mission driven)." That is, to "proceed from wonder to no wonder" as implementation knowledge is developed.

## Predictions and hypotheses

If reliable predictions define science, and testing predictions is the work of scientists, then Implementation Science is a science to the extent that 1) predictions are made and 2) those predictions are tested in practice using the scientific method. *Predictions* are made in the form of if-then statements. For example, *if* implementation supports are provided with expertise (an implementation independent variable), *then* practitioners will use effective innovations consistently with fidelity and socially significant outcomes (implementation dependent variables). A prediction can be confirmed or disconfirmed. *Hypotheses* are tentative, testable, and falsifiable explanations for observed phenomena. Hypotheses can be disconfirmed, but never "proven" by data. Thomas Huxley is quoted as saying, "The great tragedy of science–the slaying of a beautiful hypothesis by an ugly fact." Sutton and Staw (1995, p. 376) note that "Hypotheses ... serve as crucial bridges between theory and data, making explicit how the variables and relationships that follow from a logical argument [a theory] will be operationalized." For example, Einstein predicted the images of stars would appear to shift when the sun is close by. When this prediction was confirmed during a solar eclipse in 1919, the theory of relativity was not disproven, and the idea of spacetime gained credence.

# Theory

*Theory* is a source of predictions (if-then) and hypotheses (explanations of if-then relationships) that lead to observations to confirm or disconfirm theory-based predictions. The relationships between theory, hypotheses, and predictions are likely what Moll (1990) had in mind when he wrote, "Without theory it is hard to talk about practice and without practice, theory has no meaning."

Five criteria that define a theory have been outlined by Carpiano and Daley (2006, p. 565).

1. Logic: The major concepts and relations should be logically coherent. Terms must be clearly defined so that they can be understood by those examining the theory.
2. Causality: The goal of theoretically based research is to identify the systematic components of a set of factors that produce change in the phenomena being studied. Causal drivers and a sense of causal process should be clearly identified.
3. Falsification: At least some of the major propositions should be empirically falsifiable. All useful theories suggest ways in which they may be subjected to empirical assessment.
4. Scope: Although it can change over time, the scope of the theory should be clear and relatively broad. It must be focused on generic processes and not unique characteristics of any specific situation or case.
5. Productivity: The theory should promote non-obvious implications and produce a relatively large number of predictions per assumption.

Popper (1963, p. 39) adds another criterion:

6. Prohibition: Every "good" scientific theory forbids certain things to happen. The more a theory forbids, the better it is.

With respect to Carpiano and Daley's criterion regarding scope, the Improved Clinical Effectiveness through Behavioural Research Group (2006) distinguishes among grand theories, mid-range theories, and micro-theories. These are summarized in Table 1.

**Table 1. Levels of theory as defined by the Improved Clinical Effectiveness through Behavioural Research Group (2006)**

| Scope | Definition | Purpose |
|---|---|---|
| Grand or Macro Theory | A grand or macro theory is a very broad theory that encompasses a wide range of phenomena. | A grand theory is a general construction about the nature and goals of a discipline. |
| Mid-Range Theory | A mid-range theory is more limited in scope, less abstract, addresses specific phenomena, and reflects practice. It encompasses a limited number of concepts and a limited aspect of the real world. | Mid-range theory is designed to guide empirical inquiry.<br><br>Mid-range theories are made up of relatively concrete concepts that are operationally defined and relatively concrete propositions that can be empirically tested. |
| Micro Theory | A micro, practice or situation-specific theory (sometimes referred to as prescriptive theory) has the narrowest range of interest. | Focuses on specific phenomena that reflect specific practices and are limited to specific populations or to a particular field of practice. |

Based on these criteria, the Active Implementation Frameworks qualify as a mid-range theory of implementation.

With these ideas in mind, theory is a guide for practice and a source of testable predictions and hypotheses that serve to strengthen or disconfirm the relationships posited in the theory. As noted earlier, Wootton (2015, p. 393) says, "What makes it science is not that it provides an explanation but that it provides reliable predictions." To paraphrase, what makes it theory is that it provides explanations for predictions and conceptual labels for discrete facts.

## Scientific method

As noted earlier, the scientific method is defined as "principles and procedures for the systematic pursuit of knowledge involving the recognition and formulation of a problem, the collection of data through observation and experiment, and the formulation and testing of hypotheses." In this definition, there is no preference for one or another form of "collection of data through observation and experiment." For example, in Wootton's book on the history of the development of science as an idea and as a set of disciplines, repeated observations of individual examples formed the basis for the science of physics, chemistry, and so on. Bernard (1865), who wrote the first text on experimental medicine, argues strongly in favor of functional analyses of individual cases as the basis of science. Gertner (2012) describes the productivity of scientists at Bell Labs who averaged more than one new patent every day for more than 50 years with a focus on small scale experiments. There is no mention of a randomized control trial in any of these sources. Thus, good science has been and can continuc to be done using a variety of scientific methods that value predictions, observation, and replication.

## Implementation independent variables

Predictions in the if-then logical format necessarily require a way to first produce the "if." In physics, chemistry, biology, and other "hard sciences," scientists can study natural phenomena that exist everywhere (e.g., every living thing has chromosomes that can be studied at any time; chemical elements already exist and are waiting to be observed). The independent variable often exists in nature, much like the stars and the solar eclipse in the study of Einstein's prediction based on the theory of relativity. In the so-called "soft sciences," things are much more difficult: *the independent variable must be produced by the scientist.* Unlike waiting for a solar eclipse, implementation scientists cannot wait for an expert implementation team (a postulated implementation independent variable: see Chapter 14) to form and begin to function and then assess the outcomes. This may never happen in any predictable and assessable way.

In this regard Wootton (2015) distinguishes between discovery and invention. If something already exists, a scientist or explorer can discover it. America, a land mass that already existed, was discovered by Europeans in 1492. Gravity already existed before Galileo described the "law of fall" and Newton described it in a mathematical formula. Chromosomes already existed before Watson and Crick developed a framework (the double helix) to understand the data already collected by others. On the other hand, inventions are new and do not exist in nature. According to Wootton, science itself was invented in the 1600s by those who valued facts (a new idea ca.1661) over philosophy, and who used experimental methods (a new idea ca.1675) to answer questions and to replicate findings (a new idea ca.1657). Transistors did not exist before they were invented by scientists and technicians at Bell Labs. "Surveillance and containment" methods did not exist before they were invented and used by global health scientists to eradicate smallpox.

This is an important distinction because implementation scientists must be able to produce the independent variable (if this) so that predictions of its effects can be measured (then that). *The independent variable in Implementation Science is an invention.* At this point, soft-science increases in complexity because each independent variable must be created and, therefore, is a dependent variable. Consider the logic:

1. An implementation scientist must be able to produce the independent variable (if this) so that it can be studied. For example, a prediction might be that if a high-functioning Implementation Team supports practitioners' use of an evidence-based program, then the practitioners will use the evidence-based program with high fidelity and socially significant outcomes.

2. Production of the independent variable itself requires the research group to possess an adequate level of implementation knowledge and skill. For example, who produces Implementation Teams? How can the research group produce the Implementation Teams reliably and effectively within an experimental design?

   a. A contributor to the complexity of Implementation Science is that each independent variable required to test a prediction is, itself, a dependent variable in the context of a test of the prediction.

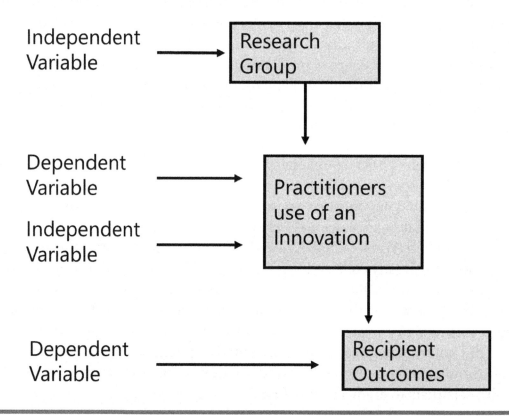

Figure 3. A logic model showing how a dependent variable at one level is an independent variable at the next level

14

The overall logic is presented in Figure 3. A research group must be sufficiently skilled in using implementation practice (the independent variable) to produce practitioners who use an innovation with fidelity (the dependent variable). At the next level, the practitioners' use of an innovation with fidelity (the independent variable) is assessed in terms of benefits to recipients (the dependent variable). In this example, the fidelity of practitioners' use of an innovation is both a dependent variable and an independent variable. Perhaps this dual role helps to explain the number of studies of fidelity and its role in producing desired outcomes and in analyzing outcome data (e.g. Bartley, Bright, & DePanfilis, 2017; Durlak & DuPre, 2008; K. D. Hurley, Lambert, Gross, Thompson, & Farmer, 2017; Naleppa & Cagle, 2010; Sanetti & Kratochwill, 2014; Tommeraas & Ogden, 2016).

How, then, can implementation independent variables be produced on purpose? Perhaps by using implementation best practices to produce them? The circularity of developing Implementation Science as a science becomes apparent—some implementation knowledge and skillful uses of best practices are required to produce implementation independent variables suitable for study.

This calls for a different perspective on developing theory and testing hypotheses and predictions in Implementation Science. For example, Galileo had a powerful (at that time) telescope built to sharpen his observations of the night sky. However, he did not have to produce the stars that were the object of the observations. The difference is implementation scientists need to "produce the stars." That is, they need to be able to produce high-functioning implementation teams if they want to study implementation teams. The independent variable is not already there waiting to be observed.

To establish implementation independent variables, Implementation Science must rely on implementation practice. Fortunately, implementation practice has been developing and improving since the middle of the twentieth century. Best practices have been summarized and operationalized, and lists of best practices have been organized into coherent frameworks to guide implementation practice in human services and other fields (for recent examples, see: Allanson et al., 2017; Blanchard et al., 2017; Blase, Fixsen, et al., 2005; Fixsen, Naoom, et al., 2005; Glennan Jr. et al., 2004; Greenhalgh et al., 2004; Meyers et al., 2012; Øvretveit, Mittman, Rubenstein, & Ganz, 2017; Schoenwald & Garland, 2013). Implementation best practices are needed to establish implementation independent variables at the right time and place and with the quality required to test predictions and hypotheses.

For example, a multi-national study of facilitation (an implementation independent variable) found no effect on organization staff use of effective innovations or on patient outcomes (Seers et al., 2018). Post hoc analyses found that facilitation was not used as intended (with fidelity) in each of the organizations (Harvey, McCormack, Kitson, Lynch, & Titchen, 2018; Rycroft-

Malone et al., 2018). Thus, the research group did not produce high fidelity examples of facilitation and, therefore, facilitation was not available for study as an independent variable.

In contrast is a large-scale study of community health workers (CHWs) who delivered individual and combined water, sanitation, handwashing (WSH) and child nutrition interventions to the homes and families of pregnant women in rural villages in Bangladesh. In this study, the fidelity of delivery of the innovation was assessed proactively from the beginning. After three months, fidelity was found to be well below the pre-set benchmarks of 80% for each independent variable. The research group made adjustments to improve the delivery of services, and the fidelity scores improved (in the 86% to 93% range). At the end of the study the multiple benefits of the combined WSH intervention were substantial (Rahman et al., 2018; Tofail et al., 2018). The research group produced high fidelity examples of the combined intervention and, therefore, the independent variable was available for study and was found to be effective for producing improvements in water quality, handwashing, sanitation, and nutrition.

As illustrated in this section, Implementation Science depends on implementation practice, and implementation best practices must be used by research groups if high fidelity independent variables are to be available to study. Assessing the fidelity (presence and strength) of an implementation independent variable is essential to any study that hopes to advance implementation as a science.

## Observation

Predictions in the if-then logical format require a way to observe the "then" to see if a prediction is disconfirmed in practice. When describing the invention of science, Wootton (2015, pp. 258-259) states, "Before the Scientific Revolution facts were few and far between: they were handmade, bespoke rather than mass produced, they were poorly distributed, they were often unreliable."..."Establishing facts depends upon instruments ... which have to be standardized."... "Precision was pointless when units of measurement were local." Centuries ago, telescopes and microscopes provided new ways to observe objects with clarity and precision that far exceeded human sensory capacity. More recently the European Organization for Nuclear Research (CERN) developed the collider and the world's most complex scientific instruments to observe the basic constituents of atomic matter. Observation can come in many forms but must be reliable and repeatable from one group of scientists to another if the observations are to inform science.

In Implementation Science, observation is a problem. Various measures exist and fit the "handmade" and "often unreliable" versions that pre-date the Scientific Revolution. C. Lewis et al. (2015) catalogued 104 existing implementation-related measures and found them lacking in reliability, validity, and conceptual clarity. Proctor et al. (2011) described potential implementation measures derived from a review of concepts in the literature. Of the eight proposed measures, three (adoption, cost, fidelity) relate to implementation; three (acceptability, appropriateness/fit, feasibility) concern the innovation and two (sustainability, penetration) relate to scaling. Weiner et al. (2017) developed new implementation outcome measures where each item concerns the innovation ("This EBP meets my approval;" "This EBP seems applicable"), similar to acceptability, appropriateness/fit, feasibility in the Proctor et al. list. Finally, reviews of the implementation research literature note that it is unusual for any measure to be used by more than one researcher (Allen et al., 2017; Fixsen, Naoom, et al., 2005).

The lack of useful and agreed-upon measures is a problem. If implementation independent variables (inventions) must be produced, then there must be some way to detect the presence and strength of the implementation independent variable in practice. Otherwise, the risk of Type III errors increases. A Type III error occurs when one is attempting to study the impact of a variable that does not exist in practice (Dobson & Cook, 1980; Harvey et al., 2018). In implementation studies, the fidelity with which implementation supports are provided is an important factor. If implementation dependent variables are to contribute to a science of implementation, then there must be commonly used measures of implementation outcomes. Pinnock et al. (2017) have proposed criteria for publishing research on implementation. The criteria include specific descriptions of intervention methods and outcomes, and specific descriptions of implementation methods and outcomes. These criteria hold promise for advancing the field.

The lack of repeated measures is a problem. Implementation is widely acknowledged as a complex process that may take several years to accomplish desired outcomes. Yet, few research studies examine implementation variables over time and use data to bring the process to light. Some examples are provided by Panzano and colleagues (Massatti, Sweeney, Panzano, & Roth, 2008; Panzano & Billings, 1994; Panzano & Roth, 2006; Panzano et al., 2004) who assessed 91 agencies every nine months for several years and identified patterns of adoption, use, deadoption, and readoption of evidence-based programs. McIntosh et al. (2016) had repeated measures of intervention fidelity across five years for over 5,000 schools and found distinct patterns for achieving, sustaining, and losing fidelity. Independent studies have documented the progress of scaling for over a decade in Scandinavian countries using repeated measures of fidelity (Sigmarsdóttir et al., 2018; Tommeraas & Ogden, 2016). The studies document the consistent fidelity resulting from the use of consistent implementation supports (Ogden et al., 2012). In other studies, repeated measures of implementation capacity development have been conducted every six months over 18 months to five years (Chaple & Sacks, 2016; Fixsen, Ward, Ryan Jackson, et al., 2018; McGovern, Matzkin, &

Giard, 2007; Ryan Jackson et al., 2018). These studies show the impact of implementation capacity on attaining and sustaining criterion performance in organizations and systems. Repeated measures are used in global health environment to track the use of nationally sanctioned innovations and to document the improvements in innovations as they are used in practice (Adondiwo et al., 2013; Thomassen, Mann, Mbwana, & Brattebo, 2015).

These longitudinal studies are not typical, but they should be. After, before and after, and one-time assessments are interesting but add little to the science of implementation. To do something once or even a few times is interesting. To be able to do something repeatedly with useful outcomes and documented improvements over decades will produce socially significant benefits for whole populations. Data on the processes of implementation over time are badly needed.

## Summary

At this point, Implementation Science is approaching the criteria for being a science. It is not yet a "system of knowledge covering general truths," nor does it make regular predictions (if-then) that are tested in practice (then-what). In general, implementation research does not systematically test theory and has few ways to generate implementation variables on purpose to study hypotheses related to theory.

Yet, the field is on the cusp of rapid and dramatic development. As described in this book, potentially powerful implementation variables have been identified. The implementation practices required to produce implementation independent variables so they are available for study have been operationalized and outlined in this book.

# Chapter 3: Definitions

To advance implementation practice and science, we need common language, common concepts, and common measures in order to promote clear communication among practitioners, researchers, and policy leaders. With these in hand, Implementation Science can be crowdsourced with many simultaneous experiences and experiments that test theory contributing to shared learning and adding to sharable data globally and across domains. Without common language, common concepts, and common measures, the current situation likely will persist where "The lack of clarity associated with construct definitions, inconsistent use of theory, absence of standardized reporting criteria for implementation research, and the fact that few measures have demonstrated reliability or validity were among the limitations highlighted in our review" (Allen et al., 2017).

*We need common language, common concepts, and common measures in order to promote clear communication among practitioners, researchers, and policy leaders.*

Some terms and phrases used repeatedly in discussions of Active Implementation are defined below. Other terms and phrases are defined in the text when they are used for the first time.

## Research evidence

Research evidence consists of "empirical findings derived from systematic research methods and analyses" (W.T. Grant Foundation, 2013). According to the U.S. Government Accounting Office (2009), systematic research methods include randomized group designs and "quasi-experimental comparison group studies, statistical analyses of observational data, and–in some circumstances–in-depth case studies. The credibility of their estimates of program effects relies on how well the studies' designs rule out competing causal explanations" (quoted from the Abstract).

## Evidence-based movement

The evidence-based movement is an international effort "to connect social scientific knowledge with policy, programs, and practices" (http://www.britannica.com/EBchecked/topic/1920806/evidence-based-policy). The purpose is to use research evidence to produce benefits to children, families, individuals, communities, and society.

## Framework

"A conceptual framework identifies a set of variables and the relations among them that are presumed to account for a set of phenomena" (Carpiano & Daley, 2006, p. 565). The Improved Clinical Effectiveness through Behavioural Research Group (2006) considers frameworks as mid-level theories that provide a broad and logically coherent set of explanatory relationships that are a source of testable hypotheses. Reviews have identified a variety of diffusion, dissemination, and implementation frameworks. Several of the so-called frameworks were never offered as "a framework" by the original authors, and only a few of the listed frameworks meet the Carpiano and Daley definition of a framework where key variables are described, and the relationships among variables predict important outcomes.

## Implementation

> **Quote from Word Origin and History** (http://www.thesaurus.com/browse/implement)
> implement 1454, from Late Latin. implementem "a filling up" (as with provisions), from Latin implere "to fill," from in- "in" + plere "to fill" (see plenary). Sense of "tool" is 1538, from notion of things provided to do work, that which "fills up" a house, etc. The verb is 1806, originally chiefly in Scotland, where it was a legal term meaning "fulfillment." It led to the wretched formation implementation, first recorded 1926.

"Implementation is defined as a specified set of activities designed to put into practice an activity or program of known dimensions. According to this definition, implementation processes are purposeful and are described in sufficient detail such that independent observers can detect the presence and strength of the 'specific set of activities' related to implementation. In addition, the activity or program being implemented is described in sufficient detail so that independent observers can detect its presence and strength. When thinking about implementation, the observer must be aware of two sets of activities (intervention-level activity and implementation-level activity) and two sets of outcomes (intervention outcomes and implementation outcomes)" (Fixsen, Naoom, et al., 2005, p. 5).

Implementation is universal, as individuals, organizations, or systems attempt to support the use of innovations in practice. The implementation activities designed to put into practice an activity or program may be haphazard and unintentional (a "do the best you can" approach), or it may be purposeful and specified well (a "do what is required" approach). Using well-specified and effective implementation supports can promote the accomplishment of innovation outcomes in practice (Brody & Highfield, 2005; G. Lewis, 2014; Metz et al., 2014). Active Implementation Frameworks help define effective implementation supports.

The extent to which the "specific set of activities related to implementation" have been operationalized has an impact on the successful use of innovations. Concepts such as "adaptation," "absorptive capacity," "modifiable periphery," "leadership," "facilitation," "stickiness," "inner and outer settings," "buy-in," and so on are encountered in the implementation literature. For implementation supports to be effective, these concepts need to be stated in operational terms that specify what to do in practice. For Active Implementation, the common activities behind these multiple concept labels are part of the operations that define Systemic Change, Improvement Cycles, Implementation Teams, and so on.

It is common to see the word "implementation" in an article when it only means "to use." For example, "We implemented the new program in the neighborhood wellness clinic" meaning "We used the new program in the neighborhood wellness clinic." In this book, the word "implementation" will only refer to implementation practices intended to support the full and effective use of innovations in practice. "Implementation" in the "to use" sense will be replaced by the word "use."

## Human services

The term "human services" refers to the full spectrum of services in which one human being (e.g., therapist, teacher, medical provider, community health worker) interacts with another (e.g., patient, student, neighborhood resident) in a way that is intended to be helpful. Human service domains include behavioral health, child welfare, community development, corrections, education, global health, health, mental health, public health, social services, substance abuse treatment, and others.

## Innovation

An innovation is anything new to an individual, organization, or human service system (Rogers, 1995). The innovation may be a therapeutic intervention, instruction method, evaluation method, management practice, clinical guideline, policy directive, improvement initiative, or other activity or program. An innovation may or may not have research evidence to support it.

Interaction-based innovations are embedded in human services and inherently are different from atom-based innovations (Fixsen, Blase, Metz, & Naoom, 2014; P. S. Jensen, Weersing, Hoagwood, & Goldman, 2005). In atom-based innovations, the science is built into the serum or seed or microchip, and the essential components of the innovation remain the same no matter who delivers it. In contrast, interaction-based innovations rely completely on whoever deliver them. As described by Modi (2011), in human services "the magic lies in the magician, not the wand."

Implementation always is in service to doing something (the innovation). The question is "what is the something?" and "how will we know if we have done it or not?" Implementation Specialists may ask, "what is the what?" or "what is your it?" or "what are you trying to do?" If there are ten people in the room, will all ten have the same answer? Or, will there be ten different answers to the question?

If "it" can be anything anyone says it is, then there is no need to bother with purposeful implementation supports. Unfortunately, poorly conceived ideas supported by haphazard management and technical assistance methods are the norm which may explain why outcomes-in-need-of-improvement are the norm in current human services.

Throughout this book, the focus is on doing what you intend to do. Implementation supports are designed to help you achieve what you intend to do. People will ask, "So how do you implement an idea or a vague policy or an ill-defined directive?" The answer is, first disambiguate the "it" and make it clear. Even standard (status quo) practices can be described and operationalized to see if they accomplish desired results when used as intended. This book provides several ways to go about that task, some even in the context of trying to implement an ambiguous "it" by clarifying what "it" is in the process of trying to use "it" in practice.

## Constant adjustment

The use of innovations in practice disturbs practices, organizations, and systems. Constant adjustment is required and is focused on the use of effective innovations and effective implementation methods that contribute positively to socially significant outcomes. Constant adjustment occurs in response to "attractors or repellers in the behavioral spaces within which a system functions" (Aldrich, 2008, p. 148). As noted by Weick (1987, p. 119), "People need to see that inertia is a complex state, that forcefield diagrams have multiple forces acting in opposed directions, and that reliability is an ongoing accomplishment."

Constant adjustment relies on organizations and systems having the capacity to search for errors and faulty operating assumptions, the capacity to learn from them, and the *ability to make needed changes* to improve intended outcomes (Kotter, 1996; Morgan, 1997; Senge, 2006; Tucker & Singer, 2015).

Constant adjustment relies on *recursive feedback* (Gilpin & Murphy, 2008; Morin, 2007; Strongman, 2013). Recursive feedback is information within a system that returns to the originating source of action, and that changes the originating source's views of problems and solutions. It is a form of learning to learn. Recursive feedback provides the means to know what changes are needed in the process of constant adjustment.

Constant adjustment *requires a goal* so that recursive feedback identifies adjustments needed to continue to approximate and optimize goal attainment. In organizations and systems, changes that are not goal-driven often are the product of, and contribute to, an "environment of turbulence, flux, fragmentation, disequilibrium and uncertainty" (Strongman, 2013). In these environments, "decisions may be distorted by asymmetric information, private agendas, and game playing by individuals and groups throughout a system. Managers evaluating the outcomes of their decisions may not know the ways in which those decisions were distorted, delayed, or derailed altogether by other actors in the system" (Sterman, 2006, p. 511). Legitimate, but competing, agendas and perspectives are a part of the implementation landscape.

## Rule-generated and contingency-shaped

When learning something new, it is helpful to have rules to follow and specific things to do in a certain way. For example, the "next right steps" in complexity theory (Stacey, 1996) or "first steps" for overcoming resistance to change (Beckhard & Harris, 1987) encourage defining specific steps to begin a process of complex change. Learning in this mode begins with clear plans and directive teaching (do this; do it this way; let me show you). Implementation Team members and staff in organizations and systems start out learning in this "receptive mode" to facilitate new learning and increase comfort for staff. This is rule-generated learning and doing.

Once the basic knowledge, skills, and abilities are in place, then the feedback from the environment has direct influence on next steps and skill development. As expertise is earned, then more nuanced and confident forms of skills emerge informed by successes and failures in day-to-day interactions with others. This is contingency-shaped learning and doing. Contingency-shaped learning in this "generative mode" is the essence of constant adjustment where the realities of a situation dictate the path to the goal under the unique circumstances found in any context.

## Get started, get better

As a corollary to rule-generated and contingency-shaped behavior, learn what to do, then do what was learned. The assumption is that we have a lot to learn, and we will learn the most by attempting to do the work and by examining the experience (get started; learn the next right steps). Once examined experience has taught us a new method or procedure, then the new learning is used at the next opportunity (get better; do the first steps; continue learning). Of course, that just exposes the next level of our ignorance and the process of learning never ends as we "get started and get better" with the next set of things forever more.

## Adapt

There are many uses of many forms of the word "adapt" in the implementation literature. Dictionary.com defines *adapt* as: 1) "to make suitable to requirements or conditions; adjust or modify fittingly," and 2) "to adjust oneself to different conditions, environment, etc." In this definition, "to make" and "to adjust" refer to change in the object or person of interest. Synonyms are listed as "fit, accommodate, suit, reconcile, conform; modify, rework, convert"– all verbs that refer to action as well. Adaptation is central to implementation as constant adjustments in practices, organizations, and systems are made on purpose to realize and improve recipient benefits. Adaptation is not done once; it is a continual goal-oriented process.

## Practice-based evidence

Practice-based evidence is evidence of processes and outcomes generated in the course of doing the work of implementation. The evidence is based on examined experience. For example, during the cholera epidemic in London in the 1800s, John Snow, a founder of modern epidemiology, "was not distracted by a fruitless microscopic search for the agent. Rather, he focused his science squarely on establishing the ways in which the disease was transmitted from person to person" (Paneth, 2004). By engaging with people in neighborhoods and observing the flow of water in the open sewers, Snow saw the fecal matter in the water (distinguished from the other garbage) and saw that fecal-contaminated water was mixing with drinking water in some neighborhood wells. Snow hypothesized that this likely was the method of transmission of the disease from an infected person to others. Acting on that observation, closing down infected water sources immediately saved lives.

Examined experience is the basis for practice-based evidence. The key is to be systematic in carrying out a plan and examining results. Most things don't work very well initially. The goal is to maximize each experience so that things work well eventually. Examination comes in many forms with evidence generated by planning and debriefing the use of, and results of, the plan; purposeful use of improvement cycles; pre-post tests of planned interventions; observations of and interviews with those who have produced worthy outcomes; and other methods for doing something on purpose and sensing the outcomes (Blase, Naoom, et al., 2005b; Naoom et al., 2006; Vrakking, 1995). Generalizing from Snow's cholera experience, Paneth (2004) concludes, "we must walk fearlessly into the heart of the epidemic to study it" and, we would add, generate practice-based evidence as we walk.

# Chapter 4: Getting Started in Practice

The foundations for the Active Implementation Frameworks were developed as the Teaching-Family Model was developed (Blase, Fixsen, & Phillips, 1984; Fixsen & Blase, 2018; Wolf, Kirigin, Fixsen, Blase, & Braukmann, 1995). The Teaching-Family Model was perhaps the first "evidence-based program" in human services. Implementation lessons were derived from the development of the treatment model; the failure of the first attempts to replicate the treatment model; the discovery of larger units for replication; the modest success of first attempts to replicate larger units; and the eventual success of replications. More than 50 years after it began in 1967, the Teaching-Family Model remains a testament to the sustainability (and continual improvement) of innovation and implementation methods, and to the value of the Teaching-Family Association for sustaining a community of practice and for managing the practitioner fidelity and organization fidelity data systems nationally. Early experience with what we now know as "implementation" was gained as attempts were made to develop and replicate the Teaching-Family Model.

*The Teaching-Family Model was perhaps the first "evidence-based program" in human services.*

In the description below the reader should note how the work to do something for the first time at one level becomes standard practice at the next level as the units of replication move from procedures to programs to organizations to a system of services. For example, the initial goal was to develop effective treatment procedures and to find a way to replicate the specific procedures from one youth or time period to another. Once the focus shifted to replicating a whole program, the replication of specific procedures became standard practice within that new focus. Capacity to replicate larger units and efficiency in doing so became the issues to be dealt with as the focus shifted.

For example, the first silicon-based transistor took years to develop and then successfully replicate the initial handmade versions. Today the production of transistors is done by machines that produce integrated circuits with about one billion individual transistors on the same size chip as the original single transistor (Gertner, 2012; Kaeslin, 2008). Larger units depend on and incorporate replications of the original units. Even with a billion transistors on a chip, each individual transistor must work to enable the larger unit to work.

## The innovation

The Teaching-Family Model began with one group home named Achievement Place by the civic group that funded and renovated a large home in a community neighborhood in Lawrence, Kansas. Achievement Place, a family-style group home for six or seven teenagers referred by the juvenile court, opened in May 1967. This event marked the beginning of several decades of research on effective treatment practices (e.g., relationship development, teaching appropriate alternative behavior, self-government and rational problem-solving, motivation systems) to help adolescents be more successful at home, in school, and in the community. This research led to the establishment of the Teaching-Family Model (a bibliography and related information are available at http://www.teaching-family.org). Achievement Place was staffed by Lonnie and Elaine Phillips, the prototype Teaching-Parents, who lived in the home and developed treatment procedures that became the subject of research studies to operationalize the methods and document the outcomes.

The Teaching-Family Model was cited as a "model program" by the American Psychological Association in its initial review of "evidence-based programs" (Roberts, 1996), as one of three evidence-based residential treatment programs in the Surgeon General's report (U.S. Department of Health and Human Services, 1999), and as perhaps the best developed and researched residential treatment model among those reviewed by the California Evidence Based Clearinghouse (James, 2011). Subsequent meta-analyses have found the Teaching-Family Model to be one of three residential treatment programs that produce positive and cost-beneficial outcomes (Lipsey & Wilson, 1998; Washington State Institute for Public Policy, 2016). The Teaching-Family Model of treatment is in current use in a variety of group home treatment, home-based treatment, treatment foster care, supported independent living, and school-based service delivery settings.

# Develop the science

The remainder of this chapter is written from the perspective of Dean Fixsen.

The first task is to get the science right to ensure an effective, useful, and usable intervention. The research and development efforts were stimulated by the Great Society Program (1964–1992), a massive national initiative supported by President Lyndon B. Johnson that focused on developing and using effective programs to solve national problems in education, housing, urban living, and so on. The Great Society programs led to support for applied research from the National Institute of Mental Health (NIMH). In 1967 NIMH was moved from the National Institutes of Health (NIH) and became an independent bureau within the Public Health Service with a focus on applied research and practice in support of the national mandate (Great Society Program).

In 1969 the first NIMH research grant was funded to support research to develop effective treatment interventions at Achievement Place. During the next 25 years, more than twenty million dollars (seventy million in 2019 dollars) was invested by NIMH, the Office of Juvenile Justice and Delinquency Prevention (OJJDP), and others to develop, replicate, and evaluate the Teaching-Family Model. Summaries of the research and development of the Teaching-Family Model are available for review and are not detailed here (Blase, Fixsen, & Phillips, 1984; Fixsen & Blase, 1993; Fixsen et al., 2001; Fixsen, Schultes, & Blase, 2016; Wolf, 2001; Wolf et al., 1995).

In the early years, the research group at the University of Kansas (KU) conducted applied research at Achievement Place to examine the use of the motivation system–points that could be earned for appropriate behavior, lost for inappropriate behavior, and earned back for learning appropriate alternative behavior. Issues that arose in the daily life of Achievement Place youths broadened the agenda to include research on self-government and rational problem-solving (Fixsen, Phillips, & Wolf, 1973; Phillips, Phillips, Wolf, & Fixsen, 1973), improving interactions with parents (Kifer, 1974), and impacting behavior at school (Bailey, Wolf, & Phillips, 1970). This research agenda established the essential components of the Teaching-Family Model (Table 2) that included relationship development (Willner et al., 1977), teaching methods (Bedlington, Braukmann, Kirigin Ramp, & Wolf, 1988; Bedlington et al., 1978; Ford, 1974), motivation system components (Phillips et al., 1971), and development of socially acceptable behavior (Maloney et al., 1976; Minkin et al., 1976; Werner et al., 1975; Wolf, 1978).

**Table 2. Components that defined the Teaching - Family Model of treatment in 1973**

| Teaching-Family Treatment Components | |
|---|---|
| Teaching | Skills Curriculum |
| Relationship Development | Advocacy |
| Motivation Systems | Generalization Procedures |
| Self-Determination | Integration of Components |
| Counseling | |

Having the data to support the essential components of the Teaching-Family Model turned out to be critical for program improvement and replication. The developers (Lonnie Phillips, Elaine Phillips, Dean Fixsen, Montrose Wolf) knew what the essential components of the Teaching-Family Model were, and we had data to support our assertions about what had to be there for anyone to claim to be using the Teaching-Family Model. Currently, the definition of essential functions is referenced as a key element of a "Usable Innovation" (Fixsen et al., 2013). The pioneering use of multiple-baseline designs (Phillips et al., 1971) and assessments of social validity (Wolf, 1978) were essential to carrying out the applied research agenda.

Getting the science right included being informed by knowledgeable and diverse perspectives of researchers, program developers, and policy makers. During the initial program development period, NIMH, OJJDP, and other federal agencies were mission driven, with the mission being to create a Great Society as envisioned in federal legislation. The research and development of the Teaching-Family Model benefited greatly from the flexibility and investment of intellectual capital from these federal agencies. At NIMH, Saleem Shah, Chief of the Center for Studies of Crime and Delinquency, had a substantial influence on the directions of the research agenda. Shah would convene groups of NIMH-funded researchers to promote shared views of problems and solutions and methods to conduct research related to the ideas that emerged from those meetings (Voit, 1995). Meetings included representatives from developers of evidence-based programs including "Fairweather Lodges" for adults with severe mental illness (Fairweather, Sanders, & Tornatzky, 1974a), Functional Family Therapy (Alexander & Parsons, 1973), Assertive Community Treatment (Stein & Test, 1978); evaluators and theorists from the Center for Research on Utilization of Scientific Knowledge (Havelock, 1969), and other researchers (Elliott, Ageton, & Canter, 1979; Liberman, 1979). The focus of these meetings and NIMH-funded research groups was on how to develop, research, replicate, and scale evidence-based approaches to solving significant social problems.

In these meetings, discussions among colleagues who were struggling with the same issues in other arenas had a direct impact on the development of the Teaching-Family Model. For example, all the research groups were struggling with how to define and operationalize treatment components; how to assess treatment processes (fidelity) to determine what contributed to outcomes; how to teach new practitioners how to do what prototype practitioners were doing so well; how to conduct research in complex applied settings; and how to connect in a meaningful way with potential users of the evidence-based programs that were being developed. The shared learning from these sessions provided indications early on that the challenges and solutions in program development and replication were universal and not unique to any one field or type of program.

## From procedures to programs

The goals of the Teaching-Family Model were clear in 1967: establish a treatment program that is humane, effective, individualized, satisfactory to participants, cost efficient, and replicable. After four years of development and research, the first few goals were being met at Achievement Place, the prototype group home treatment program. Given the applied research and service focus of NIMH, Shah and NIMH colleagues were actively engaged in helping solve difficult problems (Voit, 1995). During one of his visits to Achievement Place, Shah called our focus on discrete procedures "developing a bag of tricks" and challenged us to think of a program that consisted of evidence-based procedures and interactions that occurred 24 hours a day, seven days a week in a residential setting. He pointed out that the evidence-based procedures were being used all day every day with each youth. For example, relationship development was impacted with each interaction. Teaching appropriate alternative behavior was done proactively, reactively, and incidentally, as opportunities arose with youths interacting with one another, the Teaching-Parents, or people outside the group home.

In addition, Shah encouraged us to document the setting conditions and general infrastructure required including referral methods, funding streams, board of directors' involvement, and relationships with Juvenile Court, Child Welfare, and family support systems. What does it take to have Achievement Place have a positive impact on the lives of youths, and what does it take to operate a group home year to year? We took his advice and these programmatic elements were included in the second edition of the *Teaching-Family Handbook* (Phillips, Phillips, Fixsen, & Wolf, 1974).

Thinking of the Teaching-Family Model as a program was a significant shift. With the shift to program thinking, the task was not only to replicate findings regarding specific procedures but also to replicate the program as a whole. To this end, Mont Wolf engaged his colleagues in another community to form a non-profit organization and board of directors to operate a group home. Wolf worked for over a year with the Optimist Club to raise funds to purchase a home, secure zoning and licensing permits, renovate the home, and so on. While this was going on, an excellent couple was recruited to be the Teaching-Parents (the new name for the couples who lived in and operated a Teaching-Family group home). They enrolled in the applied master's degree program at the University of Kansas. They also spent considerable time at Achievement Place interacting with the youths and learning all they could from Lonnie and Elaine Phillips, the Teaching-Parents at Achievement Place. Finally, in 1971 the new group home was ready, the newly graduated Teaching-Parents moved in, referrals arrived from the juvenile court, and our troubles began.

## Failure to replicate the program

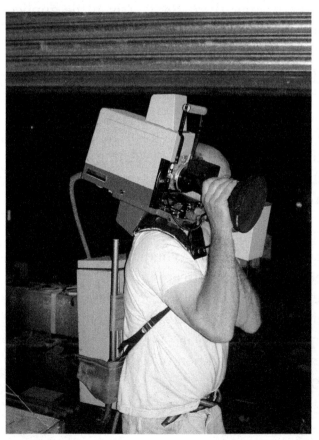

Figure 4. Figure 4. A portable video recorder in use in 1970.

Our first program implementation failure occurred when the replication attempt ended nine months later. The friends we had recruited to be on the board of directors of the new group home called us to a meeting and fired us! As humiliating and well-deserved as that was, we learned a great deal from that failure. We had been using the newly available "portable" video recording devices (Figure 4) to tape the Teaching-Parents in the replication group home and in the prototype group home. We spent countless hours analyzing the tapes and more hours in the replication group home trying to figure out what was going well and what was going wrong. As we decided on a solution, we immediately provided *in vivo* modeling and training to try to improve the interactions among staff and the teenage boys.

It was clear from the beginning that the new Teaching-Parents had learned the applied behavioral concepts in the KU graduate courses, but we had not taught them the skills

Teaching-Parents need to interact effectively with the youths. At about the same time we learned that other communities that wanted to start Teaching-Family group homes were not willing to wait a year or two for Teaching-Parents to complete graduate courses.

The developers began to resolve these program replication issues by creating a skill-based training program for Teaching-Parents. The new standard for training involved describing the essential components of the Teaching-Family Model, then having the trainees practice essential skills related to those components during a week-long preservice training workshop. Pre-post tests of knowledge and skills became standard and were a major source of feedback for improving training content and methods (Blase, Timbers, & Maloney, 1975; Kirigin et al., 1975).

Looking back, we recognize our engagement in PDSAC (plan, do, study, act, cycle) and usability testing Improvement Cycles as we applied new learning as rapidly as we could. We were learning and making progress, but not soon enough to avoid the humiliating meeting with our friends on the board. Repeated and careful analyses of the video tapes and the hours of observation and re-training finally revealed an essential function in the prototype program that none of us had seen in five years of work. The essential function was named the *teaching interaction*, an approach to teaching a wide variety of appropriate alternative behaviors. The Teaching-Parents at Achievement Place were teaching the youths appropriate behavior so skillfully we had missed it until we had the contrasting experience in the replication group home. By the end of a year of worry and failure, we had new treatment components to add to the definition of the Teaching-Family Model. We also had the beginnings of a way to assess fidelity of a comprehensive and complex treatment program (Bedlington et al., 1988; C. J. Braukmann et al., 1975).

Armed with this new information we changed the staff-training workshop to include the teaching interaction. Trainers also found it useful to use the teaching interaction during training to teach the teaching interaction and other essential treatment skills. We created a behavior rehearsal component in the workshop to assure each Teaching-Parent had the opportunity to learn and practice the skills. We also used the video technology to engage trainees in role-play scenarios before and after each workshop, and scored the tapes to test our effectiveness in teaching the teaching interaction skills. By continuing to refine staff selection and training methods we finally had our first successful replication of the prototype in 1972! In 1973 the Teaching-Parents who had staffed the failed first attempted replication decided they wanted to try again. They went through the new skill-based training program and went on to be certified Teaching-Parents in a group home in another state (Certification was earned by meeting rigorous fidelity criteria.). Their success clarified how poorly we had prepared them and how little we had known about our own evidence-based program two years previously.

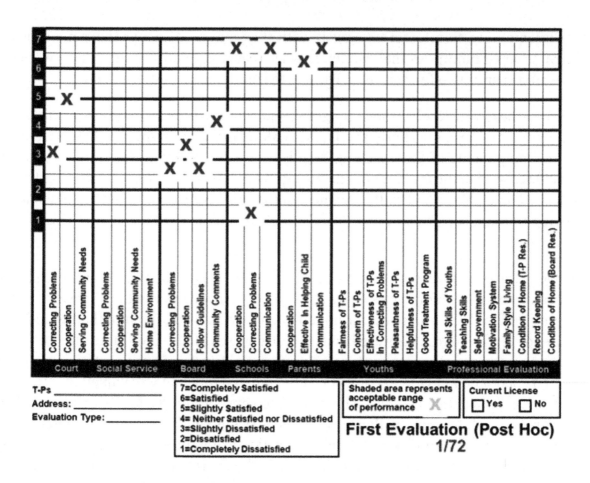

Figure 5. Post hoc results for the first (failed) attempt to replicate the Teaching-Family Model

We also learned the value of having a fidelity assessment. The Teaching-Family Model had failed in the first replication home simply because it never was in use—it was a program replication failure, not a treatment program failure. However, at the time, we did not have a way to assess the use of the Teaching-Family Model in practice. By the end of 1971, an initial version of a Teaching-Parent certification (fidelity) assessment had been developed as an indicator of the presence and quality of the Teaching-Family Model in any group home and community (C. J. Braukmann et al., 1975). Figure 5 shows the data from the first fidelity assessment, done a few months after we were fired from the first failed replication attempt. We asked the court personnel, board members, school teachers and staff, and parents to rate their interactions with the Teaching-Parents with regard to communication, cooperation, and helpfulness. The ratings were mixed but consistently low on helpfulness/effectiveness as expected. We decided to begin using the fidelity assessment as an early warning system so we could get feedback in small doses rather than all at once when we were being fired by a board.

34

Figure 6 shows the results of the first fidelity assessment of the prototype group home (Achievement Place). By 1972 the fidelity assessment included a consumer evaluation (questionnaires mailed to individual court, social services staff that included court and child welfare, board of directors, school teachers and staff with direct contact with the youths and Teaching-Parents); youth evaluation (interviews with individual youths living in the group home); and professional evaluation (direct observation by two trained evaluators). By 1975 all scores needed to be 6.0 or higher to become a certified Teaching-Parent. This is an achievable standard when the Teaching-Parents are supported by a competent Implementation Team.

We learned that fidelity defined a successful replication. Without fidelity, there is no consistent way to judge whether a program "is there" or not and therefore no way to interpret outcomes. Fidelity assessment becomes more important as the number of replications increase (Tommeraas & Ogden, 2016) and as outcome evaluations are done (Dobson & Cook, 1980).

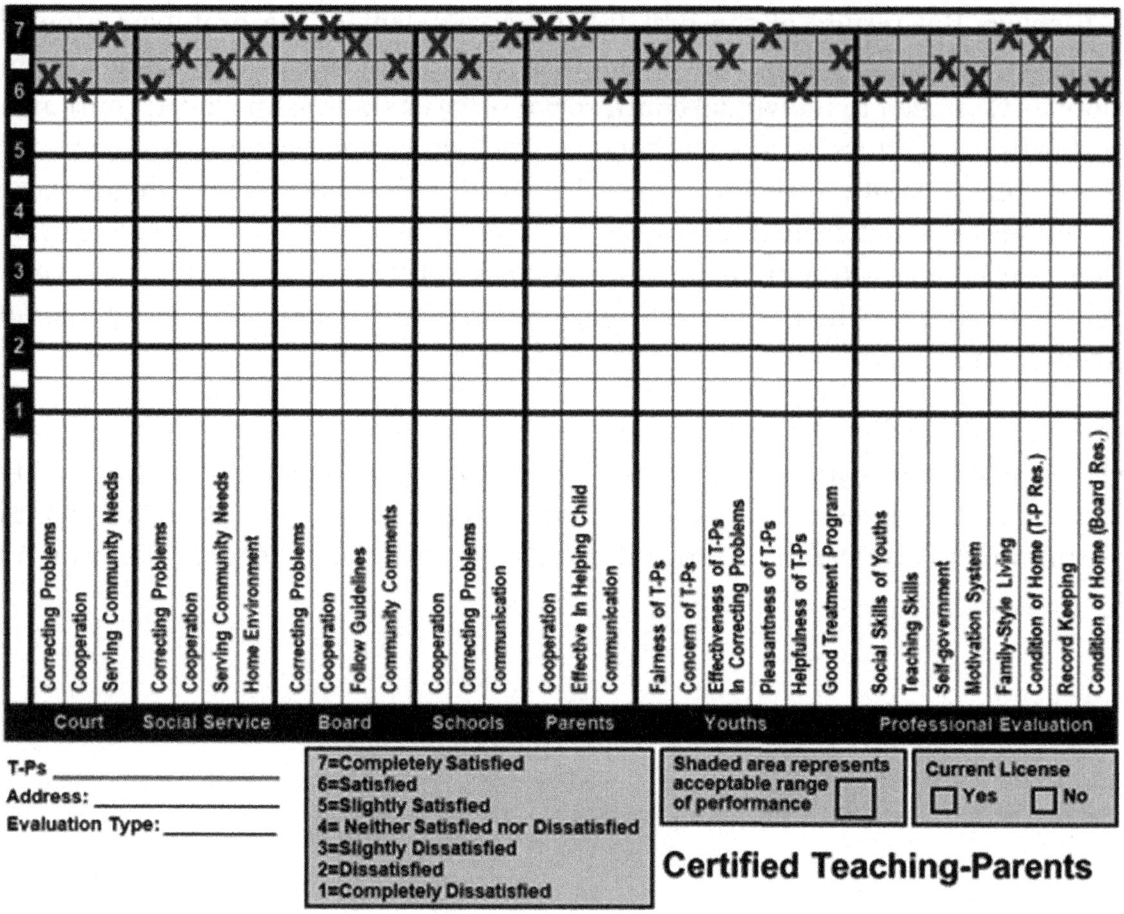

Figure 6. Results of the first fidelity assessment (1972) of the Teaching-Parents at the prototype Teaching-Family group home (Achievement Place)

## Program replication

With the skill-based training workshop and Teaching-Parent certification (fidelity) assessment in operation, and the demand for community-based group homes at a high level (the "deinstitutionalization movement" was well under way), successful replication of Teaching-Family group homes was feasible.

By the end of 1975, the developers had attempted to replicate the Teaching-Family Model in 64 group homes (Fixsen & Blase, 1993). We tracked each home for five years after the home began operating as a Teaching-Family home (i.e., the couple completed a preservice workshop offered by the staff of the Achievement Place Research Group at the University of Kansas). As we monitored their progress, we found that after five years 31 of those homes were still operating as Teaching-Family homes and 33 were closed (i.e., stopped operating as a group home or continued operating without sending new staff for Teaching-Family training).

36

The retention rate was less than 50%, and sustainability became a real concern. When analyzing these data, we found that 25 of the 64 homes were in Kansas and 39 were in 11 other states. The retention rate was about two times greater for the group homes in Kansas: 58% of the Kansas homes were still open after five years compared to only 23% of the out-of-state group homes. It seemed that our proximity to the homes was a key variable. For nearby homes, we knew much more about the operation and quality of the homes, our advice often was based on direct observation, and our communications and supports were more functional and timelier. The lesson was that the post-training support of the research team at the University of Kansas seemed to be important to the sustainability of the program.

## The concept of a Teaching-Family Site

In 1973, graduates of the KU doctoral program moved to Morganton, North Carolina, to start eight community-based group homes in Western North Carolina. Gary Timbers became the director of the Bringing It All Back Home (BIABH) Teaching-Family organization; Karen Blase was director of training; and Dennis Maloney was director of evaluation. The BIABH organization was different from the research group at the University of Kansas. BIABH had direct responsibilities for assuring administrative supports as well as treatment supports for each Teaching-Family group home. BIABH also had to work with communities to establish the homes and work with the state delinquency and mental health systems to assure licensing and adequate funding support for all the group homes. This organization became the first Teaching-Family Site and was the learning laboratory for the next set of program development lessons.

By 1975 it was clear that the North Carolina group had established an excellent organization of Teaching-Family Model homes complete with staff selection procedures, preservice and in-service training, ongoing staff coaching and consultation, staff certification evaluations, program evaluation, and Facilitative Administration (known today as Implementation Drivers). All the homes were within a couple hours' drive from Morganton; all eight of the original homes were still open and thriving (100% retention); and more Teaching-Family homes were being developed to serve youths and families in communities in the area.

The BIABH experience led to reworking the entire approach to the replication of the Teaching-Family Model. Instead of replicating the Teaching-Family Model one group home at a time, the decision was made to replicate by developing Teaching-Family Sites modeled on the North Carolina organization. A focus on site development addressed the issues of proximity, continued contact with, and frequent coaching for, Teaching-Parents as they used the treatment program, and continued attention to local political and funding changes over time.

The development of Teaching-Family replications is shown in Figure 7. From one group home in 1967 and the first attempted replications in 1971, by 1982 791 Teaching-Parent couples had completed training and had been employed in 290 Teaching-Family group homes.

## From programs to organizations

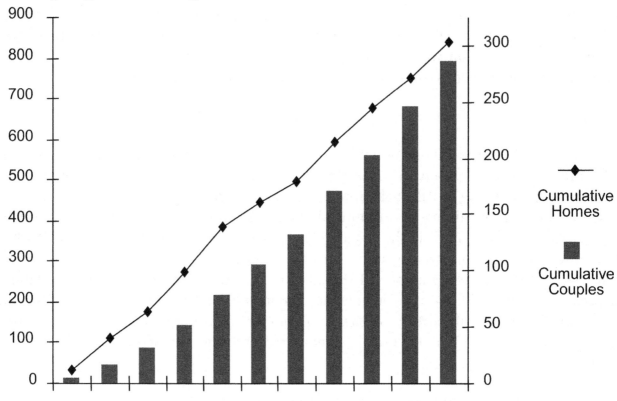

Figure 7. An annual count of the number of Teaching-Family group homes and the number of Teaching-Parents who completed training

Once the focus shifted to site development, it took a couple of years of trial and learning to figure out what was required to gain entry to whole organizations, conduct a mutual assessment so each party had enough information to make an informed choice, conduct training for the key site staff (e.g., trainers, coaches, supervisors, evaluators; now known as an Implementation Team), provide ongoing assistance and support to whole organizations, and evaluate progress toward organizational development.

Note that the organization level replications subsume group home replications, and group home replications subsume treatment procedure replications. In order to replicate organizations successfully, the initial struggles to replicate procedures and group homes had to be overcome so their replications could be accomplished with relative ease again and again from one organization to the next.

The KU research team had worked with organizations in the 1970s to help agencies develop two or more group homes in a community-based or a campus-based setting. However, the focus of these early replication efforts was on the group homes and not on organizational change and not on use of the Teaching-Family Model on an organization-wide basis. The early attempts were not very successful in working with organizations. The first organizational site success occurred when members of the research and development team moved to an agency and directly ran the program at BIABH in North Carolina. Subsequently, in 1975 five KU researchers and program developers moved to Boys Town, Nebraska, to replicate the Teaching-Family Model at Father Flanagan's Boys' Home.

The Teaching-Family Site replication at Father Flanagan's Boys' Home was instructive. It was a large and complex residential campus, not individual community-based group homes like those we had developed previously, and it was in trouble. In 1972 a small weekly newspaper in Omaha reported on Boys Town's immense wealth (over $200 million in the bank in 1971) and poor care of youths. As a side note, the now-famous Warren Buffet was the publisher of the newspaper and likely did the financial analyses in the reports; the newspaper won a Pulitzer Prize in 1973 for its investigative journalism. In response, Boys Town had suspended fund raising, changed directors, and hired two successive groups of experts to change the care of youths on campus. Each change effort had failed. At the end of 1974 Fr. Robert Hupp, the new director, contacted Mont Wolf, Lonnie Phillips, and Dean Fixsen and asked them to consider replicating the Teaching-Family Model at Boys Town. In this case, "readiness" bordered on desperation! As we discussed the possibilities, our colleagues Jerry Miller and Ed Budelman who were in the midst of deinstitutionalizing the delinquency system in Massachusetts (J. G. Miller, 1991) warned us about the dangers of organizational change and told us not to risk the reputation of the Teaching-Family Model in what likely would be a lost cause.

We were familiar with large institutions and how intractable they seem to be, resisting change of any consequence (Reppucci & Saunders, 1974). But what if we could change a large institution? Would the new standard become just as intractable, and sustain humane and effective care for decades to come? Would the Teaching-Family Model work just as well in an institutional campus setting as in a community setting? With these thoughts in mind and armed with the Teaching-Family Site learning from BIABH, Phillips became the Director of Youth Care in May 1975 and was joined by Fixsen (from KU), Karen Blase and Dennis Maloney (from the BIABH prototype Teaching-Family Site), and Richard Baron (from an attempted Teaching-Family replication in an institution in Salina, KS).

Change at Boys Town required remodeling 41 dormitory-style cottages to become family homes; eliminating cafeterias, dental offices, furniture-making facilities, and so on in favor of eating at home and going into the community for typical services; and changing the staffing from shift staff to Teaching-Parents. From November 1975 through December 1979 every aspect of Boys Town operations was changed. The five of us who moved to Boys Town did not know how to change an institution, but we did know how to develop and operate a Teaching-Family Model home.

The basis for change was the Teaching-Family Model (Fixsen, Phillips, Baron, et al., 1978). Teaching-Parents needed individual transportation, so each home had a van. Teaching-Parents needed to shop in town, so each couple had a checking account. Teaching-Parents needed access to maintenance, so building and grounds staffing was changed to do timely repairs. Teaching-Parent recruitment and hiring required ads that would attract couples to apply and required interviews that tested skills and ability to accept and act on feedback, so the human resources department was revamped. Youths needed a good education to address and compensate for learning deficits, so the instruction and behavior programs were changed in the schools on campus (Black, Downs, Phillips, & Fixsen, 1982). Each of these decisions was contested (many times with lawsuits) by Boys Town board members, affected staff, and related professional associations. Without the Teaching-Family Model as the standard and reason for making changes, and without the ardent support of Fr. Hupp, we might have lost these arguments.

In addition to the administrative changes, Teaching-Parent selection, training, coaching, and certification (fidelity) assessments, and organization administrative supports and data systems were fully in place by 1979 and part of the daily routines in the organization. As it turns out, the hypothesis about the intractability of institutions was correct: Boys Town continues as a certified Teaching-Family Site decades after the institutional change process was complete (K. D. Hurley et al., 2017; Thompson et al., 1996).

## Organization replication

The good news from these experiences was that site replication could be done, and we could establish successful Teaching-Family Sites. The bad news was that it required a scarce resource: people with PhDs and master's degrees from the University of Kansas who were highly skilled and had superb experience in developing and evaluating behavioral programs.

If the Teaching-Family Model was to have a broader impact, our task was to develop a practical site development system so that a broader range of staff could learn how to perform the key functions of staff selection, training, coaching, evaluation, and administration at a local site. Over time, essential functions were identified to replicate entire Teaching-Family Sites. The following factors came to define the site development process used to replicate the Teaching-Family Model at an organization level.

**Site selection:** *A mutual selection process (similar to informed consent) was used. It provided increasing levels of information to a potential site while asking for increasing levels of behavior from the potential site. For example, a first meeting might outline the basics of the Teaching-Family Model and the benefits of using the model with fidelity. Later meetings might ask the staff to produce budgets, minutes of board meetings, and other details regarding the organization and its operations. In these meetings, difficult issues were identified and solutions agreed on prior to agreeing to engage in site development. The mutual selection process helps the board and executive director understand and commit to the change process and prepare for the turmoil of organization change.*

**Site staff selection:** *The best candidates for the positions of Site Director, Director of Training, and Director of Evaluation (the Implementation Team) are those who have been certified Teaching-Parents and, therefore, know the treatment technology and understand the life style. It is difficult for others to learn the Teaching-Family treatment methods and learn how to change an organizaton at the same time.*

**Site staff training:** *Preservice and in-service workshops were provided to introduce site staff to Teaching-Family training, consultation, evaluation, administration, and leadership concepts and skills.*

**Site staff coaching and consultation:** *The site development team members made frequent visits to observe, provide on-site coaching, conduct information-data reviews, etc., with new site staff working in the organization. During visits the site development staff also met with the board or other responsible body to teach, inform, and troubleshoot problems that arose. On-site visits were augmented by regular communications between visits.*

**Site staff evaluation:** *The site development staff conducted regular formal reviews of site staff behavior and competencies as they engaged in staff selection, training, consultation, evaluation, and supportive administration within their organization. Verbal and written feedback informed the consultation agendas with new site staff.*

**Program evaluation:** *The site development staff conducted a "systems checkout" with direct observation, review of fidelity data, review of documents, and consumer evaluations once a year.*

**Site staff administration:** *The site development staff worked with the new site staff to facilitate the development of supportive administrative systems at a new site by* *working directly with boards, funders, and other key external consumers. The site development staff demonstrated how to identify problems, explore motivation to change administrative practices, and problem-solve so that the treatment program can be fully implemented.*

At the end of the site development process, the developing site applied for certification by the Teaching-Family Association (i.e., fidelity standards for whole Teaching-Family organizations). The Teaching-Family Association site certification process embodies the role of the association as a gatekeeper and quality control mechanism for the Teaching-Family Model. Thus, the criterion for "successful" site development is certification by the Teaching-Family Association.

The benefits of shifting the scalable unit (Barker, Reid, & Schall, 2016) from a Teaching-Family group home to a Teaching-Family Site became apparent as we tracked sustainability. As shown in Figure 8, with a focus on site development 84% of the Teaching-Family group homes sustained for six years or more. This was a marked improvement over the 17% sustainability of group homes when the focus of replication was on Teaching-Family group homes. A Teaching-Family Site included the evidence-based program and the necessary implementation supports as a unified whole–a scalable unit that could be replicated and sustained.

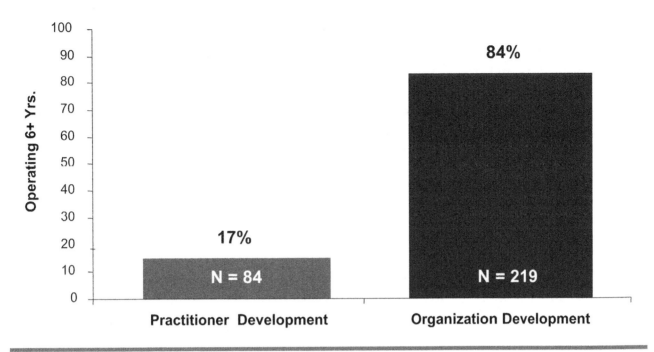

Figure 8. Sustainability of Teaching-Family group homes for six years or more comparing practitioner-focused implementation work and organization development implementation work

## Teaching-Family Association

The Teaching-Family Association is an association of site directors, Teaching-Parents, trainers, consultants, evaluators, administrators, directors, board members, and supporters that functions as a "community of practice" (Rosenheck, 2001) for the Teaching-Family Model. The Association began in 1975 when Dean Fixsen, Lonnie Phillips, and Mont Wolf convened a meeting of staff from the existing Teaching-Family Sites to discuss how to assure the quality of the Teaching-Family Model as it was being developed in agencies around the nation. The group agreed to form the Teaching-Family Association and develop guidelines and quality-assurance procedures (e.g. ethical standards; C. J. Braukmann, 1979). Each agency agreed to pay annual dues to the Association and contribute staff time to develop the standards and metrics. In addition to annual dues from the agency, annual dues were paid by Teaching-Parent couples who became members; registration fees were paid to attend the annual Teaching-Family Conference; and expenses were reimbursed for two evaluators who visited a site as part of the site certification process.

The review and certification of sites is a critical function of the Teaching-Family Association. As established by the Teaching-Family Association in 1978, site certification parallels Teaching-Parent certification processes and consists of:

1. A review of the documents pertaining to the site's actual implementation of the staff selection, training, consultation, certification (fidelity) evaluation, and supportive administration services to Teaching-Parents and group homes
2. A site consumer evaluation that asks the agency's funding sources, referral sources, board members, Teaching-Parents, trainers, consultants, and evaluators to rate and comment on the services and procedures offered by the site
3. An on-site review by two skilled evaluators who use established protocols to review and observe treatment services and documentation (e.g., group home treatment, records review; interview referral / funding agents), site services (staff selection, training, consultation, certification evaluation, and supportive administration); and conduct interviews with staff and consumers.

A developing site must meet all the criteria above in order to become a full, independent member of the Teaching-Family Association. After initial certification, document reviews are conducted annually. Site certification is renewed every three years by undergoing the entire site certification process. No service setting (e.g., group home, foster home, homebased unit, classroom) can claim to be providing Teaching-Family treatment unless it is affiliated with a certified site. The Teaching-Family Association provides a mechanism for assuring the fidelity, quality, and consistency of the actual use of the Teaching-Family Model internationally.

## Site replication: data

Between 1972 and 1995 the Teaching-Family research group at KU and members of Karen Blase's site development unit at Boys Town funded by NIMH worked with 59 agencies and organizations in an attempt to replicate Teaching-Family group homes (see Table 3). As discussed above, it took a while to conclude that the road to successful Teaching-Family Model replication was through site replication, not direct group-home replication. And, it took a few more years to puzzle through the steps involved in site development and to figure out the key functions of a site needed to replicate successful Teaching-Family group homes.

Table 3. Number of attempted Teaching-Family site replications in agencies and organizations by year (n = 59 total). Note: Starting in 1979 the site development work became more systematic. Notice how many years it took to engage 59 sites (whole organizations) in the site replication process

| Year | Number | Year | Number | Year | Number |
|------|--------|------|--------|------|--------|
| 1972 | 1 | 1980 | 4 | 1988 | 0 |
| 1973 | 4 | 1981 | 3 | 1989 | 0 |
| 1974 | 1 | 1982 | 1 | 1990 | 0 |
| 1975 | 2 | 1983 | 1 | 1991 | 2 |
| 1976 | 2 | 1984 | 1 | 1992 | 3 |
| 1977 | 3 | 1985 | 1 | 1993 | 5 |
| 1978 | 6 | 1986 | 2 | 1994 | 6 |
| 1979 | 5 | 1987 | 3 | 1995 | 3 |

## Purposeful site development

The 19 agencies for the years 1972–1978 represent the "pre-site development group" with the focus on development of Teaching-Parent competencies within individual group homes. The remaining 40 agencies represent the "post-site development group" with a focus on developing the organizational infrastructure (like BIABH) to develop and sustain a regional network of Teaching-Family group homes. Of course, the point separating the two groups is not totally clear since the site development technology evolved, rather than springing to life full blown. 1979 was chosen as the starting point for the "post" group because late 1978 marks the point when the essential functions of a Teaching-Family Site were articulated and began to be purposefully developed in partner organizations. In 1979 NIMH funded Karen Blase's site development proposal for the development of training and support for site staff. Thus, 1979 is early in the evolution process. It still took a couple of years to develop the major processes.

The results of the new site development efforts are shown in Table 4. A total of seven of 19 sites achieved certification in the pre-site development group: six (66%) were certified out of the nine that were initiated and operated by staff that had moved there from our Teaching-Family research group or was a PhD graduate from the University of Kansas and only one (10%) was certified out of the ten initiated and operated by others.

Thus, the pre-site development group results indicated that well-trained and highly skilled PhDs with superb experience in developing and evaluating behavioral programs could establish successful Teaching-Family Sites. The other staff did not fare so well.

Table 4. Results of attempted site replications before and after site development methods became more systematic in 1979

| | | Total N | Achieved Site Certification | |
| | | | Number | Percent |
|---|---|---|---|---|
| Pre-Site Development | Kansas Staff or PhDs | 9 | 6 | 66% |
| Pre-Site Development | Others | 10 | 1 | 10% |
| Post-Site Development | Kansas Staff or PhDs | 3 | 2 | 66% |
| Post-Site Development | Others | 37 | 23 | 62% |

In the post-site development group, two (66%) of the three sites operated by a group that had moved to a new location from our Teaching-Family research group or was directed by a PhD graduate from the University of Kansas were certified, the same ratio as we found in the pre-site development group. The encouraging result was that 23 (62%) of the 37 sites initiated and operated by others also achieved certification (this includes one certified site out of five attempts in 1979; removing those, the ratio is 22 out of 32 attempts or 68% certification). The percentage of sites achieving certification by the Teaching-Family Association substantially improved. With the help of a systematic site development effort, other qualified staff could replicate the Teaching-Family Model treatment and organizational support components and earn site certification by the Teaching-Family Association.

## Efficiency and effectiveness

Another set of organizational data is presented in Table 5. This table shows the average number of years that a developing site was affiliated with a site development group before it achieved certification or a decision was reached to end the site development process. In either case, a decision is made that ends the site development efforts. Across all 59 attempted replications, it took an average of 4.3 years to be certified or 3.5 years to terminate the site development process (without certification). This represents a considerable investment of resources in either case. The sub-group analysis shows that the pre-site development group required 6.4 years to achieve certification while the post-site development group that had the benefit of site development assistance required an average of only 3.7 years, a reduction of 2.7 years. The time required to reach a decision to terminate the site development process went from 3.9 to 3.1 years, a reduction of seven months. Planned and purposeful site development assistance appeared to have a noticeable impact on efficiency and effectiveness of developing new Teaching-Family Sites.

Table 5. Years to reach a site development conclusion

| | Total N | Achieved Site Certification | |
| --- | --- | --- | --- |
| | | Yes | No |
| All Attempted Replications | 59 | 4.3 Yrs. N = 32 | 3.5 Yrs. N = 27 |
| Pre-Site Development Group | 19 | 6.4 Yrs. N = 7 (37%) | 3.9 Yrs. N = 12 (63%) |
| Post-Site Development Group | 40 | 3.7 Yrs. N = 25 (63%) | 3.1 Yrs. N = 15 (37%) |

Note: A "conclusion" was either certification of the site by the Teaching-Family Association, or a decision to end attempts to develop a Teaching-Family program in that organization.

## Impact on sustainability

The shift from replicating Teaching-Family homes to replicating Teaching-Family Sites had a substantial impact on sustainability of Teaching-Family group homes. A sample of 25 group homes that were opened in 1981-82 (all associated with Teaching-Family Sites) was tracked for six years. The retention rate for the 25 group home replications (all out of the state of Kansas) was 84% (Fixsen & Blase, 1993, p. 605). This is a substantial improvement from the 23% retention rate for non-Kansas homes noted in an earlier section.

Thus, Teaching-Family homes associated with Teaching-Family Sites sustained at a much higher rate than Teaching-Family homes not associated with a site. As indicated in these examples, the timeline is long for gathering data related to efficiency and sustainability (for a recent example, see McIntosh et al., 2016). It was fortunate that the developers maintained good records for the couples, homes, and sites receiving training and assistance over the years. It takes time to see the outcomes with respect to survival and quality of services. For example, it takes about three to four years to develop a Teaching-Family Site and have it meet the certification standards of the Teaching-Family Association (Blase, Fixsen, & Phillips, 1984). Then it is necessary to follow up with each certified site to document longer-term survival and its ability to continue to meet certification standards on each ensuing triennial evaluation. This takes a minimum of six more years (two cycles of site certification reviews), so about ten years elapse before there is a clear view of these organizational outcomes. Developing and replicating effective programs requires considerable attention from groups of applied researchers and staff of service organizations over long periods of time (Wolf et al., 1995).

By 1992, 25 years after Achievement Place opened and research to develop the Teaching-Family Model began, a data-based quality assurance system was in place. As outlined in Table 6, the goal is to have certified practitioners delivering high fidelity Teaching-Family services to recipients in typical service-delivery systems. Teaching-Family Sites provide implementation supports in hospitable organization environments that facilitate high fidelity use of the Teaching-Family Model treatment services and high fidelity use of implementation supports. That is, for example, training is provided by skilled trainers who teach Teaching-Family knowledge, skills, and abilities and conduct pre-post tests of training to assure learning by practitioners. Coaching is done by coaches who have been selected, trained, coached, and assessed regarding their use of skills-based coaching in practice.

The Teaching-Family Association conducts Teaching-Family Site certification evaluations and continually updates the system to help assure that Teaching-Family Sites support the development and certification of practitioners year after year, one group of practitioners after another, in evolving human service systems. The Teaching-Family Association also convenes meetings to help assure continual examination of the Teaching-Family Model itself so that improvements are recognized and incorporated in each site and in the certification standards.

Table 6. Teaching-Family quality assurance activities and functions

| Person or Organization | Activity | Function |
|---|---|---|
| Practitioner | Provide Teaching-Family treatment services to recipients | Improve self-care, social, academic, family, and community outcomes |
| Teaching-Family Site | Provide timely implementation supports (staff selection, training, coaching, and fidelity) to multiple practitioners | Assure high fidelity Teaching-Family treatment services provided by certified Teaching-Family practitioners |
| | Provide leadership to assure a hospitable organizational environment | Assure high fidelity implementation supports; assure state system supports for the Teaching-Family organization |
| | Collect data on organization processes, fidelity, and outcomes for recipients | Use data to inform decision making and in continuous Improvement Cycles |
| Teaching-Family Association | Provide support for the development of new Teaching-Family Sites | Expand the use of the Teaching-Family Model via certified Teaching-Family Sites |
| | Conduct site certification evaluations | Assure high fidelity Teaching-Family treatment and implementation support services |
| | Convene meetings and an annual conference | Continually share knowledge and update requirements for site certification |
| | Advocate for children, youth, families, and individuals in state and national meetings | Inform policy and funding decisions to support evidence-based practices and organizations |

All activities listed below the practitioner line in Table 6 were required to establish and sustain high fidelity use of the Teaching-Family Model as the program was scaled. The linked activities and functions outlined in Table 6 are possible because the Teaching-Family Model provides a common language, common measures, and common concepts across practitioners and organizations. With so much in common, members of the Teaching-Family Association can readily communicate issues that arise, share solutions that are found, and continue to improve services and service systems even as practitioners, managers, and leaders come and go in Teaching-Family Sites.

## Practice-based culture, family, and purveyor evidence

To extend the practice-based knowledge base, in 2003-2006 we convened a series of meetings of implementation experts–culture and family experts, program developers, purveyors, implementers, and researchers. The participants had produced successful working examples of implementation methods in support of programs and practices. In the meetings they identified and operationalized essential implementation components and extended the horizons of implementation practice and science. A great deal is owed to these experts who so freely shared their triumphs, failures, and best practices with all of us.

To begin, in March 2003 Blase and Fixsen convened a meeting of experts in the area of children's mental health and cultural competence. These included individuals with expertise on African American, Asian American, Pacific Islander, Latino, and Native American cultures; the developers of evidence-based programs for children; and researchers, family members, and stakeholders. The meeting's goals were twofold. The first was to address the applicability and appropriateness of evidence-based programs for children and adolescents of different cultures and, second, to increase the capacity of systems to develop and implement culturally relevant approaches (Blase & Fixsen, 2003). At the meeting, participants developed a consensus statement of what we know and what we do not know about the relationship between evidence-based programs and cultural competence. Participants also developed recommendations for future action.

In Fall 2004, a select group of program developers (purveyors) and implementers (users) of evidence-based programs and practices was invited to attend two working meetings to explore the "craft knowledge" related to the implementation of evidence-based programs and practices (Blase, Naoom, et al., 2005b; Fixsen, Blase, et al., 2005; Fixsen et al., 2006b). The first of these meetings was conducted with the developers of evidence-based programs and practices; the second meeting was conducted with implementers of the same evidence-based programs and practices. A "purveyor" is a group of individuals representing a program or practice who actively work to implement that practice or program with fidelity and good effect. An "implementer" is a group of individuals employed by a provider organization to support the use of a particular program or practice with a group of recipients (see Fixsen, Naoom, Blase, Friedman, & Wallace, 2005 for further discussion). The concept-mapping process was used with the participants of these two working meetings. Concept mapping combines a group process (brainstorming, sorting, and rating of items generated in brainstorming) with multivariate statistical analyses (multidimensional scaling and hierarchical cluster analysis) to create conceptual maps that are then interpreted by the group(s) who generated the items (Trochim, 1994). The items and concept maps helped to operationalize many components of what are now called the Active Implementation Frameworks.

With the practice-based evidence in hand, a study examined the implementation of evidence-based programs and practices in the real world by exploring the ways in which evidence-based program developers support implementation of their programs and practices in new settings (Naoom et al., 2006). Structured interviews were conducted with a random sample of evidence-based program developers whose programs were listed on the National Registry of Effective Programs and Practices (NREPP) as well as other national registries of evidence-based programs and practices. The interview was focused on factors derived from a review and synthesis of the implementation evaluation literature. The factors were associated with successful replication and implementation of evidence-based programs and practices in new settings. The interviews were recorded, transcribed, and coded to identify similarities and differences between responses as well as themes and patterns that emerged across the participants. Results indicated that program developers provide varying degrees of support to organizations using their intervention. In addition, the results describe the extent to which program developers demonstrate varying levels of responsibility for implementation components. In general, there was an inverse relationship between the number of replications claimed and a purveyor's requirement to use an established measure of fidelity.

The final meeting was with researchers who were experts in conducting rigorous evaluations of implementation variables in typical practice settings (Fixsen et al., 2006a). The purpose of the meeting was to develop an outline for a multi-site, multi-year (ten-15 years) program of research to dramatically improve the practice and science of implementation. Based on findings from the monograph, "*Implementation Research: A Synthesis of the Literature*" (Fixsen, Naoom, Blase, Friedman, & Wallace, 2005), a focus on implementation process and outcome results could inform the implementation of quality programs and practices across domains (e.g., mental health, substance abuse, prevention). The experts concluded that the field of implementation research is still in its infancy and in need of a long-term research agenda to focus efforts on successful approaches to implementation, the various influences on implementation, and the interaction effects among implementation factors.

The information from the meetings helped to inform the ongoing work of the participants and provided detailed information about processes common among successful program developers and users. Group learning included the importance of Exploration Stage activities, the key role of coaching, the need for practical fidelity assessments, and the ways in which leadership and organization supports could be provided in supportive ways. The shared experiences on these topics (and others) augmented the learning from the review of the literature and concepts stated in the synthesis of the literature.

# Chapter 5: Strong Variables

In this chapter strong implementation variables are described and their impacts documented. To achieve socially significant outcomes for whole populations, small effects will not be sufficient. Thus, the search is for implementation variables that produce large effects and that can be reproduced on purpose using implementation best practices. The implementation components mentioned in this chapter will be described further in following chapters.

Practice-based culture, family, and purveyor evidence; case studies, surveys, and assessments have identified a vast array of potential influences on practitioners and organizations as they attempt to use innovations in practice. For example, there are lists of potential influences with respect to organization culture, implementation climate, self-efficacy, self-confidence, attitudes regarding innovations, fit with staff values, psychological readiness, strategies, and so on (Aarons, Hurlburt, & Horwitz, 2011; Damschroder et al., 2009; Durlak & DuPre, 2008; K. J. Klein & Sorra, 1996; Proctor, Powell, & McMillen, 2013). Networks have been identified as potential influences on the use of innovations on practice as a way to activate desired practice (Dearing & Cox, 2018; LeMahieu, Grunow, Baker, Nordstrum, & Gomez, 2017; Shelton et al., 2018). And so on.

*Strong variables have consequences for producing socially significant outcomes and are worth investing the time and effort to make them happen in practice so that desired outcomes can be realized.*

Potential influences, and there are many of them in the literature, are a place to begin a process to sort out implementation-specific variables from other variables. For Implementation Science to progress, potential influences need to be tested and established as actual determinants of outcomes (or not). For implementation, demonstrations of consequential validity are paramount. Strong variables have consequences for producing socially significant outcomes and are worth investing the time and effort necessary to make them happen in practice so that desired outcomes can be realized.

For implementation, many of the identified potential influences are the outcomes (not the inputs) of the Active Implementation Frameworks done well. For example, practitioners who meet the staff selection criteria, have the benefit of training and coaching done well, and receive constructive feedback from regular fidelity assessments feel efficacious, confident, respected, supported, and ready to do the work of providing innovation-based services to others. Organizations that engage in Exploration Stage activities and subsequently develop implementation capacity to support high fidelity use of innovations become high functioning organizations with a culture and climate that fully support and sustain implementation and innovations. Strategies have been identified and operationalized as Active Implementation Frameworks that are teachable, learnable, doable, and assessable in practice.

The Active Implementation Frameworks have evolved from practice where barriers must be overcome and not just documented and lamented. Starting with personnel recruitment and interview processes, practitioners who are ready, willing, and able to use innovations with high fidelity and socially significant outcomes are developed on purpose from pools of applicants. Similarly, organizations that likely are underperforming and are not only ready but sometimes desperate to change (e.g., threatened with closure or takeover) are identified in the Exploration Stage activities. In both cases, the hard work of changing structures, roles, and functions to change behavior (knowledge, skills, and abilities) is guided by Implementation Teams using Active Implementation methods. These methods can be used on purpose and replicated across countries, states, provinces, regions, organizations and individuals (Fixsen, Blase, & Fixsen, 2017).

Strong implementation variables are described below. It is recognized that other factors such as poverty, war, famine, epidemics, and so on also exert strong influences on the ability to produce socially significant outcomes (Yapa & Bärnighausen, 2018). They are not uniquely implementation factors. Likewise, major increases in funding, peacetime, and so on may make support for improvement possible but do not necessarily produce socially significant outcomes. They are strong influences but are not uniquely implementation variables.

For example, reading scores for 9-year old children in the U.S. have hovered around a score of 215 on a 500-point scale since the 1960s. As shown in Figure 9, literacy has not improved even as social conditions, politics, attention to education, evidence-based instruction, and so on have changed drastically over the decades (Grigg, Daane, Jin, & Campbell, 2003; Kutner et al., 2007; National Commission on Excellence in Education, 1983).

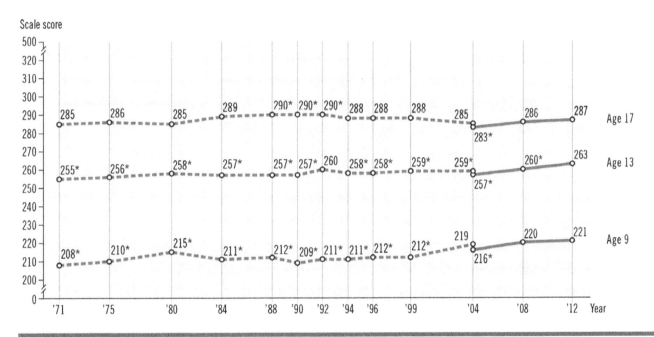

Figure 9. Literacy in the U.S. as systemically assessed by the Institute of Education Sciences (http://nces.ed.gov/nationsreportcard/subject/publications/main2012/pdf/2013456.pdf)

As shown in Figure 10, reading scores stayed about the same even though spending increased dramatically over the decades. It is not just the availability of funding; socially significant results depend on what the funds are used for. How much is invested in technical assistance that consists of providing documents, website information, and train-and-hope experiences? Spending more on things that don't work only results in outcomes-as-usual. Investments in Active Implementation supports for effective innovations have been lacking (Kessler & Glasgow, 2011; Perl, 2011; Vernez et al., 2006) and outcomes have not improved.

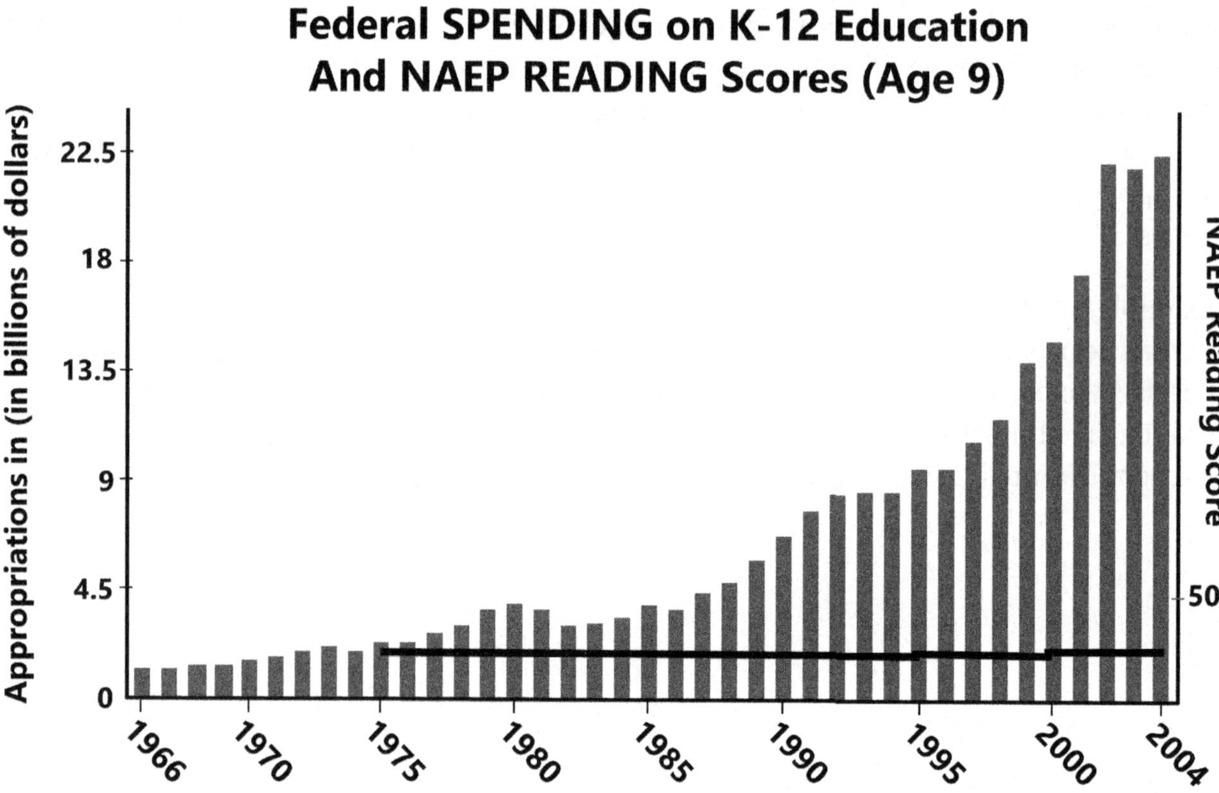

# Federal SPENDING on K-12 Education
## And NAEP READING Scores (Age 9)

Figure 10. Federal spending history and reading scores in the U.S. (http://www.ed.gov/nclb/overview/intro/index.html). Federal spending in 2012 (data not shown) was $55 billion

In health, many of the United Nation's Millennium Development Goals (2000–2015) were not achieved even with supportive global policies and unprecedented funding ($135 billion in 2014; World Health Organization, 2015) to improve health services, especially in low- and middle-income countries (LMICs). The effort continues with Sustainable Development Goals for 2015-2030. In a study of preventable death in 167 LMICs, Kruk, Gage, Joseph, et al. (2018) found that:

"15.6 million excess [preventable] deaths from 61 conditions occurred in LMICs in 2016. After excluding deaths that could be prevented through public health measures, 8.6 million excess deaths were amenable to health care of which 5.0 million were estimated to be due to receipt of poor-quality care and 3.6 million were due to non-utilisation of health care. Poor quality of health care was a major driver of excess mortality across conditions, from cardiovascular disease and injuries to neonatal and communicable disorders."

Increased access to low-quality health care is not helpful. Low-quality health care can benefit from purposively using the Implementation Drivers to effectively and efficiently improve the

56

knowledge, skills, and abilities of traditional (Tiruneh et al., 2018) and non-traditional (Jacobs, Michelo, & Moshabela, 2018; Masud Parvez et al., 2018) health service providers.

Strong implementation supports for full and effective use of innovations and for achieving socially significant outcomes are outlined below.

## Strong variables overcome weak variables

Strong variables like the components of the Active Implementation Frameworks can overcome weaker ones and can turn error variance into main effects. The Active Implementation Frameworks provide the means by which innovations can be used by an available workforce or by community members in a variety of settings. If the full and effective use of innovations in practice depends on waiting for just the right conditions and individuals to appear, scaling will be impossible to achieve in any deliberate way, and we will be left with the persistent science-to-service gap (Committee on Quality of Health Care in America, 2001; Stolz, 1981). For scaling to occur and socially significant outcomes to be realized, implementation must be in the "making it happen" mode.

Implementation Team activities provide examples of strong variables that can overcome many weak variables that have been noted in the literature as barriers to the use of innovations in practice. For implementation, an Implementation Team is engaged in creating readiness with groups, organizations, and elements of systems so that they can be engaged in supporting the full, effective, and sustained use of innovations in organizations. These activities are shown in Figure 11.

J. M. Prochaska, Prochaska, and Levesque (2001) estimate that at any given time about 20% of individuals and organizations may be ready for change. Thus, waiting for readiness is not an option for using innovations at scale to produce socially significant outcomes. Readiness must be created and nurtured by Implementation Teams so that, eventually, all individuals and organizations are ready for change and ready, willing, and able to use innovations fully and effectively in the future.

As shown in Figure 11, an Implementation Team engages in Exploration Stage work with organizations to identify those that are ready, willing, and able to proceed with developing implementation capacity to support the full and effective use of innovations to assure benefits to recipients. For the remaining organizations that are not yet ready, an Implementation Team continues to work with them to overcome barriers (leadership, stakeholder reaction) or deficiencies (e.g., knowledge, resources) so they will be ready soon or when the next opportunity arises.

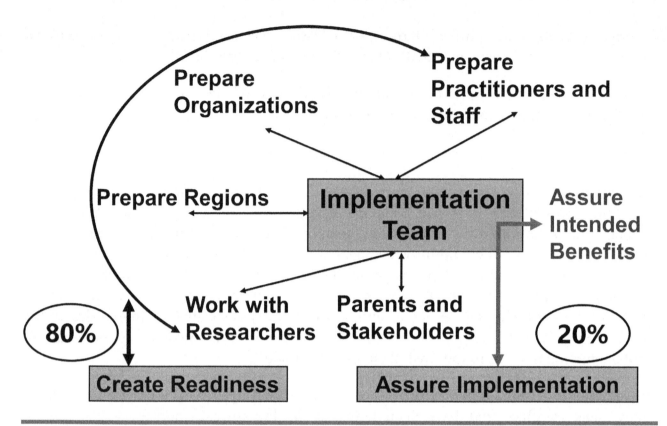

Figure 11. Implementation Team creating readiness while supporting the full and effective use of innovations

Some of the activity of Implementation Teams can be seen in Table 7. Using Nominal Group Processes (Delbecq & VandeVen, 1971; Gustafson, Shukla, Delbecq, & Walster, 1973), Fixsen, Blase, et al. (2005) collected data from 104 purveyors, program developers, and implementers (users) of a variety of evidence-based programs. In small groups, they were asked to respond to questions regarding what they did 1) while considering the possibility of using their program in a new setting (Exploration Stage), 2) after beginning to work with an organization but before evidence-based program service delivery began (Installation), and 3) after evidence-based program service delivery began (Initial Implementation). The participants generated 579 items and grouped them into concept areas (assessment, planning, etc.) called Implementation Team activities in Table 7.

Table 7. Implementation Team activities by stage of implementation. Data from Fixsen, Blase, et al. (2005)

| Implementation Team Activities | Implementation Stages | | |
|---|---|---|---|
| | Exploration | Installation | Initial Implementation |
| Assessment | 97% | 1% | 2% |
| Planning | 20% | 32% | 48% |
| Selection/Training | 3% | 31% | 66% |
| Coaching | 8% | 6% | 86% |
| Evaluation/Fidelity | 3% | 23% | 73% |
| Organization Development | 11% | 16% | 73% |
| System Intervention | 37% | 30% | 33% |

As one might expect, assessment and planning were prominent activities during the Exploration Stage, and planning, and selection of staff and preparation for evaluation and fidelity assessment were notable activities during the Installation Stage. In addition, selection, training, coaching, evaluation (fidelity), and organization development (Implementation Drivers) were intensively pursued during Initial Implementation.

A notable exception to expectations was System Intervention. It was a prominent activity during Exploration and continued unabated during subsequent stages. During Exploration purveyors (i.e., intervention-specific Implementation Teams) negotiated payment rates, licensing requirements, referral sources and rules, staffing qualifications, reporting requirements, and so on. The purveyors and program developers (Implementation Teams) had learned that these kinds of system supports were necessary for the successful use of their evidence-based program. Rather than wait for problems to arise after operations began, they had learned to initiate negotiations to develop a workable solution during Exploration and continue those efforts until the systemic issues were resolved.

Achieving a good fit between an innovation and an organization and its staff is not only assessed, it is established on purpose to create readiness during Exploration and sustain readiness in later stages. Culture and climate are established in the same way as hard-earned outcomes of using the Implementation Drivers well during the organization change process. Organization development (Leadership; Facilitative Administration) is a prominent feature of the Initial Implementation stage as the use of the innovation disturbs existing routines in the organization and leaders and managers are engaged in changing the organization to improve fit with new practitioner service delivery. Considerable activity is devoted to evaluation (Decision Support Data System) as data on staff performance (evaluation; fidelity) and organization performance are collected and used to make decisions and improvements. The data in Table 7 emphasize an important point. Exploration is important but should not be seen as a one-and-done decision to proceed. Planning continues and intensifies as the reality of using an innovation produces more problems than it solves, and System Intervention continues as attempts to create a new reality bump into system rules and regulations in unexpected ways. The importance of continued Implementation Team support was underscored by Panzano and Roth (2006) who studied 91 agencies and found that front-end (during Exploration) senior leadership support (champions) was important for making the decision to adopt an innovation but had no impact on the eventual effective use of an innovation. Thinking about things and planning what to do and how to do it during Exploration are important. However, it is unrealistic to imagine that all possible problems can be anticipated. We will not *think* our way to change, but we can *behave* our way to change by doing the work of the innovation and exposing real problems that can be solved (re-solved) in real time by leaders and Implementation Teams.

## Implementation Team outcomes

A fundamental outcome in implementation practice and science is fidelity. Fidelity is an outcome of implementation done well. If Implementation Team members use the Implementation Drivers to support practitioners well, then practitioners are more likely to use an innovation as intended. Innovations used as intended produce intended outcomes. Innovations used in unintended or haphazard ways do not produce intended outcomes. Prescription drugs, computer hardware and software, and other atom-based innovations have the essential ingredients built into them. Their effectiveness in practice does not depend on who provides them. Interaction-based innovations rely completely on a practitioner's ability to provide the essential components of the innovation consistently and effectively day after day.

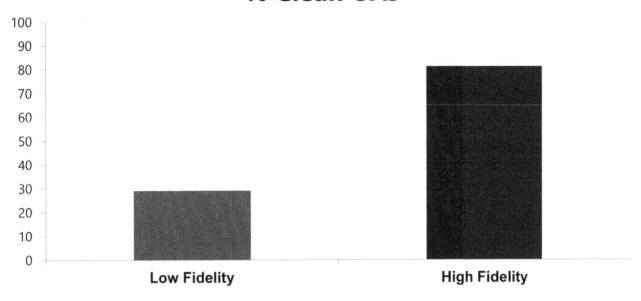

# % Clean UAs

Figure 12. Fidelity of the use of Dialectical Behavior Therapy and opiate-negative (clean) urinalyses (UA) outcomes for substance abusing patients. Data from Linehan et al. (2002)

The importance of fidelity is illustrated in Figure 12. Heroin-dependent women with borderline personality disorder were treated by therapists using Dialectical Behavior Therapy (DBT; Linehan, 1991). The women treated by high fidelity DBT therapists had 81% drug-free urine samples for one year compared to about 29% for women treated by low fidelity DBT therapists (Linehan et al., 2002). All the women "received DBT" but considerably more of those who received DBT used as intended benefited fully. Fidelity is a strong variable that makes a big difference in recipient outcomes.

Fidelity assessment and feedback are important for reducing practitioner turnover. In a large scale study conducted by Aarons, Sommerfeld, Hecht, Silovsky, and Chaffin (2009), half the practitioners received training and coaching to support their use of an evidence-based program: the other half carried on their use of services as usual (a planned mix of various service components). For half of each group, a fidelity assessment was carried out during two in-home therapy sessions each month. The results are summarized in Table 8.

**Table 8.  Fidelity improves staff retention.  Data from Aarons et al. (2009)**

| Selection, Training, Coaching and... | Practitioners Still Employed after 36 months | |
|---|---|---|
| | Evidence-based Program | Services as Usual |
| Fidelity Assessment | 58% | 27% |
| No Fidelity Assessment | 22% | 17% |

Practitioners who are selected, trained, coached, and receive regular feedback from fidelity assessments not only use an effective innovation with fidelity and produce socially significant outcomes, they also stay on the job considerably longer (58% for three years or more; 2.6 times longer than those trained and coached without the benefit of fidelity assessments).  The practitioners who had fidelity assessments also had higher scores on perceived job autonomy.  They were well prepared to do the clinical work, understood their strengths based on feedback from the fidelity assessments, and felt free to use their good skills and judgement in a more autonomous way.

The task, then, is to help assure that supports are provided so that all, or nearly all, of the practitioners are high fidelity users of innovations.  Although they are not common yet, Implementation Teams are essential to building effective, efficient, and sustainable capacity to use innovations as intended, and for establishing contexts that are more enabling and less hindering.  Implementation Team members do the work of implementation and are accountable for using implementation best practices with fidelity and socially significant outcomes.  Given the central role of Implementation Teams, the selection, training, coaching, and fidelity assessment of teams are a critical part of implementation done well.  Implementation Teams have been developed on purpose since the 1980s (Blase, 2006; Blase, Fixsen, & Phillips, 1984).

Data regarding the value of expert Implementation Teams are shown in Table 9.  An expert Implementation Team produces about 80% successful use of innovations in about three years (Brunk et al., 2014; Fixsen et al., 2001; Forgatch & DeGarmo, 2011; Ryan Jackson et al., 2018; Saldana, Chamberlain, Wang, & Brown, 2012).  Without the support of an expert Implementation Team, there is about 14% success in 17 years (Balas & Boren, 2000; Green, 2008; Lynch, Chesworth, & Connell, 2018).

**Table 9. Implementation Teams, time, and outcomes for effective innovations**

|  | Expert Implementation Team Support for Using an Effective Innovation | Support as Usual for Using an Effective Innovation |
|---|---|---|
| **Successful use** | 80% | 14% |
| **Time to accomplish successful use** | 2 - 4 years | 17 years |

As they do their work, Implementation Teams accumulate knowledge. They engage in planned and purposeful activities (the Active Implementation Frameworks); see the immediate and longer-term results; solve problems related to the use of innovations and the use of implementation supports in organizations and systems; and use the experience to develop a revised plan for the next attempt.

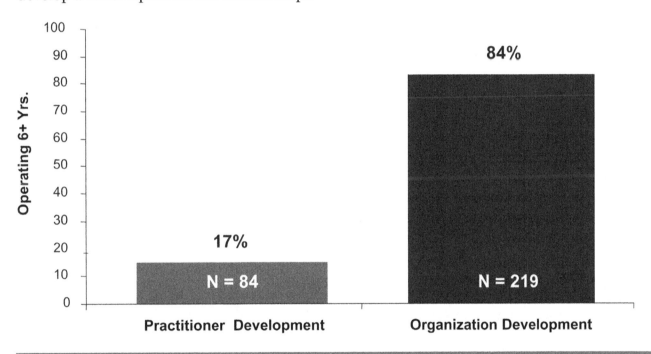

Figure 13. Program sustainability under two conditions: practitioner development and organization development. Data from Fixsen et al. (2007)

The result of accumulated knowledge can be seen in the replications of the Teaching-Family Model. As shown in Figure 13, when the focus was on practitioner development, only 17% of the group home treatment programs sustained for six years or more (Blase, Fixsen, & Phillips, 1984; Fixsen, Blase, Timbers, & Wolf, 2007). This experience led to a focus on developing whole organizations as the scalable unit so that the Implementation Team, Implementation

Drivers, and Improvement Cycles could be built into the organization as part of its ongoing operations. Under these conditions, 84% of the group home treatment programs sustained for six years or more (Fixsen et al., 2007). Organization Drivers are strong implementation variables and make a big difference in sustainability of effective implementation and innovation practices.

Fixsen and Blase (1993, p. 609) commented on the process of being planned and purposeful to maximize learning from experience:

"At [an implementation] level, the feedback loops are usually very long. [Implementation Teams] must engage in a lot of behavior over many months and years before the results can be experienced, strategies adjusted, and the new results experienced. It is at this point that the value of the integrated view becomes as apparent for program [implementation] as it is for treatment. Enough program developer [Implementation Team] staff must be present throughout the entire process in order to learn the lessons that these experiences have to offer. At least a few people have to be consistently present and personally involved in order to be contingency shaped and come to 'a new and different rational understanding [that] has more Quality' (Pirsig, 1974, p. 255)."

Being planned and purposeful seems simple enough until pressing events and crises overtake the plans, and the purpose shifts to surviving conflict and maintaining services during the turmoil of organization and system change. Yet, the purposeful (mission driven) use of the Active Implementation Frameworks and evaluation of implementation outcomes and innovation outcomes provide the pathway for continual development of evidence-based approaches to implementation practice, science, and policy. As stated by colleagues, "the Active Implementation Frameworks are the gyroscope that keeps us on track during times of change."

## Implementation Team roles

Active Implementation Teams are at the center of establishing system factors, organization capacity, and innovation fidelity and sustainability outcomes (Table 10). Expert Implementation Teams using the Active Implementation Frameworks are strong variables and can be used purposefully to produce high fidelity use of innovations. Strong Implementation Teams also use the Active Implementation Frameworks to develop high reliability organizations (Weick, Sutcliffe, & Obstfeld, 1999) with facilitative administrative practices and leadership to support the high fidelity use of innovations. This process exposes aspects of the overall system in a region, state, or nation that must be changed using Systemic Change processes so that system factors are aligned and enabling of organizations, implementation, and innovations.

Table 10. Predicted outcomes from strong and weak system, organization, and Implementation Teams.  Fixsen et al. (2005, p 59), used with permission

| System Factors | Organizational Capacity | Active Implementation Teams | Predicted Fidelity Outcomes | Predicted Sustainability Outcomes |
|---|---|---|---|---|
| Generally Enabling | Strong | Strong | High | Long Term |
| | | Weak | Low/Medium | Medium Term |
| | Weak | Strong | High | Medium Term |
| | | Weak | Low | Short Term |
| Generally Hindering | Strong | Weak | High | Medium Term |
| | | Weak | Low | Medium Term |
| | Weak | Strong | Medium/High | Short Term |
| | | Weak | Low | Short Term |

With strong Implementation Teams, strong organization capacity, and enabling system support, high fidelity is routinely achieved, and outcomes are sustained and improved with experience.  No other combination of factors in Table 10 produces high fidelity and sustained support for long-term outcomes.  Like the facilitators and change agents described by Havelock and Havelock (1973, p. 59ff), Implementation Teams function as a:

"catalyst (prod and pressure, overcome inertia, create dissatisfaction, get things started), solution giver (know what and when, where, to whom to deliver it, technical proficiency), process helper (recognize and define needs, diagnose problems and set objectives, acquire needed resources, select or create solutions, adapt or install solutions, evaluate to determine progress), and resource linker (people, time, motivation, funds)."

Van Dyke (2015) describes the ten core competencies of an Implementation Team member as:

> *"relationship development, leadership engagement and guidance, implementation instruction, implementation facilitation, intervention operationalization, team development, data-informed decision making, strategic analysis to support change, team-based project management, and coaching."*

Implementation Teams disturb the status quo and support Systemic Change by using the Active Implementation Frameworks. In the organization and Systemic Change process, Implementation Teams are the sensors that detect drift, error, and misalignment. They work to correct those issues promptly so that benefits continue to be realized (and improved) for recipients.

## Doing the work of implementation

A variety of authors have identified the need for action to support the use of innovations in practice. These authors have noted the complexity of the tasks. The suggestions for finding self-appointed or somehow-organized groups who might take on these tasks and who might intuitively know what to do and how to do leaves a lot to chance. These methods likely cannot be relied on for scaling to achieve socially significant outcomes.

Active Implementation specifies the need for Implementation Teams embedded in organizations and systems that intend to use innovations fully and effectively and sustain them on a socially significant scale. In recent years, linked Implementation Teams have been established (developing Implementation Teams so they can create more Implementation Teams) in support of Systemic Change and the use of a variety of innovations at scale (Fixsen et al., 2017; Fixsen et al., 2013). This process makes use of the practice and science of implementation to improve implementation itself. This is similar to the "virtuous circles" where crude computer hardware and software are used to create improved hardware and software (Gertner, 2012; Humble & Farley, 2011). This process turns the science and technology on itself to create improved versions of itself.

Implementation capacity in the form of linked Implementation Teams has been developed in state education systems in the U.S. In this example, Implementation Teams are developed so that they can use the Active Implementation Frameworks to create more Implementation Teams so that all teachers in all schools eventually can be supported (Fixsen et al., 2013; Ryan Jackson et al., 2018). After five years of trial and learning, the implementation capacity development process was established and replicated in four complex state education systems

(Fixsen, Ward, Ryan Jackson, et al., 2018). Figure 14 shows the results of using a purposeful process for developing Regional Implementation Teams that develop many District Implementation Teams that support schools and teachers. The staff for each Implementation Team already are employed in the state education system ("repurposed" via selection, training, coaching, fidelity), and the Implementation Teams are embedded in existing structures in the system (i.e., state, regional, district, and school organizations).

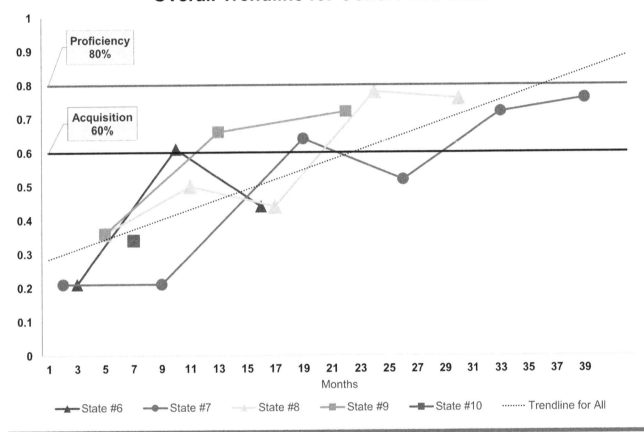

Figure 14. State Capacity Assessment (SCA) data for five states. A score of 60% is the benchmark for initial learning and a score of 80% or more is the benchmark for proficiency

The State Capacity Assessment (SCA) was developed to assess implementation capacity. The SCA is administered twice a year in each state (Fixsen, Ward, Duda, Horner, & Blase, 2015). The respondents who complete the SCA are directly involved in the change processes at the state level (e.g., deputy superintendent, cabinet members, division directors, state implementation specialists). After each administration, the respondents and others prioritize areas that need attention and develop action plans to improve those areas. The SCA is used to assess capacity in each state system and measures common aspects of implementation and scaling across uniquely configured systems.

## Investing in strong implementation variables

In the world of effective innovations, effective implementation, and enabling contexts, socially significant outcomes depend on an investment in effective implementation. "Effective implementation" is operationalized by the current version of the Active Implementation Frameworks that provide guidance for purposeful initiatives to improve the wellbeing of whole populations. The Active Implementation Frameworks continue to evolve as the use of the frameworks deepens and expands the understanding of what it takes to produce socially significant outcomes on purpose and at scale. Without purposeful use of the Active Implementation Frameworks, funders and policy makers and program directors are left with haphazard attempts to support the use of effective innovations at scale.

Developing strong implementation variables takes extra time and effort but is worth it in terms of sustainable and scalable implementation outcomes and innovation outcomes.

# Chapter 6: Usable Innovations

Usable Innovations are operationalized so they are teachable, learnable, doable, and assessable in practice. Usable Innovations are effective when used as intended. Usable Innovations have a way to detect the presence and strength of the innovation as it is used in everyday practice.

 Innovations have been the focus of implementation efforts in all fields of endeavor in human services, social sciences, agriculture, business, computing, engineering, manufacturing, and so on. Standard practices are what we do every day; innovations are something new. Innovations are deviations from standard practice. K. J. Klein and Sorra (1996) define an innovation as "a technology or practice that an organization is using for the first time, regardless of whether other organizations have previously used the technology or practice." Nord and Tucker (1987) and Rogers (1995) have offered similar definitions.

All innovations are not created equal. Some are complex (the internet; emergency obstetrics), some are technical (the steam engine; a data-entry program), and some are simple (the plow; reading aloud to a child). A big problem at the practice level is trying to figure out what is supposed to be done when attempting to use an innovation for the first time. Anyone who has read a manual to use an innovation or attempted to work with a child with autism or attempted to provide emergency obstetric services has experienced the problem. If you don't know what to do, it will be difficult to do it and, even if you are somehow successful, it will be virtually impossible to replicate the intended outcomes.

*Research on innovations rarely includes measures of the independent variable – the innovation itself. When multiple examples of an innovation must be produced to fit the requirements of a rigorous experimental design, the reader is left to wonder to what extent the innovation was present and fully in use in each instance.*

For the past few decades, evidence-based practices have been highlighted as effective innovations. The emphasis has been on the rigor of the research methods used to produce evidence in support of an innovation. Good evidence is important. If an organization is going to select an innovation for use, there needs to be some indication that the effort will be "worth it" in terms of outcomes. But it is not enough.

## Usable Innovation criteria

While debates about evidence-based programs have sharpened the focus on research methods and internal validity, the definition of an innovation has not been part of the discussion. From an implementation point of view, an innovation must be articulated so that it is teachable, learnable, doable, and assessable in practice. To produce socially significant outcomes, a Usable Innovation meets four criteria:

1. Clear *description* of the innovation
   a. Philosophy, values, and principles
      i. The philosophy, values, and principles that underlie the innovation provide guidance for all innovation-related decisions, innovation decisions, and evaluations. They are used to promote consistency, integrity, and sustainable effort across all organization units.
      ii. For example, the Teaching-Family Model philosophy emphasizes ecologically appropriate treatment (family, peer, school, community); values include providing care and treatment that is humane, effective, individualized, satisfactory to recipients and consumers, cost efficient, and replicable. It uses principles derived from applied behavior analysis concerning teaching appropriate alternative behavior, positive motivation, and self-government (Phillips et al., 1974; Wolf et al., 1995).
   b. Inclusion and exclusion criteria that define the population for which the innovation is intended
      i. The criteria define who is most likely to benefit when the innovation is used as intended, and who is not likely to benefit.
      ii. For example, Multisystemic Therapy (MST) includes youths who are a) serious juvenile offenders b) at imminent risk of placement in residential care (incarceration) and c) living with at least one parent or adult caregiver (Schoenwald, Brown, & Henggeler, 2000).
      iii. Chinman, Imm, and Wandersman (2004) stated it is important to be as specific as possible when describing whom the innovation is intended to serve. Feldstein and Glasgow (2008) suggested the

targeted populations' range of characteristics must be considered, such as age, gender, socioeconomic status, literacy, native language, and culture. Recipients often have competing demands for their attention, and pre-existing health conditions or family or work demands may make it physically challenging to follow through with encouraged actions. Thus, relevant aspects of intended recipients are a characteristic of the definition of an innovation.

2. Clear description of the *essential functions* that define the innovation
    a. Essential functions are the features that must be present to say that an innovation exists in a given application (sometimes called core intervention components, active ingredients, or practice elements).
    b. For example, McHugo, Drake, Teague, and Xie (1999, p. 820) describe the nine essential components of Assertive Community Treatment (ACT) as community locus, assertive engagement, high intensity, small caseload, continuous responsibility, staff continuity, team approach, multidisciplinary staff, and close work with support systems.
    c. Sandler et al. (2005) noted that it is a challenge to describe an innovation in enough detail to get an accurate understanding of its core components in practice. Unlike physical products where drawings or simple models of the product can be produced, human service descriptions rely on written concept statements and outlines. Elwyn, Taubert, and Kowalczuk (2007) warned against causal ambiguity where the precise reasons for successful outcomes are not understood. Problems using an innovation in new settings will be difficult to resolve if the essential functions of the innovation itself are not clear.
    d. Damschroder et al. (2009), Kilbourne, Neumann, Pincus, Bauer, and Stall (2007), Szulanski (1996), and others relate adaptability and refinement of innovations to the clarity of the core components, "the essential and indispensable elements" of the innovation itself. Greenhalgh et al. (2004) call the core components the "hard core," and the adaptable elements the "soft periphery." These authors agree that adaptation is meaningful only when the core elements are known and understood. As Kilbourne et al. (2007) stated, "Having the core elements detailed, while also providing options for implementing these core elements, is vital for optimizing both fidelity to the intervention and flexibility in its implementation."

3. *Operational definitions* of the essential functions
    a. Practice profiles (Hall, 1974; Tilly III, 2008) describe the essential functions in terms of activities that allow an innovation to be teachable, learnable, doable, and assessable in practice; and promote consistency across

practitioners at the level of actual service delivery (also known as innovation configurations; Hall & Hord, 2011; Horsley & Loucks-Horsley, 1998).

b. For example, teaching appropriate alternative behavior is an essential function of the Teaching-Family Model (P. D. Braukmann, Kirigin Ramp, Braukmann, Willner, & Wolf, 1983; Phillips et al., 1974); a teaching interaction is operationally defined as:

c. Qualitative Components
    i. Use a calm, caring speaking voice
    ii. Be enthusiastic and positive when praising
    iii. Be calm and matter of fact when offering corrective feedback
    iv. Stay in close proximity
    v. Use polite and pleasant requests (please ..., would you ...)

d. Behavior Components
    i. Initial positive statement
        1. Begin with statement of praise, empathy, affection
        2. Set a positive tone for the interaction
    ii. Name the skill (use a concept label)
        1. The focus for the interaction
    iii. Describe the inappropriate behavior (reactive teaching only)
        1. Give a specific description (a replay of what happened or was omitted)
        2. Demonstrate what cannot be described (facial expressions, gestures)
        3. Do not blame or mock the youth (be non-judgmental)
    iv. Describe the negative consequence (reactive teaching only)
        1. Mention loss of access to privileges, points, checkmarks
        2. State positive correction (earn back half the loss by practicing appropriate alternative behavior now)
    v. Describe the appropriate behavior
        1. Restate the skill label
        2. Provide specific description (exactly what to do and say)
        3. Demonstrate what cannot be described (voice tone, facial expressions)
    vi. Give a rationale
        1. Make brief, personal, believable statement
        2. Point out short-term natural benefits or harms of the skill
        3. Link skill label, behaviors, and outcomes
    vii. Request acknowledgement
        1. Check for understanding

  viii. Practice
    1. State skill label
    2. Describe/demonstrate appropriate behavior components
    3. Set up the practice "scene"
    4. Act out the scene
  ix. Practice feedback
    1. Give effective praise for parts of practice that went well
    2. Provide corrective feedback for parts that need improvement
    3. Repractice to criterion until youth are comfortable with new skill
    4. Reinforce positive consequences (positive correction: earn back half of any loss)
  x. General praise
    1. Give praise for engaging in the interaction (cooperation)
    2. Encourage the effort to learn
 e. Aarons et al. (2011) advocate for a "high degree of procedural specificity in work activities." Chinman et al. (2004) and Greenhalgh et al. (2004) recommend the development of "innovation configurations" as described by Hall and Hord (1987, 2011). As noted in the example above, innovation configurations (also known as practice profiles) provide specific examples of proficient, acceptable, and unacceptable behavior related to each core component of an innovation.

4. A practical assessment of fidelity
 a. A fidelity assessment relates to the innovation philosophy, values, and principles; essential functions; and core activities specified in the practice profiles; and is practical and can be done repeatedly in the context of typical human service systems.
 b. A fidelity assessment provides evidence that the innovation is effective when used as intended; that is, the fidelity assessment is highly correlated with intended outcomes.
 c. For example, Forgatch and DeGarmo (2011, p. 238) outline a fidelity measure (called FIMP) for the Parent Management Training Oregon model (PMTO) that assesses:
  i. Knowledge: Demonstrated understanding of PMTO content and theoretical principles
  ii. Structure: Ability to accomplish agenda activities and goals while addressing family issues. Includes maintaining orderly flow, leading without dominating, responsiveness to family, good transitions, and sensitive timing and pacing

iii. Teaching: Proficiency in strategies that promote parents' mastery and use of PMTO practices. Verbal teach includes standard pedagogical tactics (give information, make suggestions); active teach engages families in the learning process by brainstorming, role playing, and eliciting solutions

iv. Process: Provides support that promotes a safe and supportive learning context. Includes questioning that leads to insight, maintaining balance among participants, encouraging skill development, joining family's storyline

v. Overall Development: Promotes family's growth in PMTO use. Includes likelihood that family can/will use procedures, family's apparent satisfaction, likelihood of continuing, managing unique/difficult aspects of contexts/issues

d. "FIMP ratings are based on time samples of therapy sessions in which two core parenting practices are delivered: skill encouragement and limit setting. Two sessions are rated for each component, one introducing the component and another troubleshooting that component. For practitioner-certification purposes, full sessions are rated. For research and reliability assessment, segments of approximately ten minutes are sampled from video-recorded family intervention sessions. To identify segments for rating, trained assistants spot-check tapes labeled with topics, seeking segments of approximately ten minutes with content on a relevant component (i.e., skill encouragement or limit setting) and teaching activity (e.g., debriefing home practice, role playing, brainstorming for incentives or negative consequences).

e. "FIMP raters are required to be certified PMTO practitioners and are familiar with PMTO manuals and practices. During training, coders learn the coding manual, view and score video recordings, discuss agreements/disagreements with the trainer, and take the reliability test. In their study of fidelity, the FIMP raters were the PMTO trainers; sessions were randomly assigned to raters without regard to time point in training (i.e., early, mid, late)."

f. Graham et al. (2006) noted it is important to define what constitutes knowledge (the core components, operationalized) so that it can be measured in applications. A fidelity measure can be used to determine whether knowledge-based innovations have been sufficient to bring about the desired change or whether new interventions may be required. Klein and Sorra (1996) point to the ultimate criterion the extent to which intended outcomes of an innovation, used as intended, are realized in the organization. Fidelity will be discussed as one of the Implementation Drivers. Here, we are speaking of fidelity as a characteristic of the definition of an innovation. If there is no way to assess fidelity, the innovation is not a Usable Innovation.

## Evidence-based innovations

The evidence-based movement is based on rigorous research conducted on innovations. Literature reviews extensively analyze the rigor of the research and provide various tests of the degree to which an innovation is "evidence-based" or not. Since the 1990s, the focus has been on the innovation. From an implementation perspective, this is a good start. An effective innovation is one of the factors in the Formula for Success for producing socially significant outcomes.

In this chapter the focus is on Usable Innovation criteria which do not reference the rigor of the research. There are two reasons for this omission.

First, summaries of evidence-based innovations focus on the rigor of the research (use of randomized group designs; effect sizes) and do not focus on the core components of an innovation. It is uncommon to find a detailed description of an innovation in the methods section of a research article. Readers are left with a black box called "the innovation" that may have produced carefully analyzed results. As noted by multiple authors such as Dane and Schneider (1998) and Michie, Fixsen, Grimshaw, and Eccles (2009) for over 20 years, there is little empirical evidence to support assertions that the components named by an evidence-based program developer are, in fact, the essential functions necessary for producing the effects. There may be named but unnecessary components included that do not actually contribute to measured outcomes. There may be other un-named, un-measured components that are necessary and that actually produce the outcomes (P. S. Jensen et al., 2005). The mention or lack of mention of certain components by a researcher should not be confused with their function or lack of function in practice. Opening the black box takes some effort (Chorpita, Daleiden, & Weisz, 2005). Nevertheless, the evidence supporting an innovation is a factor in selecting an innovation for consideration. There is no point in attempting to provide thoughtful and effective implementation supports for an innovation that is not effective and may even be harmful.

Second, research on innovations rarely includes measures of the independent variable–the innovation itself (Durlak & DuPre, 2008; Naleppa & Cagle, 2010). When multiple examples of an innovation must be produced to fit the requirements of a rigorous experimental design, the reader is left to wonder to what extent the innovation was present and fully in use in each instance. And, potential users of the innovation are left without a useful measure of fidelity in practice.

Instead of relying on summaries of effect sizes of "evidence-based" innovations, a Usable Innovation criterion relates fidelity of the use of the innovation and outcome data. A strong correlation means that innovations that are used as intended (with high fidelity) produce intended outcomes. And, innovations that are not being used as intended produce poor outcomes or (sometimes) harmful outcomes. A Usable Innovation always has a good way (a fidelity measure) to detect the presence and strength of the innovation as it is used in practice. No innovation should be considered "evidence-based" without a fidelity assessment that meets the Usable Innovation criterion. Evidence that a fidelity measure correlates with intended outcomes at 0.70 or above is desirable (i.e., use of the innovation as intended explains about 50% of the variance in outcomes). Fidelity measures used in human services often correlate with outcomes in the 0.40 or less range.

For evaluations of fidelity and outcomes, it is preferable to display the data in a table that contrasts the top and bottom quintiles. For example, Table 11 shows the outcomes for practitioners who scored in the top or bottom quintile on Functional Family Therapy (FFT) fidelity assessments. Recidivism outcomes (number of youths who committed another felony offense during or after treatment) were greatly improved for youths treated by a high fidelity FFT therapist (8% recidivism) compared to a low fidelity FFT therapist (34% recidivism). Recidivism in the control group was 22%. High fidelity use of FFT made a big difference.

Table 11. An example of how to display fidelity and outcome scores to maximize their usefulness in practice. Based on data produced by the Washington State Institute for Public Policy (2002). Washington State's Implementation of Functional Family Therapy for Juvenile Offenders: Preliminary Findings (No. 02-08-1201). Olympia, WA: Washington State Institute for Public Policy.
http://www.wsipp.wa.gov/pub.asp?docid=02-08-1201

| Average Fidelity Score | Average Outcome Score |
|---|---|
| Top 20% of Fidelity Scores | 8% recidivism |
| Bottom 20% of Fidelity Scores | 34% recidivism |

Showing the data in this table format helps a reader select an innovation and helps a reader see the extent to which a measure of fidelity is related to measured outcomes. With the support of the Implementation Drivers, the goal is to have all practitioners meet the cutoff score for the top 20%.

Any innovation can be developed or assessed with the Usable Innovation criteria in mind. An innovation may or may not have rigorous research to support it. The keys to producing socially significant outcomes are knowing what the innovation is (Usable Innovation criteria 1-3) and having evidence that when the innovation is done as intended, it produces the intended outcomes (Usable Innovation criterion 4).

Given our experience with the Teaching-Family Model and interviews with other program developers (Naoom et al., 2006), it may take 40 or 50 attempted uses in practice before an innovation is understood and described well enough to be repeatable and effective in practice. The purposeful use of Improvement Cycles likely will reduce the time and effort required to meet the Usable Innovation criteria. The conclusion offered by McGrew, Bond, Dietzen, and Salyers (1994, p. 671) is relevant today: "Development of fidelity measures is hampered by three factors: 1) models not well-defined conceptually making it difficult to identify critical ingredients, 2) when critical ingredients have been identified, they are not operationally defined with agreed-upon criteria for implementation, 3) few models have been around long enough to study systematic variations."

Given the importance of meeting the Usable Innovation criteria, and given how few innovations currently meet these criteria, the task of developing Usable Innovations becomes the work of an Implementation Team.

### Innovations and fit with recipients

The fit between an innovation and recipients of the use of an innovation is an important topic. For the inclusion exclusion criteria for a Usable Innovation, who decides? For many human services, the funder establishes criteria for specific services to particular individuals, families, or communities. Thus, funding specifies the inclusion exclusion criteria.

At the point of service delivery, the recipient has a voice in deciding which provider and which services she will receive. The National Alliance on Mental Illness (https://www.nami.org/) uses the phrase "nothing about us without us" to emphasize the active role of the recipients of services. Karlin and Cross (2013) have scaled up effective innovations in the Veterans Health Administration (VA) system in the U.S. They discussed the value of pretreatment processes such as orientation groups to provide recipients with information about effective innovations and allow for discussion of their potential benefits for a particular veteran's problems. The introductory processes are designed to promote veterans' informed choice in the treatment planning process and to promote engagement in the therapy. The World Health Organization (WHO) recently advanced guidelines for a woman's care during childbirth (https://news.un.org/en/story/2018/02/1002781). "Achieving the best possible physical, emotional, and psychological outcomes for the woman and her baby requires a model of care in which health systems empower all women to access care that focuses on the mother and child." The WHO notes that the guidelines are in response to "disrespectful and non-dignified care [that] is prevalent in many health facilities, violating human rights and preventing women from accessing care services during childbirth."

The recipient has a voice in deciding who will provide services and how those services will be provided. A strong case has been made for the value of regular "consumer evaluations" by the recipients of services (Solnick, Braukmann, Bedlington, Kirigin, & Wolf, 1981; Wolf et al., 1995). The data from these assessments give recipients a strong voice in the evaluation of the respectfulness and quality of services they receive.

*Innovations and fit with practitioners and organizations*

A substantial literature emphasizes the importance of the fit between an innovation and characteristics of the organization or individuals associated with the organization that intends to use the innovation. As defined by Klein and Sorra (1996): "Fit describes the extent to which targeted users perceive that use of the innovation will foster or inhibit the fulfillment of their values." Often, fit and readiness are discussed together–the better the fit the more ready the organization and individuals are considered to be.

In the innovation-organization fit discussion, fit can be improved in two ways: change the innovation to fit the existing organization or change the organization to fit the innovation. Damschroder et al. (2009) state a common view that innovations need to change to fit organizations: "Without adaptation, interventions usually come to a setting as a poor fit, resisted by individuals who will be affected by the intervention, and requiring an active process to engage individuals in order to accomplish implementation." The barriers in place in a particular organization are the reasons for adapting/modifying an innovation to improve fit. Given the difficulties of knowing all this information in advance of using an innovation, Murray et al. (2010) suggest designing future innovations on purpose so that they are a good fit with existing organizations and practices.

Since this view requires innovations to be adapted to fit an organization, questions are raised about what aspects of an innovation can be adapted and why. Chinman et al. (2004) citing Backer (2002) state adaptation should be informed by well-operationalized core components that have been evaluated to demonstrate their relative contributions to outcomes. This helps to guard against adapting aspects of an innovation that are essential to producing its intended benefits. Greenhalgh et al. (2004) echo this idea by noting that the use of innovations is preceded by a lengthy period of negotiation that may impact any relative advantage an innovation may have had. Aarons, Hurlburt, and Horwitz (2011) state that the degree to which an innovation is congruent with system, organization, and provider goals and processes is likely to impact the ease with which implementation proceeds. They add that the characteristics of a given EBP may allow for more or less flexibility in intervention delivery while adhering to EBP core elements demonstrated to be responsible for treatment outcome effects. Damschroder et al. (2009) state that "The intervention is often complex and multi-faceted, with many interacting components. Interventions can be conceptualized as having 'core components' (the essential and indispensable elements of the intervention) and an 'adaptable periphery' (adaptable elements, structures, and systems related to the intervention and organization into which it is being implemented)."

The conclusion from this view is that when poor fit is encountered, the innovation must change to fit the realities within a practitioner group or an organization and, hopefully, the difficult-to-know essential elements of the innovation will be retained in the process of adaptation. Adaptation of innovations may be required and, if so, any adaptations should provide demonstrable (data-based) improvements in outcomes. In business, deviation from high fidelity (i.e., adaptation) was detrimental initially and deviation improved outcomes only after organizations had considerable experience (about 17 years) with providing high fidelity services (R. J. Jensen, 2007; Szulanski & Jensen, 2008).

## Implementation of innovations and organization change

On the other side of the innovation-organization fit discussion, fit can be created or improved by changing the organization to fit the innovation. That is, status quo organizations, already producing less-than-desirable results, need to change to improve fit with Usable Innovations. Implementation begins the Exploration Stage with the assumption that practitioner behavior, organization management, and related routines need to change to use an innovation with high fidelity. If there is poor fit, then fit is improved by changing the people (e.g., teaching new skills to ready and willing practitioners) and circumstances (e.g., employing and supporting coaches; scheduling time for fidelity assessments) in which the innovation is to be used, not just one time but from now on. The purpose of implementation is to help solve problems and to scale solutions to realize population benefits.

In this view of fit, it is assumed that the status quo will need to change to create a hospitable organization environment in which the innovation can thrive and become standard practice (the new status quo). Generally, Implementation Specialists and Team members support the use of innovations as intended (with high fidelity) to discover and deal with barriers and realize intended benefits at the earliest possible time. Organization change is discussed in the Implementation Drivers chapter. System change is discussed in the Systemic Change chapter.

# Chapter 7: Implementation Stages

Implementation is a process, not an event. The process is marked by Implementation Stages that have been identified in practice and are used to guide organization and system investments in innovations supported by Implementation Science. To use innovations and implementation in practice takes time and effort. As W. Williams (1975, p. 531) cautioned decades ago, "We have got to learn that the implementation period for complex social programs is not a brief interlude between a bright idea and opening the door for service."

 The Stages of Implementation are Exploration, Installation, Initial Implementation, and Full Implementation. Active Implementation assumes the availability of a skilled Implementation Team to facilitate the expeditious movement from Exploration to Full Implementation. Without an Implementation Team, organizations and individuals will struggle with what should be predictable issues as well as the many unpredictable issues that always arise as attempts are made to use an innovation in practice. The issues will be there with or without an Implementation Team. The question is, who will resolve stage-based issues effectively and efficiently?

*The Stages of Implementation are descriptive rather than prescriptive. By describing identifiable Stages, Implementation Teams and others can adjust their inputs to match the Stage for achieving full, effective, and sustained use of an innovation.*

The Stages of Implementation are not linear. They are additive and interactive with movement back and forth with changes in environments, people, and implementation supports. The Stages are specific to an innovation. A given organization might be in the Full Implementation Stage with one innovation and in the Exploration Stage with another. With experience, skilled Implementation Teams can anticipate and prevent issues and help move an innovation to Full Implementation more quickly across innovations within an organization and across organizations. And, organizations can learn to learn (develop "absorptive capacity") and improve their ability to identify, assimilate, and apply innovations more quickly (Cohen & Levinthal, 1990; Jiménez-Barrionuevo, Magdalena, García-Morales, Molina, & Miguel, 2011).

For example, in the Teaching-Family Model the time for whole organizations to reach site certification (organization fidelity) criteria was reduced substantially while success improved. For Teaching-Family group homes, 23% sustained for five years or more without the support of an Implementation Team, and 84% sustained for six years or more with the support of a site-based Implementation Team. And, the time to develop site-based Implementation Teams was reduced from 6.4 to 3.7 years as site development processes were operationalized (Fixsen & Blase, 2018; Fixsen et al., 2007) As the Implementation Teams doing site development gained experience, they were able to anticipate problems and do better Exploration and Installation work with organizations to help them be successful more quickly and with more certainty.

Figure 15 outlines activities within stages and notes the time required to reach Full Implementation. For the two-to-four year time frame noted in the figure, the clock starts when someone convenes the first meeting to consider using an innovation (the beginning of the Exploration Stage), and the clock stops when at least 50% of the practitioners in an organization or system are using the innovation with fidelity and socially significant outcomes (the beginning of the Full Implementation Stage). Data from the stages of implementation completion (SIC) measure (Brown et al., 2014; Saldana et al., 2012), a program performance index measure (Brunk et al., 2014), and others (Rubin, O'Reilly, Luan, Localio, & Christian, 2011; Sabatier, 1986; Swales, Taylor, & Hibbs, 2012) provide indications of similar two-to-four year time frames.

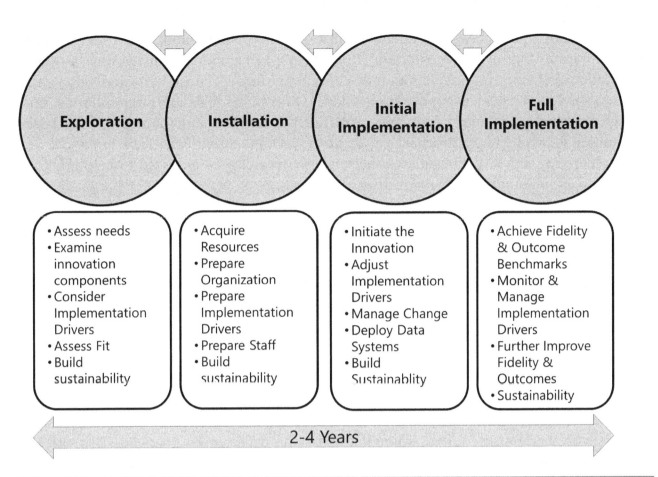

| Exploration | Installation | Initial Implementation | Full Implementation |
|---|---|---|---|
| • Assess needs<br>• Examine innovation components<br>• Consider Implementation Drivers<br>• Assess Fit<br>• Build sustainability | • Acquire Resources<br>• Prepare Organization<br>• Prepare Implementation Drivers<br>• Prepare Staff<br>• Build sustainability | • Initiate the Innovation<br>• Adjust Implementation Drivers<br>• Manage Change<br>• Deploy Data Systems<br>• Build Sustainablity | • Achieve Fidelity & Outcome Benchmarks<br>• Monitor & Manage Implementation Drivers<br>• Further Improve Fidelity & Outcomes<br>• Sustainability |

2-4 Years

Figure 15. Interactive, non-linear, and additive Implementation Stages

It has been clear for decades that initiating and using innovations in practice takes time. Somehow, someone needs to know that certain goals are not being reached, and there is something new out there that may help reach those goals more effectively and efficiently. Communications regarding innovations are part of diffusion processes. Then someone needs to learn what the innovation is and how it might be used in the context of current work. Learning more about an innovation is a part of dissemination processes. Then someone needs to figure out how to use an innovation to solve the problem or reach the goals that led to the interest in using an innovation. Then someone needs to solve all the problems that arise when practitioners attempt to use the innovation in practice. Then someone needs to learn how to juggle resources and standard operating procedures to embed the innovation in the organization to sustain benefits to generations of recipients. Effective and sustained use of innovations as intended are a result of implementation processes. When the "someones" are different people who come and go during the process, there is little hope for achieving socially significant outcomes. Expert Implementation Teams are needed.

Implementation incorporates and builds on diffusion and dissemination activities as part of the Exploration Stage of implementation. Rogers (1995) describes a diffusion process where information about innovations is communicated with the hope of encouraging individuals and organizations to consider using the innovation. Once individuals and organizations have enough information to move from pre-contemplation to contemplation, they may begin preparation for action (J. M. Prochaska et al., 2001; J. O. Prochaska & DiClemente, 1984). As they prepare for action, various dissemination resources may be accessed to help inform a decision to use an innovation (Brownson et al., 2012).

Diffusion and dissemination activities are going on all the time. Some may be purposeful and targeted (e.g., campaigns to encourage medical personnel to wash their hands before interacting with a patient), while other activities are more general (e.g., briefs, conference presentations, website descriptions of information). Diffusion and dissemination activities result in about 14% uptake of innovations after about 17 years (Balas & Boren, 2000; Green, 2008).

Once advances in knowledge and evidence are established, it takes time for that information to be diffused and disseminated. For example:

"A group of reviewers compared the time when evidence became available that clot- busting thrombolytic therapy saved lives among patients who experienced heart attacks, with the recommendations of experts in review papers and chapters in text books (Antman, Lau, Kupelnick, Mosteller, & Chalmers, 1992). Their disturbing finding was that there was a 13-year gap between reliable evidence first becoming available and its adoption by even half of experts in their proffered advice on patient management" (Freemantle & Watt, 1994, p. 133).

Diffusion and dissemination are necessary but they are slow and uncertain processes when the goal is to use an innovation with fidelity and socially significant outcomes (Aladjem & Borman, 2006; Chapin Hall Center for Children, 2002; Taylor et al., 2014).

Much of the diffusion and dissemination literature is aimed at getting information to practitioners and convincing them to use innovations. From an implementation point of view, this is insufficient. Implementation Leadership, Organization Support, and Competency Drivers are essential to effective and sustained use of innovations. Given the necessity of changes in the status quo, the people in charge of organizations and systems need to be involved from the beginning. Thus, the point of entry for implementation work is the executive leadership of an organization or of a system that incorporates many organizations.

The Stages of Implementation outlined here are descriptive rather than prescriptive. By describing identifiable Stages, Implementation Teams and others can adjust their inputs to match the Stage for achieving full, effective, and sustained use of an innovation. Too often, precious time and resources are wasted on trying to insist that organizations and practitioners use an innovation when they have not yet decided it is a good idea (Romney, Israel, & Zlatevski, 2014).

Poorly-informed or half-hearted attempts to appear to do what is mandated consume enormous resources and yield few socially significant outcomes. For example, a multi-country and multi-year study of the impact of facilitation found that the lack of understanding, buy-in, and support from staff and senior leadership likely contributed to low fidelity use of facilitation and to the lack of improved patient outcomes in long-term nursing care organizations (Harvey et al., 2018; Seers et al., 2018). Even in well-funded research studies, a memorandum of understanding is no substitute for the engaging discussion and informed agreements that are the result of Exploration Stage activities. Stage-based activities are briefly outlined in this chapter.

## Non-linear and interactive

Stages are descriptions of activities designed to fit immediate circumstances that occur during the implementation process. Logically, Exploration begins before Installation, and both are precursors to Initial Implementation. Full Implementation presumes Initial Implementation. For Implementation Teams, the pattern is followed in a linear way to initiate an innovation in an organization or system. Once an innovation is established, the stages are non-linear. Full Implementation may be reached only to have major changes in leadership and funding result in turnover of high fidelity practitioners leaving the Implementation Team to start over with Installation and Initial Implementation Stage activities once again. The value of knowing the Stages is that Implementation Teams can recognize the change and promptly and purposefully adjust their activities accordingly.

A common error is scheduling the introduction of an innovation with timing dictated by a funding contract or mandate. Policy makers and funders do not yet recognize the negative effects of their grant making and policy making when they require services to be provided by an organization within a few weeks or months of receiving funding. In effect, the conditions of funding require skipping Exploration and Installation work and starting right away in the Initial Implementation stage. Then, the same funders and policy makers lament the lack of outcomes of their new initiatives. From an implementation view, these are predictable poor outcomes. Organizations are not ready, willing, or able to use the innovation as intended and not able to produce socially significant outcomes because the required innovation is adopted quickly in name but is not in use.

When organizations and individuals are required to attempt to use an innovation without planning, then leaders and managers are faced with holding meetings to understand the innovation and required implementation supports (Exploration after the fact) and to see what resources are needed and try to find them (unanticipated Installation) and try to accommodate the use of the innovation where it does not fit with standard operations (haphazard Initial Implementation). Within typical three-to-five year funding constraints, perhaps 5%-to-15% of organizations and practitioners can accomplish this on their own (Aladjem & Borman, 2006; Glisson, 2007; Grimshaw & Eccles, 2004; Kontoghiorghes, 2004; Rossi & Wright, 1984; Taylor et al., 2014). This is not a good way to try to achieve socially significant outcomes on a useful scale.

Instead of haphazard methods, Implementation Teams attend to a series of planned activities, beginning with the Exploration Stage activities.

## Exploration Stage

Exploration Stage activities include shared communication about the strengths and needs of recipients; identification of possible effective innovations that might help fill the gaps in current approaches; assessment of the Implementation Drivers needed to support practitioners and others; discussion of resources required and their sources; and so on. The result of Exploration is a common understanding and acceptance of the innovation and of the required implementation supports, and a collective decision to proceed (i.e., mutually informed agreement).

### Involve executive leadership

Based on the work of Rogers (1995), the idea of having a champion to initiate and sustain the use of innovations is pervasive in the literature. A champion is someone who convenes meetings and promotes the use of an innovation and helps to create interest and to inspire and legitimize change. In longitudinal studies, champions help get things started, but typically do not continue in that role once the work begins in an organization or system (Panzano et al., 2004). Nevertheless, champions tend to be enthusiastic and inspirational initiators and are important to identify and support during Exploration.

Initial discussions may begin with champions or others in an organization, but executive leadership needs to be approached and included at an early point. As noted throughout the descriptions of implementation, the use of effective innovations and effective implementation supports almost always requires changes in organizations and systems as well as practices. Those changes subsequent to a decision to proceed will require participation of executive leadership in Systemic Change and Practice-Policy Communication Cycles. Thus, executive leaders' and staff understanding of the likely changes and agreement to participate in Systemic Change processes are keys to a mutual decision to proceed.

## Involve stakeholders

During the Exploration process, an Implementation Team assures contact with stakeholders and leaders who need to be informed and who likely will participate in decision making during Installation and Initial Implementation. "Assures contact" means an Implementation Team schedules as many meetings in as many locations as required to make it convenient for key individuals and groups to participate in the Exploration process and decision making. The support of stakeholders over the two-four years it takes to reach Full Implementation has substantial and positive impact on outcomes (Mutamba et al., 2018; Spoth & Greenberg, 2011). That support begins during the Exploration process.

Exploration discussions are a good time to air differences and resolve old issues with the Implementation Team members present to mediate the discussion and to focus energy on doing the next thing well. For example, staff and management issues, union grievances, difficulties working with a board of directors, poor community relations, differing interpretations of funding and licensing requirements, lack of trust among leaders, and similar issues have been part of various Exploration Stage discussions over the years. There is no way to have a better past; there is a way to honor diverse views and to create a better future by working together to establish effective implementation supports for an effective innovation so that identified needs in the community can be satisfied.

## Establish need for change

During Exploration it is especially important to identify the need for change. What is so compelling that leaders and others will invest time and energy and persist while current ways of work are changed, and the organization is changed, and the system is changed to use an innovation to satisfy the need? Preventable deaths, inequalities of various kinds, unacceptable outcomes related to significant investments, threats of closure or loss of funding, unacceptable return on investments, and so on should be documented during Exploration. The documentation can serve as a constant reminder of need, especially when the change process is underway and uncertainty abounds. The other factors outlined below are important for Exploration, but establishing and documenting need is a critical factor (Wang, Saldana, Brown, & Chamberlain, 2010) for sustaining interest and effort while changes are made.

## Consider risk and risk management

While exploring the potential use an innovation, leaders and stakeholders in an organization must consider the risk of disrupting the organization as well as their ability to manage those risks (Nutt, 2002; Panzano & Roth, 2006; Panzano et al., 2004; Tucker & Singer, 2015). Experienced Implementation Teams clearly identify anticipated risks and the methods for managing risks. For example, fewer recipients may be served during Initial Implementation to assure time for training and coaching each cohort of practitioners in the organization. If fewer recipients are served, what are the implications for revenues and expenses and relationships with referral agents, and how can the risks be managed? Existing contracts may be in place that dictate certain activities and products that are counterproductive to establishing the Implementation Drivers in the organization. How amenable are the funding agents and the contractors to "suspending the rules" for a year while their staff are taught new skills to produce the intended products in new ways (Peters & Waterman, 1982; Rhim, Kowal, Hassel, & Hassel, 2007)? These are important considerations that influence decisions to use and support the use of innovations in organizations and systems and need to be part of the Exploration Stage discussions.

## Consider contextual factors

Damschroder et al. (2009) discuss Exploration and readiness in terms of modifiable and non-modifiable contextual factors. For Active Implementation, what is deemed to be "modifiable" depends on the presence and skill of an Implementation Team.

Skilled teams are able to teach more during and after Exploration and, therefore, have fewer non-modifiable "readiness" requirements for selecting organizations. The team members are competent and confident enough to deal with considerable variability in the conditions present at startup.

Less experienced Implementation Teams must select for those dimensions they cannot yet teach comfortably after a selection decision is made. For example, less experienced teams sometimes are wary of their ability to change the hearts and minds of leaders so they select for receptive leadership deep into the organization; they gain confidence as they have more experience with Systemic Change methods.

Inexperienced teams or individuals have to guess what to select for. They have to spend more time finding (hoping for) just the right non-modifiable (for them) conditions to assure an organization is ready, willing, and able to attempt to use an innovation. As noted previously, this likely contributes to the 14% success in 17 years that is the norm for successful use of an innovation.

For any Implementation Team, there are less-readily modifiable factors (compelling need, good judgment, minimally adequate resources, willing leadership, stakeholder support) that must be assessed so the team knows where to focus time and attention initially if a decision is made to proceed.

## Assess and create readiness

The Exploration Stage is not just to assess readiness; it is designed to create readiness. Creating readiness for change in individuals and organizations is an important part of the work and effectiveness of Implementation Teams. Prochaska, Prochaska, and Levesque (2001) found that at given point in time, about 20% of individuals and organizations in their studies were "ready for change." Thus, creating readiness is an essential function for uses of effective innovations and a core activity in the Exploration Stage. Clarifying goals, establishing collaborations, locating and developing resources, securing agreements, and so on are good uses of Exploration Stage discussions. Van Meter and Van Horn (1975) note that the extent of Exploration may depend on the extent to which there is goal consensus among the participants and by the amount of organizational change that is required. Experienced Implementation Teams help to develop consensus as needed and can inspire confidence as they describe how organization change can be initiated and managed to accomplish the goals.

When an Implementation Team is not available, funding agencies can help create readiness by conducting contracting meetings in new ways to help potential applicants prepare to use an innovation with fidelity and socially significant outcomes. Implementation-informed meetings are held with potential applicants to explain the innovation (see the Usable Innovation criteria: Chapter 6) and the Implementation Drivers (Chapter 8). For those organizations that are interested, subsequent meetings ("Drivers conversations") are held so that each organization can describe in the application for funding each Implementation Driver and how the organization intends to assure the full and effective use of each Driver (Robbins & Collins, 2010).

The Drivers conversations process lacks the follow-through coaching and problem solving that would be provided by an Implementation Team. Nevertheless, the process does help to assure that each applicant understands the expectation that the Drivers will be in place in the organization, and fidelity of the use of the innovation will be assessed along with recipient outcomes. The typical "paper exchange" process (send out a request for proposals, review the proposals, fund the ones that look the best on paper) is replaced by an "information exchange" meeting process where many of the Exploration Stage and Installation Stage activities are carried out prior to granting funds. Good grant writers are no substitute for the engaging discussion and informed agreements that are the result of Exploration activities prior to making funding decisions.

**Exploration takes time**

Exploration discussions with a group often go on for a number of months to assure understanding and agreement with what needs to be done to make full, effective, and sustained use of an innovation. The length of the Exploration Stage depends on the resources allocated (time, people) to the process and participants' access to information and authority to make decisions. In a sample of 42 organizations that eventually had one or more practitioners meet fidelity criteria, Exploration time averaged 10.7 months (Saldana & Schaper, personal communication, October 1, 2018). Many Implementation Teams "end" the Exploration process with the signing of a Memorandum of Understanding (MOU) to celebrate the beginning of the intensive work together.

## Installation Stage

The Installation Stage involves acquiring or developing the resources needed to fully and effectively engage in the new ways of work. Resources and activities during Installation are focused on creating new job descriptions and pay scales; establishing interview methods and preparing interviewers to select practitioners and staff to do the new work; employing people to do the work; developing data collection sources and protocols; establishing access to timely training; preparing a coaching-service delivery plan; and so on. While these topics are discussed and debated during the Exploration Stage (promises made), the resources must materialize during the Installation Stage (promises kept). Many of the resources to be acquired or developed during the Installation Stage are listed below.

1. Practitioner-related
   a. Job description and salary scale
   b. Recruitment ads and interview protocols
      i. Employing and preparing interviewers to use best practices
   c. Training content and methods
      i. Employing and preparing trainers to use best practices
   d. Coaching-service delivery plan
      i. Employing and preparing coaches to use best practices
   e. Fidelity assessment protocol
      i. Employing and preparing assessors to use best practices
2. Organization-related
   a. Organization chart to situate the Implementation Team next to executive management in the structure
   b. Roles and functions of directors and managers
      i. In relation to practitioners using an innovation

  ii. In relation to Implementation Team members supporting practitioners and organization leaders
 c. Policies and procedures revised as needed
 d. Referral processes adjusted to fit innovation inclusion-exclusion criteria
 e. Processes to support the innovation funding
 f. Union contracts to support competency development and fidelity assessment
 g. Executive team standing agenda item related to Implementation and the innovation

3. System-related
 a. Accreditation and certification standards adjusted
 b. Requirements for contracting and funding adjusted
 c. Requirements for reporting and accountability adjusted

4. Community-related
 a. Meetings with key stakeholders to invite their understanding, support, and participation

Of course, not all of the items on this partial list will be completed by the time work begins with recipients. However, these factors need to be considered from the beginning. Organizations often think of effective innovations as "plug and play" and are surprised by the need for preparation and resources and change once work begins (Schrenker & Cooper, 2001). Many attempts to use effective innovations end at this stage because the "plug" and the "play" are not equally prepared. Implementation Teams help organization and system leaders and stakeholders anticipate resource and organization needs during the Exploration Stage. Thus, planning for resources is part of Exploration; acquiring the resources and having them in place is the work of the Installation Stage.

**Leadership challenges**

Because of the changes required, the Installation Stage is replete with adaptive leadership challenges. The attention given to the innovation and implementation supports may lead to dissatisfaction among existing staff members who feel devalued and ignored in the rush to do the new things. Some stakeholders who were enthusiastic advocates during Exploration do not follow through on promises they made. Funders get anxious when funds are being spent and no "real work" with recipients has started. And so on.

Implementation Team members and leaders need to be ready to exercise adaptive leadership to resolve these issues as supports for the new ways of work are being developed. Knowing that adaptive issues abound during Installation and Initial Implementation, Implementation Teams use this as an opportunity to develop the adaptive leadership capacity in an organization and establish the Practice-Policy Communication Cycles from the beginning of the process. The issues give the Implementation Team and leaders many opportunities to teach, learn, and practice the new ways to provide adaptive and effective leadership in the organization.

### Establishing Implementation Drivers

A challenge during the Exploration and Installation stages is finding or developing the expertise to use the Implementation Drivers to select, prepare, and support the first group of practitioners. Very few organizations or systems already have a functioning Implementation Team in place. As a result, accessing outside expertise is a good option to get started (Nord & Tucker, 1987). This is the approach Ogden and colleagues used to initiate the use of effective innovations in Norway. Too many overqualified staff were recruited to be the first practitioners. Once a program was underway, they recruited "home grown" staff who had been high fidelity practitioners to be the first members of an Implementation Team (e.g., trainers, coaches, fidelity assessors) to support the next generations of practitioners as they scaled nationally (Tommeraas & Ogden, 2016). However, very few evidence-based practices or innovations have purveyors (program-specific Implementation Teams) that support the effective use of an innovation. Thus, most organizations and systems are left to "do it yourself." That approach has not proved to be very effective (Brown et al., 2014; Durlak & DuPre, 2008; Vernez et al., 2006).

Funders are becoming aware of the need to fund Implementation Teams as part of the funding for innovation-related initiatives. Once funding becomes common, then Implementation Teams will be common. In the meantime, it is important to access groups that are expert in Active Implementation and evaluation to provide direct or indirect support during the Exploration, Installation, and Initial Implementation Stages.

## Initial Implementation Stage

The Initial Implementation Stage begins when the first practitioners attempt to use an innovation with recipients for the first time. Active Implementation staff refer to this as the awkward stage where the new ways of work are not comfortable for practitioners, managers, and leaders. It "doesn't feel right" to interact with others in the new ways, and "it is confusing" when the units within an organization are not yet fully functional and integrated. Very few attempts to use innovations are able to successfully negotiate the difficulties encountered during Initial Implementation where the challenges are many, the supports for change are weak, and the inertia of the status quo is strong.

During the Initial Implementation Stage, newly selected practitioners and staff are attempting to use newly learned skills (e.g., the innovation; the Implementation Drivers) in the context of an organization that is just learning how to change to accommodate and support the new ways of work. This is a fragile stage where the awkwardness associated with trying new things and the difficulties associated with changing old ways of work provide strong motivations for giving up and going back to the familiar, comfortable, and well-supported status quo. The status quo is powerful and resilient and readily bounces back from efforts to change it (Jalava, 2006; Oser, 2000; Zimmerman, Lindberg, & Plsek, 1998; Zucker, 1987).

## Establishing practitioner competence and confidence

Implementation Teams using the Implementation Drivers are essential to success (80% vs. 14% success as referenced previously) during the Initial Implementation Stage. Implementation Teams assure the Implementation Drivers are in place to develop the staff competencies required by an innovation, help administrators adjust organization roles and functions to align with the innovation and implementation supports, and help leaders in the organization and system address challenges and fully support the process of using the innovation and incorporating the necessary implementation supports.

As a way to counter awkwardness, Implementation Teams develop competence and build confidence by selecting staff who are ready to use the effective innovation and are enthusiastic about the support they will receive; training staff so they have the basic knowledge and skills to engage in the new ways of work; coaching staff as they interact with recipients to help them use their new skills in practice; and conducting assessments of the performance of staff using the skills in practice (fidelity) as a way to provide reassurance to practitioners and offer more systematic feedback to staff, coaches, and administrators. Implementation Teams develop competence and bolster confidence in the midst of change. Without access to skilled Implementation Team support it is difficult, in just a few months, to learn the innovation; learn how to provide highly effective staff selection, training, coaching, and fidelity assessments; and change organization operating procedures to accommodate and support practitioners using the innovation with fidelity. Without support during this fragile time, it is difficult for learn what to do and do it effectively to stay ahead of the mounting obstacles to change (Sterman, 2006).

## Establishing organization supports

Organization leaders and Implementation Team members help to change organizations to create conditions that are supportive. Supportive and Facilitative Administration (an Implementation Driver) can mean anything: helping administrators change staff schedules, developing relevant meeting agendas, reassigning staff to new functions, and so on in order to fully support the practitioners and others who are attempting to use innovations. It also may mean helping to establish data systems to support data-based decision making by practitioners, coaches, administrators, and others; and helping to intervene in external systems when impediments are encountered or problems need to be resolved at an executive level.

While supportive Facilitative Administration can mean anything in a general sense, it is always specific in a given context; it is *this* meeting that is getting in the way of using the innovation as intended; it is *this* coaching schedule that is insufficient for supporting high fidelity; and so on. Solving one problem does not necessarily solve *the* problem, but each problem and solution helps managers and leaders become Facilitative Administrators who routinely put support for practitioners and recipient outcomes first. Having a list of possible barriers is good but means little once the specific obstacles appear daily as the change process begins (who knew!).

Implementation Teams help leaders expand their skills to effectively solve technical management issues and resolve difficult adaptive issues where the problems are vague and solutions are not clear. This often involves establishing new communication patterns so that critical information from coaches and Decision Support Data Systems (an Implementation Driver) is timely and accurate. In their studies of use of innovations, VanDeusen Lukas et al. (2007, p. 315) found that "Senior leaders steered change through the organization's structures and processes to maintain urgency, set a consistent direction, reinforced expectations, and provided resources and accountability to support change. They set the path for other model elements and for the interactions among those elements in the larger organization." These are adaptive leadership skills.

During Initial Implementation the basic functions of each of the Implementation Drivers are established. They increasingly become Integrated and Compensatory in an organization. As the awkwardness is overcome, and the organization faces and resolves problems as part of the routine, then the Active Implementation Drivers become embedded in the organization and become the standard way of work in support of using one or more innovations with fidelity and socially significant outcomes.

## Full Implementation Stage

The Full Implementation Stage is reached when at least 50% of the practitioners in an organization meet fidelity criteria on a given day. The 50% is a benchmark established by the Active Implementation Research Network as an indicator of Full Implementation. That is, if the goal is to have 20 practitioners use an innovation in an organization, Full Implementation is reached on the day when 10 (50%) of those practitioners are at or above fidelity criteria. It often takes two to four years to reach Full Implementation when it is achieved at all (Brown et al., 2014; Brunk et al., 2014; Fixsen et al., 2007; Sabatier, 1986; Swales et al., 2012)

The first time the 50% benchmark is reached is cause for celebration. However, it likely will not be sustained for very long. Once a high fidelity practitioner leaves, it will take a few months for the replacement to be selected, trained, coached, and finally meet fidelity criteria. In the meantime, if that one high fidelity practitioner was the tipping point for reaching the 50% benchmark, then the organization will fall short of the 50% benchmark. If key people on the Implementation Team leave, the Competency Drivers may suffer, and it may take longer for practitioners to meet and sustain high fidelity performance. Eventually, for the few organizations that reach and sustain Full Implementation, the new ways of providing innovation-based services become the standard ways of work and the implementation supports become the standard way the organization functions (Fixsen & Blase, 2018). The use of the innovation and the Implementation Drivers becomes the new status quo.

## Sustaining high fidelity use of innovations

Notice that sustaining Full Implementation requires two things: it requires using the Implementation Drivers effectively to routinely generate new high fidelity practitioners, and it requires keeping current high fidelity practitioners employed. If high fidelity practitioners leave faster than new ones can be developed to meet fidelity standards, then the 50% criterion for Full Implementation will never be reached or sustained. The practitioner pool is draining faster than it is being filled. Fortunately, practitioners who experience fidelity assessment and feedback stay in their positions longer. The leadership and Organization Drivers are designed to keep improving supports for practitioners so they can continue to provide high fidelity results for many years, even when doing demanding work (Aarons et al., 2009; Glisson, Schoenwald, et al., 2008; Strouse, Carroll-Hernandez, Sherman, & Sheldon, 2004).

Embedding Implementation Teams and the Drivers in organizations are essential to the ongoing success of using an innovation. Practitioners, staff, administrators, and leaders come and go, and each new person needs to develop the competencies to do the work effectively. Managers and administrators need to continually adjust organizational supports to facilitate and improve the work of practitioners. Systems continue to change and impact organizations and practitioners. Innovations continue to be added, and those already in place continue to be improved. The number of variables and complexity of issues provide a range of technical and adaptive issues that require constant attention and resolution. The work of Implementation Teams is to ensure that the gains in the use of effective practices are maintained and improved over time and through transitions of leaders and staff.

Much more is known and written about the Exploration Stage and Installation Stage since even haphazard attempts to use an innovation encounter the need to make a decision to proceed (or not) and must secure resources to support the use of an innovation. Less is known about Full Implementation for two reasons. First, because few organizations assess fidelity and, therefore, have no way to know if they meet the 50% requirement. Second, because even when fidelity is assessed, few organizations have Implementation Teams that use the Active Implementation Frameworks skillfully to meet and sustain high fidelity performance by the majority of practitioners. Nevertheless, Full Implementation is required to have any hope of reaching scale and producing socially significant outcomes.

## Assessing stages

The stage-based activities described above require some way of knowing what Implementation Stage an innovation is in within an organization. Indicators of stages are summarized in this section.

### Active Implementation benchmarks

Active Implementation benchmarks are used to assess stages. The benchmarks are general and apply to the use of any innovation. Exploration begins when the first meetings are held to discuss the possible use of an innovation to reach an aspirational goal or fulfill a need. Installation begins when individuals and groups are organized to secure required resources to support the use of a selected innovation. Initial Implementation begins when the first newly trained practitioner attempts to use the selected innovation for the first time in interactions with an intended recipient. Full Implementation begins when 50% of all intended practitioners in an organization meet the criteria for high fidelity use of the innovation. The stages do not have end points since they tend to overlap and flow back and forth for many years as people change (back to Exploration as new people are onboarded); resources change (back to Installation to secure what is needed); and events overset the best laid plans (back to Initial Implementation with an exodus of high fidelity practitioners).

### Stages of implementation completion

A detailed and operationalized assessment of stages has been developed for the Treatment Foster Care Oregon (TFCO) program (formerly known as multidimensional treatment foster care; MDTFC). The Stages of Implementation Completion (SIC) instrument (Brown et al., 2014; Chamberlain, Brown, & Saldana, 2011; Saldana & Chamberlain, 2012; Saldana et al., 2012) operationalizes the activities that organizations complete as they prepare for and begin to use TFCO. The SIC is specific to TFCO. The SIC yields three scores including the proportion of tasks completed, the time spent completing the implementation tasks, and the final implementation stage achieved. Although the SIC provides a sequential list of identified activities, scoring of the instrument takes into account the non-linear and recursive nature of activity completion (e.g., activity 3.6 in Table 12 may occur before activity 2.3). The SIC stage-related activities are listed in Table 12 and are organized by the Active Implementation Stages.

Table 12. Stages of Implementation Completion (SIC) measure for Treatment Foster Care Oregon (TFCO). The categories and items from Chamberlain, Brown, & Saldana (2011) are organized in this table by Active Implementation Stages

**Active Implementation Stages**
**TFCO SIC Activities**

**Exploration Stage**
1 Engagement
1.1 Date site is informed services/program available
1.2 Date of interest indicated
1.3 Date agreed to consider implementation
2 Consideration of Feasibility
2.1 Date of first contact for pre implementation planning
2.2 Date first in-person meeting/feasibility call
2.3 Date Feasibility Questionnaire is completed

**Installation Stage**
3 Readiness Planning
3.1 Date of cost/funding plan review
3.2 Date of staff sequence, timeline, hire plan review
3.3 Date of foster parent recruitment review
3.4 Date of referral criteria review
3.5 Date of communication plan review
3.6 Date of in-person meeting
3.7 Date written implementation plan complete
3.8 Date service provider selected
4 Staff Hired and Trained
4.1 Date agency checklist completed
4.2 Date first staff hired
4.3 Date Program Supervisor trained
4.4 Date clinical training held
4.5 Date foster parent training held
4.6 Date Site consultant assigned
5 Adherence Monitoring Processes in place
5.1 Date data tracking system training held
5.2 Date of first program administrator call

**Initial Implementation Stage**

6 Services and Consultation Begin
6.1 Date of first placement
6.2 Date of first consult call
6.3 Date of first clinical meeting video reviewed
6.4 Date of first foster parent meeting video reviewed
7 Ongoing Services, Consultation, Fidelity Monitoring and Feedback
7.1 Dates of site visits
7.2 Date of implementation review
7.3 Date of final program assessment
8 Competency
8.1 Date of certification application
8.2 Date certified (met fidelity criteria)

**Full Implementation Stage**
No items

In studies using the SIC measure, 53 sites (organizations) were enrolled in the study (Chamberlain et al., 2011; Saldana et al., 2012) and all had sufficient time to complete the SIC stages one to three (3.8 Date service provider selected). Of the 53 sites, 22 (42%) made it past stage three and began to hire and train staff. The remaining sites did not complete Exploration and Installation activities and did not attempt to use TFCO.

The TFCO findings are similar to the results obtained by Panzano et al. (2004). At nine-month intervals Panzano and colleagues followed a group of 91 agencies that had committed to and were funded to use one of several evidence-based programs in a state mental health system. All 91 agencies engaged in Exploration and Installation activities, but 44 never used a selected program (i.e., did not reach the Initial Implementation Stage). Within 24.2 months, 12 of the 47 agencies that initially did use a selected program ended their use of the evidence-based program. This left 35 (38%) of the original 91 agencies that reached Initial Implementation and continued to use an evidence-based program for four years (Massatti et al., 2008), a ratio similar to the 42% found in the TFCO studies.

An analysis of a larger SIC data set was conducted for 42 new TFCO sites that successfully completed competency items 8.1 and 8.2 (Saldana & Schaper, personal communication, October 1, 2018). Note that this analysis looks at the history of a select sample of sites that reached SIC stage eight and excludes from the larger SIC data set all discontinued and in-progress sites and all the "expansion sites" that already were using TFCO in their organization. For the 42 sites that reached SIC stage eight, the median time to reach stage eight (competency; at least one practitioner met fidelity criteria) was 1,533 days (50.4 months; 4.2 years).

The time frame resulting from the SIC analysis is a good fit with the two to four years typically required to move from Exploration to Full Implementation as noted in the discussion of Implementation Stages. At a more micro level, as shown in Table 12 the specific SIC items align with the discussion of the Stages of Implementation. Exploration and Installation are important, and few organizations make it through Initial Implementation. The SIC measure is useful and helps to operationalize key activities that mark progress toward Full Implementation for the few organizations that make it that far. While it was developed specifically for TFCO, the SIC items provide a format that can outline key activities for other innovations.

## Active Implementation stages in practice

Engaging in stage-appropriate action requires planning and organization. The information provided about each stage offers guidance for supporting an organization determined to make full and effective use of a selected innovation. Some tools to support the work at each stage are outlined in this section.

### Heptagon tool

The heptagon tool provides a useful guide for discussions during exploration (Blase, Kiser, & Van Dyke, 2009; Van Dyke, Kiser, & Blase, 2019). The heptagon tool (Figure 16) helps to operationalize many of the "pre-conditions" specified by Kilbourne et al. (2007): the "identification of the need for a new intervention for a target population; identification of an effective intervention that fits local settings (e.g., mission of organization and benefits to the organization) and the intended target population (e.g., behavioral risks and culture); identifying implementation barriers; and drafting a user-friendly manual of the intervention." The heptagon tool also operationalizes the seven system factors that Greenberg, Domitrovich, Graczyk, and Zins (2005) recommend considering in the pre-planning stage: a) need for change; b) readiness for change; c) capacity to effect change; d) awareness of the need for change; e) commitment or engagement in the change process; f) incentive for change; and g) history of successful change.

The dimensions of the heptagon tool are a good fit with many of the readiness items developed for use in global health settings. For example, the I-RREACH (Intervention and Research Readiness Engagement and Assessment of Community Health Care) tool is used in meetings and interviews with leaders, stakeholders, and potential recipients to obtain information regarding basic community descriptions, leadership, community programs, local understanding of the issue, resources and planning, perceived fit of the intervention with community objectives, infrastructure and technology, and readiness for community-based research (Maar et al., 2015).

Information and documentation is focused on the community, relevant governance, staff, structure and programs, infrastructure and technology, as well as resources. Key stakeholders generally are individuals who could have a negative or positive effect on the implementation of the intervention. Many of these key stakeholders may be affected by the intervention through training, changes in practice, or additional responsibilities.

The heptagon tool can be used by a staff group in an organization in a self-guided discussion or in a discussion led by an Implementation Team. The dimensions and items for discussion draw attention to the factors that often are cited as facilitators and barriers to using innovations and producing intended benefits. During Exploration, sub-committees can be formed to focus on one or two dimensions and develop information for decision making by the group.

As shown in Figure 16, need, evidence, fit, usability of the innovation, capacity to implement, resource availability, and capacity to collaborate are key dimensions to consider. As the discussion proceeds to answer questions about the dimensions outlined in the heptagon tool, it is likely that the composition of the organization and stakeholder group will change to include people who have knowledge of relevant factors. The literature emphasizes securing "buy-in" and support from relevant stakeholders for the proposed new ways of work (e.g., effective implementation supports for effective innovations). This begins during Exploration Stage communications where local information is shared with the Implementation Team and with other members of the local group who also may be hearing the information for the first time.

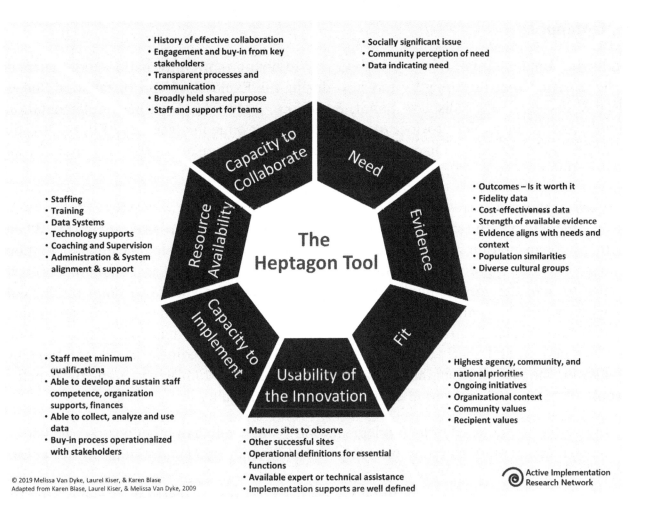

- History of effective collaboration
- Engagement and buy-in from key stakeholders
- Transparent processes and communication
- Broadly held shared purpose
- Staff and support for teams

- Socially significant issue
- Community perception of need
- Data indicating need

- Staffing
- Training
- Data Systems
- Technology supports
- Coaching and Supervision
- Administration & System alignment & support

- Outcomes – Is it worth it
- Fidelity data
- Cost-effectiveness data
- Strength of available evidence
- Evidence aligns with needs and context
- Population similarities
- Diverse cultural groups

**The Heptagon Tool**

Capacity to Collaborate

Need

Resource Availability

Evidence

Capacity to Implement

Fit

Usability of the Innovation

- Staff meet minimum qualifications
- Able to develop and sustain staff competence, organization supports, finances
- Able to collect, analyze and use data
- Buy-in process operationalized with stakeholders

- Highest agency, community, and national priorities
- Ongoing initiatives
- Organizational context
- Community values
- Recipient values

- Mature sites to observe
- Other successful sites
- Operational definitions for essential functions
- Available expert or technical assistance
- Implementation supports are well defined

© 2019 Melissa Van Dyke, Laurel Kiser, & Karen Blase
Adapted from Karen Blase, Laurel Kiser, & Melissa Van Dyke, 2009

Active Implementation Research Network

Figure 16. The Heptagon Tool to guide exploration discussions.
© 2019 Melissa Van Dyke, Laurel Kiser, and Karen Blase, used with permission

## ImpleMapping

Conducting ImpleMap interviews is a good way to obtain more information about current implementation-specific strengths and gaps during the Exploration and Installation Stages (Blase & Fixsen, 2013; Salisbury, Sundt, & Boppre, in press). Creating implementation supports in human service provider organizations is not done in a vacuum. Efforts already are underway using the do-it-yourself approaches that characterize the vast majority of current attempts to use innovations in human services.

Every organization has areas of strength, areas of overlap, gaps, and degrees of integration and fragmentation with regard to current implementation and improvement efforts. When creating implementation capacity in a "new" organization (i.e., developing Implementation Teams to provide supports that are effective, integrated, efficient, and sustainable), it is good practice to map the current implementation landscape. The goal is to build on current strengths and collect information to inform planning the best path toward developing implementation capacity in *this* uniquely configured provider organization. The ImpleMap interview process and sharing of results also helps to create readiness in organizations by highlighting the current strengths and gaps in their implementation activities and the benefits of supporting the implementation of innovations systematically.

The ImpleMap is conducted by an Implementation Team member or other person who knows the Active Implementation Frameworks very well and can interpret and summarize key points quickly (https://www.activeimplementation.org/resources/implemap-exploring-the-implementation-landscape/). The ImpleMap is used during the Installation Stage, after an organization has decided to use an innovation. It leads to a more specific and in-depth discussion of the dimensions listed in the heptagon tool and action planning for how to assure each dimension will be in place when needed.

| INTERVENTION | WHAT | HOW | WHO |
|---|---|---|---|
| Enter the name of each intervention provided by the respondents.<br><br>You may know the intervention by another name, but record the name used in this provider organization.<br><br>Ask questions to get information about the vetting process (who, how decisions are made to use one innovation or another) | Ask about the "core innovation components" as they are described by the respondents.<br><br>Core intervention components are the critical functions that define a Usable Innovation. | Ask about the Implementation Drivers.<br><br>Implementation Drivers are components related to:<br>- developing staff competency (selection, training, coaching, performance assessments);<br>- organization supports (Decision Support Data Systems, Facilitative Administration, systems interventions); and<br>- leadership supports (technical and adaptive). | Ask about the person accountable for providing each Implementation Driver.<br><br>Record the name, position, and physical location of each person. |

The ImpleMap guide in Table 13 outlines questions that are asked in a non-judgmental way. The questions are not intended to be asked in a linear fashion. Conversations with respondents take on a life of their own. Some respondents will volunteer considerable information about one intervention so the questions proceed from left to right on the grid in no particular order. The goal is to arrive at a good "picture" of how implementation has been attempted in the organization. Asking each question in some fixed order is not the goal.

**Assessing Implementation Drivers best practices**

As preparations are made for the first newly trained practitioners to use an innovation when interacting with recipients, the support of the Implementation Drivers becomes essential. The use of the Competency Drivers, Organization Drivers, and Leadership Drivers in practice can be assessed every three months during the first year, twice a year for the next five years, and annually thereafter. The results of each assessment provide data for action planning to establish each Driver, for Practice-Policy Communication with executive leadership to assure organization and leadership support for the use of the Drivers as intended, and for continual improvement of each Driver and all the Drivers working in harmony. Regular assessments keep implementation in the forefront as innovations are used and improved in practice (Fixsen, Ward, Blase, et al., 2018).

In studies using the Assessing Drivers Best Practices measure, the data correlate highly with fidelity of use of innovations and discriminate between different approaches to providing implementation supports (Fixsen, Ward, Blase, et al., 2018; Metz et al., 2014; Ogden et al., 2012).

**Implementation Quotient for organizations**

The benchmark for Full Implementation is to have 50% of all the practitioners in an organization providing services that meet fidelity criteria. While this is a difficult criterion to meet, it also means that half of the practitioners are functioning at less than minimum fidelity standards. Thus, overall, the recipient outcomes for the organization will be vastly improved at the 50% mark but still fall short of what could be achieved if all practitioners were functioning at high fidelity. Given turnover and length of time to reach fidelity, having 100% of the practitioners meeting fidelity standards is not likely to be achieved in interaction-based human services. Yet, provider organizations and systems should work to approximate 100% fidelity to maximize benefits to recipients.

The Implementation Quotient measure was developed to provide an organization level assessment of fidelity that takes competency development and turnover into consideration (Fixsen & Blase, 2009). In the calculations below, note that the focus is on the practitioner *positions* and the current occupant of each position. This requires a statement at the beginning of the process about the intentions of an organization regarding the use of an innovation. In the example below, 41 group homes were being managed by the organization. In another example, there were 48 clinical positions in an organization, and the plan was to have them begin to use the innovation sequentially, with 12 in a cohort. Full Implementation (six of the 12 or 50% meet fidelity) had to be achieved with one cohort before the organization began training and coaching for the next cohort. In that case, 48 was the Allocated Position N for the organization since the intention was to have all 48 positions occupied by practitioners using the innovation in the organization.

At a given point in time (June 30 and December 31 each year in the example below), an Implementation Quotient on that day is calculated using the formula below.

Determine the number of practitioner positions allocated to the eventual use of the innovation in the organization (Allocated Position N = _____).

At a point in time:

Assign a score to each allocated practitioner position: <u>Score</u>

| | |
|---|---|
| Practitioner position vacant | = 0 |
| Practitioner in position, untrained | = 1 |
| Practitioner completed initial training | = 2 |
| Practitioner trained + receives weekly coaching | = 3 |
| Practitioner met fidelity criteria: as of this month | = 4 |
| Practitioner met fidelity criteria: ten of past 12 months | = 5 |

Sum the scores for all practitioner positions (Practitioner Position Sum = _____).

Divide the Practitioner Position Sum by the Allocated Position N.

The resulting ratio is the "Implementation Quotient" for that innovation in that organization.

Figure 17 shows the use of the Implementation Quotient for ten years to track implementation progress in one organization. In this example, the organization consisted of 41 group homes, and the intention was to use the innovation (the Teaching-Family Model) in each group home. Thus, 41 is the "Allocated Position N" at every point in time in Figure 17. The use of the innovation was supported by a competent Implementation Team that began working with two group homes in November 1975 and used that experience to inform a range of changes in the organization to eventually support all 41 group homes. The data in Figure 17 begin in December 1975, just after implementation of the Teaching-Family Model homes began in two group homes in the organization.

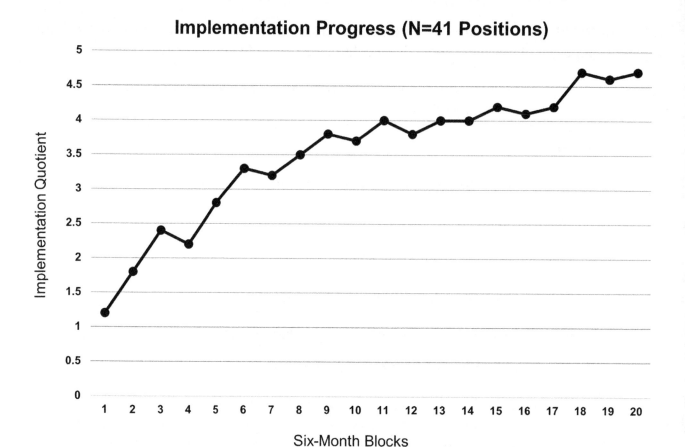

**Implementation Progress (N=41 Positions)**

Figure 17. Implementation quotient for ten years in one organization. Data from Fixsen, Phillips, et al. (1985)

As shown in Figure 17, the Implementation Quotient improved from an organization-wide average of about 1.0 (practitioner in position, untrained) to a score of 4.5 (practitioner met fidelity criteria: as of this month) after about eight years. The score of 4.5 was sustained for 18 months at the end of the ten-year period data collection period shown in the graph.

By July 1977, the Decision Support Data System was established and stable in the organization (Fixsen, Collins, Phillips, & Thomas, 1982). An outcome measure was derived from the Decision Support Data System and included a mix of youth behavior in the community and school grades and attendance. Outcomes for individual measures were transformed to a seven-point scale where a score of seven indicates zero occurrence of problem behaviors (e.g., runaway, police contact) or outcomes in the top quintile for all 41 group homes for positive behavior in the community and at school. The results for each group home were summed and averaged across the 41 group homes. As shown in Figure 18, implementation quotient and outcome scores were calculated every six months on the last day of the month from 1977 through the end of data collection in 1985. A Spearman rank correlation of 0.95 was found between the Implementation Quotient and the summary outcome scores for youths calculated over 15 six-month blocks.

In early 1980, about four years after beginning to use the innovation in the organization, over 50% of the practitioners (22 out of 41) met fidelity criteria in a given month (the definition of Full Implementation). As shown in Figure 18, at that time the average Implementation Quotient score for all 41 group homes was a 3.0 (practitioner trained and receives weekly coaching). The value of the Implementation Quotient is that it serves as a reminder that the work is not done even when Full Implementation is reached. At the point where 50% of the practitioners meet fidelity criteria, the remaining 50% do not meet criteria and outcomes for the organization are still not what they could be. For example, in the 41 group homes the score for youth outcomes did not reach six on the seven-point scale until 1984, at the point when the Implementation Quotient score was nearly 4.0.

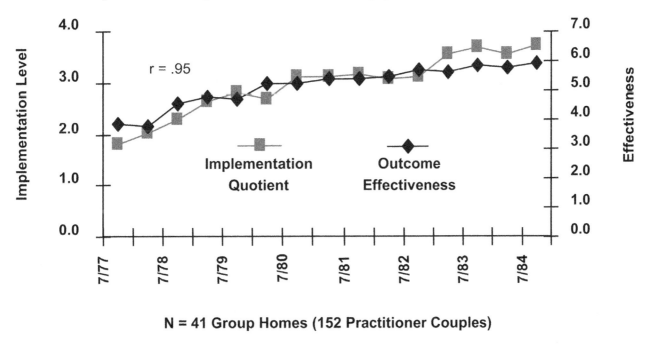

N = 41 Group Homes (152 Practitioner Couples)

Figure 18. Implementation quotient and youth outcomes in one organization. Data from Fixsen, Phillips, et al. (1985)

A total of 152 Teaching-Parent couples staffed the 41 Teaching-Family group homes over the 7.5 years where Implementation Quotient and youth outcome scores were available. An accurate count of youths is not available, but an estimate is about 4,000 different youths resided with the 152 Teaching-Parent couples who staffed the 41 group homes during the 7.5 years. By 1984 nearly all of the original leaders and initial Implementation Team staff had been replaced by new staff while scores sustained and improved.

Outcomes for a whole population are difficult to improve when the practitioners and recipients come and go with regularity. The value of the Implementation Drivers is made apparent as constant adjustments are made to reduce the impact of transitions. The goal is to maintain treatment and outcomes in the midst of "starting over" with each transition of staff or recipients. The Implementation Quotient is a reminder of implementation outcomes in service to realizing innovation outcomes.

# Chapter 8: Implementation Drivers Overview

Innovations are, by definition, new ways of work. To use an innovation, practitioners must be able to learn how to do the new ways of work in practice. New ways of work are disruptive to practitioners and organizations that must change in subtle or radical ways to accommodate and support the use of an innovation by practitioners. Initiating and managing disruptive organization change is the work of leadership and Implementation Teams. In Active Implementation, the Implementation Drivers are defined, and criteria are provided for assessing Competency Drivers, Organization Drivers, and Leadership Drivers.

Michie and colleagues (Michie et al., 2013; Michie, van Stralen, & West, 2011) have outlined behavior change methods that roughly correspond to the Implementation Drivers. Their "behaviour change wheel" also includes policy-related behavior change components that fit into the Systemic Change framework in Active Implementation (Chapter 15). The Implementation Drivers organize and operationalize many of the behavior change methods outlined by Michie and colleagues.

*In human services, newly learned innovation-relevant skills often have a short shelf life and even with fidelity checks and improvements over time, the investment in teaching and learning lasts only as long as a well-prepared high-fidelity practitioner remains in that position in human services.*

# Interaction of innovations, context, and Drivers

Innovations may be simple, complicated, or complex: they may require less or more of the Implementation Drivers done less or more skillfully. As explained by a business person, when considering the use of an innovation, the choice is to either smarten up the workforce or dumb down the innovation. Beginning with the Industrial Revolution and steam-driven textile mills that replaced cottage industries, manufacturing has been busy dumbing down innovations to the point where robots now perform many of the required simple and complicated tasks in manufacturing processes, on assembly lines, and in warehouses.

"Dead simple" innovations, seen as "plug and play" (Schrenker & Cooper, 2018), are said to be those that have removed as many barriers to usage as possible. Elwyn et al. (2007) call this "sticky knowledge" where the design of the innovation itself "overcomes the barriers to transfer." In this sense, dead simple innovations and sticky knowledge are self-implementing: if you know it, you can do it. As Schrenker and Cooper (2018) document, for plug and play innovations to work, both the plug and the play have to be standardized to a high degree to assure interoperability across multiple situations. This may be out of reach for many current human service applications that are interaction-based and complex.

In human services, newly learned innovation-relevant skills often have a short shelf life, and even with fidelity checks and improvements over time, the investment in teaching and learning lasts only as long as a well-prepared high-fidelity practitioner remains in that position in human services. The more complex and demanding the intervention (e.g., the more procedural adequacy, clinical judgment, and System Intervention that are required), the more important the Implementation Drivers are for promoting consistent use and realizing intended outcomes of those interventions over time and across practitioners.

In interaction-based human services, careful analysis and thought is required to determine how to use innovations in practice. It is best to do this thinking before attempting to begin using an innovation. For example, Table 14 shows the interaction between the context in which an innovation is used and the skills required to use an innovation. Innovations that are greater departures from standard practice and used outside typical contexts likely will require more careful consideration and more precise use of the Competency, Organization, and Leadership Drivers. On the other hand, innovations (dead simple; sticky) that are close to standard practice and within existing skill sets of typical practitioners and conducted within a familiar context may require less precise attention to the Implementation Drivers.

**Table 14. Support required for innovations of varying complexity**

|  | Close to Current Skills | Requires New Skills |
|---|---|---|
| Familiar Context | Little departure from standard practice. Less Intensive Support Required | Significant departure from standard practice. More Intensive Support Required |
| Unfamiliar Context | Changes required in standard organization operating procedures. More Intensive Support Required | Significant changes required in practitioner and organization behavior and operating procedures. Very Intensive Support Required |

The categories in Table 14 are reflected in the work of Nord and Tucker (1987), who distinguish between routine and radical innovations. Routine innovations are similar to what an organization has done before. Radical innovations are very different and require significant change and disruption of the status quo. They noted that radical innovations require more changes in fundamental systems, new types of knowledge, and new types of specialists which lead to more uncertainty, less agreement, and greater involvement of top management. The more radical the innovation, the more learning and unlearning that must take place. Nord and Tucker (1987, p. 24) concluded, "Few organizations can perform radical innovation without, in essence, forming a new organization." Support for radical innovation requires the creation of a new unit (an Implementation Team) "in which new personnel are recruited and which has its own source of resources and enough time to work through the implementation stage."

The judgements required to place innovations in Table 14 are made by Implementation Team members and organization leaders during the Exploration Stage when the use of an innovation is being considered. In each quadrant, the goal is to support high fidelity use of an innovation with socially significant outcomes: the intensity and precision of implementation supports are adjusted to achieve the goal.

Some examples of innovations that require more or less complex skills to be used in more or less familiar contexts are provided in Table 15.

Table 15. Examples of innovations of varying complexity

|  | Close to Current Skills | Requires New Skills |
|---|---|---|
| Familiar Context | A literacy innovation that requires a teacher to use new curriculum materials with students in a classroom | A heart transplant innovation that requires team members to use new methods in a surgical suite |
| Unfamiliar Context | A maternal health innovation that requires a midwife to attend to prenatal, obstetric, and postnatal care of mothers and babies in rural and extremely low-resource settings | A HIV/AIDs innovation that requires community health workers to go door to door in a community and follow a protocol to discuss prevention of unsafe sexual encounters |

Implementation Drivers are the heart of the change processes that support the full, effective, and sustained use of innovations in complex human service environments.

## Active Implementation Drivers

Hall and Hord (1987) and Greenhalgh et al. (2004) have noted three ways to support the use of innovations in practice: letting it happen, helping it happen, and making it happen. Many implementation attempts take a "letting it happen" approach, relying on passive diffusion of information through networks and communication patterns (e.g., publication of articles; conferences; champions).

Other efforts that take a "helping it happen" approach are more proactive, providing ready access to useful summaries of the literature, websites aimed at practitioner and policy audiences, and persuasive communications in the form of social marketing. The idea is to get relevant information into the hands of prospective innovation users so they are better informed and more likely to find ways to use the innovation in their daily practice. Technical assistance services fall into the helping it happen category. Letting it happen and helping it happen approaches result in about 5% to 15% use of innovations as intended (Aladjem & Borman, 2006; Green, 2008; Kontoghiorghes, 2004; Shojania & Grimshaw, 2005; Tornatzky, Fergus, Avellar, Fairweather, & Fleischer, 1980).

"Making it happen" approaches are quite different. They offer purposeful, active, and persistent supports for using innovations as intended and producing promised results in practice. Active Implementation is a "making it happen" approach that is mission driven and does not stop until the goal of using and sustaining Usable Innovations in practice is reached.

A review of the implementation evaluation literature (Fixsen et al., 2005) found evidence in support of several factors that seem to drive full and effective uses of innovations. Since then, experience and research have built on and expanded the knowledge base. The Implementation Drivers include Competency Drivers, Organization Drivers, and Leadership Drivers and have been associated with consistent innovation use and achievement of intended benefits (Fixsen, Blase, Naoom, & Wallace, 2009). In addition, the various components (e.g., coaching, Facilitative Administration, adaptive leadership) are integrated and focus on using the innovation as intended (e.g., with fidelity). Furthermore, strengths in some components can be used purposefully to compensate for weaknesses in other components without compromising outcomes.

The Implementation Drivers are required to produce, sustain, and improve the effectiveness and efficiency of innovations as they are used in practice.

As noted in the definition of implementation, an innovation is one thing, and implementation is another thing altogether (Fixsen, Naoom, et al., 2005). Like computer software and hardware, they are very different yet need to work together to produce reliable outcomes. The idea of evidence-based implementation methods is new and, *as an innovation*, implementation methods themselves need to meet the Usable Innovation criteria. Fidelity of the use of the innovation is important as one of the criteria for a Usable Innovation. Logically, fidelity of the use of Implementation Drivers is important as well. Practical assessments of the Implementation Drivers have been developed (Fixsen, Ward, Blase, et al., 2018) and tested (Ogden et al., 2012). The strong links between the Implementation Drivers assessment (implementation fidelity: fidelity of the use of the drivers) and intervention assessment (innovation fidelity: fidelity of the use of an innovation) are being established in practice (Metz et al., 2014; Ward et al., 2017; Ward et al., 2015).

The Active Implementation Drivers are shown in Figure 19. An innovation is a new way of work that must be learned by those who will do the work (practitioners). The Competency Drivers summarize how practitioners are introduced to an innovation and are supported in their efforts to use it as intended (with fidelity). Innovations that meet the Usable Innovation criteria inform the content for the Competency Drivers (selection, training, coaching).

To be repeatable and sustainable, the uses of an innovation by practitioners and the uses of the Competency Drivers almost always require changes in organization roles, functions, and structures. The Organization Drivers describe how administrators and managers sense the need for change (coaching, fidelity, Decision Support Data System) and make changes (Facilitative Administration, System Intervention) to fully support practitioners' uses of innovations (with fidelity). The third leg of the triangle involves Leadership Drivers to initiate the uses of innovations, support the constant changes required to align organization components with intended outcomes, and constructively cope with unintended outcomes, adaptive challenges, and wicked problems that arise.

All three components need to be in place and fully functioning to produce and sustain consistent uses of innovations by practitioners and reliable outcomes for the intended recipients of an innovation. After a few years, the Implementation Drivers and the innovation practices become the new ways of work in an organization and, eventually, become the standard ways of work. Using innovations as intended is the work of practitioners. Using Implementation Drivers as intended is the work of an Implementation Team.

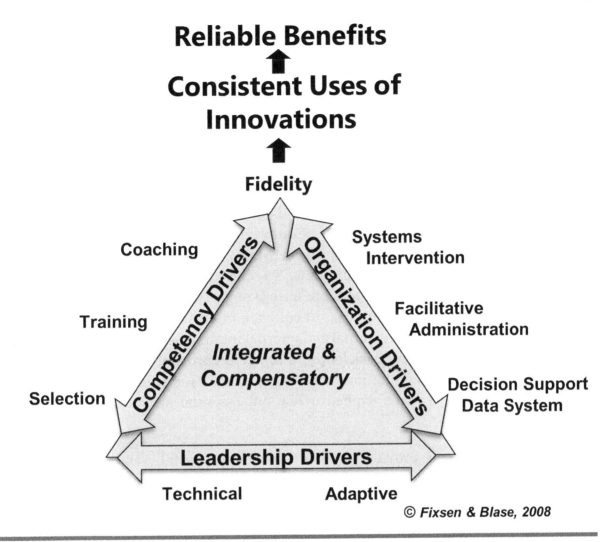

**Reliable Benefits**

**Consistent Uses of Innovations**

Fidelity

Coaching

Systems Intervention

Competency Drivers

Organization Drivers

Training

Facilitative Administration

*Integrated & Compensatory*

Selection

Decision Support Data System

**Leadership Drivers**

Technical

Adaptive

© *Fixsen & Blase, 2008*

Figure 19. The Implementation Drivers for developing practitioner competency, establishing hospitable organizations, and providing leadership for using innovations with fidelity and socially significant outcomes

The Implementation Drivers triangle (Figure 19) has fidelity at the top as the essential link between the Implementation Drivers and the innovation; that is, between implementation outcomes and innovation outcomes. Innovation outcomes cannot be interpreted without knowing the fidelity with which an innovation is being delivered. Poor outcomes may be the result of high fidelity use of an ineffective innovation or may be the result of an effective innovation used poorly in practice (i.e., with low fidelity) (Lipsey, 2009). Without a measure of fidelity, there is no way to attribute good (or poor) outcomes to an innovation (Naleppa & Cagle, 2010). High fidelity is the outcome of using the Implementation Drivers well and results in consistent uses of an innovation within and across practitioners and reliable benefits to recipients. A description in a methods section of an article is no substitute for a measure of the innovation (independent variable) as it is used in practice (fidelity).

## Integrated and compensatory

Organizations using the Active Implementation Frameworks are learning organizations. They use innovations on purpose; they support the use of innovations on purpose; they teach new staff members innovation and implementation best practices; they collect data on effectiveness and efficiency; and they use data to make better decisions, improve practices, and improve benefits. Teaching, learning, learning to learn, and improvement are hallmarks throughout a learning organization (Marsick & Watkins, 2003; Senge, 2006).

Given the changing socio-political, economic, and cultural contexts in which organizations operate, nothing is expected to stay the same. Complexity theory (Morgan & Ramirez, 1983; Stacey, 2002; Weick et al., 1999) points to the need to be aware of uncertainty and unexpected conditions in society, systems, and organizations. To cope with "environments where change is imminent and frequent," Dooley (1997, pp. 92-93) suggests some general guidelines for organizations: "a) create a shared purpose, b) cultivate inquiry, learning, experimentation, and divergent thinking, c) enhance external and internal interconnections via communication and technology, d) instill rapid feedback loops for self-reference and self-control, e) cultivate diversity, specialization, differentiation, and integration, f) create shared values and principles of action, and g) make explicit a few but essential structural and behavioral boundaries."

The Implementation Drivers provide ways to respond purposefully and constructively to changes that are inevitable and to the guidelines described by Dooley. Leadership Drivers, Competency Drivers, and Organization Drivers enhance one another in multiple ways in response to internal and external change and uncertainty. With reference to Dooley's guidelines, Implementation Teams "cultivate diversity, specialization, differentiation, and integration" as managers and leaders also conduct selection interviews and teach sections of training workshops; coaches and trainers also do fidelity assessments and data management; and so on. Leaders and Facilitative Administrators make use of Decision Support Data Systems to detect trends and "instill rapid feedback loops for self-reference and self-control." Leaders use Systems Interventions to "enhance external and internal interconnections via communication and technology." Leaders, managers, trainers, coaches, and fidelity assessors work together in an integrated fashion to "create a shared purpose" and "create shared values and principles of action." The use of data in action planning and Improvement Cycles helps to "cultivate inquiry, learning, experimentation, and divergent thinking." And, the Active Implementation Frameworks "make explicit a few but essential structural and behavioral boundaries."

The Implementation Drivers are integrated so that each supports the others. And, they are compensatory in that a weakness in one (e.g., training) can be accommodated by

116

strengthening others (e.g., coaching and fidelity assessment). For example, as the Teaching-Family Model expanded, it required considerable attention to maintain high fidelity use of recruitment, selection, training, and coaching of Teaching-Parents, the married couples and their children who lived and worked in Teaching-Family group homes. For a time, there were enough couples applying for each opening to allow the selection criteria to be satisfied. Later, when the economy improved dramatically, the pool of applicants was reduced and couples who did not meet all the selection criteria were hired. To compensate, more time was spent on behavior rehearsals during training; coaching time was doubled for couples leaving training; and fidelity assessments were scheduled to occur more frequently to provide feedback to coaches and Teaching-Parents. With the compensatory supports in place, high fidelity use of the Teaching-Family Model was reached in a timely way, and benefits to the youths living in the group homes were maintained.

In another example, the Decision Support Data System detected changes in outcomes associated with practitioner turnover in Teaching-Family group homes. An analysis showed that one or even two turnovers of Teaching-Parent couples during a 12-month period were associated with only a modest reduction in youth outcomes. However, three turnovers in a 12-month period were associated with a sharp drop in youth outcomes. Knowing this, Assistant Teaching-Parents (staff who completed Teaching-Parent training, worked eight hours a day in a group home, and did not live there) were given extra coaching, and a fidelity assessment for assistant Teaching-Parents was developed to assure their high fidelity use of the Teaching-Family Model. Subsequently, after a second turnover of Teaching-Parents within a year, the staffing by skilled Assistant Teaching-Parents was increased in that group home to avoid a reduction in benefits to youth. This provided the consistency and continuity that was needed to maintain adequate outcomes until the Teaching-Parent position was stabilized. Leaders, managers, and Implementation Team members participated in planning and carrying out the plan to compensate for unexpected and rapid turnover of Teaching-Parents in a group home.

Given the complexity of providing interaction-based services in capricious operating environments, the Active Implementation Frameworks provide a way to sense changes and a way to rapidly and purposefully compensate for those changes without losing sight of the mission and goals.

## Implementation Drivers in practice

In organizations there are structures, roles, and functions. The Implementation Drivers are functions. The functions can be performed in a variety of roles and structures in an organization provided they remain highly integrated and mission driven with a focus on fidelity and consistently good and improving outcomes.

An Implementation Team is embedded in an organization, and the Implementation Drivers are carried out by a variety of people who are Active Implementation experts in addition to doing other work. Figure 20 gives a realistic view of how the staff in an organization perform all the Drivers functions in a variety of ways. The individuals involved in selection, training, and so on change over time as staff and interests change. The constant is the Drivers done well with improvements made at every opportunity. This is because every key staff person has an understudy who is learning to do the work of implementation along with doing the work of providing services to practitioners or recipients. In this way, an organization builds in redundancy of skills without duplication of effort and can maintain itself and even provide staff to seed similar organizations in a network (Brunk et al., 2014; Fixsen & Blase, 2018; Tommeraas & Ogden, 2016). Redundancy in this sense is not wasted effort but an investment in the future.

Assessing Drivers Best Practices (ADBP) is a measure of the Implementation Drivers as they are used in organizations (Fixsen, Ward, Blase, et al., 2018). The measure serves as an assessment of fidelity of the use of the Drivers. For example, is an Implementation Team using the Implementation Drivers as intended? If the ADBP score is high, then good support is being provided to practitioners who are attempting to use an innovation in a typical human service setting. If the innovation is effective and is being used with fidelity, then socially significant outcomes are being produced for recipients of those services. This logical chain is a key to any successful use of innovations and improvable outcomes for recipients. If poor outcomes are being produced, why is that? Is it an implementation support problem or an innovation effectiveness problem? The answer can be known if the fidelity of the use of the Implementation Drivers is known and if the fidelity of the use of the innovation is known. If fidelity is low at either point, an Implementation Team knows where to look for solutions.

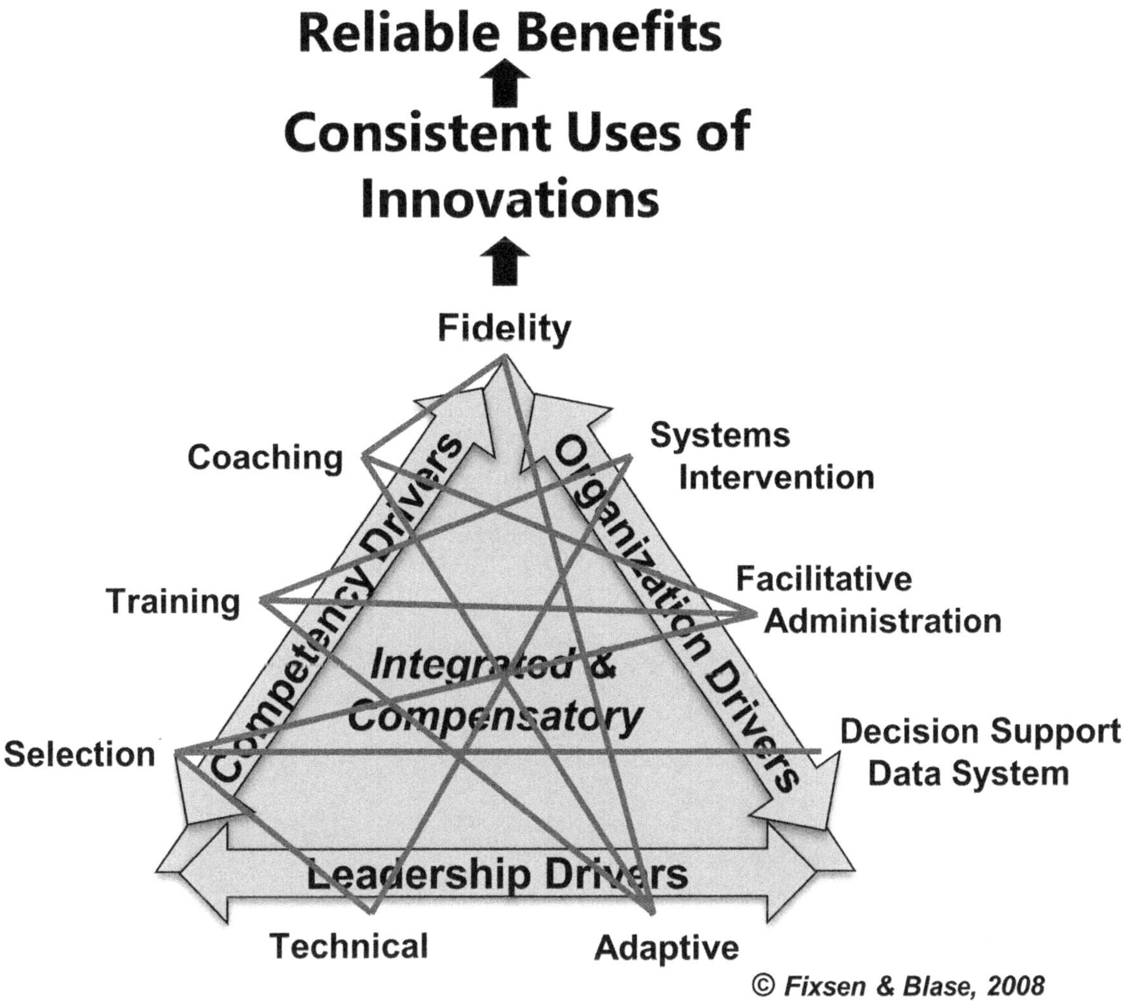

Figure 20. How Implementation Driver functions are actually provided in an organization

# Chapter 9: Implementation Competency Drivers

Competency Drivers are key to practitioner behavior change. By definition, an innovation is new to practitioners and organizations. Thus, practitioners (and others) need to learn the new ways of work required by an innovation. Staff selection, training, coaching, and fidelity assessments are frequently cited in the literature as important ways to assure skilled use of innovations. Mentioned less often, and equally important, is the integration of these components. There are occasions when practitioners leave training and find their new knowledge and skills are not supported by their supervisor ("That's not how we do things in my unit."). In an integrated approach, coaches (and supervisors) are prepared to support and expand the knowledge and skills introduced in training. Innovations that have been operationalized and meet the Usable Innovation criteria provide the information needed to inform the content of selection, training, coaching, and fidelity assessments.

The Competency Drivers are essential to achieving intended outcomes. If practitioner behavior does not change, then outcomes will not change. If the use of the Competency Drivers does not result in behavior change, then forget the rest of the Active Implementation Frameworks and focus attention on behavior change. The ability to reliably change practitioner behavior is the heart of implementation work. The ability to eventually produce socially significant outcomes for whole populations starts there.

*The Competency Drivers used as intended are essential supports for practitioners learning to use an innovation. If the Drivers do not produce intended innovation-related competencies, then socially significant outcomes will not be produced.*

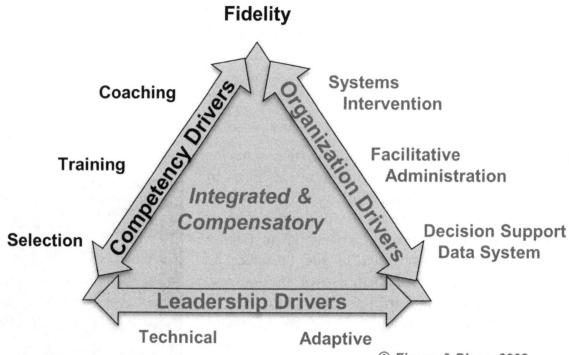

**Fidelity**

Coaching

Systems
Intervention

*Competency Drivers*

*Organization Drivers*

Training

Facilitative
Administration

*Integrated &
Compensatory*

Selection

Decision Support
Data System

Leadership Drivers

Technical          Adaptive

© *Fixsen & Blase, 2008*

In the following sections we describe Competency Drivers in detail. The Competency Drivers used as intended are essential supports for practitioners learning to use an innovation. If the Drivers do not produce intended innovation-related competencies, then socially significant outcomes will not be produced. Thus, selection, training, coaching, and fidelity are the heart of behavior change and the heart of implementation done well. For new Implementation Teams and others, this is the place to focus any initial attempts to use Active Implementation and develop implementation capacity. Organization change and aspects of system change may get the headlines, but behavior change supported by the Competency Drivers get the results.

Developing and sustaining high fidelity use of innovations is an essential role of an Implementation Team. The team assures the use of the Competency Drivers to achieve this goal. The Competency Drivers are well-used in practice (Blase, Maloney, & Timbers, 1974; Chamberlain, 2003; Fixsen & Blase, 2018; Kirigin et al., 1975; Martino, Ball, Nich, Frankforter, & Carroll, 2008; Martino, Gallon, Ball, & Carroll, 2008; Ogden et al., 2005; Schoenwald et al., 2000) and supported by research evidence (Aarons et al., 2009; Fixsen, Naoom, et al., 2005; Joyce & Showers, 2002; W. R. Miller & Mount, 2001; Webster-Stratton, Reid, & Marsenich, 2014).

Michie and colleagues (Michie et al., 2013; Michie et al., 2011) have outlined behavior change methods that roughly correspond to the Implementation Drivers. Their "behaviour change wheel" also includes policy-related behavior change components that fit into the

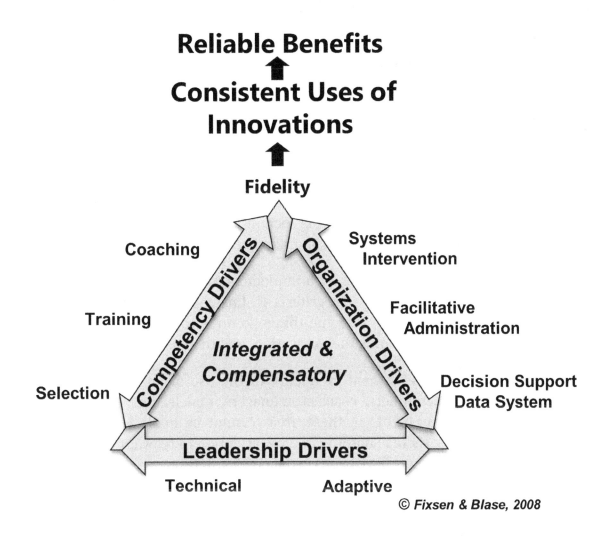

**Reliable Benefits**

↑

**Consistent Uses of Innovations**

↑

Fidelity

Coaching

*Competency Drivers*

*Organization Drivers*

Systems Intervention

Training

Facilitative Administration

*Integrated & Compensatory*

Selection

Decision Support Data System

**Leadership Drivers**

Technical

Adaptive

© *Fixsen & Blase, 2008*

Systemic Change framework in Active Implementation. The Implementation Drivers described in this chapter organize and operationalize many of the behavior change methods outlined by Michie and colleagues.

The descriptions of the Implementation Drivers provide rationales, data, and details for how to use the Drivers. It might seem overwhelming for an organization that is attempting for the first time to use the Drivers to support the full and effective use of an innovation. The rule is to "get started and get better." A group can get started with coaching, for example, knowing that direct observation and teaching innovation-related skills are essential to competent coaching. Later on, after coaching is established and functioning at a rudimentary level, a coaching-service delivery plan and the use of coaching data for improvement can be developed. And selection and training can be improved to ease the workload of coaches.

As noted previously, the Implementation Drivers triangle has fidelity at the top as the critical link to consistent use of innovations and reliable production of outcomes.

## Staff fidelity

The goal of the fidelity Driver is to assess the use of an innovation in practice. Fidelity assessments provide indicators to answer the questions: Are we doing what we intend to do? How do we know? Does it make a difference? Fidelity sets a minimum standard for using an innovation. Developing a fidelity assessment was described previously as a dimension of a Usable Innovation. Fidelity is described in this section as an implementation Competency Driver; that is, the use of fidelity assessments in practice.

Without a fidelity assessment, why bother with implementation supports? If any use of an innovation is acceptable, and there are no criteria to link the use of an innovation with outcomes, then training and coaching become things to do if you choose to and are not a means to an end. Just say you are doing the innovation, and there is no argument.

For implementation, regular assessment of fidelity of the use of an innovation provides essential information to practitioners, coaches, managers, and leaders. Without a good assessment of fidelity, improvements in these areas cannot be made with any certainty. Without fidelity assessments, there is nothing to draw attention to relevant problems and no way to assess when those problems have been solved (Weick, 1987).

### Fidelity assessment

If the intention is to use an innovation, is it being used in practice as it was intended to be used? Is there a way to assess the presence and strength of the innovation for every practitioner who is using the innovation? Does the use of the innovation as intended matter in terms of outcomes; that is, do high fidelity scores equal excellent outcomes; do low fidelity scores equal poor outcomes? Answers to these questions are critical to enable purposeful implementation, improvement, scaling, organization change, and system improvement. In this chapter we will focus on the use of fidelity for the purpose of assessing the quality of implementation supports and the use in improvement.

A practical measure of fidelity highly correlated with outcomes is part of each Usable Innovation. With a strong correlation (e.g., 0.70 or better), if fidelity is known, then future outcomes can be predicted. Instead of lamenting poor outcomes a year from now, fidelity brings the (predictable) future into the present where there is an opportunity to create a better future by improving fidelity now. If you know fidelity (high or low), you have a good idea of what the outcomes will be (excellent or poor). If a measure is not available, or the measure is not practical to use in the daily practice environment, it is up to an Implementation Team to create a workable fidelity measure and improve it with experience. Having no way to assess fidelity is not an option in implementation practice or science.

Fidelity criteria are minimum criteria: that is, if a practitioner is doing these things with this level of quality, then recipient benefits should be apparent. As practitioners continue to meet fidelity criteria, they begin using the innovation in nuanced ways that go beyond the minimum criteria and provide excellent examples of the innovation done with extreme expertise and decidedly improved outcomes. They move from rule generated to contingency shaped behavior. Skilled practitioners can deviate from the basic fidelity criteria in ways that maintain the integrity of the innovation while adding value in particular instances (Szulanski & Jensen, 2006). A person who has learned to play the scales and read music may meet minimum fidelity criteria for a piano player but is not yet an accomplished pianist. Like pianists, high fidelity experienced practitioners are artists whose work can be studied to expand knowledge of the innovation and supports for its uses in practice (Wolf et al., 1995).

## Fidelity first

There is a continuing discussion about "fidelity first" or "adapt to adopt." Active Implementation focuses on fidelity first. It is assumed that initially there will be a poor fit between an interaction-based Usable Innovation and any existing staff group, organization, and system. It is assumed that the existing organization structures, roles, and functions that support existing (less than desirable) outcomes will need to change so that newly designed organization structures, roles, and functions will support an innovation that produces better outcomes. Thus, when attempting to use an innovation, the goal is to use the essential components of a Usable Innovation with high fidelity and change the organization to fit the innovation. The status quo is powerful; fidelity is a lever for change.

To improve fit, Implementation Teams support practitioners as they attempt to use an innovation with fidelity first. The focus on using an innovation with fidelity compels attention to the ways in which the existing organization or staff group's typical ways of work do or do not fit with the use of an innovation. And, it compels attention to the Implementation Drivers and the extent to which leadership, competency development, and organization routines need to be changed or created to increase organization- and staff-fit with the effective innovation. It is uncomfortable to change the ways of work of organizations and staff groups; it is much easier to change aspects of innovations that staff groups say "don't fit" with status quo ways of work. However, if an innovation meets the Usable Innovation criteria, then the essential components are just that—essential to producing desired outcomes. They need to be put in place with fidelity if benefits are to be realized.

For example, basic emergency obstetric and newborn care (BEmONC) methods are complex and well-established. The fidelity of the use of BEmONC and its outcomes were studied in 134 health centers, covering 91 rural districts of Ethiopia (Tiruneh et al., 2018). With improved implementation supports for staff and clinic organizations, the BEmONC fidelity score (zero to ten scale) increased from 4.3 at baseline to 6.7 at follow-up. At the same time the 134 health centers' rates for safe delivery practices and dealing with complications during birth increased from 24% to 56%. The essential components of BEmONC were not adapted to somehow fit better with each of the 134 health centers. Instead, staff practices and operations within each health center were changed to deliver the essential components of BEmONC with higher fidelity. Improved supports for higher fidelity use of BEmONC led to improved health outcomes for mothers and babies.

From the beginning use of an innovation in an organization, an Implementation Team identifies the specific staff, organization, and system routines, ways of work, and regulations that need to change to make full and effective use of a given innovation and the others to come. As emphasized throughout, fidelity is a key indicator of selection, training, and coaching effectiveness. It also is a major source of feedback for Implementation Teams to improve those Implementation Drivers over time. Fidelity serves a similar role in informing leadership and managers regarding organization changes needed to improve the use of an innovation and its outcomes.

With fidelity as a central defining feature, needed changes in practice and organization routines quickly become apparent, and fidelity serves as a source of continual feedback on progress for organization change.

Fidelity has many benefits for the operation of organizations and systems. Stacey (1996, p. 10) notes, "Complex adaptive systems consist of a number of components, or agents, that interact with each other according to sets of rules that require them to examine and respond to each other's behavior in order to improve their behavior and thus the behavior of the system they comprise. In other words, such systems operate in a manner that constitutes learning." As Yeaton and Sechrest (1981, p. 161) point out, the sets of rules (defining features of complex interventions) require "both monitoring to detect lapses and mechanisms to repair them." When fidelity detects lapses and the mechanisms to repair lapses consist of constructive use of the Implementation Drivers, then trust is developed.

Thus, fidelity assessment changes the relationship between practitioners and managers and employers. Jalava (2006, p. 62) notes, "Interactions with those we endow with trust are liberated from anxiety, suspicion, and watchfulness and allow for more spontaneity and openness. We are released from the necessity of monitoring and controlling every move made by others." With coaching support and fidelity assessment, managers and others know how well practitioners are doing and can be in a supportive role instead of a command, control, and compliance role. And, the use of fidelity data for improvement supports the development and operation of a learning organization (Edmondson & Moingeon, 1998). Doing work with fidelity means doing work consistently and reliably producing socially significant outcomes. With an effective organization and system that supports the routine use of implementation supports for innovations, then directors and managers can trust the processes for producing excellent outcomes and can direct their attention to continual improvement.

Fidelity is not a characteristic of a practitioner. There is no expectation that, once established, high fidelity performance will continue. Thus, regular assessments of fidelity are required to assess the degree to which an innovation currently is used as intended. It is expected that fluctuations in fidelity scores will lead to continual changes and refinements in organization supports for practitioners. With fidelity as a criterion, leaders in an organization are on a continual quest to find ways to improve selection, training, coaching, administrative practices, policies and procedures, and so on so that all practitioners can use an innovation fully and effectively on a consistent basis, now and in the future.

## Measures of fidelity

The critical features of fidelity assessments have been summarized (Carroll et al., 2007; Fixsen, Naoom, et al., 2005, pp. 47-52; Sanetti & Kratochwill, 2014; Schoenwald & Garland, 2013). The components of fidelity assessments can be categorized as shown in Table 16. Every fidelity assessment identified to date fits into the dimensions of Table 16.

**Table 16. Method to categorize fidelity assessment items and some examples**

| Type of Assessment | Direct Observation | Record Review | Ask Others |
|---|---|---|---|
| Context<br><br>Prerequisites that must be in place for an innovation to be used | | Staffing qualifications or numbers, practitioner-recipient ratio, supervisor-practitioner ratio, location of service provision, prior completion of training | Interview practitioners regarding their experience regarding the prerequisites in the organization |
| Content<br><br>The extent to which the practitioner uses the essential components of the innovation and avoids those activities proscribed by the Usable Innovation criteria | Recipient and practitioner agree on a plan of action (e.g., treatment plan); practitioner follows agenda during therapy session; the practitioner sets up behavior rehearsal for skill teaching and learning | Electronic records review of number of contacts, list of innovation-related services delivered | Recipients' reports that the practitioner asked certain questions or prompted certain actions |
| Competence<br><br>The level of skill shown by the practitioner in using the essential components of the innovation while interacting with a recipient | The practitioner capitalizes on teaching opportunities; uses a respectful tone of voice; balances teaching and relationship development; is sensitive to timing given the context of the individual and ongoing interactions; adjusts to recipient's current life situation | | Recipient interview regarding feeling respected, clear communication, helpfulness during interactions with a practitioner, care and concern, solve problems, achieve aspirations |

The critical dimension of fidelity assessment is *direct observation of competence* as a practitioner (teacher, therapist, community health worker) interacts with others (student, patient, family) in the service delivery setting (classroom, clinic, village). Record reviews, when they are complete and accurate, provide information on what services were provided, by whom, when, where, and so on. They do not provide information on the quality with which the services were delivered. Direct observation permits an assessment of quality of services as they are delivered in practice, including nuances such as assessing omissions and missed opportunities as well as delivering essential components at the wrong time. For example, the World Health Organization has developed guidelines for respectful treatment of women during pregnancy and childbirth. "Respectful" services that relate to the guidelines are difficult to assess without direct observation of woman-staff interactions and without asking women how satisfied they are that the health provider staff were respectful to them (ask others).

Developing fidelity measures is facilitated by having a Usable Innovation where the operational definitions of essential components provide strong indicators of what to measure. Fixsen, Hassmiller Lich, and Schultes (2018) provide information on developing a fidelity measure. An example of a measure based on Table 16 was developed by the Pulmonary Hypertension Association (Gray, Onyeador, & Wirth, 2018). Other examples of newly developed and practical measures of fidelity are available (King-Sears, Walker, & Barry, 2018; Rahman et al., 2018; Tiruneh et al., 2018).

In another example, the water, sanitation and hygiene (WSH) interventions in Bangladesh (Masud Parvez et al., 2018) included monthly fidelity assessments described as "spot checks and survey that captured reported behaviors of interest, as well as the presence, functionality, condition, and signs of use of the delivered hardware. Structured observations consisted of the spot checks of technologies plus direct observation of the behavioral practices of interest." Direct observation of the innovation's essential components provided evidence regarding the presence and strength of the innovation's use in each cohort using the WSH innovation in low-resource village environments.

Fidelity measures are expected to improve with use. Natural variation of practices occurs and is used as a basis for modifications with scrutiny over a long enough period of time to see if the modifications are beneficial to recipients. The fidelity instrument is revised to reflect the beneficial variations in practices by the practitioners and coaches who are faced with solving real problems every day. In addition, new concepts and methods may be defined, operationalized, and finally included in the fidelity assessment protocol. These improvements also are used to add more specificity to the selection interview protocol, preservice workshop training curriculum, and coaching protocols.

## Fidelity processes

An Implementation Team is responsible for assuring the availability of competent fidelity assessors (selection, training, and coaching of fidelity assessors) and establishing fidelity assessment plans. A specific person is responsible for coordinating the quality and timeliness of coaching processes for practitioners using an innovation. Every practitioner using an innovation has regular fidelity assessments.

Some specific examples from the use of the Teaching-Family Model are below. It should be mentioned that the Teaching-Family examples were accomplished in the context of operating service organizations in typical service delivery systems in U.S. states and Canadian provinces. Funding for services, staffing, and accountability/compliance requirements were about the same as for other agencies providing services in a human service system (Weinrott, Jones, & Howard, 1982). The difference was that staff in Teaching-Family organizations had implementation-informed roles and skills as Implementation Team members integrated in the organizations to establish, manage, and support service delivery in the agency.

For example, intensive (two-family caseload; about 15 hours per week per family), short-term (three-four months) Teaching-Family treatment is provided to families who have one or more children who have been removed from home (30 days or less) or have been scheduled to be removed from their home due to abuse, neglect, delinquency, or similar reasons. The program was funded as residential treatment with the "residential bed" located in each child's own home staffed by Family Specialists (practitioners). Fidelity assessments for Family Specialists include the following dimensions (see Table 16 for the outline):

### Context: Criteria for certification as a Family Specialist

1. Completion of the 60-hour preservice training
2. Completion of pre-assessment training that explains to the practitioner the entire fidelity assessment process and the uses of the information
3. Participation in a complete initial fidelity assessment at about six months

### Content: Criteria for certification as a Family Specialist

1. Minimum of one-year of use of the Teaching-Family Model for in-home, family-based treatment
2. Minimum of one-year of in-service training and on-going coaching by a supervisor-coach trained in the Teaching-Family Model
3. Meet all criteria on the annual fidelity assessment

## Competence: Criteria for certification as a Family Specialist

1. Assessment by the recipients of the treatment services (ask others) Within two weeks of the termination of treatment (for any reason) in each family, a specially-trained professional assessor visits the family home and privately interviews each parent and each child (seven years old or older) who was the direct recipient of the services of the Family Specialist. Interview questions are asked about cooperation, communication, concern, and respect for the family.

2. Assessment by other direct consumers and stakeholders of the services (ask others) Within two weeks of the termination of treatment in a family, a consumer assessment questionnaire is sent to each "consumer" and stakeholder outside the family. The list is unique to each family and usually includes social service agency staff (referring caseworker, mental health or juvenile justice specialists related to the child and family), school staff (teachers, counselors, principal associated with the child), employers, and support staff (agency colleagues who have regular contact with the Family Specialist). Each "consumer" directly interacted with the Family Specialist at some point during the intensive treatment period. Questions ask about cooperation, communication, helpfulness, and effectiveness.

3. Observation of ongoing treatment by two specially trained fidelity assessors (direct observation) When a fidelity assessment is due, the professional assessment occurs about 30 days after initiating services with a family. The professional assessment is based on a one-hour pre-meeting to review the treatment plan for the family and progress to date, and a two-hour (minimum) observation of the Family Specialist while she is involved in providing treatment in a family home. Using a 23-item assessment scale (rated on a 1-7 Likert scale that asks "How satisfied are you that ..."), the evaluators rate the Family Specialist's treatment-related behavior along the following dimensions. The note "(*CJ)" indicates an item to assess clinical judgement.

   - Treatment planning–understanding of the treatment plan, treatment plan fits the family's treatment needs, (*CJ) treatment plan is effectively implemented in interactions with the family
   - Relationship development–expresses warmth and concern, attends to emotional content, able to engage family members, (*CJ) effectively fits the family context
   - Teaching–use of teaching interaction components, balance of teaching between children and parents, matched skills between parents and children, use of contingencies, use of conceptual feedback, (*CJ) perceives and

responds to teaching opportunities, (*CJ) creates teaching opportunities, (*CJ) effectiveness of teaching given the treatment plan, (*CJ) intervention is intensive but not too intrusive

- Intervention progress–behavior of the children re: any child welfare (or other referral) concerns, behavior of the parents re: any child welfare concerns, helps family members see their progress, (*CJ) Family Specialist judgement is accurate in assessing family progress
- Clinical judgement–see the items marked "(*CJ)" in each of the areas above: these are pooled to provide an assessment of the Family Specialist's ability to do the right thing at the right time with the right person for the right reason

4. Review by two specially trained fidelity assessors (record review)
- Record keeping–case files are complete, prompt in meeting paperwork deadlines, quality and content of documents in the file

Verbal feedback to the Family Specialist with a focus on descriptive praise occurs immediately after the family visit or within 24 hours. A written report is provided within ten working days, and a meeting with the practitioner and coach to review the report is scheduled within five working days after that. All the information is entered in the Decision Support Data System.

A Family Specialist who meets the fidelity criteria in each of these areas at 12 months is "certified" by the Teaching-Family Association. Family Specialist certification is re-earned annually.

Managing the schedule of fidelity assessments requires considerable attention and planning, thus the need for a person who is responsible for assuring fidelity assessments. As noted in the example, each practitioner has a unique schedule related to the date she completed training. With dozens of practitioners, this presents scheduling problems for interviewing family members, surveying consumers, and assuring two trained assessors will be available when the practitioner and family will be together. Plans often are disrupted by illness, changes in family schedules, and so on. Backup plans are made routinely to assure the fidelity assessments are done in a timely manner.

# Using fidelity data for improvement

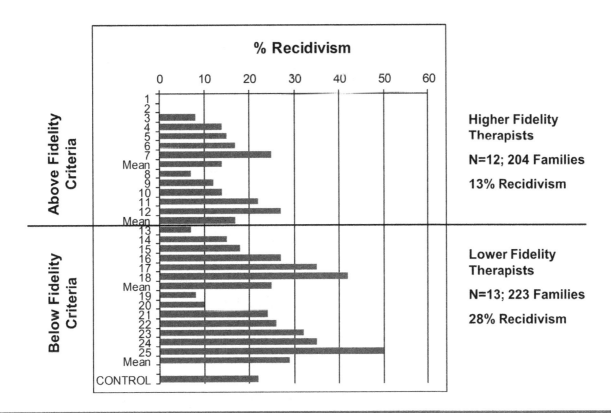

Figure 21. A revised display of the original data produced by the Washington State Institute for Public Policy (2002). Washington State's Implementation of Functional Family Therapy for Juvenile Offenders: Preliminary Findings (No. 02-08-1201).

Figure 21 shows fidelity data and recipient outcomes for 25 therapists using Functional Family Therapy (FFT), a well-established evidence-based program (Alexander & Parsons, 1973; Sexton & Alexander, 2000). The Washington State Institute for Public Policy (2002), also known as WSIPP, conducted a study of the effects of FFT with families who had one or more youth in the juvenile justice (delinquency) system. Overall, there were no significant differences between the experimental and control groups, although the data on reduction of felony offenses came close at p = 0.08. This led to a post-hoc analysis of the fidelity of the use of FFT and felony recidivism outcomes. The results for each of the 25 FFT therapists are shown in Figure 21. For example, Therapists 1 and 2 had the highest levels of fidelity and none of the youths in the families they treated committed another felony offense (an excellent outcome). Therapist 25 had the lowest fidelity score, and 50% of the youths in the families he or she treated committed another felony offense (a poor outcome).

With respect to the fidelity questions (Are you doing what you intend to do? How do you know? And, does it make a difference?), it is clear that fidelity of the use of the innovation makes a difference. On average, higher fidelity equals 13% recidivism and lower fidelity equals 28% recidivism. Notice that low fidelity is not a neutral event; the 13 low fidelity therapists produced some harm with recidivism rates (28%) that were worse than the control group (22%). With that as a background, how can the data in Figure 21 be used to improve outcomes for therapists, organizations, and the system?

## Fidelity and practice

The first and immediate use of fidelity data is to inform the practitioner and her coach. These are the only people in an organization who know the detailed day-to-day interactions between the practitioner and the recipients. They are in the best position to do what is required to improve the use of an innovation, achieve higher fidelity scores, and produce improved outcomes to recipients. Competent coaching support for making changes in below-fidelity areas is a priority for improvement.

Fidelity assessments that occur several times a year provide feedback to the practitioner and the coach on progress and areas that need improvement. Any fidelity assessment score that is less than criterion requires further work by the practitioner and his coach. Coaching is intensified until the criterion performance is achieved.

## Fidelity and coaching

Feedback to a given coach is based on the results of the fidelity assessments for all of the practitioners being coached by that coach. What if Therapists 1-12 in Figure 21 were coached by Coach A and the others had Coach B? Then this would indicate a coaching problem. For this reason, the results of the fidelity assessments for all of the practitioners being coached by a given coach are used as feedback to that coach. Looking across the most recent ten fidelity assessments, have the practitioners served by a given coach performed particularly well in some areas? Have they had problems using a particular innovation-related skill (e.g., teaching or relationship development)? Have they typically met certification criteria on their first attempt? The fidelity assessments provide the information to help answer these questions and provide a clear basis for helping a coach improve her skills.

## Fidelity and Implementation Drivers

What if Therapists 1-12 were employed in Clinic A and the others were employed in Clinic B? This would indicate a Competency, Organization, and Leadership Drivers problem. For this reason, the results of fidelity assessments for all of the practitioners employed by an agency or unit within an agency provide excellent information for the entire Implementation Team and organization leaders and staff. For example, the trainers review the results of the first post-training fidelity assessments (perhaps at month three for some innovations) to see where the practitioners generally have greatest strengths and most common areas for improvement. Any common areas for improvement then become the target for changing training curricula and enhancing trainer skills as well as reconsidering administrative supports for practitioners and Implementation Team members within the agency. And, the recruitment and selection process would be scrutinized and Therapists 1-12 would be interviewed to see what attracted them to the position and what they found to be helpful during the employment process. The goal is to have more new hires that are like Therapists 1-12.

### Fidelity and organization improvement

The fidelity instruments are an excellent tool for overall quality improvement. Once or twice a year the training, coaching, assessment, and administrative staff meet to review the results of the fidelity assessments for all of their agency's practitioners. Are there particular strengths across all the evaluations? Are there common problems or deficiencies? Are there innovative practices that have been used by high fidelity and experienced practitioners that should be operationalized and replicated? Is the fidelity observation protocol still getting at the important aspects of the desired treatment in families? And so on. The training, consultation, assessment, and administrative staff then decide what, if any, modifications need to be made in their selection criteria and processes to find more of the best candidates and hire fewer of the ones who take undue amounts of coaching time to achieve fidelity standards. They also look at the balance between training and coaching to see if some of the common problems being experienced at the coaching level could be addressed more directly at the preservice workshop training level. In addition, they look for any aspects of the practitioners' work that could be facilitated administratively to relieve paperwork, sharpen communication patterns, better use available technology, fill gaps in staffing, increase longevity, etc.

### Fidelity and usability testing

What if 1,000 FFT therapists were needed to reduce felonies by youths in the state, and the 25 therapists in Figure 21 are the 25 in the first cohort? In that case, fidelity data would inform decisions regarding where to develop capacity in the organization employing the 25 therapists. Then the capacity development decisions would be put into place and tested with the next cohort of 25 therapists. This process would be repeated until at least 80% of the therapists had the support they needed to reach fidelity criteria in a reasonable time. Once the bugs are ironed out and the capacity is developed in a way that is repeatable, then the scaling to 1,000 FFT therapists can begin.

**Training fidelity assessors**

Purveyors of evidence-based programs have learned complex skills sets in order to help staff at new sites learn how to use an innovation's core components with fidelity and socially significant outcomes for recipients and the community. For some purveyors, their implementation plan for a new site includes teaching the staff members many of these complex skill sets so the implementation site can become self-sufficient with respect to staff selection, training, coaching, assessment, and administrative supports (the Implementation Drivers).

The Implementation Drivers apply equally to this next level of purveyor activity. That is, staff selection, training, coaching, fidelity assessment, leadership, and administrative supports are as important for developing excellent trainers, coaches, evaluators, and administrators as they are for developing high fidelity practitioners. A problem arises because: a) only a few trainers, coaches, evaluators, and administrators are needed for a new implementation site, b) it is difficult to organize and justify the expense of training a few people, and c) the roles are complex and not amenable to preparation in a training workshop and coaching experience. Yet, people need to be prepared for these roles in a systematic manner that can be reliably reproduced from one implementation site to another.

These practical issues led to a 3-2-1 tutorial system for training staff at new implementation sites to be trainers, coaches, evaluators, and administrators. The following describes the training for an evaluator who assesses practitioner fidelity (direct observation of a practitioner's skills while he is working directly with a recipient, interview of parents and children regarding practitioner behavior during the intervention, mail out questionnaire to consumers and stakeholders associated with the children, families, and practitioner).

An essential element of the 3-2-1 tutor's behavior is "active modeling" where the tutor (the already qualified assessor in this case) a) previews what is about to happen, b) has the trainee engage in behavior rehearsals as needed to teach basic skills, c) does the activity in practice with the trainee present to see how it is done, and d) debriefs with the trainee afterward to review what happened and explain any variations that may have occurred. As the trainee gains skill, the prep time turns into a quick review of what needs to happen, the trainee takes on more of the lead role in doing the activity, and the debriefing portion becomes more of a self-examination. This active modeling role is used to help new staff carry out the complex roles needed to maintain a self-sufficient implementation site. Readers will recognize this as a variation of the "I do, We do, You do" training and coaching method common in some fields.

*Qualifications of a fidelity assessor*

*Currently employed as a qualified program manager, coach/supervisor, or trainer, or as a high-fidelity practitioner.*

Training

1. Full participation (i.e., pre-fidelity assessment meeting, in-home assessment, assessment write-up, post-assessment meeting) in a minimum of six fidelity assessments conducted with a certified primary assessor as a co-assessor/trainer (tutor):
    a. Three assessments as a secondary fidelity assessor
    b. Two assessments as a primary-in-training fidelity assessor
    c. One assessment as a solo primary fidelity assessor
2. Verbal and written feedback will be provided by the co-assessor/trainer.

Qualifying

1. The Assessment Review Committee (three people who are expert fidelity assessors) will decide to grant or withhold "primary fidelity assessor status" based on a review of any information including:
    a. The written feedback provided over the six or more training assessments
    b. The "assessor consumer" feedback from the training assessments (i.e., responses from the practitioners whose behavior was assessed)
    c. The write-up of the solo primary fidelity assessment
    d. The verbal statements by the co-assessor/trainer on the solo primary fidelity assessment including pre- and post-assessment meetings.
2. The review of the write-up of the solo primary fidelity assessment can include a discussion of items such as:
    a. The fidelity assessment summary—are the themes important? are the examples relevant to the themes? is there a positive emphasis with at least a five-to-one ratio of strengths to areas that need improvement? is improvement-related feedback brief and constructive? is the summary an accurate and reasonable reflection of the actual ratings and comments in the body of the report?

b. Appropriate advice—in the summary and in the in-home report is the advice specific, technically sound, and in a conceptual feedback style (with any score of five or less)? do the ratings and comments match? is the language clear and free of confusing sentences or ideas? are the ratings and comments discrete and not the product of double jeopardy?

c. Evaluation management—were timelines met? are formats consistent? are the data accurate? is the editing complete with respect to clarity of writing, grammar, spelling, etc.?

d. Clinical judgment—judge the assessors' judgments about the judgments made by the clinical staff person(s) being evaluated

Using the 3-2-1 training method allows preparation of new fidelity assessors as an ongoing activity that is minimally disruptive to the organization and to practitioners. Similar methods are used to prepare new trainers, coaches, leaders, and others.

## Fidelity over time and scale

Fidelity is not a characteristic of practitioners, nor is it a characteristic of organizations. It is something to work for every day. McIntosh et al. (2016) conducted a study of fidelity of the use of Positive Behavior Interventions and Supports (PBIS) in 5,331 schools in 37 states in the U.S. PBIS is a whole-school innovation that has a history of research, development, and expansion since the 1990s. PBIS fidelity assessments and a national system of data collection are well-established and used by over 25,000 schools in the U.S. and globally. The 5,331 schools in the study had collected fidelity data over a five-year period.

The results showed four patterns of fidelity of PBIS use over five years. "Sustainers" (29% of the schools) met fidelity criteria in the first year and maintained high levels of fidelity for five years. "Slow starters" (13% of the schools) did not meet fidelity criteria in years one-three but did by years four and five. "Late abandoners" (24% of the schools) met fidelity criteria in years one-three then dropped sharply in years four and five. "Rapid abandoners" (34% of the schools) met fidelity criteria in year one but not in years two-five. Overall, 42% of the 5,331 schools met and sustained fidelity criteria by years four and five.

The PBIS "blueprint" recommends the use of the Implementation Drivers and provides information and training at annual conventions. However, there is no systematic assurance of the use of the Implementation Drivers to support the use of PBIS in every school. More recent implementation and scaling efforts by PBIS focus on developing Implementation Teams at the school district (organization) level to support the use of PBIS in all schools in a district. This is a step toward assuring the use of the Implementation Drivers to support each school.

Tommeraas and Ogden (2016) studied fidelity as the Parent Management Training–Oregon model (PMTO) was scaled. PMTO was initiated in Norway in 2004 and its use has expanded with subsequent generations of therapists. PMTO makes full use of the Implementation Drivers and has an established and required fidelity measure (Forgatch et al., 2005). All the materials were translated to Norwegian, and the first-generation practitioners were trained, coached, and assessed by staff from Oregon. Subsequent generations of therapists increased in number and were supported by first-generation practitioners who became "home grown" trainers and coaches in Norway.

Ogden and colleagues had a thoughtful approach to scaling from the beginning and assured the use of the Implementation Drivers in support of each generation of PMTO practitioners in Norway (Ogden et al., 2012). Tommeraas and Ogden (2016) found no decrease in practitioner fidelity from the first to subsequent generations as scaling occurred over ten years, and no decrease in outcomes produced for children and families. Fidelity of the use of PMTO was high in the beginning and remained high even as practitioners changed and as the use of the innovation expanded. The constant was implementation support provided by competent Implementation Team members, first from Oregon and then from "home grown" team members in Norway. This approach has been replicated in other countries with equally socially significant outcomes for fidelity and recipients (Sigmarsdóttir et al., 2018)

Fidelity assessment is the key to assessing organization functioning. As an important source of recursive feedback, it is the reason for making organization changes and the way to assess the success of those changes.

## Fidelity and Implementation Teams

The Teaching-Family Model established certification (fidelity) standards for Teaching-Family Sites (organizations of Teaching-Family group homes) in 1978. The standards and methods of directly observing site (organization) staff behavior, reviewing records, and surveying staff and consumers (asking others) are described elsewhere (Fixsen & Blase, 2018; Fixsen, Blase, Duda, Naoom, & Van Dyke, 2010) and can be found on the Teaching-Family Association website (https://teaching-family.org/). Once site certification criteria are met, the Teaching-Family Association conducts annual reviews of documents (e.g., pre-post training data; fidelity assessment reports) and conducts a complete re-certification review every three years. An outcome of moving to site development as the unit for replication and scaling was a marked increase in sustainability (group homes still operating as Teaching-Family group homes after six years), from 17% retention of Teaching-Family group homes pre-site development to 84% retention of homes post-site development (see descriptions in a previous chapter).

Multisystemic Therapy Services, Inc.® (MSTS), the implementation and scaling group for MST treatment, has established "network partners" (like Teaching-Family Model Sites) in the U.S. and other countries. After several years of experience and the development of a functional Decision Support Data System, MSTS developed the MST Program Performance Index (PPI). Brunk et al. (2014) described the development of the PPI and reported its use in practice over two years. They found that 84% of the MST teams associated with a network partner that scored in the top 25% on the PPI sustained for the two-year period of the study, compared to 57% of the MST teams associated with a network partner that scored in the bottom 25% on the PPI.

The Teaching-Family Model sites and MSTS network partners included the innovation and an Implementation Team to support the use of the innovation as the scalable unit (Barker et al., 2016). Thus, in a high functioning organization (i.e., certified Teaching-Family Site; MST network partner scoring in the top quartile on the PPI), Implementation Drivers were provided competently for each treatment unit (Teaching-Family group home; MST team). Under these conditions, about 85% of the treatment units in the two programs sustained their high fidelity use of the innovation. For PBIS, where the use of Implementation Drivers was recommended but not assured by an Implementation Team, retention was 42% for two years or more (29% for five years with an additional 13% meeting and sustaining fidelity in years four and five). The outcome for no or poor support from an Implementation Team for PBIS (42% retention) is between the 15% retention found for Teaching-Family group homes with no support and the 57% retention for MST teams with less than optimal support as assessed by the PPI.

At the beginning of the current evidence-based movement, McGrew et al. (1994, p. 671) stated , "Development of fidelity measures is hampered by three factors: 1) models not well-defined conceptually making it difficult to identify critical ingredients, 2) when critical ingredients have been identified, they are not operationally defined with agreed-upon criteria for implementation, 3) few models have been around long enough to study systematic variations." The Teaching-Family Model, MST, PBIS, and PMTO are among the models that are well-defined, are operationalized, and have been around long enough to develop practical assessments of fidelity at the practitioner level and, for the Teaching-Family Model and MST, at the organization level. Practice-based evidence is accumulating as these and other effective innovations are scaled up, and new levels of implementation and scaling issues are encountered, solved, and replicated repeatedly in practice.

The development of fidelity assessments for whole organizations of innovation users is a big step forward for implementation and scaling. It allows the scalable unit of replication to be bigger and more meaningful and have that unit include the Implementation Drivers capacity to sustain and improve itself. These are essential to scaling to reach whole populations (Fixsen et al., 2017).

## Fidelity assessment in practice

Fidelity assessment requires planning and organization. Table 17 provides a list of key aspects to consider as fidelity assessment is established for the first time in an organization determined to make full and effective use of a selected innovation.

Table 17. Best practices for assessing fidelity in organizations

| Best practices for fidelity assessments | In Place |
|---|---|
| Accountability for performance assessment measurement and reporting system is clear (e.g., a lead person is designated and supported) | |
| Transparent Processes—Proactive staff orientation to the process and procedures used for performance assessment | |
| Performance assessment measures are highly correlated with (predictive of) intended outcomes | |
| Performance assessments are conducted on a regular basis for each practitioner | |
| The organization has a practical and efficient performance assessment measurement and reporting system | |

| | |
|---|---|
| Performance assessment measures extend beyond the measurement of context and content to <u>competence</u> (e.g., competency requires observation) | |
| Use of <u>multiple data sources</u> (e.g., practitioners, supervisors, consumers) | |
| Positive <u>recognition</u> processes in place <u>for participation</u> (e.g., performance assessment is seen as a source of data to improve quality; not a punitive process) | |
| Performance assessments of practitioners are used to <u>assess the effectiveness of coaching</u> | |

## Staff Selection

The goal of the Selection Driver is to have practitioners who are ready, willing, and able to do what the innovation requires and who are enthusiastic about participating in the process of learning and using the innovation as intended. Advice from business leaders is that organizations should be difficult to get into and easy to get out of. Once a person is hired or promoted or reassigned, then the organization has an obligation to that person. If the decision to hire the person was a poor one, the person consumes considerable time and effort as supervisors, managers, human resources staff, administrative staff, and others try to help the person do the intended work in spite of the person's apparent lack of skill or motivation. The best way to solve these problems is to prevent them with a good Staff Selection process. The process applies to people being hired as new practitioners and to people already employed in an organization who are asked to volunteer to begin using an innovation.

Much has been written about the readiness of practitioners to use an innovation and the importance of the fit between the innovation and practitioner values, beliefs, psychological states, and so on (Aarons et al., 2011; Proctor et al., 2009; Stetler, McQueen, Demakis, & Mittman, 2008). In Active Implementation, these factors are assessed and created in the selection process. If newly hired or reassigned staff are "resistant" to change; are a poor fit with doing the work required by an innovation; are reluctant to be coached or refuse to participate in fidelity evaluations, then the selection process needs to be reconsidered and improved. For example, applicants who don't value dignity, privacy, confidentiality, and freedom from harm and mistreatment during labor and childbirth likely are a poor fit with innovations that emphasize respectful and inclusive obstetric care as recommended by WHO. Philosophically opposed applicants can opt out of consideration for WHO-compliant obstetric service positions and choose to work in other services instead. In addition, applicants who value professional autonomy above all else likely are a poor fit with the training, coaching,

142

fidelity, Facilitative Administration, data-driven leadership, and other aspects of a high reliability organization. Those applicants can opt out of consideration as well. Thus, the use of the term "mutual selection"-the candidate and the organization choose each other or not in the recruitment and selection process.

Staff selection in human services often is overlooked as an essential implementation variable. However, that is changing. Protocols that include best practices (e.g., work samples in a structured interview process) are being used effectively (Maloney et al., 1983; Wroe et al., 2017). Philosophy, values, readiness to learn, and other dimensions are readily assessed during the selection process. There is no such thing as resistant staff (blame the practitioner); there is only lack of preparation (be accountable for using the Implementation Drivers effectively), and lack of attention to the Selection Driver.

Selection consists of recruitment and interviewing. The procedures noted below apply equally to candidates already employed in an organization and to candidates seeking employment in an organization.

## Staff recruitment processes

Human resources staff can do advertising and can screen applicants for basic qualifications (e.g., completed application, academic background, years of experience). When advertising to recruit applicants, it is advantageous to include information on the training and coaching support and opportunities to learn innovative practices. The offer of professional development and support in the recruiting ads has been attractive to many applicants. Advertising for people already employed in an organization might take the form of an email alerting staff about the intended use of an innovation and providing the name of a person to contact if anyone is interested.

Candidates who complete the paper submission process and meet minimum qualifications are engaged in an interview process.

## Staff Selection processes

For interviewing, a detailed summary of 85 years of research on interview practices (Schmidt & Hunter, 1998) found that tests of "general mental ability" (the ability to quickly learn and use new information and skills) were the best predictors of future job performance. They found that work-sample measures (e.g., role plays) and using a structured interview process were among the best ways to assess general mental ability. Similar findings resulted from a meta-analysis (McDaniel, Whetzel, Schmidt, & Maurer, 1994) that clearly supported the predictive advantages of structured behavior-based interviews (behavioral vignettes, role plays, in-box exercises) compared to the usual alternatives. The Implementation Team is responsible for assuring the availability of competent interviewers (i.e., the selection, training, coaching, and fidelity of interviewers) and establishing recruitment and selection plans. A specific person is responsible for coordinating the quality and timeliness of interview processes for practitioners using an innovation.

The following example of a best practices interview process is conducted by those who have a stake in hiring the person; that is, those who will "live with" the person who is hired. Typically, interviewers include a coach or trainer who knows the innovation well and has a "feel for" successful (and unsuccessful) practitioners, a manager or director responsible for the use of an innovation, and a practitioner who has met fidelity criteria.

A good-quality interview process includes:

- Initial phone call: ten minutes to describe the position, the use of the innovation, and supports for using the innovation as intended; 40 minutes asking the applicant about relevant experience, asking for self-ratings on verbal and written communication experience and abilities, and asking the applicant to respond to simple scenarios that provide examples of the kinds of work to be done using the innovation; ten minutes asking the applicant questions about her resume or other application materials related to experience and qualifications, and answering any questions the applicant may have.
  - o Look for candidates who are engaging and enthusiastic; who ask questions related to the innovation and not just the position (salary, benefits); who exhibit knowledge, skills, and abilities that are a good fit with the innovation.
  - o Invite a promising applicant for an in-person interview.
- In-person interview–Part 1: ten minutes for discussion to answer any questions the applicant has about the position, the work to be done, and the supports provided to do the work with fidelity; 20 minutes asking the applicant to respond to more complex scenarios taken from the experience of practitioners. The interview is conducted in a conversational and friendly way with some humor and banter to help the applicant relax and display her best behavior.
  - o Look for candidates who are engaging and enthusiastic; who exhibit knowledge, skills, and abilities that are a good fit with the innovation; and who provide reasonable responses to the scenarios. The scenarios elicit hints about an applicant's personal philosophy and values that can be explored further with a few observations and questions.
  - o Look for candidates who ask questions about the duties required, the support they will receive to learn and do the work well, and the opportunities to expand their knowledge base.

- o For many candidates, this is the end of the interview process. They have not met the standards of the interview team. Let the candidate know when a decision will be made and how they will be contacted.
  - o For candidates who still look like potentially good hires, take a quick break and then begin Part 2.
- In-person interview–Part 2: 40 minutes to conduct two role plays (see Chapter 10 for details). The role plays are the most telling aspect of the interview process. Perhaps two or three candidates out of ten who make it to the in-person interview also excel in the role play scenes and are hired. There always seem to be one or two surprises in each group of candidates–apparent stars who fade quickly during the role plays. For each role play, the lead interviewer (role play leader) presents a situation (complicated, but not too difficult) and asks the applicant to put her/himself in the role of the practitioner. The second interviewer (confederate) plays the role of the intended recipient of the innovation services (child, parent, patient, community member). The role play is scripted so the confederate knows what to say and not say as the applicant engages the "recipient." At the end of role play #1, the lead interviewer provides descriptive praise for two or three aspects on the applicant's behavior and provides constructive criticism of one thing the applicant did or omitted. After assuring understanding of the appropriate alternative behavior, the lead interviewer re-starts the role play at a point where the applicant has an opportunity to engage in the new behavior with the "recipient." Then do role play #two–and repeat the process. 20 minutes for questions and next steps.
  - o During the role plays, the interviewers pay close attention to how well the candidate accepts the positive descriptive feedback and the constructive critical feedback. Candidates who deny doing the positive things or want to argue about the content of the critical feedback likely will not accept coaching very well and are poor candidates for demanding practitioner positions.
  - o For those candidates who do well during the role plays and incorporate the feedback in the re-practice part, engage them in a discussion about what the experience was like for them and put the role play experience in the context of how training, coaching, and fidelity assessments are done in the organization.

## Staff Selection in practice

Staff recruitment and selection requires planning and organization. Table 18 provides a list of key aspects to consider as selection with implementation in mind is established for the first time in an organization determined to make full and effective use of a selected innovation.

Table 18. Best practices for recruitment and selection of new and existing staff in organizations

| Best practices for recruitment and selection of staff | In Place |
|---|---|
| Accountability for development and monitoring of quality and timeliness of selection services is clear (e.g., lead person designated and supported) | |
| Job description for human resource staff; clarity re: accountability and expectations | |
| Prerequisites for employment are related to "new practices" and expectations (e.g., basic group management skills) | |
| Interactive Interview Process is used | |
| • Behavioral vignettes and role plays | |
| • Assessment of ability to accept feedback | |
| • Assessment of ability to change own behavior | |
| Interviewers who understand the skills and abilities needed and can assess applicants accurately | |
| A regular process in place to feed forward interview data to training staff and administrators and coaches (integration) | |
| A regular process in place to feed back from exit interviews, training data, turnover data, opinions of administrators and coaches, and staff evaluation data to evaluate effectiveness of this Driver | |

## Staff training

The goal of the Training Driver is to teach practitioners the knowledge, skills, and abilities required to begin using an innovation. Training for new hires or reassigned staff who successfully complete the selection process is a critical step toward using an innovation with fidelity. No practitioner should be asked to use an innovation without first completing training. This means that training is done as needed, and not on some fixed schedule–a challenge for some organizations and a topic for leadership and Facilitative Administration.

146

Thus, a practitioner position stays "open" until a practitioner completes training. Untrained staff are not asked to "fill in" by working with recipients.

The training content is informed by the information developed to meet the Usable Innovation criteria. However, even then, there are choices to be made about what foundation information should be presented and practiced in training, and what safely can be left for coaches to teach on the job. Philosophy, values, inclusion-exclusion criteria, essential components, what to do and say to use the innovation (from practice profiles), and the methods and content of fidelity assessments all inform the content of training. While the content is innovation specific, the methods of training are universal and apply across all innovations that require more than a little behavior change on the part of practitioners.

A member of the Implementation Team is accountable for assuring that training is timely, done as intended, and improved over time. Highly competent individuals provide training (e.g., trainers who have deep content knowledge and effective training skills). Trainers who teach sections of a preservice workshop may be coaches, managers, fidelity assessors, practitioners who have met fidelity criteria, and others who are immersed in doing the work of assuring the full and effective use of an innovation in an organization.

Trainers do not just stand and deliver. Like teaching in general, evidence-based training is interactive with many opportunities to elicit responses from trainees (Hattie, 2009; Ward et al., 2017). An effective trainer:

1. "Provides clear instruction" operationalized as the trainer stating a) what participants should learn and b) why the learning concept is important
2. "Demonstrates instructional tasks" operationalized as the trainer modeling skills a) explicitly (e.g., step by step), b) consistently (e.g., repeatedly), and c) with examples and non-examples
3. "Engages participants in meaningful interactions with content" operationalized as the trainer using a variety of materials and strategies to a) generate new knowledge, b) extend critical thinking, and c) promote reflection by all participants on their own learning, effort, and understanding
4. "Provides prompt and accurate feedback" operationalized as the trainer communicating verbal and nonverbal positive and encouraging responses appropriate to a participant's a) effort, b) behavior, or c) engagement with content
5. "Adjusts to participants' responses to instruction" operationalized as the trainer demonstrating flexibility in a) pacing the lesson, b) redirecting off-task behavior, or c) incorporating additional practice based on participants' responses
6. "Provides multiple methods and opportunities for participants to practice" operationalized as the trainer a) checking for understanding, and b) using a variety

of methods and activities to engage participants through individual and group responses

7. "Adjusts to participants' engagement with instruction" operationalized as the trainer purposefully a) adjusting the physical environment, b) access to materials, or c) the manner of instruction in response to an observable participant need

## Staff training processes

The Implementation Team is responsible for assuring the availability of competent trainers and establishing training and professional development plans. In every case, each trainer is prepared (selected, trained, coached, fidelity to be a trainer) by the Implementation Team. A specific person is responsible for coordinating the quality and timeliness of training processes for practitioners using an innovation.

Training is 1) skill-based, 2) includes opportunities for practice in the form of behavior rehearsals for essential skills, and 3) includes both positive and constructive feedback to participants. Note that behavior rehearsals are different from the role plays described for Staff Selection (see Chapter 10 on this topic). In behavior rehearsals, the trainees are not "playing a role." They are working on what to do and say when interacting with others as soon as training ends. In training, the skills are practiced and re-practiced until criteria for competence are reached (training criteria similar to the criteria used in fidelity assessments). As competency trainers say, Day One of training is done when Day One skills are learned (sometimes at 10 pm for a given trainee).

Behavior rehearsals require preparation of the "scenes" and preparation of the behavior rehearsal leader and confederate (Dreisbach, Luger, Ritter, & Smart, 1979). These are not opportunities to "stump the trainee" but are intended to help newly employed practitioners learn critical skills needed for their first encounters with real recipients of the innovation-based services. Preparation is everything to assure a constructive experience for practitioners. Coaches often volunteer to participate in the behavior rehearsals to help assure trainees' receptivity and responsiveness to feedback, and to initiate the coaching relationship.

The immediate outcome of training is demonstrated gains in innovation-related knowledge and skills as measured before and after training. Since the purpose of training is to teach the knowledge, skills, and abilities required to begin using an innovation, the first question to ask is, Did the trainers accomplish this goal? Pre-post tests of knowledge and skills are hallmarks of training as an Implementation Driver (Collins, Brooks, Fixsen, Maloney, & Blase, 1976; Navarro-Haro et al., 2018; Reinke, Herman, Stormont, Newcomer, & David, 2013). Pre-post assessments of skills rely on behavior rehearsals similar to those used in the practitioner selection and training processes (C. J. Braukmann, Kirigin-Ramp, Tigner, & Wolf, 1984;

Kirigin et al., 1975). Video recording makes pre-post assessments of complex skills practical in typical organizations; innovation-related interactions can be recorded before and after training, then scored at a later time (Forgatch et al., 2005).

Figure 22 shows the results of six training workshops where role play scenes were used to assess key skills just before and just after a one-week training workshop (Collins, Brooks, Daly, et al., 1976; Collins, Brooks, Fixsen, et al., 1976). These were the first workshops delivered in an organization that was just beginning to use the Teaching-Family Model.

During these workshops, trainers were being trained at the same time trainees were being trained. The goal was to have trainees at 80% or better on the post-training assessment. This goal was finally reached after the tenth workshop (data not shown) and sustained at that level for many years (data not shown). The data from each workshop was fed back to the trainers so that they could improve their training skills and curricula after each workshop (P. D. Braukmann et al., 1983).

If pre-post tests are done, then it is training; otherwise, it is an information-sharing meeting. Training content is refined over time by using Improvement Cycles based on information from pre-post tests of training, coaching logs, and fidelity assessments (part of the Decision Support Data System). The goal of training is to facilitate coaching and shorten the time required to meet fidelity criteria. The constant monitoring of training via the Decision Support Data System provides the avenue (a data-based pathway) for continuing to work toward this goal.

# Training

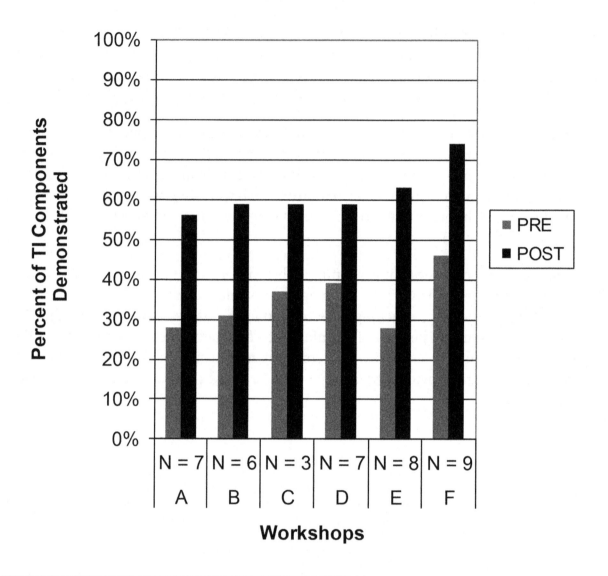

Figure 22. Pre-post results of six training workshops. "TI" are Teaching Interaction components that are essential functions within the Teaching-Family Model (Collins, Brooks, Daly, et al., 1976)

Given the emphasis on skill development, a training session may have readings that can be completed by trainees prior to a training session, followed by a brief introduction to the skills to be learned, and explanations of why they are important. Perhaps 40% of training time is spent in behavior rehearsals to begin teaching and learning the innovation-related skills. Discussion time interspersed with behavior rehearsals allows time to revisit the information that was provided in the readings and brief introductions. This process helps to develop common language for describing the essential components of the innovation as the skills are being taught and learned. The skill required of trainers cannot be overestimated. Trainers need to be content experts and skilled teachers. The preparation of trainers is an important step in the implementation and scaling processes.

## Selection of trainers

The best candidates for trainers are practitioners who have met fidelity criteria. They know the innovation in detail and are aware of the art and science that underpins excellent performance. Examples are readily available from their real-life experience, and answers to questions can be provided with context. In more mature organizations, nearly all of the leadership positions (e.g., directors of training, coaching, operating units, the organization) are filled with individuals with this history. With preparation for delivering content and engaging in behavior rehearsals, different individuals can teach sections of the preservice training without losing continuity for the trainee practitioners.

In an organization using an innovation for the first time, trainers need to be selected and developed. It is critical to have trainers who have in-depth knowledge of the innovation, even if the trainer needs to be contracted to do the training. If a contracted trainer is used, part of the contract should include training local staff to participate as trainers-in-training and for the contracted trainer to share materials and training knowledge with the local staff. As shown in Figure 22, there may be less than satisfactory results for a while, but this process will set the path to fairly rapid development of knowledgeable and skilled trainers.

## Staff training in practice

Staff training requires planning and organization. Table 19 provides a list of key aspects to consider as innovation-informed training is established for the first time in an organization determined to make full and effective use of a selected innovation.

**Table 19. Best practices for training new or existing staff in organizations**

| Best practices for training | In Place |
|---|---|
| <u>Accountability</u> for development and monitoring of quality and timeliness of training services <u>is clear</u> (e.g., lead person designated and supported) | |
| <u>Timely</u> (criteria: Training occurs <u>before</u> the person attempts to or is required to use the new program or practice) | |
| Skill-based training methods are used | |
| • Behavior rehearsals | |
| • <u>Qualified</u> behavior rehearsal leaders who are <u>content</u> experts | |
| • <u>Practice</u> critical interactions skills <u>to criteria</u> | |
| Trainers have been trained and coached | |
| Outcome data collected and analyzed (pre- and post-testing) of knowledge and/or skills | |
| <u>Performance assessment measures</u> collected and analyzed <u>related to training</u> (e.g., schedule, content, processes, qualification of trainers) | |
| Feed forward of pre-post data to coaches/ supervisors | |
| Feedback of pre-post data to selection and recruitment | |

## Staff coaching

The goal of the Coaching Driver is to support practitioners' learning as they use an innovation with fidelity in their interactions with recipients. Coaching and fidelity assessment are the eyes and ears of implementation of any innovation in an organization. Fidelity is quality assurance; are we doing what we intend to do? how do we know? does it make a difference? Fidelity sets a minimum standard for using an innovation. Coaching is the way to see the details regarding how an innovation is used and help practitioners initially meet and then routinely exceed that standard. High expectations are set by fidelity standards; low tolerance for error is set by coaching. The result is a high level of consistency and dependable socially significant outcomes.

With the exception of coaching, the Competency Drivers are episodic. Practitioners encounter selection once during the hiring process, participate in training once as they anticipate using an innovation, and participate in fidelity assessments a few times each year. Coaching is constant. If a practitioner is using an innovation, then scheduled and unscheduled coaching support is being provided according to the coaching-service delivery plan (explained later).

Coaching is essential because most skills needed by successful practitioners can be assessed during selection and introduced in training but really are learned on the job with the help of a coach. An effective coach provides "craft" information along with advice, encouragement, and opportunities to practice and use skills specific to the innovation (e.g., engagement, using an innovation in the setting, clinical judgment). The full and effective use of innovations requires behavior change at the practitioner, supervisory, and administrative support levels. Training and coaching are the principal implementation methods by which behavior change is brought about for carefully selected staff in the beginning stages of implementation and throughout the life of evidence-based practices and programs and other innovations. Organizations make use of data to establish and improve coaching methods.

Every key position in a high functioning organization has a coach (Drucker, 2004). New directors, managers, coaches, trainers, fidelity assessors, and so on have a coach to help them use new skills in typical practice settings. In this section the focus is on coaching for practitioners. The general principles apply more broadly to any coaching to help assure the use of meaningful skill sets by any staff member.

## Related research

With the recognition of the importance of coaching, research on coaching has helped to solidify and refine the knowledge base. Meta-analyses continue to identify coaching as a critical addition to training if practitioner fidelity and recipient outcomes are to be produced (Dunst, Bruder, & Hamby, 2015; Joyce & Showers, 2002; Kretlow & Bartholomew, 2010; Stormont, Reinke, Newcomer, Marchese, & Lewis, 2014). Recent studies (Dorsey et al., 2018; Driscoll, Wang, Mashburn, & Pianta, 2011; Kraft & Blazar, 2017; Reinke et al., 2013; Walsh, Ryan, & Flynn, 2018; Webster-Stratton et al., 2014) that purposefully use coaching and proactively assess coaching and outcomes provide more evidence regarding the key role of coaching when practitioners are learning to use an innovation with fidelity and socially significant outcomes. For example, Driscoll, et al. (2011) found that, when compared to a control group, pre-school teachers who had in-person coaching in addition to training and web-based resources were 13 times more likely to use the innovation with children. Joyce and Showers (2002) found that coaching was the difference between 5% (training only) and 95% (training and on the job coaching) use of an innovation in practice (fidelity assessment). Competent coaching makes a big difference.

Studies that include direct observation of coaching behavior consistently identify key aspects of coaching such as direct observation of performance, feedback in an innovation-consistent manner, modeling, behavior rehearsal, and personal/emotional support (Dorsey et al., 2018; Martino, Gallon, et al., 2008; Reinke et al., 2013; Schoenwald et al., 2004; Webster-Stratton et al., 2014). Some specific coaching skills are being operationalized and studied in functional analyses of coaching. For example, Saldana, Chamberlain, and Chapman (2016) operationalized coaching as reinforcement of a) efforts, b) relationships and roles, and c) small steps toward goal achievement done by coaches who a) use strength-focused language, b) notice normative appropriate behavior, c) observe and reinforce, and d) take opportunities to smile and laugh. Coaches (n=51 in nine agencies) were taught (selected, trained, and coached) to use the defined approach to coaching, and *fidelity to the coaching methods* was assessed. About six months after training, the first fidelity assessment was conducted and 14% had coaching fidelity scores in the 80-100% range; two years after training 47% of the coaches met the 80% benchmark. Learning to be an effective coach takes time and effort, and not everyone is suited to be an excellent coach.

It has been clear for some time that coaching is essential for developing knowledge, skills, and abilities related to innovations. The clarity of the data has improved, the definition of coaching has improved, and training and evaluation of coaching behavior have improved so that there is greater agreement and certainty regarding what constitutes "coaching" and its outcomes.

## Coaching processes

The Implementation Team is responsible for assuring the availability of competent coaches (selection, training, coaching and fidelity assessment of coaches) and establishing coaching-service delivery plans. A specific person is responsible for coordinating the quality and timeliness of coaching processes for practitioners using an innovation. Every practitioner using an innovation receives coaching support at least once a month. New practitioners often receive coaching several times a week until new skills become more natural and fidelity criteria are met. In general, the more important the outcome and the greater the risk poor performance poses to a recipient, the more frequent and intensive the coaching must be. The ratio of coaches to practitioners often is in the 1:4 to 1:6 range for intensive interaction-based human services (C. J. Braukmann et al., 1984; Chamberlain, 2003; Girard, 2013; Schoenwald et al., 2004).

After a few decades of research related to training teachers, Joyce & Showers (2002) began to think of training and coaching as one continuous set of operations designed to produce actual changes in the classroom behavior of teachers. One without the other is insufficient. Behavior change is difficult for most people (for example, some people hire personal coaches to help them exercise more or change their eating behavior or stop smoking). With newly learned behavior there are several simultaneous problems that must be faced:

- Newly learned behavior is awkward compared to performance by a master practitioner. Joyce and Showers (2002) estimate that initial acquisition of the skills related to an innovation of medium complexity requires repeated daily trials in a classroom environment over a period of eight-ten weeks. Blase, Fixsen, and Phillips (1984) note that it takes about 8–12 months for Teaching-Parents to learn and use the complex skills to meet all fidelity criteria in a Teaching-Family group home treatment program. Physicians who want to be general surgeons are required to complete five years of residency (intensive coaching) and engage in at least 850 operative procedures to meet fidelity criteria (http://www.absurgery.org/default.jsp?certgsqe_training). Coaching is not a short-term investment in high-quality services. It is continuous and essential to support consistent services and reliably beneficial outcomes.
- Newly learned behavior is fragile and needs to be supported in the face of reactions from recipients and others in the service setting. When faced with difficulties or negative reactions, the impulse is to seek the comfort of the familiar and give up trying to do the unfamiliar and uncomfortable innovation. A good coach is the counterbalance to this impulse and can help practitioners cope with the difficulties while they improve competence and instill confidence as new skills develop.
- Newly learned behavior is incomplete and will need to be shaped to be most functional in a service setting. Saldana et al. (2016) describe in detail an R³ coaching process that includes: Reinforcement of effort, Reinforcement of relationships and roles, and Reinforcement of small steps to support practitioner learning on the job. Practitioners who routinely meet fidelity standards are a good indicator that innovation-specific knowledge, skills, and abilities are being learned. Coaching continues to expand those skills so they become embedded and nuanced in ways that benefit more recipients more of the time.

In addition to helping to establish new behavior in the service environment, emotional and personal support for a practitioner is another role for a coach (Reinke et al., 2013; Spouse, 2001). In interaction-based innovations, practitioners *are* the intervention. Usable Innovations inform when and how practitioners interact with recipients and stakeholders, but it is the practitioner who delivers the innovation through his or her words and actions in face-to-face encounters with recipients. In the transactional interplay between practitioner and recipient, each affects the other in complex ways. Intensive services require high levels of trust and sharing. Eventually, a practitioner's own personal issues are encountered in the service setting ("I felt like I lost my own baby all over again!"). Thus, emotional and personal support are part of coaching to help practitioners through temporary issues.

The overall components of coaching are listed in Table 20 along with estimates of coaching support. Practitioners who are just learning how to use an innovation in practice require more time and attention to the development of skills and judgement–an extension of training. As skills and judgement develop and become natural, more time is devoted to reflection based on a practitioner's observations of his own interactions with recipients. With coaching, the practitioner learns what to look for in his own behavior as the innovation is used and then can accurately report more accurately what was done and not done. Personal support remains at a fairly low level throughout. The purpose of personal support is not to provide counseling for chronic personal issues; the goal is to provide personal support to cope with frustrations and temporary issues impacting performance (Reinke et al., 2013; Schoenwald et al., 2004).

**Table 20. Estimates of changes in coaching support as competency for using an innovation is established**

| Component of Coaching | New Practitioner | Met Fidelity at Least Twice |
|---|---|---|
| Teaching innovation-related skills and judgement | 60% | 20% |
| Reflection based on practitioner's observations | 20% | 60% |
| Personal support for issues impacting performance | 20% | 20% |

To be effective, coaches' feedback to staff is based on direct observation (e.g., face to face, audio or video recording) and at least one other data source such as:

- Individual or group reflection
- Product or document review
- Interviews with key stakeholders

Direct observation is essential for coaching regarding any interaction-based innovation that requires skillful use of an innovation to produce intended outcomes. Newly trained practitioners falter with the words to say and things to do and often miss opportunities to use their new skills. They do not recognize the cues (good judgement) to step in and use (or not use) parts of the innovation. Errors of omission are difficult to detect without direct observation of the practitioner and the recipient interacting with one another. Direct observation also provides information on the quality components (tone of voice, proximity, respectful language, body movements, use of humor) and other nuances that may not be described as part of an innovation but still may influence outcomes (P. S. Jensen et al., 2005).

**Coaching-service delivery plan**

A written plan outlines the coaching supports provided to staff who carry out the program or practice including requirements for coaches to be experts in delivering the program or practice, frequency of coaching, and coaching methods. A coach's adherence to the plan is reviewed at least three times a year with the data entered into the Decision Support Data System.

Agency staff assess effectiveness of coaching quarterly through the use of two or more of the following data sources:

- Practitioner fidelity (percent of practitioners who reach fidelity 3, 6, 9, and 12 months after completing training and beginning to use an innovation in practice)
- Coach fidelity (adherence to the coaching-service delivery plan)
- Satisfaction surveys (e.g., clarity of communication, helpfulness, availability) from those being coached (two-three times a year for a new coach; annually thereafter)
- Observations of coaches conducting coaching activities (direct observation by the supervisor of coaches and a member of the Implementation Team)

Coaching effectiveness data are entered in the Decision Support Data System and are used to inform improvements in recruitment, selection, and training of coaches and other implementation supports for coaches.

A comprehensive coaching system is comprised of a Usable Innovation, the necessary Facilitative Administration supports and other activities and supports as specified by the Implementation Drivers, and a coaching-service delivery plan. The coaching-service delivery plan is a proactive approach to purposeful and supportive coaching. It details the responsibilities of both the coach and the practitioner. It specifies the coaching elements that will promote quality service delivery via support for the practitioner or other staff and serves as the basis for further professional development.

A sound coaching system relies on multiple sources of data including qualitative reports of activities, observations, and the voice of the practitioner as well as data related to service delivery timeliness, perceived quality and helpfulness of the service by stakeholders, and outcomes of service provision. By developing a coaching-service delivery plan and adjusting it over time—always with the goal of improved support for practitioners and service to recipients—the coach and practitioner can partner in this quality improvement process.

As an Implementation Team engages in the planning of the coaching-service delivery methods and processes, they consider the following:

- Description of the concepts, skills, or areas to be coached (based on the Usable Innovation and practice profile)
- Details of the coaching processes (e.g., direct observation, documentation review)
- Expected frequency of coaching. Frequency is adjusted as practitioners or coaches gain experience and grow in their skill competency (e.g., pre-fidelity, after meeting fidelity criteria twice, after meeting fidelity criteria consistently for two or more years)
- Specification of required documentation (e.g., written feedback after each coaching visit) and data to be collected or reviewed and the timeline for submission by the coach (to whom, by when)
- Outline of the format of each post-coaching event. For example, the coach provides a verbal summary during a face-face meeting with the practitioner or at least within 24 hours of a direct observation and provides a brief written summary of observations and recommendations within five working days
- Details of the plan for monitoring the coach's adherence to the coaching-service delivery plan; who, how, how often, and when will the plan be reviewed?
- Schedule for reviewing coaching data, analyzing data for continuous improvement of coaching processes and outcomes, and analyzing coaching data in the context of the overall Decision Support Data System; at least twice each year

## Coaches and organization change

Coaches are accountable for removing obstacles to high fidelity use of an innovation. So far, the focus has been on the lack of practitioner skills as an obstacle, and on methods to observe, teach, and reinforce skills on the job as a way to overcome that obstacle. That is one consistent obstacle. There are many other potential obstacles that hinder the use of an innovation as intended. Scheduling of time, supervision that is not coaching, frequency and content of meetings, employment and salary standards, content of staff meetings, expense reimbursement guidelines, administrative staff support, and so on and on are all potential obstacles.

Coaches see specifically what is getting in the way of practitioners using an innovation with fidelity. Coaches are accountable for meeting with leaders, administrators, and staff to foster changes in the organization structure, roles, and functions to remove those obstacles. Coaches prompt facilitative administrative changes. The goal is to align organization ways of work so that they fully support the use of an innovation by practitioners. Doing the work required of an innovation is difficult enough for practitioners without asking them to do the work in spite of an organization's status quo operations.

Agreement from leaders to engage in these kinds of organization changes is secured by the Implementation Team during the Exploration Stage activities. Agreement is reinforced by the coaching-service delivery plan that is established during the Installation Stage and strengthened during the Initial Implementation Stage. It is the task of the Implementation Team to assure that the voices of the coaches are heard and that obstacles are removed as quickly as practicable. At Teaching-Family Sites each Teaching-Parent couple in a group home needed their own checking account and their own van for transportation to promote teaching and learning in the community. Finance departments and boards of directors had to change their policies and procedures to enthusiastically support these needs. Getting agreement to make the changes during Exploration was one thing; getting the changes made internally for each and every Teaching-Family group home now and in the future required additional effort.

Coaches have an essential role in implementation of innovations and creating organization support for practitioners' high fidelity performance. Coaches are the eyes of the organization and see what is needed to improve supports for practitioners so that innovation can be used consistently and with socially significant outcomes. With continual improvement in supports, continual improvements in outcomes for recipients can be realized.

## Selection of coaches

The best candidates for coaches are practitioners who repeatedly have met fidelity criteria for using the innovation (Blase, Fixsen, & Phillips, 1984; Martino, Gallon, et al., 2008). Staff trained as coaches without detailed knowledge of the innovation and its uses in practice are at a disadvantage. For example, Mutamba et al. (2018, p. 11) found, "The supervisors (primary health workers in our example) were new to the intervention as were the VHTs [village health team members]. Although they were trained as supervisors, they had no direct experience delivering the intervention, which greatly limited their ability to supervise VHTs. Therefore, their supervisory role may not have been to the standard desired."

While asking high performing practitioners to become coaches is disruptive to the practitioner corps, it is the right thing to do to develop implementation capacity. The advice is to recruit too many overqualified people to be the first practitioners so they can learn the innovation, meet fidelity criteria, and within a year or two become the next sets of trainers, coaches, managers, and directors as the use of an innovation begins to scale (Ogden et al., 2005; Tommeraas & Ogden, 2016). High fidelity practitioners know the innovation, the nuances of its use in practice, and how it feels to be a practitioner. Given that coaches need to have a thorough understanding of the innovation, high fidelity practitioners have a head start. During the interview process, candidates for coaching roles are asked to display their knowledge of the innovation and their willingness to learn the innovation thoroughly (if not currently familiar with it).

The in-person portion of the interview includes role plays that require the candidates to demonstrate their coaching skills (see the Selection Driver for more information on interviews). The interview team provides feedback to determine how well the candidate gives and receives feedback. During the role plays for coaches, the interview team looks for a candidate's ability to accurately observe and describe behavior; ability to put a concept label on a set of discrete activities and generalize the concept to new sets of activities; ability to give rationales and provide constructive feedback; ability to organize and conduct a behavior rehearsal to teach a new skill; and judgement about when to teach and when to listen to practitioner reflections. In addition, the interview team looks for quality components such as tone of voice, posture, facial expressions, pleasantness, and engagement. An overview of a process for training, coaching, and assessing fidelity of coaches is outlined by Martino, Gallon, et al. (2008).

Stormont, Reinke, Newcomer, Marchese, and Lewis (2015) surveyed the literature on coaching in education. In 29 studies that evaluated coaching and its outcomes, they found coaching activities often were described in general terms such as "provision of feedback" or "support." More specific coaching activities included modeling, practice, team teaching, role play, and goal setting. There was virtually no information included in the studies regarding the skills required to serve as coaches, how coaches are trained, and the amount and type of coaching provided. The practice profile developed by Van Dyke (2015) and the study by Saldana et al. (2016) detail many of the skills required of competent coaches.

**Staff coaching in practice**

Staff coaching requires planning and organization. Table 21 provides a list of key aspects to consider as coaching for performance is established for the first time in an organization determined to make full and effective use of a selected innovation.

## Table 21. Best practices for coaching in organizations

| Best practices for coaching | In Place |
|---|---|
| <u>Accountability for</u> development and monitoring of quality and timeliness of <u>coaching services is clear</u> (e.g., there is a lead person who is accountable for assuring coaching is occurring as planned) | |
| Coaches are <u>fluent</u> in the <u>innovation(s)</u> | |
| There is a <u>written coaching-service delivery plan</u> (where, when, with whom, why) | |
| Coaches use <u>multiple sources of information</u> for feedback to practitioners | |
| • Coaches directly observe practitioners using the innovations(s) (in person, audio, video) | |
| • Coaches <u>review records</u> to obtain information to inform coaching | |
| • Coaching <u>information</u> is obtained from <u>interviews</u> with others associated with the practitioner | |
| Accountability structure and processes for coaches | |
| • <u>Adherence</u> to coaching-service delivery plan is <u>regularly reviewed</u> | |
| • Evidence that practitioners' abilities to deliver the intervention routinely improve as a result of coaching | |
| • Multiple sources of <u>information used</u> for feedback to coaches | |
| o Satisfaction surveys from those being coached | |
| o Observations of each coach by an expert/master coach | |
| o Performance (fidelity) assessments of those being coached as key coaching outcome | |
| Coaching data are reviewed and inform improvements of other Drivers (feedback function) | |

# Chapter 10: Role Play and Behavior Rehearsal

Teaching and assessment of complex behavior regarding interaction-based innovations requires equally complex methods to elicit relevant interactions and judgments. Role plays and behavior rehearsals are used for these purposes during Staff Selection interviews, staff training for competency, pre-post assessments of learning during training, teaching during coaching, and so on. Given the multiple uses, the role plays and behavior rehearsal methods are described in this chapter and only referred to in other chapters.

Role plays and behavior rehearsals are similar procedures with different purposes. Role plays elicit snippets of behavior that can be assessed during an interview. There is no expectation that the candidate will use components of an innovation in a role play scene. The purpose is to assess judgement and coachability during the interview. On the other hand, behavior rehearsals are designed to have practitioners practice key innovation-related behavior until competency criteria are met, either in training or in coaching sessions. For behavior rehearsals, the focus is on using an innovation with fidelity.

Procedurally, they require considerable preparation of the role play / behavior rehearsal leader and the confederate and thoughtful description of the scenes. The role play / behavior rehearsal leader must be skilled at observing and describing behavior and giving descriptive praise and constructive feedback in a pleasant way (Dancer et al., 1978). The confederate must be skilled at acting out the role, following the advice of the candidate even if it goes far off topic, and not giving unplanned clues to "right answers" or otherwise "help the candidate." The scenes must be realistic examples of

> *Role plays and behavior rehearsals are similar procedures with different purposes. Role plays elicit snippets of behavior that can be assessed during an interview to assess judgement and coachability. On the other hand, behavior rehearsals are designed to have practitioners practice key innovation-related behavior until competency criteria are met to use an innovation with fidelity.*

situations encountered by practitioners (typically events that have occurred in practice and that are well-known to the interviewers) without being too complicated.

## Scenes

An example of role play scenes used in the interview process for hiring new Implementation Specialists (Implementation Team members) is provided here. The interviewer and role play leader roles often are carried out by the same person in an interview.

### Instructions to the interviewer

*Prepare the applicant by stating that we are going to present some "real life" role-play situations based on the work we have done. Introduce the confederate. Prior to each role play, give the applicant the instruction sheet and answer any questions after the applicant has read it. State a couple of times that we are not looking for any specific procedures; "there are no right answers: so just do what you think is right to be helpful."*

*Take notes during the role play. After the role play has concluded, offer positive feedback on one or two things that the applicant said or did related to the specific role play. You also can offer positive feedback on one or more of the following generic skills: ability to offer empathy, active listening skills, respect for the person and team members, asking follow-up questions to get relevant information (e.g., second-hand observation skills), non-judgmental statements, hopeful words, attending to feelings, clinical judgement, ability to arrive at "next right steps," and ability to get buy-in for next right steps. Spend most of the time on the positive things the applicant did.*

*Then, pick one concept area and offer constructive feedback. Describe what the applicant said or did that needs to change ("what you said/did was …;" describe the appropriate alternative behavior clearly ("another way of saying/doing that is …;" label the skill ("this is an example of …;" provide a rationale for why the appropriate alternative behavior is an improvement ("the reason this is important is …);" ask the applicant to practice doing/saying the appropriate alternative behavior with you ("to make sure you've got it"), answer any questions the applicant may have; then restart the role play at a point where the applicant can use the "new skill" in the interaction with the confederate.*

*Pay close attention to the applicant's abilities in each of the concept areas during the interactions with the confederate and with the Interviewer. Also, carefully note the applicant's ability to accept praise, accept critical feedback, learn the new skill you*

164

teach, and use that new skill in the re-start of the role-play situation.  This is a mini-training session and a mini-coaching session wrapped up in one, so pay careful attention to how teachable/coachable the applicant is (a "general mental ability;" the ability to quickly learn and use new information and skills).

At the end of a re-started role play, offer only positive statements about how the applicant performed.  Then, move on to the next role play.


### Instructions to the role play leader

The following role play asks the applicant to engage an Implementation Team member in problem-solving to get past didactic teaching.

Problem-solving consists of engaging the confederate in SOCS–identifying the situation, generating options, considering the consequences of each option (i.e., advantages and disadvantages), and generating one or more possible solutions.

During the role play, take notes on how the applicant engaged the confederate in constructive problem-solving instead of complaining; what advice the applicant had for solving the problem; and what help the applicant offered to solve the problem (try to get quotes of what he/she said).  Also note the extent to which the applicant is willing to take responsibility for helping to use those solutions in practice (e.g., all "you do" or do solutions include "we do?").

After the role play has concluded, offer positive descriptive feedback on any skill components that were used.  If none were used, offer praise for ability to offer empathy, active listening skills, clarity of instructions, or other generic skills.

Then provide constructive criticism on one or more missing components related to SOCS, engagement, and taking responsibility.  In general, try to get the applicant to do as much of the problem-solving interaction as possible without overwhelming the applicant.  Then restart the role play at a point where the applicant can use the "new skill" in the interaction to do problem- solving with the confederate.

When giving constructive criticism, pay close attention to the applicant's ability to accept praise, accept critical feedback, listen and learn the new skill you teach, and use that new skill in the re-start of the role play situation.  This is a mini-training session and a mini-coaching session wrapped up in one, so pay careful attention to how teachable/coachable the applicant is.

At the end of the re-start, offer only praise for trying again and engaging in the process (no matter how well or poorly the applicant performed).

### Instructions to the confederate

You are the leader of an Implementation Team that has just started working with a provider organization. You have engaged the leadership of the organization and are working with the staff to establish Implementation supports for practitioners in the organization. You are very frustrated and upset that the people in the organization are not following your advice (Theme of this role play: You have been providing only didactic training with no active modeling or observation-based coaching). You have made presentations to them; you had them do homework on Active Implementation and report what they learned at meetings; you have developed reminder cards; and so on. The people in the organization still are not preparing leadership, developing competencies, and changing organization practices as required (i.e., not changing their behavior).

Make statements to the Implementation Specialist about how working with this group is a waste of your time, and how you are willing to move on to work with another organization if the Implementation Specialist agrees. Make statements about how you have tried everything and nothing seems to work.

You start by complaining about the lack of progress. Be excited and a bit angry at first. Then calm down once the Implementation Specialist interrupts your monologue or asks a question. Be positive and accepting of any advice.

## Instructions to the applicant (Implementation Specialist)

*You are an Implementation Specialist and the leader of efforts to establish an Implementation Team that will work with several organizations to establish implementation supports for practitioners. You have been working with the Implementation Team for several months. You are meeting with the leader of the Implementation Team who has told you he/she is frustrated with lack of progress.*

*Respond to the situation as you see fit. There are no right or wrong approaches. Don't worry about the specifics (names, places, events). Make it up along with any other information you want and [confederate name] will go along with you in the role play.*

# Chapter 11: Implementation Organization Drivers

Innovations are new ways of work. They require changes in practitioner behavior, and changes in the operations of organizations that support them. To sustain and improve socially significant outcomes, organizations provide many supports for the use of effective innovations and effective implementation. Existing organizations are not designed for these purposes so they must change to provide a hospitable and supportive environment so that intended outcomes can be realized consistently and sustained across cohorts of practitioners and recipients (Bertram, Suter, Bruns, & O'Rourke, 2012; Corrigan, Steiner, McCracken, Blaser, & Barr, 2001; Cummings et al., 2017; Schoenwald et al., 2008; Tucker & Singer, 2015).

## Organization defined

*An organization "employs" practitioners and Implementation Team members to do the work that meets the goals and mission of the organization. "Employs" means "a) to engage or make use of the services of (a person) in return for money; hire; b) to provide work or occupation for; keep busy; occupy; and c) to use as a means" (http://www.dictionary.com/). An organization is said to have common purpose, coordinated effort, division of labor, and hierarchy of authority (Schein, 1992). An organization may take many forms and may be large or small, well-resourced or volunteer, local or multinational, public or private, for profit or not for profit, or place-based or virtual, and may have sub-units that are tightly or loosely coupled, and so on. Organizations are knowable, scalable, and improvable.*

*While the immediate focus is on practitioners who deliver services, organization functioning and system functioning and societal factors exert their influences and must be accounted for as an innovation is used with fidelity, scaled, improved, and sustained.*

Organizations "employ" staff. This is an important point. In human service systems, there always is an organization of some kind with staff of some kind. For example, the Safe Motherhood Action Groups (SMAGs) are made up of volunteer and paid community members who were "employed by" Neighbourhood Health Committees in rural Zambia (Jacobs et al., 2018). The researchers themselves were "employed by" the School of Public Health at the University of Zambia to carry out the research methods as they interacted with the Neighbourhood Health Committees and SMAG members. In any organization (e.g., a Neighbourhood Health Committee, a School of Public Health) the Implementation Drivers (e.g., Staff Selection, leadership) are always present and always at work, haphazardly or on purpose.

Some researchers describe organizations in terms of inner and outer settings (Aarons et al., 2011; Damschroder et al., 2009; Fernandez et al., 2018; Greenhalgh et al., 2004). For Active Implementation, the inner setting is the organization that "employs" those who are intended to use an innovation, and the outer setting is the world beyond that organization. Implementation exerts strong influence on those in organizations, and organization staff are accountable for influencing those beyond the organization (the System Intervention Driver) to improve alignment and integration of relevant factors with the use of an innovation. If the system itself is attempting to use an innovation, then the system is the organization that "employs" those intended to use the innovation. In those cases, the system is the inner setting, and the socio-political-economic world beyond that organization is the outer setting.

## Organization Drivers overview

The Organization Implementation Drivers are Facilitative Administration, Decision Support Data Systems, and System Intervention.

- Facilitative Administrators look for ways to support practitioners' use of an innovation. Any impediment to achieving and sustaining high fidelity use of an innovation is the concern of Facilitative Administrators.
- Decision Support Data Systems include granular information regarding the use of an innovation and the use of the Implementation Drivers and their proximal outcomes. Data systems also include molar information that sums up the granular information and adds information regarding the overall effectiveness and efficiency of the organization. The data are used immediately and over the longer term to support decision making at every level of an organization.

- System Intervention is expected and planned for from the beginning. Barriers that are beyond the immediate control of an organization are common when innovations are being attempted for the first time and sustained over the long term. It is incumbent on leaders within an organization to work with groups and individuals external to an organization to clear away system barriers and strengthen system facilitators.

These and other factors impact the full and effective use of innovations to produce socially significant outcomes. While the immediate focus is on practitioners who deliver services, organization functioning and system functioning and societal factors exert their influences and must be accounted for as an innovation is used with fidelity, scaled, improved, and sustained (Hanney, Kuruvilla, Soper, & Mays, 2010).

The following sections operationalize the Organization Drivers: Facilitative Administration, Decision Support Data Systems, and Leadership.

## Facilitative Administration

Facilitative Administration sometimes is confused with the Leadership Drivers. While there are similarities, the difference pertains to the scope of influence. Leaders are the executive staff who can change structures, roles, and functions within an entire organization, and who regularly interact with other organizations, systems, and community groups outside the organization. On the other hand, administrators and managers have more limited authority and can change roles, functions, and operating procedures in one or more sub-units within an organization. While individuals may at times be both administrators and leaders, for implementation purposes the functions are distinct.

Facilitative Administrators look for ways to support practitioners' use of an innovation. Any impediment to achieving and sustaining high fidelity use of an innovation is the concern of Facilitative Administrators. In their study of health providers, Foote and Town (2007, p. 1640) found, "Contractors lack the infrastructure to manage implementation of advances in EBM [evidence-based medicine], especially when the process of change is administratively complex (e.g., assuring relevant information/ data; aligning policies, practices, and incentives; providing education and support for changes)." Facilitative Administration is essential to using innovations with fidelity and socially significant outcomes.

A major impediment to the use of an innovation is low fidelity use of the innovation. To remove this impediment, Facilitative Administrators assure timely access to the Competency Drivers delivered effectively. For example:

171

- Practitioner vacancies are anticipated so that recruitment, interviewing, and selection of a new practitioner can be completed before the departure of an experienced practitioner
- Training is scheduled to begin promptly after a new practitioner is hired so that untrained staff never have to "fill in" when interacting with recipients
- Competent coaches are scheduled to visit each practitioner according to the coaching-service delivery plan with some slack in the schedule for unplanned visits as needed
- Qualified staff are scheduled to conduct fidelity assessments on the schedule required for each individual practitioner based on the date of completing training and subsequent performance (e.g., six times a year starting in the second month post training; once a year after fidelity requirements are met consistently)
- Data review meetings are scheduled for weekly review of progress, quarterly review of coaching and fidelity data, and two times a year review of all the Decision Support Data System information regarding the people and progress in the unit(s) and the whole organization
- Redundancy of skills is maintained with cross training and mentoring available for interested staff, especially high fidelity practitioners who aspire to be coaches or directors

Another major impediment to high fidelity uses of an innovation is existing practices within an organization. Any barrier to practitioners making full and effective use of an innovation in the organization becomes a problem to be solved as quickly and as permanently as practicable. Facilitative Administrators are problem-solvers (Tucker & Singer, 2015) and an innovation being used for the first time (Initial Implementation) in an existing organization will produce a steady stream of problems to be solved. For example:

- Scheduling time for staff to do new things requires cancelling or changing existing meetings and events and putting new ones on the calendar
- Scheduling time for staff to learn new roles and functions while still attending to recipients served by the organization in the standard way; supporting learning and doing the new things while continuing to support the old things is a challenge until all services are new services
- Assuring coverage for key activities when practitioners, coaches, and so on are absent (planned or unplanned) requires staff with redundant skills and is difficult for preparation and scheduling of staff
- Existing resources and space must be reallocated or reassigned to support the new ways of work, and hurt feelings need to be assuaged to maintain morale and performance

- Working within the budget while assuring effective support for practitioners is a challenge
- Meeting agendas and communication patterns need to be altered to make room for new topics and new language and different individuals in attendance
- Business office and administrative units likely will be confused about new payments, reimbursement methods, forms, and so on; and accuracy and promptness may decline

A typical agenda for a Facilitative Administration meeting regarding an important and persistent issue allots five minutes to describing a problem; five minutes to reviewing relevant data; 30 minutes to discussing possible solutions; ten minutes to operationalizing a solution that will be attempted; and ten minutes to assigning tasks, setting deadlines, and assuring access to needed information, data, and decision makers. The focus is on solving problems, not admiring problems (e.g., 50 minutes bemoaning the issue and ten minutes on what might be done instead). For less serious issues or repetitive issues, two or even three issues may be dealt with in a similar fashion in a one-hour meeting.

Resolution of issues impacting practitioner performance lead to changes in policies and procedures that impact all operating units within an organization. In one organization, the directors named the policy manual "Reflections of Current Best Practice" to emphasize that best practice and the judgement of high fidelity practitioners and coaches (doing the right thing) took precedence over descriptions in the policy manual (doing things right). The manual was updated periodically to reflect the evolving best practices.

## Capacity development

Facilitative Administrators are the front line for the full and effective use of innovations and for organization change. Managers (Facilitative Administrators) are accountable for aligning administration and services with the mission and goals of the organization as exemplified in the use of a chosen effective innovation. The work of change must be done while balancing critical factors at the practice level (Fu, Flood, Rousseau, & Morris, 2018):

- Advocacy for change *and* responsibility for staff morale
- Monitoring for administrative and funding purposes *and* coaching for fidelity and outcome purposes
- Accountability for high fidelity use of an innovation to benefit recipients *and* accountability for capacity development

The last item cannot be emphasized enough. Using an innovation with fidelity for the first time in an organization that is simultaneously using the Implementation Drivers for the first time requires considerable change in many aspects of the organization. Competent trainers and coaches who know the innovation thoroughly are in short supply. For example, in a mental health services replication study in Uganda, Mutamba et al. (2018) found that the supervisors who served as coaches were new to the intervention. Although they were trained to be supervisors (coaches), they had no direct experience delivering the intervention and their effectiveness as coaches was limited. Once the problem was detected, the directors recruited expert therapists who had previously participated in using the intervention in this region and initiated a "supervision of supervisors" approach to coaching.

It is desirable to have high fidelity practitioners move into training and coaching roles. These "home grown" staff know the innovation well and know the organization well and can learn the additional skills to be competent trainers and coaches. Capacity development within an organization and within a system depends on home grown staff (Fixsen & Blase, 2018; Mutamba et al., 2018; Tommeraas & Ogden, 2016). The consequence of moving practitioners into new Implementation Team roles is that high fidelity practitioners who produce excellent outcomes for recipients are replaced by new practitioners who are in the process of acquiring the skills to eventually be high fidelity performers. If high fidelity equals excellent outcomes and low fidelity equals poor outcomes (a requirement of a Usable Innovation), then recipient outcomes may be slow to improve for the overall organization given this self-induced turnover of practitioners.

Even though coaching service delivery plans can be adjusted to intensify coaching for newly trained practitioners, and other drivers supports can be adjusted to maximize selection, training, fidelity, administrative supports, and leadership encouragement, there still will be a gap before high fidelity and great outcomes are achieved by a new practitioner. This is true for any staff position, of course, but matters most for practitioners since they are the only ones who directly provide effective innovation services that benefit recipients. Encouraging high fidelity practitioners to take on new Implementation Team roles delays overall organization outcomes in the short run but adds to sustainable and scalable outcomes in the longer run (Fixsen & Blase, 2009).

*Related research*

In the literature, Facilitative Administration (front line management; VanDeusen Lukas et al., 2007) is described as assuring employee skills and opportunities to use an innovation and removing obstacles by promptly responding to employees' concerns and complaints regarding innovation use (K. J. Klein, Conn, & Sorra, 2001; K. J. Klein & Sorra, 1996). Aarons et al. (2011) discuss the need to have practitioner record-keeping and productivity requirements fit the innovation. And, Weiner (2009) recommends adjusting work schedules, unit workload expectations, workflow, and production levels to improve their fit with the use of an innovation.

In a series of studies starting in the 1990s, Glisson and colleagues have noted the importance of low-conflict work environments marked by cooperation, role clarity, and personalization. The desired mix of high morale and high productivity occurred when practitioners had managers who encouraged mutual support, developed their individual abilities, maintained positive interpersonal relationships, and motivated staff to succeed while doing stressful work in human services. Using an Organizational Social Context measure, Glisson, Landsverk, et al. (2008, p. 110) conducted a study of over 1,000 clinicians in 100 mental health clinics and found that in the highest-functioning organizations studied (10% of the clinics in the sample), "High clinician morale can be maintained in the face of high work environment stress if the organizational machinery is well-oiled and working to support the clinicians' efforts." Assuring well-oiled machinery to support practitioners is the work of Implementation Teams using the Implementation Drivers so that all organizations can be high functioning, not just 10% of them. Facilitative Administration is key to achieving this goal.

These and other studies point to the critical role of Facilitative Administration in the context of the day-to-day work of managers and practitioners (Fernandez et al., 2018; Gifford et al., 2018; N. J. Williams, Ehrhart, Aarons, Marcus, & Beidas, 2018). With respect to implementation, managers also may be coaches. In that case, the role of a manager representing the organization needs to be separated from the role of a coach supporting the full and effective use of an innovation. This has worked well in organizations where conveying management messages is done in one meeting (e.g., the latest on travel reimbursement rates, new forms for documenting admissions and departures, new schedule for holidays, revised emergency procedures), and coaching is done in separate individual meetings. Managers are careful to maintain trust and do not use the more personal and detailed information gained from coaching visits as a reason for making management decisions about a given practitioner.

*Facilitative Administration in practice*

Facilitative Administration requires planning and organization. Table 22 provides a list of key aspects to consider as Facilitative Administration is established for the first time in an organization determined to make full and effective use of a selected innovation.

Table 22. Best practices for Facilitative Administration in organizations

| Best practices for Facilitative Administration | In Place |
|---|---|
| A leadership and Implementation Team is formed | |
| The leadership and Implementation Team has Terms of Reference that include <u>communication protocols</u> to provide feedback to the next level "up" and describes from whom feedback is received (Practice-Policy Communication protocol) | |
| Policies and procedures are developed and revised to <u>support the new ways of work</u> | |
| The team uses feedback and data to improve the Implementation Drivers | |
| • Solicits and <u>analyzes feedback</u> from staff | |
| • Solicits and <u>analyzes feedback</u> from "stakeholders" | |
| • Reduces <u>internal administrative barriers</u> to quality service and high performance assessment implementation | |

## Decision Support Data System

The name of this driver says it all: use data to support decision making at every level within an organization. Typically, organizations have data on finances and compliance-oriented activities so that they can maintain and increase services and funding. Funders require careful collection and entry of financial information with regular internal and external audits to assure accuracy and validity. While funding is important, the data most useful to support the full and effective use of innovations in organizations often are not available. It is rare to find organizations that have data on how skillfully and respectfully practitioners actually deliver intended services and data on how skillfully and respectfully Implementation Teams support those practitioners.

A systematic review of Lean improvement applications in health (Lean is continuous improvement methods based on Improvement Cycles such as those described in Chapter 13) revealed few consistent measures of practitioner behavior and little use of data to improve whole organizations (D'Andreamatteo, Ianni, Lega, & Sargiacomo, 2015). Yet, if practitioners do not deliver services as intended, then outcomes likely will not improve as intended. In research and evaluation, a range of relevant data may be collected for a program independently of an organization. For example, WSH (an integrated behavioral model for water, sanitation and hygiene and child nutrition in low- and middle-income countries) has an impressive array of data that are systematically collected and used to improve the approach to WSH and its outcomes. However, the data collection and use are not embedded in organizations in affected communities (Masud Parvez et al., 2018; Tofail et al., 2018). In these cases, the data are short term and used for the benefit of a research project (a worthy goal) and are not used to improve organization functioning and sustain benefits for a population of recipients (necessary for sustainability and scaling).

Active Implementation data are used to improve support; never to levy sanctions. If data are useful and used for improvement of supports for staff, then data collection improves in quality and usefulness as everyone anticipates the next helpful data point. Otherwise, it is easy for staff to "game the system" to give the appearance of participation while avoiding sanctions (A. Donaldson et al., 2014; Saliba et al., 2003; Westphal, Gulati, & Shortell, 1997).

A word of caution about the use of data and the difference between *assessment of* and *accountability for*. Active Implementation includes collecting and using data for feedback and improvement. To be useful, data-based feedback is always constructive and supportive. For example, fidelity is an *assessment of* practitioner performance and data regarding a practitioner is promptly fed back to the practitioner so he can see the results. *Accountability for* improving fidelity resides with the Implementation Team that provides training and coaching to develop practitioner competencies. Perhaps coaching frequency needs to be increased or needs to focus on neglected dimensions of a practitioner's use of an innovation. Perhaps other team members need to join a session or two to assess how well the coach is providing coaching support. In any case, *accountability for* improving fidelity rests with the Implementation Team and Facilitative Administrators.

Active Implementation team members comment that accountability for practitioner performance "rolls uphill." If for some reason the Implementation Team is not able to provide the needed support, accountability for Implementation Team performance resides with leadership in the organization. And, if leadership is not able to provide needed support, then accountability shifts upward via the System Intervention driver. Practitioners produce the benefits an organization is expected to (paid to) produce with recipients. Other staff (Implementation Team members, leaders, administrators, members of the board of directors, system administrators) are accountable for supporting practitioners so they have the knowledge, skills, and abilities and other support they need to do their job as effectively and efficiently as possible.

Given the lack of implementation-relevant data currently available in an organization, it may take a few years to develop a relevant, accessible, and actionable Decision Support Data System. In its more mature state, a Decision Support Data System includes information about staff, data from the use of each of the Implementation Drivers (e.g., pre-post training scores, fidelity scores), organization variables (e.g., recipient engagement, expenses, staff turnover), and data regarding recipient proximal and distal outcomes.

For data to be used, they must be trusted. Executive leaders and administrators must gain experience with the new data generated from use of the Implementation Drivers and proximal and distal recipient outcome measures. Why are pre-post training scores important? What is all the fuss about fidelity scores? How can we use implementation capacity assessment data to inform action plans? It is interesting to watch the non-verbal behavior of board members who are relaxed and attentive during presentations of decision support data, then scoot up to the table and lean forward to look at the latest financial data. They understand and trust the financial data. After a few years, they have the same trust in the program data.

### Related research

Decision Support Data Systems (evaluation systems with a purpose) produce evidence about the appropriateness, effectiveness, and efficiency of practice. A Decision Support Data System is part of the feedback and improvement processes (Rycroft-Malone, 2004) and is used to assess the benefits (e.g., recipient services; employee satisfaction and morale) produced by and received by an organization as a result of using an innovation (K. J. Klein & Sorra, 1996). Others note the importance of including data on the quality of the program as it is delivered (intervention fidelity; Greenberg et al., 2005), the quality of implementation supports provided to practitioners (i.e., implementation fidelity), and indicators that the intended populations are being reached (Feldstein & Glasgow, 2008). Using data for decision making and continuous quality improvement is commonly noted in the literature (Chinman et al., 2008; Damschroder et al., 2009; VanDeusen Lukas et al., 2007).

The collection and use of data as feedback on past decisions and as prompts for new decisions is an important Implementation Driver. For many decades, the leaders of organization and system change have described the central role of timely and accurate feedback as a governing mechanism in complex systems (Ashby, 1956; Morgan & Ramirez, 1983; Senge, 2006). At a granular level, timely and accurate feedback is a key factor in behavior change (Baer, Wolf, & Risley, 1968; Michie et al., 2011; Saldana et al., 2016). At an organization level, Hysong, Best, and Pugh (2006) conducted structured interviews with over 100 staff employed in six Veterans Affairs Medical Centers selected because they had high (n = 3) or low (n = 3) adherence to six clinical practice guidelines. They reported, "High performers provided timely, individualized, non-punitive feedback to providers, whereas low performers were more variable in their timeliness and non-punitiveness and relied on more standardized, facility-level reports. The concept of actionable feedback emerged as the core category from the data, around which timeliness, individualization, non-punitiveness, and customizability can be hierarchically ordered" (p 1).

Some examples include the Teaching-Family Model data systems (Fixsen & Blase, 2018; Fixsen et al., 2001; Fixsen et al., 1982), MST data systems (Brunk et al., 2014; Schoenwald, Halliday-Boykins, & Henggeler, 2003; Schoenwald ct al., 2004; Schoenwald, Sheidow, et al., 2003), and Multidimensional Treatment Foster Care data systems (Chamberlain, 2003; Chamberlain et al., 2011; Chamberlain, Moreland, & Reid, 1992). Data systems at Thresholds, a psychiatric rehabilitation center, have been used to support decisions for many years (Bond, Miller, Krumwied, & Ward, 1988; Dincin & Witheridge, 1982; Drake et al., 2009). Other Decision Support Data Systems have been used across organizations in a state human service system to guide selection and use of evidence-based practice components (Chorpita, Bernstein, & Daleiden, 2008; Chorpita et al., 2005).

*Decision Support Data System in practice*

Figure 23 shows the multiple sources of and uses of data in a Decision Support Data System. At the treatment unit level, the data collection and feedback loops are more immediate and frequent to help sustain a high level of quality services for every recipient. At the Implementation Team level, the data regarding practitioner performance and outcomes is fed back to improve team functioning and supports for practitioners. At the organization and system level, the data are summed up to inform decisions about staffing, funding, and so on, and to draw from and contribute to the evidence base for the field in general.

Figure 23. Multiple levels of data in use in a Decision Support Data System.
Based on Blase and Fixsen, 2004

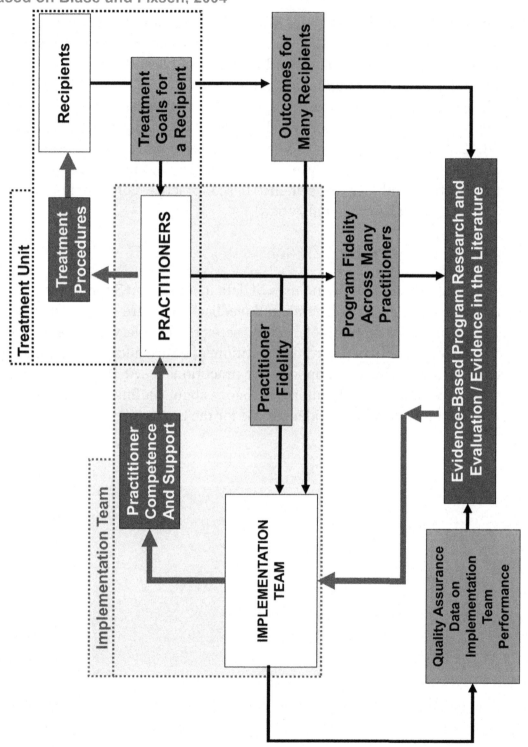

A Decision Support Data System requires planning and organization. Table 23 provides a list of key aspects to consider as a Decision Support Data System is established for the first time in an organization determined to make full and effective use of a selected innovation.

Table 23. Best practices for a Decision Support Data System in organizations

| Best practices for a Decision Support Data System | In Place |
|---|---|
| Accountability for measurement and reporting system is clear (e.g., lead person designated and supported) | |
| Includes information related to intermediate and longer-term desired outcomes | |
| Includes process measures (performance and fidelity assessment) | |
| Measures are "socially important" (e.g., academic achievement, clean urinalyses, incidence of sepsis) | |
| Data are: | |
| • Reliable (standardized protocols, trained data collectors) | |
| • Reported frequently (e.g., weekly, quarterly) | |
| • Built into practice routines (e.g., on the agenda for each meeting) | |
| • Collected from and available to actionable units (e.g., OB-GYN clinic staff, classroom teachers, parent advocacy groups) | |
| • Widely shared with organization personnel | |
| • Regularly shared with recipient groups and community stakeholders | |
| • Used to make decisions (e.g., training needed, coaching improvements, organization supports) | |

## System Intervention

Not all performance and implementation problems can be solved within an organization. There are many licensing rules and regulations, requirements that accompany funding, professional accreditation standards, referral issues, state and federal laws and mandates, and so on. Any of these may affect the ability of an organization to assure the full and effective use of an innovation and reliably realize the intended benefits. It is incumbent on leaders within an organization to work with groups and individuals external to an organization to clear away system barriers and strengthen system facilitators. System barriers are common when innovations are being attempted for the first time. The need for System Intervention is to be expected and planned for from the beginning and is an important role for leadership within an organization.

Some issues may be resolved readily. Others may take a few years. The important thing is for the leaders to persist until any key issue is resolved. For example, in the early days of the Teaching-Family Model, regulations were encountered regarding the staffing of a group home. Several states required a certified social worker to be the director of a licensed group home. In Teaching-Family homes, the Teaching-Parents are the directors and the staff along with an Assistant Teaching-Parent; being a social worker was not part of the selection criteria. In these cases, Teaching-Family Site staff (directors, Implementation Team members) convened meetings with state licensing and regulation staff, described the program and the outcomes, and outlined the training, coaching, and certification (fidelity) assessments for Teaching-Parents. In every case, state regulators granted exceptions for licensing Teaching-Family Model group homes that met these conditions.

In Active Implementation there is awareness of intervening "up one, down one, and out five." This means engaging in System Intervention activities (up one) to help system leaders and staff learn how to better support the use of organizations using effective innovations with fidelity and socially significant outcomes. It also means assuring the Implementation Drivers are in place in the organization (down one) so that practitioners routinely meet fidelity criteria, and recipients consistently benefit. This experience provides the information needed to present to system leaders and staff regarding specific impediments and facilitators. The work that is done at each level is done with the future in mind (out five years). Patience and persistent System Intervention attempts often are required to get the Implementation Drivers fully in place and functioning at a high level with the purposeful support of the systems external to the organization.

For example, Ethiopia identified high death rates for mothers and newborns in remote villages due to the lack of attended births (Spicer et al., 2014). To respond to this need, United Nations agencies and other groups supported government planning to dramatically increase the number of qualified midwives (3,500 new midwives). When it became apparent that newly educated midwives were reluctant to go to the remote areas of greatest need, the staff in the regional units quickly identified impediments and facilitators and provided that information to government leaders and staff (the System Intervention Driver at work). In the next few years the maternal and child health units began a) recruiting women from the remote villages (selection), b) supporting their education as midwives (Competency Drivers), c) providing protected housing when they returned to the village, d) assuring access to education for their children, and e) helping the husbands find relevant jobs in the area (all related to Facilitative Administration, Systems Intervention, and leadership). When they did all these things, midwives went back to their villages, and many stayed. They also became role models for girls and women in the villages, providing additional value to Ethiopia.

## Related research

System Intervention is concerned with issues that impact organization functioning and can only be resolved by interacting with others outside the organization. Examples of the need for System Intervention include coordination of resources and capacity development across provider organizations and within community groups (Spoth & Greenberg, 2005); working with local media to motivate community members to take part in efforts to reduce risk factors and promote protective processes in the community (Hawkins, Catalano, & Arthur, 2002); and reducing barriers and encouraging seamless transitions between program elements and services for those individuals with complex needs and many providers (Bertram et al., 2012; Bruns & Walker, 2010; Feldstein & Glasgow, 2008). In each case, Implementation Teams encounter organizational boundaries that require commitments of resources by, or the cooperation of, others to affect change and sustain benefits to recipients. The long-term outcome is the promotion of integration among units within a system (VanDeusen Lukas et al., 2007).

The targets of System Intervention were outlined in a review of the literature. Watson et al. (2018) noted that "complex health interventions extend into and interact with the larger environment they are embedded within." They conducted a systematic review of the implementation literature to discover common facilitators and barriers. They identified eight influential contextual factors "outside the boundaries of the implementing organization/s:" 1) professional influences, 2) political support, 3) social climate, 4) local infrastructure, 5) policy and legal climate, 6) relational climate, 7) target population, and 8) funding and economic climate.

System Intervention was apparent in a study of a five-year intervention to improve obstetric triage. D. M. Goodman et al. (2018) evaluated the impact of an obstetric triage improvement program on reducing hospital-based delay in a referral hospital in Accra, Ghana. Baseline data collected to monitor obstetric triage capabilities revealed significant delays in patient assessment on arrival. A triage training course was provided and monitoring of quality improvement provided evidence of systemic barriers to reducing triage wait times. System Intervention led to the construction of a free-standing obstetric triage pavilion that opened a year later with dedicated midwives as staff. In a busy low-resource hospital, wait times were subsequently reduced, quality of services improved, and the implementation process was sustained under local leadership during transition to a new hospital.

Implementation Teams supporting several evidence-based programs have learned to convene meetings with funders and regulators before beginning work in a state or other jurisdiction. For example, the Behavior Tech company that supports the use of Dialectical Behavior Therapy (DBT) negotiates acceptable payment rates with insurance companies in a state before providing training for any therapists to work in a state. The MSTS group that supports the use of Multisystemic Therapy negotiates acceptable referral methods and payment rates before developing a MST team in a jurisdiction.

These and other purveyor groups participated in structured meetings based on Nominal Group Processes to document implementation activities in organizations attempting to use their evidence-based programs (Blase, Fixsen, et al., 2005; Blase, Naoom, Wallace, & Fixsen, 2005a). The results shown in Table 24 indicate that over one-third of all System Intervention activities occurred during the Exploration Stage of implementation, then continued throughout the Installation and Initial Implementation Stage processes of using effective innovations for the first time. For innovations that do not have the support of experienced purveyors like Behavior Tech and MSTS who anticipate and resolve many issues during the Exploration process, the only choice for others is to encounter systemic problems, then reactively use the System Intervention driver to rectify those problems.

Table 24. Implementation Team activities by stage of implementation (Exploration, Installation, Initial Implementation). Data from Fixsen, Blase, et al. (2005)

| Implementation Team Activities | Exploration Stage | Installation Stage | Initial Implementation Stage |
|---|---|---|---|
| Assessment | 97% | 1% | 2% |
| Planning | 20% | 32% | 48% |
| Selection/Training | 3% | 31% | 66% |
| Coaching | 8% | 6% | 86% |
| Evaluation/Fidelity | 3% | 23% | 73% |
| Organization Development | 11% | 16% | 73% |
| System Intervention | 37% | 30% | 33% |

As noted in Table 24, System Interventions began during Exploration and continued during Installation and Initial Implementation. Systems are designed to support current organizations that produce current results. Innovations and the use of Active Implementation supports are disruptive to the status quo, and systems interventions continue long after Full Implementation is reached for any organization. The methods to convene groups and intervene in system issues outside an organization are discussed more fully in the section on the Leadership Driver.

*System Intervention in practice*

System Intervention requires planning and organization. Table 25 provides a list of key aspects to consider as Systems Intervention is established for the first time in an organization determined to make full and effective use of a selected innovation.

## Table 25. Best practices for Systems Intervention in organizations

| Best practices for Systems Intervention | In Place |
|---|---|
| <u>Leadership intervenes</u> when needed to resolve system issues the effectiveness of work in the organization (e.g., Directors meet with state leaders on issues at that level) | |
| <u>Leadership engages</u> and nurtures multiple "champions" and "opinion leaders" outside the organization | |
| Leadership objectively <u>documents</u> barriers and <u>reports</u> barriers to "next level up" | |
| Leadership makes <u>constructive recommendations</u> to "next level up" to resolve barriers | |
| Leadership develops <u>formal processes</u> to establish and use Practice-Policy Communication protocols (e.g., linking communication protocols to give and receive feedback from the practice level of the organization) | |
| Leadership creates time-limited, barrier-busting capacity by: | |
| • Using Transformation Zones (build capacity and resolve issues in a manageable slice of the system) | |
| • Doing usability testing (plan-do-study-act cycles with small groups) | |
| Leadership creates optimism and hope by regularly communicating successes | |

# Chapter 12: Implementation Leadership Drivers

The importance of leadership is noted in just about every discussion of implementation. The absence of leadership support is a well-documented barrier, and success is attributed to the presence of leadership support. For example, Szulanski (1996, p. 31) described the difficulties faced by leaders who encounter "The reluctance of some recipients to accept knowledge from the outside (the 'not invented here' or NIH syndrome) ... Lack of motivation may result in foot dragging, passivity, feigned acceptance, hidden sabotage, or outright rejection in the implementation and use of new knowledge."

For decades the quality of leadership was noted after the fact (Drucker, 2004; Kaiser, Hogan, & Craig, 2008; Kotter, 1996). That is, good leaders were identified by the good work that had been accomplished with their support; poor leaders were identified by their less than desirable outcomes. Post hoc analyses and speculation may provide some guidance but are not necessarily predictive.

For implementation, leadership must be identified, nurtured, and developed so that socially significant outcomes can be achieved and sustained in the future (Baron et al., 1984; Day, 2000; de Vries & Manfred, 2005). Initially, it is necessary to identify good leadership during the Exploration Stage activities. The individuals already in executive leadership positions must be engaged; make informed decisions to invite the use of effective innovations and effective implementation; and agree to fully participate in the process to change the status quo and develop an aligned and integrated organization. For example, Figure 24 shows implementation capacity data from 195 school district organizations in the U.S. Leadership is the strongest driver because the permission of already established leadership is required to organize and conduct a capacity assessment. The leadership score, therefore, is a product of the selection process and not the result of a leadership development process.

*While finding leadership at this key Exploration decision point is essential for beginning the process, it is not enough. Implementation Teams must be able to develop and nurture good leadership so that socially significant outcomes can be achieved and sustained in the future.*

While finding leadership at this key Exploration decision point is essential for beginning the process, it is not enough. Implementation Teams must be able to develop and nurture good leadership so that socially significant outcomes can be achieved and sustained in the future (i.e., leadership as a Usable Innovation) as leaders make changes in the context of "an environment full of personnel rules, social stressors, union stewards, anxious administrators, political pressures, interprofessional rivalry, staff turnover, and diamond-hard inertia" (Fisher, 1983, p. 249).

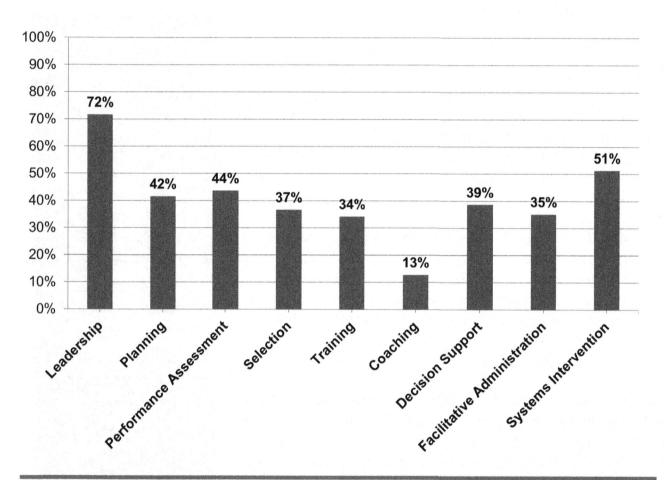

Figure 24. District capacity assessment data from 195 school district organizations. Data from the State Implementation and Scaling up of Evidence-based Programs Center, Fixsen and Ward (2016)

The only certainty regarding leadership is that people in leadership positions will come and go. For example, in education in the U.S., 25% of the 100,000 school principals turn over each year (School Leaders Network, 2014), and the average tenure of district and state school superintendents is about three years (https://www.brookings.edu/wp-content/uploads/2016/06/SuperintendentsBrown-Center9314.pdf). Leadership turnover and uncertainty were notable challenges during the eight-year process of transitioning HIV/AIDS prevention programs from donor funding to in-country funding in India (Sgaier et al., 2013). If innovations are to be used fully and effectively, sustained, and improved to provide socially significant outcomes over time, then leadership must not just be found, it must be developed and nurtured in a purposeful way.

## Technical, adaptive, and transformational leadership

A useful way to think about leadership and implementation of innovations is provided by Stacey (1996, 2002) as interpreted by Zimmerman et al. (1998). The fundamental message is that managers and leaders of organizations need to have a diversity of approaches that correspond with the diversity of simple, complicated, and complex problems they face. The complexity of finding solutions must match the complexity of the problem that is faced (Snowden & Boone, 2007).

In Figure 25 leadership options are defined in terms of agreement and certainty regarding issues and solutions. The vertical axis displays a continuum of agreement about an issue or solution within the group, team, or organization. The horizontal axis displays a continuum of certainty regarding those issues and potential solutions. Moderate levels of disagreement and uncertainty define the zone of complexity. For simple and complicated issues and solutions, typical leadership and management approaches are effective. In the zone of complexity, leadership characterized by high creativity, innovation, and breaking with the past is needed to create new modes of operating in order to develop solutions.

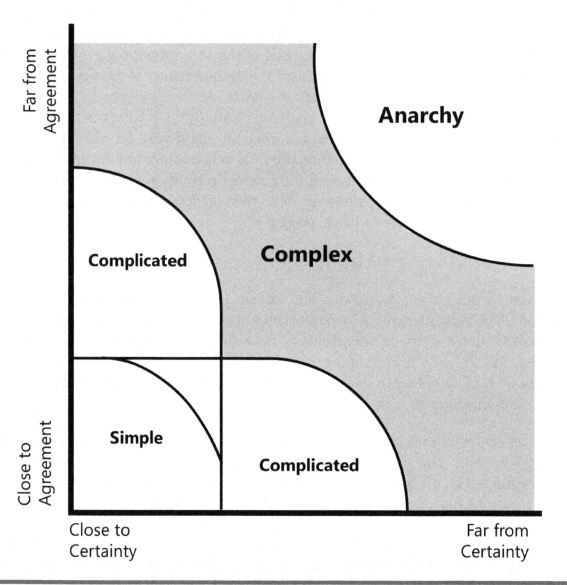

Figure 25. The Stacey (1996) matrix for considering problems and solutions; the figure was developed by Brenda Zimmerman (1998), Schulich School of Business, York University, Toronto, Canada. Used with permission

In Figure 25, there are several zones identified:

Close to agreement, close to certainty: In this region, familiar management techniques can be used to convene existing staff groups to analyze data and propose solutions that fit within existing skill sets. Leaders can develop specific paths of action (work plans) to achieve outcomes, and outcomes can be monitored and work plans adjusted until the problem is solved. The goal is to repeat what has worked in the past to improve future efficiency and effectiveness.

Damschroder et al. (2009) describe this style of leadership in terms of goals and feedback and a learning climate where "goals are clearly communicated, acted upon, and fed back to staff and alignment of that feedback with goals ..."

Far from agreement, close to certainty: Some issues have a great deal of certainty about identified problems and desired outcomes but high levels of disagreement about how to solve the problems and achieve those outcomes. Clear vision and a sense of shared mission are insufficient in this context. In this case, leaders engage in coalition building, negotiation, and compromise to create agreement regarding an organization's new work agenda and direction.

Damschroder et al. (2009) describe this style of leadership in terms of learning climate: A climate in which "leaders express their own fallibility and need for team members' assistance and input; team members feel that they are essential, valued, and knowledgeable partners in the change process; individuals feel psychologically safe to try new methods; and there is sufficient time and space for reflective thinking and evaluation (in general, not just in a single implementation)."

Close to agreement, far from certainty: Some issues have a high level of agreement about the problem but not much certainty as to the cause and effect linkages to create the desired outcomes. Leaders respond by creating a strong sense of shared mission or vision (not a work plan). Comparisons among possible solutions are made and evaluated against the mission and vision for the organization. In this region, the goal is to be mission driven and head towards an agreed upon future state even though the specific paths (work plans) cannot be predetermined.

"Rycroft-Malone (2004) states, "Leaders have a key role to play in transforming cultures and are therefore influential in shaping a context that is ready for change. Transformational leaders, as opposed to those who command and control, have the ability to transform cultures to create contexts that are more conducive to the integration of evidence into practice. These types of leaders inspire staff to have a shared vision and do so in a stimulating, a challenging, and an enabling way. This, in turn, results in clear roles and effective teamwork and organizational structures. The significance to implementation and change is that effective leaders have the ability to bring the 'science' component of healthcare practice (the application of science and technology) together with the 'art' component (the translation of different forms of practice knowledge) into caring actions."

Far from agreement, far from certainty: Situations where there are very high levels of uncertainty and disagreement, often result in breakdown, anarchy, and chaos. The traditional methods of planning, visioning, and negotiation are insufficient in these contexts. Leaders look for patterns and attempt to achieve at least modest agreement to try something to see if it works. Needless to say, this is a region that organizations and systems should avoid as much as possible.

Snowden and Boone (2007, p. 71) advise, "In the chaotic domain, a leader's immediate job is not to discover patterns but to stanch the bleeding. A leader must first act to establish order, then sense where stability is present and from where it is absent, and then respond by working to transform the situation from chaos to complexity, where the identification of emerging patterns can both help prevent future crises and discern new opportunities... Because outcomes are unpredictable in a complex context, leaders need to focus on creating an environment from which good things can emerge, rather than trying to bring about predetermined results and possibly missing opportunities that arise unexpectedly."

Much of the work of implementation is done in the zone of complexity, the large area in Figure 25 that is short of chaos (anarchy) but beyond traditional command and control management approaches. Rittel and Webber (1973) discuss the zone of complexity in terms of wicked problems that are difficult to define, value-laden, not right or wrong but good or bad (better or worse), and not solvable. Each attempt to solve a wicked problem leaves traces and impacts the nature of "the problem" and changes the options open for resolution. It is said that wicked problems "fight back" when you try to solve them (e.g., previously unknown pro and con issues arise, and groups materialize and mobilize for and against).

The various leadership styles come together in implementation leadership contexts. There is not one or the other; they are mixed together as implementation proceeds from Exploration to Full Implementation to scaling and sustainability for whole populations. Note that problems in the zone of complexity are not solvable in any permanent way. The best that can be hoped for is resolution: the opportunity to (re)solve complex problems again and again. This is important for leaders of organizations and systems to understand: the task of leadership is never done.

## Related research

Morgan and Ramirez (1983) propose "action learning" as a form of leadership to cope with complex problems posed by changing circumstances and unexpected events in the zone of complexity. They propose establishing enabling conditions that focus on outcomes and not processes (mission driven) and generate only as much structure as necessary to accomplish the mission. In this mode, inquiry is the primary method for discerning patterns and acting on success. They caution that action learning requires variety in the form of multiskilled and interchangeable teams that systematically deal with errors in all parts of the system. Team members directly interact with the problem and attempted solutions and search for faulty assumptions and ineffective operations to increase agreement and certainty. In Active

Implementation, this is the role of the Implementation Team and leadership of an organization and system. Chapter 15 on Systemic Change explores this further.

Tucker and Singer (2015) note the role of engaging staff in identifying issues and developing solutions. In their study, engaging staff in identifying problems resulted in a decrease in performance. Only when leaders subsequently engaged in problem-solving did performance improve. Thus, action learning is an important part of leadership to improve outcomes.

Marzano, Waters, and McNulty (2005) review the literature and expand the idea of action learning and describe leadership for "second order change" to define problems and find solutions when neither one is obvious (lack of agreement; lack of certainty). Under these conditions, individuals and groups have to learn new approaches that break with the past, operate outside existing norms, and conflict with prevailing values. They refer to this as transformational leadership because leaders must confront group identity, challenge values and beliefs, and challenge expertise and competencies as they attempt to develop shared vision and goals.

For example, Huaynoca, Chandra-Mouli, Yaqub Jr., and Denno (2013) outlined the national effort in Nigeria to introduce a comprehensive approach to HIV-prevention education and general sexual health at the secondary levels of education. The authors noted that the evidence-based "content was clear and was seen as credible. However, it conflicted with prevailing values and norms in some quarters and was difficult to implement." Nevertheless, over several years government leaders and others continued to convene groups, found paths to increase agreement and certainty, and eventually produced desired outcomes.

In their review and synthesis of the literature, Kaiser et al. (2008) further operationalize "transformational leadership" behavior. Transformational leaders develop a clear vision and group goals, set high standards, model the new roles and functions, and establish relationships that foster change. The result is harmony, cohesion, and team functioning where self-interest is aligned with group interests. The Practice-Policy Communication Cycles provide leaders with recursive feedback to help leaders break from the past and shift into a problem-solving mode that is mission driven and responsive to immediate- and longer-term outcomes.

## Leading in the zone of complexity

The definitions of leadership by these authors are a good fit with Stacey (1996) and Zimmerman et al. (1998). Recognizing the complexity of problems and solutions helps to reduce anxiety and to avoid attempting tame solutions to wicked problems. Stacey says problems in the zone of complexity often lead to "a classic double bind: in situations far from certainty and agreement we vainly endeavor to behave in ways that are viable only close to certainty and agreement" (p 7). This approach "hardly ever works. We end up paying lip service to the latest saving recipe, while we rush about doing something quite different under the pressure of events ... The first response must, therefore, be to identify the culprit and tighten the controls on performance. But this does not work and, as a result, confusion, frustration, insecurity, hostility, and fear increase as one recipe after another fails to do what we expect it to" (p 8). "In other words, the very steps we take to cope with increasing uncertainty and dissension themselves provoke more uncertainty and dissension, and this in turn makes us look even harder for the next saving recipe ... leading us to yet another turn on the uncertainty screw" (p 9).

Implementation is synonymous with change–change in practitioner behavior; change in organization policies, procedures, and ways of work; and change in contextual system structures, roles, and functions. Implementation operates in the zone of complexity as Full Implementation criteria and scaling criteria are reached and sustained in a system. A goal of leadership is to move toward higher levels of agreement and lower levels of uncertainty as the full and effective use of an innovation becomes the way of work in an organization and, eventually, in a system. Elwyn (2007) cautions, "Change management ... is not for the fainthearted, or those lacking curiosity and creativity in their approach to problems. For busy clinicians and managers, attempting to get to terms with intangibles like knowledge capital may seem too much to take on when the to-do list is already full."

## Leadership and challenges

There are significant leadership challenges related to choosing, implementing, sustaining, and improving innovations in practice. For Heifetz and Laurie (1997), the zone of complexity requires adaptive leaders who clarify values, develop new strategies, and learn new ways of operating. As noted by Stacey and Zimmerman, technical challenges, while complicated and challenging, are well-defined, fairly certain, generally agreed upon, and able to be addressed with current strategies and often with more traditional top-down leadership. The term "adaptive" references the types of challenges that require revising and rethinking values, beliefs, and current ways of work. They are likely to generate feelings of loss, grief, disloyalty, and incompetence (Blase, Fixsen, Sims, & Ward, 2015). Adaptive challenges often surface legitimate but competing agendas for which solutions are not likely to be found by relying on mandates, 'to do' lists, and project management plans (Rittel & Webber, 1973).

The distinction between adaptive and technical challenges is a useful one since it draws attention to the challenges resulting from a lack of certainty and agreement about the problem definition and, therefore, the potential solutions. Adaptive challenges can emerge from attempts to engage in more technical work where attempted solutions only seem to add to the problem. Large-scale, sustained change certainly has all the conditions necessary for generating adaptive challenges.

Heifetz, Grashow, and Linsky (2009) note that technical challenges may be very complex and important, but can be addressed by current knowledge, authoritative expertise, and organization structures and processes. In contrast the distinguishing features of adaptive challenges include lack of a clear agreement on the definition of the challenge, and uncertainty about solutions that are unlikely to be found in the current knowledge base and current ways of work. Adaptive work is required when there are legitimate but competing agendas that challenge deeply held beliefs and values that can generate feelings of loss, incompetence, and disloyalty. Requiring changes in people's beliefs, habits, and loyalties is a messy process. And new learning is required while acknowledging and dealing with feelings of loss and incompetence. While change initiatives are always a mix of technical and adaptive challenges, one of the biggest mistakes is to treat an adaptive challenge with a technical approach.

Adaptive leadership requires acknowledging that to improve socially significant outcomes leaders must not only engage the hearts and minds of practitioners and stakeholders by addressing adaptive challenges, they also must change the actions and patterns of behavior (mental models) of administrators, providers of professional development, and policy makers (e.g., administrative supports and routines, policy guidance) and engage in systems change.

Six broad approaches to addressing adaptive challenges were summarized by Heifetz and Laurie (1997). As described by Blase et al. (2015) they include:

- Getting on the Balcony. This requires stepping up onto the metaphorical balcony to survey the broader context and relevant history, the patterns, data, emerging themes and processes. This ability to be both involved in the work and observing it more broadly is viewed as a prerequisite for the remaining strategies. The danger is becoming mired solely in the day-to-day efforts and unable to identify adaptive challenges and broader leverage points for change
- Identifying the Adaptive Challenge. This requires diagnosing, identifying, and naming the adaptive challenge(s). This work occurs through gathering information, identifying points of conflict that may be proxies for differing norms and values, and leadership understanding that they, too, are contributing to the adaptive challenge.
- Regulating Distress. Regulating distress requires attending to pacing and sequencing the change and setting priorities. There needs to be a continuing sense of urgency while not overwhelming those doing the work.
- Maintaining Disciplined Attention. In many ways this is a corollary to regulating distress. One way of avoiding tension is to return to comfortable ways of work, even

when those ways of work are not resulting in desired outcomes. A key to forward progress is recognizing work avoidance and redirecting energies back to the difficult work at hand.

- Giving the Work Back to the People. This involves creating conditions to let groups and individuals take the initiative in addressing challenges. This is a shift away from a hierarchical system of leaders leading and others taking direction and following. This means rewarding risk-taking, engaging in trial and learning, and encouraging meaningful participation in defining challenges and proposing solutions.
- Protecting All Voices. Sometimes the most insightful perspectives are provided in uncomfortable ways. When people are mustering the courage to speak their truth and perhaps offer critical insights, they may not always choose the right time and place to do so. Or they may cover their anxiety by speaking so passionately that their way of communicating gets in the way of what they are trying to say. There is a need to hear all voices and continue to focus on what is being said while helping to regulate how issues are being communicated.

## *Competency Drivers and adaptive challenges*

Blase et al. (2015) summarized many of the leadership challenges associated with developing and using the implementation Competency Drivers in organizations. Organizations sometimes indicate that they already use many of the Implementation Drivers to create change in their organizations. That is, they select staff, provide professional development opportunities, and "coach"; and increasingly they have outcome data available. However, they may or may not be using these levers for change in an "implementation-informed" way that is more likely to result in improved fidelity, sustainability, and functional improvement processes.

The very act of ensuring that Competency Drivers (i.e., selection, training, coaching, fidelity) are in place, implementation-informed, and integrated can create adaptive challenges. And fortunately, the recommended approaches for addressing adaptive challenges can be facilitated by, and incorporated into, the use of the Implementation Drivers. Thus, the Installation and Initial Implementation Stages provide many opportunities for teaching and learning leadership skills.

A common implementation-informed core feature for all the Competency Drivers is the collection and use of data to shine a light on successes and challenges–including adaptive challenges. But it is not the stand-alone availability of data that generates change in behavior and addresses adaptive challenges. Rather, it is the integrated use of data for improvement with collective accountability for the proximal outcome of good fidelity and more distal results of improved outcomes.

Examining two of the Competency Drivers illustrates the importance and value of an implementation-informed approach to these drivers and the interplay with adaptive challenges and strategies to address them.

## Staff Selection

Implementation-informed Staff Selection involves being clear about the knowledge, skills, and values that will be needed in the setting–including those needed to implement an evidence-based or evidence-informed innovation (Blase, Fixsen, Maloney, & Phillips, 1984; Blase, Fixsen, & Phillips, 1984; Reiter-Lavery, 2004).

With respect to adaptive challenges and strategies to address them, implementation-informed selection processes can help identify adaptive challenges that are likely to arise by hiring particular applicants. The scenarios, vignettes, and role plays serve a dual purpose. They provide the interviewers with information about the "fit" of the applicant with the current culture, practices, and expectations, and they provide applicants with the opportunity to assess their own comfort and competencies as well. This mutual selection process may result in applicants opting out of consideration. And while no applicant will be a perfect "fit," the interview process can feed information forward to administrators, coaches, and trainers about a new employee's strengths and developmental needs.

If there is a consistent and knowledgeable person participating across all interviews, it creates the opportunity for that person to get on the balcony. They have been "in the action" but also can more broadly assess the available workforce and consider implications for recruitment practices, hiring timelines, suitability of candidates overall, and the implications for training and coaching intensity for new teachers and staff.

## Fidelity assessments

Inclusion of fidelity as a core feature of effective implementation is a lightning rod for adaptive challenges. Perhaps adaptive challenges arise because of the history of staff evaluations as a pro forma compliance activity or being used, or perceived as being used, punitively. This is in sharp contrast to an implementation-informed use of fidelity data as a system diagnostic to critically analyze how the Implementation Drivers can be improved to support practitioners in achieving higher fidelity and improved recipient outcomes. Fidelity assessments also may cut to the heart of differing philosophies (e.g., behavioral and philosophical approaches to solutions).

However, use of fidelity data helps to maintain disciplined attention by redirecting supports for practitioners back to accomplishing the hard work at hand. Getting on the balcony work is facilitated when fidelity data are reviewed over time and across practitioners. This view and the discussion of the data not only highlight patterns and systemic issues but also can regulate distress if the data reviews are implementation-informed. This means that the fidelity data reviews from the balcony are not related to shaming and blaming practitioners but are directed at critically analyzing the Implementation Drivers and determining how to improve their effectiveness in order to better support practitioners. And while taking the fidelity data to those who generated them and asking for practitioner input and perspectives might be uncomfortable, there are benefits to giving the work back to the people so advice about what's working to support them and what else may be needed is as close to the action as possible.

## *Leadership in practice*

Leadership requires planning and organization. Table 26 provides a list of key aspects to consider as leadership is established for the first time in an organization determined to make full and effective use of a selected innovation.

## Table 26. Best practices for leadership in organizations

| Best practices for leadership | |
|---|---|
| Technical leadership | In Place |
| Leaders within the organization provide specific guidance on technical issues where there is sufficient clarity about what needs to be done | |
| Leaders within the organization are very good at giving reasons for changes in policies, procedures, or staffing | |
| Leaders within the organization are actively engaged in resolving any and all issues that get in the way of using the innovation effectively | |
| Leaders within the organization are very good at focusing on the issues that really matter at the practice level | |
| Leaders within the organization are fair, respectful, considerate, and inclusive in their dealings with others | |
| Adaptive leadership | |
| Leaders within the organization continually look for ways to align practices with the overall mission, values, and philosophy of the organization | |
| Leaders within the organization convene groups and work to build consensus when faced with issues on which there is little agreement about how to proceed | |
| Leaders within the organization establish clear and frequent communication channels to provide information to practitioners and to hear about their successes and concerns | |
| Leaders within the organization actively and routinely seek feedback from practitioners and others regarding supports for effective use of the innovation | |
| Leaders within the organization are actively involved in: | |
| • Conducting employment interviews | |
| • Participating in practitioner training | |
| • Conducting performance assessments of individual practitioners | |
| • Creating more and better organization-level assessments to inform decision making | |

# Chapter 13: Improvement Cycles

Improvement cycles are critical to continued use of effective innovations and are an essential part of using effective implementation methods. To use innovations and Implementation Drivers in practice is to invite problems. Achieving socially significant outcomes is affected by big problems such as changes in the economy or social expectations, and by local problems like working conditions, salary expectations, staff turnover, leadership changes, and so on. The influence of these environmental factors is coupled with the need to continually improve the usability and effectiveness of an innovation and of the Competency, Organization, and Leadership Drivers to produce and scale socially significant outcomes.

Implementation and improvement are Siamese twins joined at the heart. To "choose one" is folly. Improvement science needs Implementation Science. Improvement methods themselves must be used as intended (with fidelity) if they are to be effective in practice. Taylor et al. (2014) conducted a review of 73 published studies that reported application of plan, do, study, act, cycle (PDSAC) methods. PDSAC is used as the acronym to note the importance of each component. One attempt rarely succeeds so the C for cycle is a critical component. Taylor et al. found that only two (3%) of the 73 studies included all five components of PDSAC. While all 73 had a plan. there was virtually no indication of how well the plan was done. Only seven studied results in a systematic way; two indicated how they acted on the information/data; and 14 reported conducting an ensuing cycle. Thus, if improvement methods are to be used fully and effectively in practice, then implementation methods must be used to assure their use as intended. This point has been made by others who have studied the use of improvement methods in practice (Khodyakov et al., 2014; Leis & Shojania, 2017; Marshall et al., 2017; Øvretveit et al., 2017; Oyeledun et al., 2017; Reger, Gustafson, DeMarie, & Mullane, 1994; Shojania & Grimshaw, 2005; Westphal et al., 1997). Given the emphasis on

*Implementation science needs improvement science. No matter how successful attempts are to achieve socially significant outcomes, there always is room for improvement. There are no perfect innovations, totally effective implementation methods, or completely enabling policies.*

doing things as intended (i.e., with fidelity) throughout the Active Implementation Frameworks, improvement science needs Implementation Science.

> Thought is born of failure. Only when action fails to satisfy human needs is there a basis for thought. To devote attention to any problem is to confess a lack of adjustment which we must stop and consider. And the greater the failure is, the more searching the kind of thought which is necessary (Whyte, 1944).

Implementation science needs improvement science. No matter how successful any attempts may be to achieve socially significant outcomes, there always is room for improvement. There are no perfect innovations, totally effective implementation methods, or completely enabling policies. Implementation is a world of imperfection that is constantly striving for noticeable improvement. Improvement cycles are based on trial and learning approaches to problem-solving in all aspects of implementation.

Complexity science notes we continually operate in an "environment of turbulence, flux, fragmentation, disequilibrium and uncertainty" (Brachthauser, 2011, p. 222) where implementation and improvement are required to establish and sustain desired outcomes (Humble & Farley, 2011). Practitioners, organizations, and systems are constantly adjusting to align resources to support the use of effective innovations and effective implementation. Constant adjustment relies on organizations and systems having the capacity to search for errors and faulty operating assumptions; the capacity to learn from them; and the ability to make needed changes to improve intended outcomes (Kotter, 1996; Morgan, 1997; Senge, 2006). Constant adjustment requires a goal. And, practitioners and organization managers and system leaders use feedback to identify adjustments needed to continue to approximate and optimize goal attainment.

In the early days of attempting to use evidence-based programs in typical practice settings, there was debate about the need to replicate an innovation exactly vs. the need to adapt an innovation to local circumstances to promote acceptance and use. Those arguing for the former assumed that, because an evidence-based innovation had research to support its effectiveness, the same results could be expected when employing it in practice. While this assumption still has some currency in intellectual debates, the issues have been settled in interaction-based human service practice: there is no such thing as exact replication, and no laboratory-developed innovation delivers in practice all the benefits one expects. In dynamic environments, where shifts occur with respect to public policy, funding, workforce availability, leadership, personal and family dynamics, and community values, even the most agile organizations face challenges in sustaining innovations and outcomes.

202

Even so, evidence-based innovations offer higher expectations for socially significant outcomes than innovations that are not evidence-based. Innovations that meet the Usable Innovation criteria have the practical information and supports needed to get started; fidelity assessment and outcome data can then be used to refine innovation use and better support use of innovations over time. This iterative process of improvement is to be expected and is part of the ongoing work of an Implementation Team.

Implementation Teams make use of the plan, do, study, act (PDSA) Improvement Cycle designed to detect and correct errors and strengthen facilitators *en route* to realizing desired outcomes. PDSA cycles sometimes are referred to as trial-and-learning cycles. In implementation work, PDSA cycles can assume two forms (rapid-cycle and usability testing) that are distinguished by time frames (rapid or longer term) and scope of issues (small or medium).

The PDSA Improvement Cycles were originally used in manufacturing and business settings (Shewhart, 1939) to reduce error and have since been employed in a wide variety of human service settings. Rapid-cycle uses of PDSAC require frequent opportunities to do what was planned, study what has been done and the results of doing it, and act on that information to make changes to improve the next plan. Note that rapid-cycle use of PDSAC includes the assumption of clear accountability for achieving the desired outcomes. This is a good fit with the "making it happen," mission-driven approach inherent in the Active Implementation Frameworks. For example, rapid PDSA cycles are well-suited to making improvements in teacher instruction behavior or therapist behavior from one day or week to the next. In these cases, plans can be adjusted and results monitored on a frequent basis, allowing for rapid improvements to be made. As part of an Implementation Team, coaches can use PDSA cycles to expand the skills and improve the outcomes of practitioners.

## Plan, do, study, act (PDSA) Improvement Cycles

Having a plan is important. "Napoleon allegedly said that no successful battle ever followed its plan. Yet Napoleon also planned every one of his battles, far more meticulously than any earlier general had done. Without an action plan, the executive becomes a prisoner of events. And without check-ins to re-examine the plan as events unfold, the executive has no way of knowing which events really matter and which are only noise" (Drucker, 2004, p. 61). It also is said that no plan survives its first encounter with reality.

Leaders plan how to begin an improvement initiative, are prepared to manage the change process once the plan is launched, and never lose sight of the original goal. This logic is at the heart of improvement and implementation. When attempting to use an innovation in practice, the expectation is that changes in related activities and routines will be required in expected and unexpected ways. The Active Implementation Frameworks provide the basis for "the plan:" reality quickly presents problems to be solved. For example, the plan is to use Implementation Drivers to support the full and effective use of a Usable Innovation.

For Active Implementation the Improvement Cycles are based on PDSAC logic as shown in Figure 26. Note that each component of PDSAC includes activities related to developing and using an innovation and developing and using Active Implementation supports.

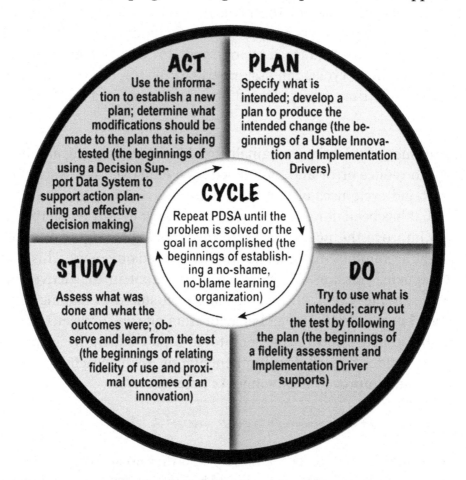

Figure 26. PDSAC for implementation and innovation development and improvement. Thanks to Heather Wire and the WHO Collaborating Center for Research Evidence for Sexual and Reproductive Health for production of this graphic

## Rapid cycle problem -solving

PDSA cycles can be done rapidly one person or method at a time. Rapid cycles are helpful for situations that are repeated frequently, such as engagement strategies with recipients, the use of medication protocols, methods for conducting coaching, and so on. These activities provide many opportunities each day or each week to plan, do, study, act, and try again to solve a problem or reach a goal.

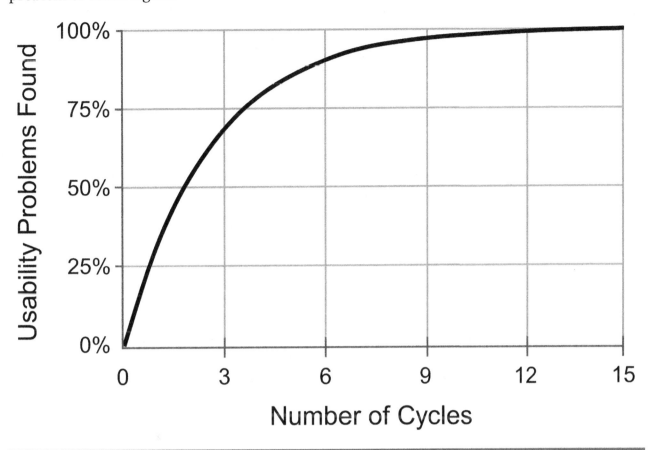

Figure 27. Improvement Cycles with a small number of users and a few iterations to improve complex processes. Nielsen (2000).

The key to using PDSAC effectively is to use PDSAC as intended, that is, with fidelity to the PDSAC process. There are many instances of planning and doing, and few instances of studying and acting. Cycling planning and doing without studying and acting can be frustrating and end up with a lot of unimproved do-do. Rapid cycle PDSAC methods can lead to vastly improved methods and outcomes after a few weeks of trial and learning.

Nielsen (2000) and others have stated that five cycles produce about 85% of the benefit that might be found after 12 or more iterations (Figure 27). In Active Implementation use, Implementation Teams focus on the cycle; that is, how many attempts have been made to solve a problem? What progress has been made? How well-documented is the use of PDSAC? The number of cycles is an indicator of persistent mission-driven support by an Implementation Team.

As shown in Figure 27, it only takes a few users to find nearly all of errors in a complex program (in these cases, web sites or computer software). Perhaps three to five users identify about 80% of all the errors eventually found by many more users. Similar data may be produced eventually for interaction-based programs in human services. The only certainty is the 0-user data point—we will not get better if we don't try.

## Usability testing

PDSAC in the form of usability testing is employed for more comprehensive or complex innovations (Akin et al., 2013; Genov, 2005; Henton et al., 2014). Usability testing is PDSAC using small groups of people or units and studying more complex processes and outcomes over longer periods of time (months or years). If each cycle shows improvement or not, then progress is being made. It is just as important to know what *does not work* as it is to know what *does work* when attempting to solve problems.

In the early years of the development of the Teaching-Family Model (see Chapter 4), usability testing was being done in a haphazard way as outcomes for cohorts of group homes were studied (Fixsen & Blase, 2018). A more purposeful, disciplined approach is recommended to achieve results more quickly. For innovations and implementation methods, "negative findings at any point may be cause for reconceptualization of the intervention design. Thus, the process is not linear. It has a recursive feature in which, though progress may be made over time, an intervention may be revised and retested iteratively until it reaches a benchmark for efficacy" (Fraser & Galinsky, 2010, p. 462).

Usability testing work is carried out expeditiously with just a few "cases" to permit rapid adjustments and rapid learning. For example, the Iowa Model was developed to guide clinicians as they attempt to use evidence to improve health care outcomes: "The practice is first implemented with a small group of patients, and an evaluation is carried out. The EBP [Evidence-Based Practice] is then refined based on evaluation data, and the change is implemented with additional patient populations for which it is appropriate. Patient/family, staff, and fiscal outcomes are monitored. Organizational and administrative supports are important factors for success in using evidence in care delivery" (Titler et al., 2001, p. 139). Only when an innovation has been used effectively with a few individuals in a few iterations is it then considered for use with many. This process saves time and resources for organizations and saves exposing recipients to ineffective innovations. Fit with practitioners, recipients, and organizations is not assumed or lamented; it is developed on purpose.

Mutamba et al. (2018) followed a similar path in Uganda.

"To contextualize a psychological treatment, we followed the four components of the REP [Replicating Effective Programs] framework: pre-conditions, pre-implementation, implementation, and maintenance and evolution. A three-step process involved reviewing health services available for nodding syndrome-affected families and current evidence for psychological treatments, qualitative formative research, and analysis and documentation of implementation activities. Stakeholders included members of affected communities, health care workers, therapists, local government leaders, and Ministry of Health officials. Detailed written, audio, and video documentation of the implementation activities was used for content analysis.

During the pre-condition component of REP, we selected group interpersonal therapy (IPT-G) because of its feasibility, acceptability, effectiveness in the local setting, and availability of locally developed training materials. During the pre-implementation component, we adapted the training, logistics, and technical assistance strategies in conjunction with government and stakeholder working groups. Adaptations included content modification based on qualitative research with caregivers of children with nodding syndrome. During the implementation component, training was shortened for feasibility with government health workers. Peer-to-peer supervision was selected as a sustainable quality assurance method. IPT-G delivered by community health workers was evaluated for fidelity, patient outcomes, and other process-level variables. More than 90% of beneficiaries completed the treatment program, which was effective in reducing caregiver and child mental health problems. With the Ministry of Health, we conducted preparatory activities for the maintenance and evolution component for scale-up throughout the country."

Thus, Usability Testing (planning and preparation; trial and learning) with a small sample of practitioners, agencies, and stakeholders led to modifications that preserved effectiveness of the innovation while discovering how to support the use of the innovation in particular settings, low- resource or otherwise. Some refer to this as "contextualizing" innovations and support. For example, Hirschhorn et al. (2015) set out to measure the impact of the BetterBirth program on EBP (Essential Birth Practices) and maternal-neonatal morbidity and mortality. They found "The adaptive study design of implementation, evaluation, and feedback drove iterative redesign and successfully developed a SCC [Safe Childbirth Checklist]-focused coaching intervention that improved EBPs [Essential Birth Practices] in UP [Uttar Pradesh, India] facilities. This work was critical to develop a replicable BetterBirth package tailored to the local context."

In another example Harrison and Grantham (2018) used a "team redesign" process to improve chronic care and prevention outcomes, and ease provider burden. In a description of the results of this process, they stated, "Besides making small adjustments to cope with setbacks, redesign and system leaders engaged in more thorough organizational learning. They examined contextual challenges underlying setbacks and posing risks to the delivery system as a whole. Their responses to challenges helped strengthen the redesign's prospects, improved the delivery system's position in its labor market, and helped the system prepare to meet emerging requirements for value-based care and population health."

By whatever name, Usability Testing is a critical part of practice and program development and implementation. The need for common concepts and common language to promote clear communication is evident in every review of the implementation literature.

Usability Testing in human services is PDSAC work that occurs across longer time frames and addresses issues with more interactive components. Usability Testing is done with iterative groups of four or five individuals or units (Akin et al., 2013; Fixsen, Hassmiller Lich, et al., 2018; Genov, 2005). For innovation development or capacity building, the number of iterations equals the number of opportunities to learn, adjust, and learn again. For example, assume 40 people need to be trained, and training capacity needs to be developed. Capacity to do training well means having skilled trainers as members of an Implementation Team who:

- Know the material well
- Can deliver it effectively to adult learners
- Have developed behavior rehearsal opportunities
- Know how to carry out the behavior rehearsal leader and confederate roles so that trainees have the opportunity to practice essential skills (Collins, Brooks, Daly, et al., 1976; Dreisbach et al., 1979) (see Usable Innovation criteria), and
- Have created useful pre-post training tests of knowledge and skill development.

# Training

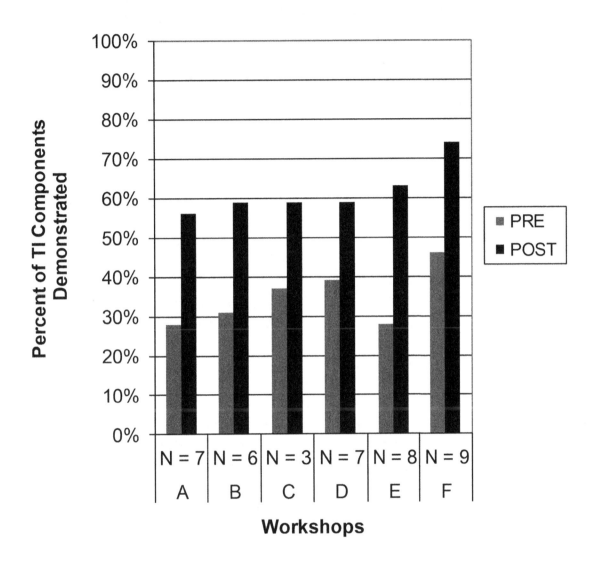

Figure 28. Pre-post results of six training workshops. "TI" are Teaching Interactions, essential components of the Teaching-Family Model. Collins, et al. (1976)

If training is provided to all 40 people at one time, there is only one opportunity to develop training capacity. Any lessons learned have to wait until the next cohort needs to be trained. If the focus broadens from not only training 40 people but also to developing effective and durable training capacity, then training should be done with iterative groups to maximize learning opportunities for trainers. The usability testing format shown in Figure 28 provides six times more opportunities for the trainers to build their capacity and refine training materials and procedures based on their results, as they move through training the cohort of 40 people in smaller groups of 3 to 9.

Figure 28 shows the results from repeated training workshops provided to a few trainees in each workshop. During this time the trainers were learning to be better trainers, and the context of training was being adjusted with each iteration. In subsequent workshops the post-training scores reached the 80% benchmark and remained in the 80-100% range thereafter.

## Fit, adapt, adjust, tailor

Innovations are new ways of work in any organization or system. Problems are expected as innovations are considered and their first uses are attempted in practice. Anticipating problems is built into the Active Implementation Frameworks. For example, attempting to skip Exploration and Installation and moving right into Initial Implementation is not a good idea. Assigning staff to "just do it" instead of engaging in Staff Selection processes is not a good idea. The problems associated with "lack of buy-in," "poor fit," and "resistance to change" are the anticipated results of "lack of planning and preparation" during Exploration and Staff Selection. Even so, there always will be unanticipated problems when attempting to introduce or sustain an effective innovation in the unique environment of any organization or system. Unexpected problems are an expected part of the implementation process. Solving problems is the work of using the Improvement Cycles.

"If you wish to make an improved product, you must already be engaged in making an inferior one" (Varella, 1977, p. 921). The quote from Varella is a good fit with Implementation Team members and Implementation Specialists (Van Dyke, 2015) who often say "get started, get better." Get started by using the best available implementation and innovation methods and persist in doing that work with fidelity. Then experience the responses from individuals and units within an organization that seem to impede progress. Work then commences to overcome those impediments identified by those individuals in those units to get better outcomes. Note that this process focuses on real problems and real people in the actual setting where the plan is to use the innovation.

Use of the Improvement Cycles involves practitioners, managers, and directors in ways that encourage participation and buy-in while solving problems (i.e., tailoring the local circumstances) to support high fidelity use of an innovation (Hirschhorn et al., 2015; Prince, Hines, Chyou, & Heegeman, 2014). PDSAC methods are important in this regard since the focus is on repeating the process (cycles) until a solution is found. Simply identifying problems and engaging stakeholders leads to dissatisfaction unless the problems are solved in the process (Tucker & Singer, 2015; Wilson, Dell, & Anderson, 1993).

From an Implementation Team perspective, the best thing is to experience similar problems from one setting to another. These similar problems then move to the list of expected problems, and planned solutions become part of the improved approaches to implementation. Over the years this is how the Installation Stage was discriminated as separate from the Exploration Stage as unexpected problems securing Exploration-promised resources arose consistently and became expected problems and put into a stage of their own.

Pérez, Van der Stuyft, Zabala, Castro, and Lefèvre (2016) noted, "Classical fidelity dimensions and conceptual frameworks do not address the issue of how to adapt an intervention while still maintaining its effectiveness." Either on purpose or haphazardly, adaptation is accomplished by using PDSAC. For implementation: Plan to use an innovation as intended; Do the innovation with Implementation Driver supports to attempt high fidelity use of the innovation; Study the fit with existing practitioner behavior, organization operating procedures, and system influences; Act on the information to tailor practitioner behavior, modify organization routines, and adjust system practices to improve fit; and develop a plan to assess the impact of those changes in the next Cycle. If there is something about the innovation that attracts attention in this process, then the innovation itself becomes the focus of PDSAC to arrive at an adapted-but-still-effective version of the innovation. However, the initial focus is on adapting the context to fit the use of the innovation with fidelity so that desired results can be obtained.

## High expectations, low tolerance for errors

As noted in these examples, Improvement Cycles provide methods for detecting and correcting errors to produce improved practice, implementation, and policy methods and socially significant outcomes. The PDSAC methods originally were developed to reduce error and increase quality in manufacturing. In the 1920s and 1930s, telegraph and telephone innovations required transformers, amplifiers, switching mechanisms, and other devices to allow communications to flow. Initially the lines and cables and devices were mounted on telephone poles on city streets. This became unsightly and the cables and devices were buried underground. When the devices were on telephone poles, they were easy to access to service or replace components when a failure occurred. When the components were buried, the cost of repair and replacement increased dramatically resulting in the demand for more reliable devices. This put a premium on methods for detecting and correcting errors during the manufacturing process to produce more reliable outcomes (Shewhart, 1931, 1939).

In manufacturing, high quality is attained by reducing error. Setting high standards has become the norm in human services (e.g., the Millennium Development Goals and Sustainable Development Goals set by the United Nations; achievement standards set by government education agencies). Equal emphasis has not been given to reducing error (e.g.

medical error remains the third leading cause of death in the U.S.; literacy scores for nine-year-old children in the U.S. have churned around a mediocre mean of 215 on a 500-point scale since the 1960s). Errors can be reduced by the use of implementation methods that emphasize high fidelity and the use of Decision Support Data Systems and coaching systems for continuous adjustment of supports for and uses of innovations. Low fidelity is the equivalent of manufacturing error and results in wasted time and effort and leads to unreliable (sometimes harmful) outcomes.

Six Sigma is a statistic-driven version of PDSAC originally applied to manufacturing atom-based products where error rates could be reduced to three defects per million units of production (99.99% success). Three sigma represents 66,800 defects per million units (93% success). Outside of atom-based manufacturing applications, results of Six Sigma improvement methods in interaction-based human service applications often result in outcomes in the range of 20-60% success for reducing cycle times, wait times, and usage error (Kwak & Anbari, 2006). This translates to about 400,000 defects per million units in interaction-based applications. Error rates have a big impact on the ability to achieve socially significant outcomes: there is room for significant improvement in human services.

By focusing on eliminating error, manufacturing processes have improved in ways that exceed all expectations. For example, attempts to manufacture the first transistors on silicon chips resulted in about one usable transistor out of 100 silicon chips that were made—a very high error rate. They discovered many sources of contaminants and subsequently developed ultra-clean manufacturing plants to eliminate those contaminants. They learned how to produce nearly error-free silicon-based transistors; the transistors were arranged in integrated circuits; and those integrated circuits then were used to manufacture even better silicon chips and more reliable integrated circuits containing a billion or more transistors (Gertner, 2012; Kaeslin, 2008). By eliminating error, Silicon Valley engineers and scientists created a virtuous circle and got better and better at getting better by using their improved products to make the next generation of even better products.

# Improving socially significant outcomes

Three themes for improvement strategies are embedded in the various Active Implementation Frameworks: 1) improvement of an innovation, 2) improvement of the implementation supports for the uses of innovations in practice, and 3) improvement of the organization and system contexts in which change occurs. These themes map onto the Formula for Success where Effective Innovations x Effective Implementation x Enabling Contexts = Socially Significant Outcomes.

As noted in the Six Sigma examples, variability is the enemy of quality. Low fidelity is the equivalent of manufacturing error and results in wasted time and effort and leads to unreliable (sometimes harmful) outcomes. Errors can be reduced by the use of Active Implementation methods that emphasize high fidelity and the use of Decision Support Data Systems and coaching systems for continuous adjustment of supports for and uses of innovations.

> **For Active Implementation:** Plan to use an innovation as intended; Do the innovation with Implementation Driver supports to attempt high fidelity use of the innovation; Study the fit with existing practitioner behavior, organization operating procedures, and system influences; Act on the information to tailor practitioner behavior, modify organization routines, and adjust system practices to improve fit; and develop a plan to assess the impact of those changes in the next Cycle.

The need to attend to improvement strategies has been a consistent part of the implementation literature for many decades. Van Meter and Van Horn (1975, pp. 450-451) surveyed the field and noted, "The problems of implementation are overwhelmingly complex and scholars have frequently been deterred by methodological considerations. Relative to the study of policy formulation, the analysis of the implementation process raises serious boundary problems. It is often difficult to define the relevant actors. Furthermore, many of the variables needed to complete an implementation study are difficult–if not impossible–to measure. Unlike legislative and judicial arenas where votes are often recorded, decisions in an administrative setting are frequently difficult to isolate. Finally, a comprehensive analysis of implementation requires that attention be given to multiple actions over an extended period of time, thus involving an enormous outlay of time and resources."

Decades later Greenhalgh et al. (2004, p. 615) came to a similar conclusion: "Context and 'confounders' lie at the very heart of the diffusion, dissemination, and implementation of complex innovations. They are not extraneous to the object of study; they are an integral part of it. The multiple (and often unpredictable) interactions that arise in particular contexts and settings are precisely what determine the success or failure of a dissemination initiative."

Improvement strategies are a way to contend with the acknowledged complexity inherent in any attempt to use an innovation in practice. The applications of PDSAC logic to interaction-based innovations are important for achieving and sustaining socially significant outcomes. Innovations can be improved, implementation methods can be improved, and enabling contexts can be improved using PDSAC logic as a guide. Then the improved versions can be used to produce the next generation of even better processes and outcomes. Instead of haphazardly "tinkering toward utopia" (Tyack & Cuban, 1995) or "groping along" (Golden, 1990), changes in each factor of the Formula for Success can be planned, assessed, and improved on purpose.

## Related research

In the following sections we use the terms originally used by the authors who are cited. Note how the different terms could be replaced by PDSAC or usability testing without losing the meaning. We suggest using PDSAC and usability testing in the interest of establishing common concepts, common language, and common measures to promote communication to advance the practice and science of implementation. We have left the variety of other terms in the information provided below to preserve the authors' original statements.

### Improving innovations

Any innovation is a work in progress and subject to refinement in practice. Sandler et al. (2005, p. 132) states, "The prototype development and testing phase begins with the further refinement of the service concept into a more detailed service blueprint that captures every aspect of how the service will be implemented ... Over time, the specific details of the service under development can be fleshed out via an iterative process of prototype development and testing. Although research on prototype development and testing in a services context is still in its infancy and little work has explored what methods are best to use given the characteristics of the new service under consideration, there are a variety of ways that organizations can develop and test aspects of the prototype."

Damschroder et al. (2009) offer specific advice for improving innovations. "Adaptability relies on a definition of the 'core components' (the essential and indispensable elements of the intervention itself) versus the 'adaptable periphery' (adaptable elements, structures, and systems related to the intervention and organization into which it is being implemented) of the intervention ... A component analysis can be performed to identify the core versus adaptable periphery components, but often the distinction is one that can only be discerned through trial and error over time as the intervention is disseminated more widely and adapted for a variety of contexts. The ability to trial is a key feature of the plan-do-study-act quality improvement cycle that allows ... individuals and groups to build experience and expertise, and time to reflect upon and test the intervention, and usability testing (with staff and patients) promotes successful adaptation of the intervention."

Kilbourne et al. (2007, p. 6) recommend usability testing and suggested that any innovation "can be tested for clarity and functionality within a few intervention sites. During this process, the organizations can identify five to eight patients to participate in a full intervention cycle, and study investigators should collect information on feasibility, acceptance, and any problems with the overall package, so that the package can be refined based on their input."

Usability testing also is suggested by Pronovost, Berenholtz, and Needham (2008, p. 964) who state: "The interventions must fit each hospital's current system, including local culture and resources. While there is no formula for redesigning care processes, certain tactics seem effective. Informed by evidence and our experiences, we developed a "four Es" approach to improve reliability: engage, educate, execute, and evaluate. This differs from the established plan-do-study-act cycle, in that it is applied only to the whole project and not to each step within it. Also, while the plan-do-study-act cycle approaches change linearly, the four Es recognises the importance of culture change, contextual factors, and engaging staff in the project." The authors are describing usability testing. They further recommend physically walking through the steps to observe what is done, barriers to doing the work, and better understand the context in which an innovation is being used.

Usability testing is a purposeful way to develop a Usable Innovation and demonstrate its value in practice. Establishing functional relationships between "using the innovation as intended" and "innovation outcomes" is an important first step for any innovation. If an innovation "works" (i.e., high fidelity use equals excellent outcomes; low fidelity equals poor outcomes) with a few recipients in a usability test, then it is ready for use on a broader scale for practice or research purposes. If it "doesn't work," then it is time for the next cycle of usability testing.

## Improving implementation supports

There is a need for improvement of implementation strategies to support the use of innovations in practice. For example, Stith et al. (2006, p. 613) note, "There are a number of sources of variability that may undermine fidelity ... These sources of variability may be diverse and could be influenced by the community, agency, practitioner and/or setting. Sources of variability could be features of the program (e.g., program length), program content (e.g., the amount of material presented), characteristics of the participants (e.g., socioeconomic status), or limitations of the organizational environment (e.g., adequate supervision or technical assistance). Identifying these sources of variability and taking steps to minimize their effects may help to maximize successful program implementation in community agencies. Pre-testing possible modifications to overcome barriers may also enhance fidelity."

More specific advice for making improvements to implementation methods to support the use of innovations in practice is offered by Sandler et al. (2005, p. 139) who suggest the use of "input from key stakeholders (organizational experts, providers, consumers, and cultural experts) to identify potential sources of variability in implementing the core components of the intervention in service agencies. Sources of variability might include features of the program (e.g., session length), aspects of the manual (e.g., amount of material to present), characteristics of participants (e.g., cultural differences), or constraints of the organizational environment (e.g., time allocated to supervision). These sources of variability are potential barriers to consistent high fidelity implementation in the service delivery setting." The strategy of seeking input from relevant stakeholders also is evident in the work of others (Chinman et al., 2008; Glisson & Schoenwald, 2005; Greenhalgh et al., 2004; Hawkins et al., 2002; Spoth & Greenberg, 2005).

Damschroder et al. (2009) "describe four essential activities of implementation process that are common across organizational change models: planning, engaging, executing, and reflecting and evaluating. These activities may be accomplished formally or informally through, for example, grassroots change efforts. They can be accomplished in any order and are often done in a spiral, stop-and-start, or incremental approach to implementation; e.g., using a plan-do-study-act approach to incremental testing. Each activity can be revisited, expanded, refined, and re-evaluated throughout the course of implementation."

Each use of the selection, training, coaching, fidelity, and other Implementation Drivers provides ongoing opportunities for improvement. Each use can be improved based on the findings from the last use or the last ten uses. The Decision Support Data System is used to collect the information in actionable forms. The use of the data for feedback to the Implementation Team is noted in the descriptions of the Implementation Drivers.

**Improving organization and system functioning**

Organizations and systems are complex and changeable. Chinman et al. (2008) make an appeal for a purposeful PDSAC approach to organization and system change: "Given that few, if any, programs achieve perfect outcomes during the initial implementation, what can be done to improve the program's effectiveness in the future? There is a great opportunity to learn from previous implementation efforts when processes and outcomes of a program are well documented."

Glisson and Schoenwald (2005) offer advice on how to make improvements and add guidance about who is to do the work of improvement. They identify change agents who have been trained and prepared for their role in creating fit, solving problems, and overcoming barriers to realizing intended outcomes. To improve supports for the use of innovations in practice, Glisson and Schoenwald (2005, p. 254) state, "Participatory decision-making is used in all four phases by the change agent who provides the opportunity for input from service providers and community opinion leaders into decisions about service implementation and community support. Participatory decision -making is essential to the development of teamwork, continuous quality improvement (CQI), and other ARC [Availability, Responsiveness and Continuity] intervention components. Participatory decision-making has been recognized for many years as a critical step in organizational and community development efforts that provide the foundation for constructive, problem-solving environments. "Conflict resolution at the interpersonal-, intergroup-, and interorganizational levels is used ... to mediate differences in opinion or competing interests that threaten efforts to address the targeted problem. Work with community groups and personal relationships with service providers, judges, school officials, and other community opinion leaders are essential to effective conflict resolution."

Soliciting input is always a good step; using input to make improvements and asking for more input is an even better step. Goal-oriented PDSAC, used on purpose by Implementation Teams, provides a way to make experience and stakeholder input count. Stakeholders define problems, and they judge the methods to solve problems and the progress toward solving problems (Best et al., 2012; J. J. Hurley, 2012; Stage, 2008; Tucker & Singer, 2015; Willner et al., 1977; Wolf, 1978).

The Systemic Change framework (Chapter 15) uses PDSAC and usability testing logic as a foundation for initiating and managing change in organizations and systems. For example, the Practice-Policy Communication Cycle is a way to incorporate stakeholder experience in executive decision making so that organization and system change can better support practitioners and Implementation Teams. Recursive feedback that is part of monthly Practice-Policy Communication can be used as the "study" component of an Improvement Cycle that includes any aspect of an organization or system that impedes achievement of socially significant outcomes.

## Improvement Cycles in practice

An example of an approach to establishing usable interventions and implementation supports is provided below. Note how PDSAC is used on purpose to develop simultaneously the innovation and the implementation supports for the innovation in an education context (Fixsen, Hassmiller Lich, et al., 2018).

The process outlined below employed nine teachers over the course of four months. In a usability testing format (Figure 29), the Implementation Team worked intensively with three teachers at a time to maximize the learning and to quickly make use of learning in the work with the next group of three teachers. This provides many more learning and improvement opportunities for the Implementation Team compared to one experience with nine teachers.

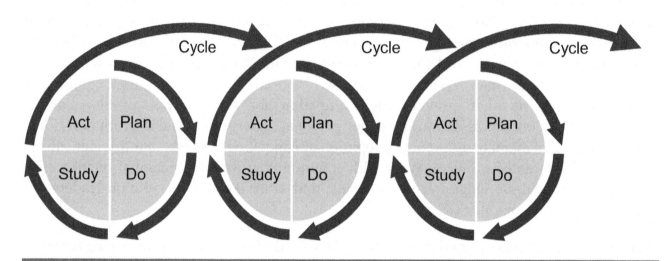

Figure 29. Usability testing with repeated iterations to develop a solution to a problem or achieve an aspiration

## Iteration #1

Plan: The state legislature just passed a law mandating new standards for Grade Three literacy. The state department of education asked faculty of the state university to summarize the research on early literacy instruction with an emphasis on instructional practices that might be useful for children and students from age three through Grade Three. The research summary specified the following two instruction practices found to be effective in the literature (e.g., Hattie, 2009):

- Effective instructors encourage high levels of student engagement with education content
- Effective instructors provide frequent, prompt, and accurate feedback to students when they respond

A Practice Profile was drafted to identify expected, developmental, and poor examples of instructional behavior related to each of the instruction practices.

<u>Do:</u> To begin the process, the Implementation Team contacted a nearby school district. After some Exploration Stage work with principals and teachers, they secured the cooperation of nine K-3 teachers and their principals. The teachers agreed to try to use the instruction methods, participate in training, allow two people to observe their classroom every day for two weeks, give students a weekly quiz related to literacy content taught that week, and participate in up to one hour of de-briefing discussion during each week. In a meeting with the teachers and their principals, a schedule was developed so Teachers One-Three would participate during Month One, Teachers Four-Six would begin to participate in Month Two, and Teachers Seven-Nine would begin to participate in Month Three.

Just prior to Month One, the Implementation Team developed a two-hour training workshop to review and discuss the literature regarding the two key instruction practices, created video tapes to model the two key components, and developed "behavior rehearsal scenes" to provide opportunities for teachers to practice the skills in a mock classroom. At the beginning of Month One the Implementation Team provided the training to Teachers One-Three and debriefed with the teachers at the end of training to obtain their opinions of the training methods and content.

Prior to Month One, the Implementation Team drafted four fidelity items to assess the use of the two key instruction practices. During the behavior rehearsal section of training, one member of the Implementation Team used the items to observe teacher instruction in the mock classroom. The items were modified based on those observations. The "fidelity scores" related to teacher instruction at the end of training were analyzed to see how training could be improved next time.

Immediately after training, the three teachers began using the instruction practices in their classrooms. Starting on the third day and every other day thereafter, the Implementation Team observed each classroom for two hours with two members of the team simultaneously observing one classroom at a time. The team members used the Practice Profile outline to note instances of expected, developmental, and poor examples of instruction. At the end of Week One and again at the end of Week Two, two members of the Implementation Team did a teacher instruction fidelity assessment using the four items developed prior to training and modified during training. Each teacher provided the Implementation Team with the average scores for the weekly student quiz related to literacy content taught that week.

At the end of each week, two Implementation Team members met with the three teachers as a group to discuss the instruction practices. Teachers provided their perspectives on what was easy or difficult for them to do in their interactions with students. Implementation Team members offered suggestions for using the instruction practices based on their observations of all three teachers. Implementation Team members began drafting a coaching-service delivery plan based on teachers' input.

Study: At the end of Weeks Two and Three the Implementation Team met to consider the information being developed. The information and data being gained from the experience with the first three teachers were used to revise the innovation and improve implementation supports as noted in the Act section.

Act: Based on classroom observations and comments from teachers, the Implementation Team re-defined the key instruction components of the innovation. The Implementation Team expanded the component, "Instructors encouraging high levels of student engagement with education content" to include "provides explicit instruction" and "models instruction tasks." The Implementation Team drafted a Practice Profile (including the new components) with detail based on the classroom observations. A draft of the Practice Profile was reviewed with the three teachers, and their ideas were included regarding how to define expected, developmental, and poor examples of use of each component of the innovation.

The Implementation Team compared notes on the fidelity assessments to see if they agreed or not on scoring each of the four items. Agreement was not good, so the fidelity items were revised to be more specific, and the number of items was increased to include the new components being operationalized in the Practice Profile. A protocol for how a fidelity observer should enter the classroom and conduct the observation was drafted for use in subsequent fidelity observations. The fidelity scores and the scores for the weekly student quizzes were summarized. No discernable relationship between the two was apparent.

As noted above, the Implementation Team began studying training during and after the training session for Teachers One-Three. In Week Three the team began work on how to improve training methods and how to include the new content in training for the next three teachers.

**Iteration #2**

Plan: The Implementation Team met with the principal and teachers to set the time for a two-hour training workshop for Teachers Four-Six. The Implementation Team discussed the work during Month One and invited questions about the classroom observations and the de-brief times.

Do: In Month Two, the Implementation Team provided the revised training to Teachers Four-Six. The training content was based on the expanded essential components. The revised training methods were based on the experience and feedback from Teachers One-Three.

The Implementation Team provided a two-hour training workshop to review and discuss the literature regarding the key instruction practices, model the key components, and provide opportunities for Teachers Four-Six to practice the skills in a mock classroom. During training, practice continued until the teachers felt competent and confident. The Implementation Team debriefed with the teachers at the end of training to obtain their opinions about the training methods and content.

During the behavior rehearsal section of training, one member of the Implementation Team used the revised fidelity items to observe teacher instruction in the mock classroom. The fidelity items were modified further based on those observations.

To collect pre-post training data, a version of the behavior rehearsal (used in training) was conducted individually for each teacher just prior to training. The teacher's behavior was scored using the fidelity criteria. The scores for each fidelity item prior to training and during the last behavior rehearsal at the end of training were analyzed to see the extent to which teachers improved instruction skills during training. The data provided direction on how training could be improved next time.

Immediately after training, Teachers Four-Six began using the instruction practices in their classrooms. Starting on the third day and every other day thereafter, the Implementation Team observed each classroom for two hours with two members of the team jointly observing one classroom at a time. For Teachers One-Three, one observation per week was conducted. During the observations, the team members used the Practice Profile outline to note instances of expected, developmental, and poor examples of instruction.

Two members of the Implementation Team did a fidelity assessment. The new fidelity assessment was used for assessments of Teachers One-Six each week to gain more experience with the items and to continue to develop the observation protocol. Each teacher provided the Implementation Team with the average scores for the weekly student quiz related to literacy content taught that week.

At the end of each week, two Implementation Team members met with the six teachers to discuss the instruction practices. Teachers provided their perspectives on what was easy or difficult for them to do. Implementation Team members offered suggestions for using the instruction practices based on their observations of all six teachers. Implementation Team members revised the coaching-service delivery plan based on teachers' input.

Study: The Implementation Team now has two months of information from Teachers One-Three and one month of information from Teachers Four-Six. In Month Two, Teachers One-Three were gaining experience and using the innovation with confidence in their interactions with students. The Implementation Team began seeing more nuanced versions of the four key components of the innovation.

The pre-post training data were summarized to see where training produced more or less improvement in teachers learning the instruction skills. Those data were compared to the ongoing fidelity assessments to see if the post-training scores for teachers predicted later fidelity scores.

The fidelity scores for the six teachers and the scores for the weekly student quizzes were summarized. A pattern emerged indicating a possible relationship between higher fidelity scores and better scores on student quizzes.

Act: Based on observations and teacher comments, the Implementation Team again re-defined the key instruction components of the innovation. The Implementation Team expanded the component, "Effective instructors provide frequent, prompt, and accurate feedback to students when they respond" to include "corrects errors by modeling a correct response" and "limits corrective feedback to the task at hand." These new components were included in the draft Practice Profile. The draft of the Practice Profile was reviewed with the six teachers, and their ideas were included regarding how to define expected, developmental, and poor examples of use of each component of the innovation.

The Implementation Team compared notes on the fidelity assessments to see if they agreed or not on scoring each of the items. The items were revised to be more specific, and the number of items was increased to include the new components being operationalized in the Practice Profile. The protocol for how a fidelity observer should enter the classroom and conduct the observation was revised based on the experiences with all six teachers.

The pre-post training data summary made it clear that trainers were more effective when teaching the instruction components related to delivering information to students. However, the trainers were producing mixed outcomes when teaching instruction components related to providing feedback to students after they responded. The Implementation Team developed new behavior rehearsal scenarios to provide more training on those skills.

## Iteration #3

Plan: The Implementation Team met with the principal and teachers to set the time for a two-hour training workshop for Teachers Seven-Nine. The Implementation Team discussed the work during Months One and Two and invited questions about the classroom observations and the de-brief times.

<u>Do</u>: In Month Three, the Implementation Team provided the revised training to Teachers Seven-Nine. The training content was based on the expanded essential components and practice profiles. The revised training methods were based on the experience and feedback from Teachers One-Six. The Implementation Team debriefed with the teachers at the end of training to obtain their opinions of the training methods and content.

During the behavior rehearsal section of training, one member of the Implementation Team used the revised fidelity items to observe teacher instruction in the mock classroom. The fidelity items were modified further based on those observations.

Pre-post training data were collected by using a version of the behavior rehearsal (used in training) individually for each teacher just prior to training. The teacher's behavior was scored using the revised fidelity criteria. The scores for each fidelity item prior to training and during the last behavior rehearsal at the end of training were analyzed to see the extent to which teachers improved instruction skills. The data provided direction on how training could be improved next time.

Immediately after training, Teachers Seven-Nine began using the instruction practices in their classrooms. Starting on the third day and every other day thereafter, the Implementation Team observed each classroom for two hours with two members of the team simultaneously observing one classroom at a time. For Teachers One-Six one observation per week was conducted. During the observations, the team members used the Practice Profile outline to note instances of expected, developmental, and poor examples of instruction.

For Teachers One-Nine, at the end of Week One and again at the end of Week Two, two members of the Implementation Team did a fidelity assessment. The revised fidelity assessment was used for assessments of Teachers One-Nine each week to gain more experience with the items and to continue to develop the observation protocol.

At the end of each week, two Implementation Team members met with the nine teachers to discuss the instruction practices. Teachers provided their perspectives on what was easy or difficult for them to do. Implementation Team members offered suggestions for using the instruction practices based on their observations of all nine teachers. Implementation Team members revised the coaching-service delivery plan based on teachers' input.

<u>Study</u>: The Implementation Team now has three months of information from Teachers One-Three, two months of information from Teachers Four-Six, and one month of information from Teachers Seven-Nine. With daily use of the new instruction methods in the classroom, Teachers One-Six were using the innovation with confidence in their interactions with

students. As each teacher "made the new skills her own," the Implementation Team began seeing nuanced versions of the key components of the innovation.

Fidelity scores for Teachers One-Three and Four-Six seemed to be improving from the first week after training to Month 3. The continued revision and expansion of the fidelity items made these data difficult to interpret, but the impression from observations and teacher reports seemed to confirm the fidelity information. The fidelity scores and the scores for the weekly student quizzes were summarized. Analysis of Month Three data for all nine teachers resulted in a positive correlation of 0.50 between fidelity scores and student quiz outcomes.

For two teachers in the Teachers Four-Six group, fidelity scores were good and their student outcomes were outstanding! The Implementation Team and teachers met to review the classroom observations and to engage the teachers in discussion of their instruction practices. It turned out that in the previous year these two teachers had been mentored by the same master teacher. During their induction into teaching, they had been taught to stand by the door and greet each student by name as he/she entered the classroom at the start of the school day and again after lunch period (Embry & Biglan, 2008). They felt this "primed the pump" and helped with student engagement.

The pre-post training data were summarized to see where training produced more or less improvement in teachers learning the instruction skills. Those data were compared to the ongoing fidelity assessments to see if the post-training scores for teachers predicted later fidelity scores.

Act: Based on observations, the Implementation Team again re-defined the key instruction components of the innovation. The Implementation Team expanded the key components to include greeting each student by name at the beginning of the school day. This new component was included in the draft Practice Profile. The draft of the Practice Profile was reviewed with the nine teachers, and their ideas were included regarding how to define expected, developmental, and poor examples of use of each component of the innovation.

The Implementation Team compared notes on the fidelity assessments to see if they agreed or not on scoring each of the items. The items were revised to be more specific, and the number of items was increased to include the new "greeting component" being operationalized in the Practice Profile. The protocol for how a fidelity observer should enter the classroom and conduct the observation was revised based on the experiences with all nine teachers.

The pre-post training data summary showed that trainers produced better outcomes when teaching instruction components related to providing feedback to students after they responded. However, there was need for further improvement. The Implementation Team decided to revise how they were giving feedback to teachers during training (e.g., focus comments on the positive behavior; model expected behavior prior to asking the teacher to practice again) during the behavior rehearsal scenarios.

Cycle: After four months, the Implementation Team was refining the fine points of the Practice Profile, assessing pre-post training knowledge and skills of teachers participating in training, using a good set of items to assess instruction practices in the classroom, and collecting information to correlate fidelity scores with student quiz scores. The innovation still needed improvement but met the basic criteria for a Usable Innovation.

# Chapter 14: Implementation Teams

Expertise is required to purposefully and effectively use the Active Implementation Frameworks to support using innovations so that they can produce intended outcomes reliably and repeatedly. This expertise is developed in Implementation Teams that are formed in organizations and systems. An Implementation Team has three-five members who work closely with the executive leadership of an organization. The team members are experts regarding identifying and developing Usable Innovations, experts in their own use of the Active Implementation Frameworks and their ability to teach others to use the frameworks, and skilled at initiating, facilitating, and managing system change processes.

Implementation Teams "make it happen" in a purposeful, constructive, and mission-driven way. In this process, existing staff and stakeholder groups in an organization or system are included in the various activities, discussions, and decisions. Especially in the first few years of practice, organization, and system change, the staff and stakeholders are an important source of information and help to guide the Implementation Team toward key leverage points and help to balance urgency and the pace of change. In this way, staff and stakeholders are co-developers of implementation supports for effective innovations and will sustain the implementation work for decades to come.

*Given the scope of responsibilities and depth of knowledge and skills, Implementation Teams sound like unicorns or other mythical creatures. There is no magic. It is hard work. The hard work is going on right now in nearly every organization to improve quality, follow clinical guidelines more closely, make organization functioning more efficient and less costly, improve patient relations, and so on.*

Co-development of implementation capacity is guided by the principles of Active Implementation. The implementation processes are clear: the task is to work together to develop the necessary implementation-informed roles and functions to achieve the goals of change in the status quo and its outcomes. Various facilitated participatory processes, such as co-creation, co-production, and co-design, which engage citizens and service users in the process of better understanding the problem to be solved and better exploring, defining, and agreeing on suitable solutions, are best suited for Exploration Stage work and general capacity development (Bombard et al., 2018; Metz & Albers, 2014; Voorberg, Bekkers, & Tummers, 2015). These approaches may be used to support groups to increase agreement and certainty about effective innovations to be implemented with fidelity and socially significant outcomes (Hawkins et al., 2002; Spoth & Greenberg, 2011; Stacey, 2002; Wandersman, 2003; Zimmerman et al., 1998). Once a decision is made to proceed, then co-development is guided by the Active Implementation Frameworks during Installation and Initial Implementation activities to achieve desired outcomes for recipients.

Unfortunately, Implementation Teams are not commonly available and take effort to develop so that they are functional and effective. Too often individuals and groups are asked to perform Implementation Team tasks without adequate preparation. The "just do it" and "get it done" and "work together" approaches lead to haphazard and unsustainable uses of effective innovations in practice and rarely produce socially significant outcomes. Decades of evidence consistently show that about 5-15% of attempts to use effective innovations may succeed (at least for a while) in the absence of purposeful implementation supports (Aladjem & Borman, 2006; Fairweather, Sanders, & Tornatzky, 1974b; Glisson, 2007; Green, 2008; Greenhalgh et al., 2004; Joyce & Showers, 2002; Lynch et al., 2018; Rossi & Wright, 1984; Tornatzky et al., 1980).

## Implementation Team definition

Implementation Teams are essential to scaled use of effective innovations. An Implementation Team consists of three-five people who are accountable for assuring the Active Implementation Frameworks are used as intended in organizations and systems in support of effective innovations. There may be more people on a team but, like any other functional team (Walker, Koroloff, & Schutte, 2003), the core group assures effective, efficient, and sustained functioning as an Active Implementation Team.

- Active Implementation Team members know the science and practice of implementation. They are able to use the Active Implementation Frameworks effectively and efficiently to affect change in practitioner behavior and organization and system functioning to directly improve benefits to recipients.

- Active Implementation Team members have the skills to build the capacity of others to effectively use the science and practice of implementation. By investing in the development of implementation capacity, individuals, organizations, and communities become equipped to successfully initiate, guide, and sustain their change efforts, continue to improve their system, and generalize the learning to future change efforts (Van Dyke, 2015, p. 3).
- Active Implementation Team members work closely with leadership and Implementation Teams. Leaders and team members work together closely to initiate and manage change processes, continue the operations of status quo services while establishing new and improved services, and embed new ways of work in organizations and systems to sustain and expand benefits to recipients.

Implementation Team members are guided by values that are based on accountability and effectiveness in the context of making it happen in human services and include being team-oriented; driven to develop implementation capacity; data-based practitioner-scientist; improvement-centered; ethical; and culturally competent.

## Competencies

Implementation Teams have been developed on purpose since the 1980s (Blase, Fixsen, & Phillips, 1984; Fixsen, 1978) and their impact on implementation outcomes have been assessed (Fixsen & Blase, 2018; Fixsen et al., 2007; Ogden et al., 2012; Tommeraas & Ogden, 2016). The process of developing Implementation Teams has matured and the competencies learned by Team members have become clearer as experience has been gained in multiple domains (Ryan Jackson et al., 2018).

Figure 30 outlines the competencies required of successful Implementation Team members.

# Active Implementation Practice Competencies

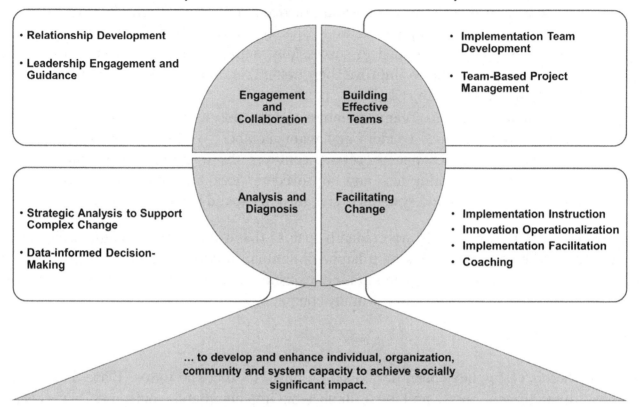

- Relationship Development
- Leadership Engagement and Guidance

Engagement and Collaboration

Building Effective Teams

- Implementation Team Development
- Team-Based Project Management

Analysis and Diagnosis

Facilitating Change

- Strategic Analysis to Support Complex Change
- Data-informed Decision-Making

- Implementation Instruction
- Innovation Operationalization
- Implementation Facilitation
- Coaching

... to develop and enhance individual, organization, community and system capacity to achieve socially significant impact.

Figure 30. Essential components of Implementation Team member competencies that have been operationalized in a Practice Profile (Van Dyke, 2015)

In Figure 30 the ten core competencies of Active Implementation Practice (Van Dyke, 2015) are relationship development, leadership engagement and guidance, implementation instruction, implementation facilitation, intervention operationalization, team development, data-informed decision making, strategic analysis to support change, team-based project management, and coaching. In any one situation, an Active Implementation Team member is likely to draw upon multiple core competencies simultaneously to analyze and respond; for example, using data for decision making (data-informed decision making) may occur while facilitating an Implementation Drivers' analysis (implementation facilitation) (Van Dyke, 2015, p. 6).

A Practice Profile guides building the competencies of Active Implementation Team members by providing a detailed description of the core components of Active Implementation practice. For example, pages 11–39 of Van Dyke (2015) detail the knowledge, skills, and abilities related to Acceptable Performance, Developmental Performance, and Unacceptable Performance of

Implementation Team members regarding each of the essential components outlined in Figure 30.

Like other skills, Implementation Team member skills must be teachable, learnable, doable, and assessable in practice. The Assessing Drivers Best Practices (ADBP) measures are used to evaluate Implementation Team performance in practice (Fixsen, Ward, Blase, et al., 2018; Ogden et al., 2012). Implementation Team functioning (use of the Implementation Drivers) is highly related to practitioner fidelity outcomes (Metz et al., 2014; Skogøy et al., 2018; Tommeraas & Ogden, 2016).

The Implementation Team member core competencies described by Van Dyke (2015) encompass and expand the skill sets identified over the past several decades (Table 27).

**Table 27. Core competencies for an Implementation Team member. Adapted from Van Dyke (2015), used with permission**

| Structure | … in place … | … so that the Implementation Team… | … can produce… |
|---|---|---|---|
| Implementation Team Structure | Three to five members are selected to serve as an accountable structure for facilitating stage-based implementation<br><br>Members are mutually selected into their roles<br><br>Members may include program developers or purveyors, if needed for their content expertise<br><br>Members represent various levels and perspectives of the system<br><br>The composition and functions of the team likely will shift as implementation progresses<br><br>A "Terms of Reference" (or internal memorandum of understanding) is in place with an accompanying communication protocol | Contains one or more members who know the intervention/ strategy, implementation, improvement processes and systems change methods<br><br>Includes the individuals needed to get the work done, but remain nimble enough to forge ahead and complete necessary stage-based activities in a timely manner<br><br>Can affect change simultaneously at multiple levels of the system<br><br>Is accountable for their work and has clarity on the parameters and authority of their activities [in relation to other teams working on the same change effort]<br><br>Can make decision or has access to those | Documentation of functional Terms of Reference<br><br>Documentation of linked communication protocols so that implementation decisions are aligned within the system boundaries<br><br>Documentation that membership includes individuals that represent various levels and perspectives of the system<br><br>Indicators of an evidence-based selection process, team functioning and decision making, communication, structure, and membership |

| | | with decision-making power | |
|---|---|---|---|
| **Core Competencies** | **… in place …** | **… so that the Implementation Team…** | **… can produce…** |
| Know the intervention /strategy (Formal and Practice Knowledge) | Demonstrate knowledge, skills, competencies related to assuring the ongoing high fidelity use of an effective innovation related to the problem and context<br><br>Demonstrate fluency in the effective innovation<br><br>Operationalize less-well defined features of the innovation or strategy (meets Usable Innovation criteria) | Can promote implementation and integration of effective innovations with a full appreciation of the core components, underlying theories, philosophies, and nuance of the approaches<br><br>Can facilitate discussions related to "form" vs. "function;" adjustments or "adaptations" (to include when it is time to reach out to the innovation expert (or program developer)<br><br>Can develop the necessary implementation infrastructure (Drivers; Teams) | Intervention/strategy performance assessment /fidelity assessment data<br><br>Systematic feedback from clients, supervisors, and managers related to purpose and experience of the innovation<br><br>Practice Profiles for interventions when additional development is necessary for effective use in practice |

| Core Competencies | ... in place ... | ... so that the Implementation Team... | ... can produce... |
|---|---|---|---|
| Know Implementation (Formal and Practice Knowledge) | Demonstrate knowledge, skills, abilities related to stage-based activities<br><br>Demonstrate knowledge, skills, abilities related to Drivers, Stages, Improvement Cycles<br><br>Demonstrate use of implementation best practices (can be observed or self-report)<br><br>Demonstrate use of knowledge, skills and abilities related to infrastructure / Drivers analysis<br><br>Demonstrate use of knowledge, skills and abilities to support the development of adaptive leadership skills to support necessary changes | Can successfully guide the implementation process, attending to the key activities of each stage to create a successful foundation for the activities of the next stage<br><br>Can facilitate the development and institutionalization of implementation capacity throughout the organization and system<br><br>Can support and ensure that other levels of the system know their role in supporting the intervention / strategy | Implementation Stages Assessment<br><br>Assessment of Drivers Best Practices<br><br>Systematic feedback from "line staff," supervisors, and managers related to the available supports in place to develop competencies and the organizational and systems environment (barriers and facilitators) |

| Core Competencies | ... in place ... | ... so that the Implementation Team... | ... can produce... |
|---|---|---|---|
| Know Improvement Cycles | Demonstrate active use of skills and abilities to apply Improvement Cycles<br><br>Demonstrate active use of required communication skills and abilities to support problem-solving, receiving feedback, and providing conceptual feedback to promote advanced, nuanced thinking<br><br>Demonstrate action planning (PDSAC)<br><br>Demonstrate use of data for decision making<br><br>Demonstrate functional engagement of leadership<br><br>Demonstrate institutionalized feedback loop including practice-policy feedback loops | Can support the ongoing use of assessment and data (e.g., Drivers analysis) to improve competencies and the organization and system context<br><br>Can identify and address problems and barriers (to include general capacity issues)<br><br>Can develop and follow-through on action planning<br><br>Can model commitment to and the use of conceptual feedback (to support on-going improvement) | Assessment of Drivers Best Practices<br><br>Evidence of successful use of practice-policy feedback loops<br><br>Evidence of functioning communication protocols<br><br>Systematic feedback from recipients, "line staff," supervisors, and managers related to the ease of communicating barriers and facilitators and the responsiveness of the system in addressing barriers |

| Core Competencies | ... in place ... | ... so that the Implementation Team... | ... can produce... |
|---|---|---|---|
| Know Systemic Change | Active use of knowledge, skills, and abilities related to Systemic Change, system building<br><br>Focus on system components such as:<br><br>• Context<br>• Mindsets (values, assumptions, attitudes, mental models)<br>• Connections among units | Can be engaged in and support efforts to improve access, reach, or scale<br><br>Can be engaged in strengthening, improving, and promoting the development of additional relationships and connections across different system actors to support critical systems components (resulting in improved "user" experience and increased efficiencies)<br><br>Can become more skilled at influencing decision makers (increased understanding of how decisions are made within the system, who participates, and who can influence decision makers)<br><br>Can be engaged in and facilitate efforts to adjust policies, practices and procedures that regulate system behavior | Evidence of increased and improved implementation capacity and infrastructure supports<br><br>Evidence of improved relationships/connections across key system units and partners<br><br>Evidence of increased understanding of who and how decisions are made within the system and increased success in efforts to influence decisions<br><br>Evidence of necessary adjustments to system policies<br><br>Evidence of functioning feedback mechanisms across system actors<br><br>Systematic feedback from key system partners related to the ease of communications and the responsiveness of the partner organization in addressing barriers |

| | | Can be engaged in and support efforts to increase awareness of attitudes, values, and beliefs that direct current system behavior and practices | |
|---|---|---|---|
| | | Can be engaged in and facilitate efforts to strengthening feedback mechanisms across various system actors | |

Given the scope of responsibilities and depth of knowledge and skills outlined in Table 27, Implementation Teams sound like unicorns or other mythical creatures. There is no magic. It is hard work. The hard work is going on right now in nearly every organization to improve quality, follow clinical guidelines more closely, make organization functioning more efficient and less costly, improve patient relations, and so on. The people are there, the effort is there, the will is there, the funds are there—what is missing is implementation expertise to align, integrate, and leverage current efforts so the hard work pays off more often for more beneficiaries.

## Implementation Team selection criteria

Given the key role of Implementation Teams and the multiple functions of team members, members are selected using best practices. In an interview process involving discussion, scenarios, and role plays, Implementation Team members are selected for their general skills and abilities. The experience of candidates may have been successful or not; the important thing is that they have some experience doing something in each area.

- Using or supporting the attempted use of one or more different innovations or evidence-based practices
- Using data and presenting data for problem-solving and improvement of organization and system functioning
- Using interpersonal communication (verbal and written) and collaboration skills
- Accepting and responding to critical feedback constructively

237

- Building and developing teams;
- Supporting attempts to use innovations or evidence based practices in human service settings; and
- Recognizing and responding to important issues, needs, and data (good judgement).

Each candidate may not have experiences related to all of the areas but should possess some experience with each skill or ability and be excellent in several.

An important consideration is to select team members who have a variety of strengths so the team as a whole can be successful in the complex world of change. Each person can add to the "collective competency" of a team (Zaccaro, Blair, Peterson, & Zazanis, 1995). Once a team is formed, the shared competencies lead to redundant knowledge, skills, and abilities within a team where the whole (group knowledge) is reflected in each part (individual team member) (Morgan & Ramirez, 1983). Redundancy does not mean duplication of effort.

Selection, as an implementation variable, is an Implementation Driver and described fully in Chapter 9.

## Implementation Team operations

Implementation Team members are accountable for assuring the full and effective use of innovations. However, the members do not do all the work themselves. They do it, find it, or create it. For example, an innovation may not be well known to the team. In that case, they can find those who are experts in the innovation and include them in designing implementation supports for the innovation (e.g., content for training and coaching). Or, an innovation may be a good idea that does not meet any of the Usable Innovation criteria. In that case, the Implementation Team engages in usability testing (an Improvement Cycle) to create a Usable Innovation. With each experience of doing it, finding it, or creating it, the Implementation Team gets stronger with a larger and more varied set of knowledge, skills, and abilities.

A critical mass is the minimum number of people on a team needed to effectively and efficiently conduct a range of required activities and sustain effectiveness and efficiency during growth and change.

Keeping in mind that implementation is for solving problems and achieving and sustaining goals for whole populations, Implementation Teams are *teams* and not individuals who might occasionally work together. When an individual is the "change agent," all of the learning and

238

skill and institutional memory is gone when that person leaves the position. On the other hand, teams are sustainable (Klest, 2014; Walker et al., 2003) with sufficient critical mass to replenish themselves as staff turnover occurs in the team (Morgan, 1997). Structurally they are a unit within an organization, their roles are part of the organization, their functions are included in policies and procedures, and their knowledge, skills, and abilities are regularly assessed.

The three-five individuals who are the Implementation Team are accountable for assuring the Implementation Drivers are in place, are functioning as intended, and are improving with experience and data. As shown in Figure 31, they do not do all the work themselves but they are accountable for seeing that it is done. In an aligned and integrated human service organization, people who work full time in other positions are prepared to provide sections of training workshops, do fidelity assessments, conduct selection interviews, re-write policies and procedures, and so on to assure each of the Implementation Drivers is done as intended with and for all practitioners and others in the organization. An organization may have 500 employees and an Implementation Team of five or six people who assure others are prepared to do their part as needed to support each practitioner (e.g., be trained as a trainer, be prepared to be a high reliability fidelity assessor).

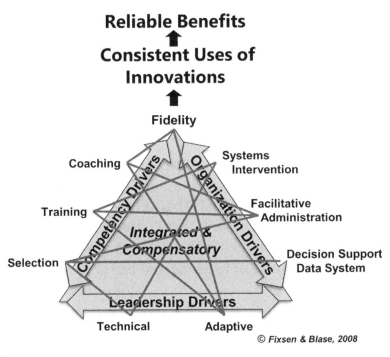

Implementation Teams are an essential part of an organization structure to support full and effective use of innovations within an organization or system. Implementation Teams are the creators of capacity and coherence in otherwise fragmented organizations and systems. In this process, Implementation Teams deal with contradictions and paradoxes. Creating capacity and coherence in otherwise fragmented organizations and systems requires constant adjustment while balancing multiple goals, objectives, and preconceptions.

Figure 31. Implementation Drivers in practice with distributed Implementation Team functions

# Implementation Teams and behavior change

Implementation science, practice, and policy are new to most human service organizations and systems. Knowledge and the use of the implementation knowledge need to be taught and understood initially, then expanded as action planning and execution begin. Using Active Implementation requires considerable face time with practitioners, organization staff, and system staff as well as continual communications between in-person meetings. The interactions provide opportunities for two-way teaching and learning. While teaching, the Implementation Team members need to learn about the people and the context to enhance their effectiveness as intensive implementation support providers.

The Active Implementation teaching and learning method is simple in concept and complex in practice. Teaching Active Implementation entails cycling between a) description and direction, b) Socratic inquiry, c) facilitated discussion and debate, and d) selective recognition of signs of progress.

1. Description and direction: The Implementation Team members name, define, and describe the overall goal and processes for reaching that goal. These statements (often PowerPoint presentations supplemented with handouts) are direct and prescriptive with clear linkages between the concepts, behavior of individuals and groups, and goal attainment.
   a. Implementation science, practice, and policy are not well known or understood. Unambiguous descriptions of the Active Implementation Frameworks and their applications in practice are an essential starting point: this is what needs to be done, this is how to do it, and this is what it means for you and your organization.
   b. Components of the Active Implementation Frameworks are the organizing concepts for all the work that follows. The Implementation Team members return to these concepts repeatedly in many contexts. There is no expectation that the practitioners, organizations, and systems will "get it" the first time or even the third or fourth time they hear it or try to use it. Repeated exposure to the organizing concepts is an essential feature of teaching and learning Active Implementation.
   c. The Active Implementation Frameworks provide the common concepts, common language, and common measures that promote clear communication vertically and horizontally within an organization and system. Alignment and integration are facilitated as a result ("everyone is on the same page").
2. Socratic inquiry: After presentations and during meetings, the Implementation Team members invite discussion and debate of the key points in the description and consider challenges to the descriptions and directions provided.

a. The role of the Implementation Team members is to ask interesting questions about how the concepts might apply to the current work of a unit in the organization.

"Socratic inquiry" is a method for open-ended inquiry in which participants ask probing questions, question their assumptions, and develop a deeper understanding of a topic.

b. True to Socratic inquiry, there is little attempt to lead the conversation one way or another. It is up to the group to use their reasoning to answer questions and respond to one another as they take in the description and direction and consider the implications for their own work. ("OK, what do you make of this information? Is this relevant at all to what is going on here? Can you explain more of your thinking?").
    i. Implementation Team members may reframe topics that arise in a Socratic discussion ("Are we talking about the intervention now? Is that a State policy issue or is it something that can be dealt with locally? That sounds like performance assessment and fidelity; is that what you mean? Could resistance relate back to the Exploration Stage or the Staff Selection Driver?").
        A. Reframing topics helps to relate the experiences of practitioners, organizations, and systems to particular aspects of the Active Implementation Frameworks.
    ii. Implementation Team members pay close attention to the learners' level of understanding of the implementation frameworks. They also tune into where the frameworks are a good fit, where there are obvious challenges, and how readily the group is willing to consider alternative ways of work to approach solving persistent problems. The status quo is strong and resilient and comfortable, so it may require a few iterations and false starts before new ways of work begin to be used and produce results.
c. As the descriptions and directions are repeated over several occasions, and as the practitioners, organization staff, and system staff gain understanding and experience, the conversations deepen and become more sophisticated (e.g., bringing linkages among components into the conversation; integrated and compensatory).
    i. The practitioners, organization staff, and system staff come to see where more and more of their current activities/ problems/ successes fit into the frameworks. The frameworks become more "real and relevant" with each discussion.

241

3. Facilitated discussion: Based on the information gained through Socratic inquiry, Implementation Team members facilitate organized discussions with practitioners, organization staff, and system staff.
   a. The Implementation Team members use the specifics gained through Socratic inquiry to contextualize how they teach the concepts embedded in the frameworks, then use the frameworks to help make sense of the specifics.
      i. The heart of teaching Active Implementation is the use of current and contextual examples to exemplify the conceptual frameworks and the use of the conceptual Active Implementation Frameworks to organize and explain contextual examples.
   b. The agenda is designed to identify and describe strengths and how those strengths relate to the overall frameworks; identify and describe challenges; and explain again why overcoming those challenges is critical to carrying out the components of the frameworks to achieve the goals of the practitioners, organization staff, and system staff.
   c. In facilitated discussions the Implementation Team members re-state the frameworks (again!) and relate current specifics to the components of the frameworks. This is an example of moving from making lists (facilitators, barriers, complaints) to making sense (the frameworks).
   d. Facilitated discussions occur repeatedly as the process of developing implementation capacity unfolds. The theme always is the same (the concepts related to the frameworks) while the topics change to focus on what needs to be taught and learned to allow the work to progress at each point in time (just enough, just in time).
      i. The complexity of the discussion increases as the work progresses and the levels of understanding of the conceptual frameworks expand. One may think of this as moving from a quick sketch to a fully completed painting by a landscape artist.
4. Selective recognition: As the first three steps are repeated (many times), the practitioners, organization staff, and system staff move from a receptive mode (I am listening and learning the information) to a generative mode (I am understanding and using the information in novel ways). Organization and system staff begin using the concepts in conversations with one another, in statements in meetings, and in written documents.
   a. Any generative use of the concepts is heavily reinforced by the Implementation Team members (moving from rule-generated to contingency-shaped behavior).
      i. The (usually unprompted) generative uses of the concepts embodied in the frameworks are the first indication of "understanding" and preparation for action. This is an exciting development!

242

ii. The accuracy and completeness of the generative uses of the concepts are the next order of business. Shaping on the accuracy and completeness of generative uses of the concepts usually can be approached tangentially by "agreeing" with the generative statement and adding the more accurate and complete information as part of the "agreement" statement.

   A. Make the agreement as descriptive and as complimentary to the person as possible! This is a big deal!

iii. It is OK to go on to explain further "what the person said" to clarify any important errors in the generative statement. Often, whatever is incomplete or slightly inaccurate doesn't really matter in the context and the restatement of "what the person said" can leave out those parts (keep them in mind for a later facilitated discussion instead of attending to it in the moment).

"Descriptive praise" describes the appropriate behavior (what the person said or did, like an instant replay), adds a concept label (labels the behavior as an example of some aspect of the Active Implementation Frameworks), provides a rationale (importance of the concept for facilitating and supporting change), and a generalization statement (when you do this in these kinds of situations, then these good things are more likely to happen).

   A. Any correction that is needed typically is done by adding some information a few minutes later–there is no way Implementation Team members want to "make a person wrong" when the person has just (for the first time!) used a concept in a generative mode!

The components of 1) description and direction, 2) Socratic inquiry, 3) facilitated discussion and debate, and 4) selective recognition of signs of progress are used repeatedly in various meetings with expanding groups of Implementation Teams, organization staff, and system staff. Often these meetings occur over a period of a few months before enough members of the group are in a generative mode regarding the concepts and the uses of the concepts in their daily practices.

Teaching Active Implementation takes skill and "active patience." The Implementation Team members need to be confident in their knowledge of Implementation Science and best practices. The patience that is required does not mean standing by waiting for things to happen. Active patience is required to begin in a directive-prescriptive mode to set the stage; back off to allow people to struggle with the ideas and the potential application of the ideas; step back into a more directive "teaching role" in facilitated discussions; then step up the intensity of action planning as sufficient glimmers of generative uses of the concepts begin to appear among multiple members of the group. The Implementation Team members work hard to produce the desired results while remaining patient with the process. Each group starts at a different place and requires more or less cycling through the components of teaching method. For this process to be effective:

1. Good judgment is required and needs to be exercised at each point–when to be directive or Socratic, when to teach or back off and let them struggle, when to move into action planning and doing. Sophisticated Implementation Team members often describe how they "leaned in" at some point in a discussion, that is, exercised the judgement to be more directive and capture a teachable moment in the midst of an otherwise Socratic group discussion.
2. The Implementation Team members always are expecting the best while holding low tolerances for errors that potentially derail the process. High expectations and low tolerances do not translate into punitive behavior. They do translate into more intensive work done by Team members in a positive and supportive way to reduce errors and improve results.
3. The Implementation Team members have a propensity to move more quickly into action while maintaining a willingness to back up and use one or more of the Active Implementation teaching components when action is not forthcoming.
   a. The Implementation Team members err on the side of urgency.
   b. Adequate preparation is continually assessed against the ability to do the work of implementation competently and confidently.

With the emergence of reasonably accurate generative uses of the concepts associated with Implementation Science, organization change, and system reinvention, a new Implementation Team is ready to move more fully into action planning and creating implementation capacity in the organization, state, or national department. To proceed to action planning prematurely is an invitation to failure. Ultimately, it is the daily decisions of those closest to the action that determine the fate of human services (Darling-Hammond & McLaughlin, 1995; Leonard-Barton & Kraus, 1985). Those people are practitioners, organization staff, and system staff, not Implementation Team members. Thus, intensive work using the Active Implementation teaching and learning methods can lead to long-term generalized implementation capacity that is effective and sustained in an organization, state, or national department.

## Related research

Years ago the Center for Research on Utilization of Scientific Knowledge (CRUSK) was perhaps the first organized group to attempt to define, develop, and support the use of identified implementation methods in practice and research (Havelock, 1969; Tornatzky et al., 1980). Havelock and Havelock (1973) wrote a book on training for change agents to support the use of innovations in practice. They noted that change agents "advocate, organize, and agitate" to produce change. They trained change agents to be catalysts (prod and pressure, overcome inertia, create dissatisfaction, get things started), solution givers (know what and when, where, to whom to deliver assistance; technical proficiency), process helpers (recognize and define needs, diagnose problems and set objectives, acquire needed resources, select or create solutions, adapt or install solutions, evaluate to determine progress), and resource linkers (people, time, motivation, funds). They defined many functions of modern Implementation Teams.

In an intensive and iterative study of teams, Walker et al. (2003) conducted systematic direct observations of 72 meetings of 26 teams functioning under a variety of conditions in human services. The teams functioned as change agents to identify, organize, and assure the coordinated delivery of individualized services for children with serious behavioral and emotional problems and for their families. Many of the supports Walker et al. (2003) identified for team development and sustained high-functioning can be found in the Active Implementation Frameworks with an emphasis on Exploration Stage considerations, Leadership Drivers, Competency Drivers, Organization Drivers, and Improvement Cycles.

Based on the observed performance and outcomes of the teams, they identified the necessary conditions for high-functioning teams:

a. Team adheres to meeting structures, techniques, and procedures that support high quality planning,
b. Team considers multiple alternatives before making decisions,
c. Team adheres to high fidelity use of well-defined practice models,
d. Team adheres to procedures, techniques and/or structures that work to counteract power imbalances between and among providers and families,
e. Team facilitates training and coaching to help others learn the philosophy underlying the practice models and the specific procedures and skills that help them to be strengths-based, culturally competent, and family-centered while also managing meetings effectively.
f. Team uses structures and techniques that lead all members to feel that their input is valued,
g. Team builds agreement around plans despite differing priorities and diverging mandates, and manages conflict,
h. Team builds an appreciation of strengths, and
i. Team planning reflects cultural competence.

They noted the extent to which "the necessary conditions are in place at the organizational and system levels provides a means for pushing accountability upward as well as downward" (p 11). They identified different configurations of organization and system support for teams:

1. The independent team (low organization support, low system support),
2. The single agency program (high organizational support, low system support),
3. Newly developing system of care (high or low organizational support, low to moderate system support) and
4. Integrated system of care (high organizational support, high system support).

Independent teams tended to be led by a few highly committed individuals who often "did it themselves" in the absence of organization and system supports. This led to uncertainty on the part of families being served and likely lessened the impact of services provided by the committed few. They noted the members of the single-agency program approach (with low system support) experienced relatively greater stress because they were constantly negotiating exceptions with counterparts in other agencies and systems with no end in sight. Thus, Systemic Change is essential for teams to function and sustain their impact on recipients.

Community development teams (CDTs) also share many of the goals and activities of an Implementation Team. Saldana and Chamberlain (2012) describe how CDT members help community leaders and potential implementing agencies understand and successfully launch an innovation (Exploration Stage, Installation Stage, Initial Implementation Stage); orient the site leadership toward fidelity and help make adjustments both within the organization and the practice to improve the chances of success (Facilitative Administration; Improvement Cycles); help the organization develop innovation-specific data collection methods and use data to monitor fidelity and change behavior (Decision Support Data System); and establish the capacity to assure timely and effective training, coaching, and data collection (Implementation Drivers). An evaluation of the CDTs showed modest impact on the use of an effective innovation (Brown et al., 2014). However, the data are difficult to interpret without an assessment of the fidelity of CDT functioning (i.e., the presence and strength of the independent variable–the CDT–at each site).

Facilitation has been defined as "a deliberate, interactive process of problem-solving and support that occurs in the context of a recognized need for assistance" (Smith et al., 2018). Elledge, Avworo, Cochetti, Carvalho, and Grota (2018) conducted a review of the literature regarding the central role of "facilitation" in the uptake of innovations in clinical settings. They listed "facilitator skills" as:

- Planning: identifies the practice issue; develops a strategic plan; frames knowledge to make it understandable; increases awareness related to practice issue
- Leading: develops strategic partnerships; supports administrative (fiscal and contract) management; navigates systems; engages stakeholders
- Monitoring: manages the project; problem-solves; mediates; communicates with stakeholders; provides ongoing support
- Evaluating: assesses outcomes

A multi-national randomized controlled trial attempted to test different methods of facilitation (Seers et al., 2018). There were no statistically significant differences in patient outcomes between the groups. However, the data are difficult to interpret without an assessment of the independent variable–facilitation in each organization–to provide an indication of its presence and strength within each human service organization. Nevertheless, facilitation is viewed as a critical component of leading change efforts (Berta et al., 2015).

The view of the role of an Implementation Team corresponds with the role of a change agent in the ARC (Availability, Responsiveness and Continuity) approach (Glisson & Schoenwald, 2005). Like Implementation Teams, ARC change agents span organization and system boundaries to share information among individuals, groups, organizations, and communities; provide updates about innovation efforts; diagnose problems in the process of improving services; motivate community interest in innovation; create interpersonal networks that include community opinion leaders; reinforce efforts to improve services; and prevent discontinuance of improvement strategies that are working.

The PARIHS framework (Rycroft-Malone, 2004) also acknowledges the need for organized facilitation of implementation, and notes that the purpose of facilitation can vary from a focused process to achieve a specific task to a more complex, holistic process of enabling teams and individuals to analyze, reflect, and change their own attitudes, behaviors, and ways of working. As the approach moves toward holistic, facilitation is increasingly concerned with addressing the whole situation. To fulfill the potential demands of the role, facilitators likely will need a wide repertoire of skills and attributes (Seers et al., 2018; Smith et al., 2018; Van Dyke, 2015).

Others note the complexity involved in using innovations in practice without describing who is supposed to have the knowledge, skills, and abilities to put into action the components outlined in the framework. For example, Damschroder et al. (2009) propose that successful implementation usually requires an active change process aimed to achieve individual and organizational level use of the intervention as designed. Hoped-for local champions or external-change agents are expected to establish and manage processes that are aimed at producing the use of an innovation as intended. Aarons et al. (2011) have framework components that describe the extensive work required to assess a broad range of psychological characteristics of practitioners and managers, and assess organizational fit, readiness, culture, and climate. This work is said to be conducted by "interorganizational networks" that encourage the implementation of innovations.

Chinman et al. (2004) emphasizes the key role of a community coalition for planning successful implementation, and Wandersman et al. (2008) identify innovation-specific support (innovation-specific capacity building) and general support (general capacity building) provided by those community coalitions. A community coalition can include activities such as providing information about an innovation before an organization decides if it wants to adopt and providing technical assistance once the innovation is in use.

## Assessing Implementation Team functioning

As teams begin to function, Implementation Team assessment is conducted with the Assessing Drivers Best Practices measure (Fixsen, Ward, Blase, et al., 2018). This measure provides indicators of the presence and strength of the Implementation Drivers as they are used to support practitioners. Organization- and system-change outcomes of Implementation Teams can be measured repeatedly with capacity assessments that have been in use in education systems (Fixsen, Ward, Duda, et al., 2015; St. Martin, Ward, Harms, Russell, & Fixsen, 2015; Ward et al., 2015) and other systems (Glisson, Green, & Williams, 2012; R. M. Goodman, McLeroy, Steckler, & Hoyle, 1993; McGovern et al., 2007).

As teams develop, the Active Implementation Team that is developing new teams (noted as Ai Experts in Table 28) can use the "look fors" outlined below to organize observations of Implementation Team meetings and organize constructive feedback to team members.

**Table 28.** Key elements of an Implementation Team meeting. Based on original work by Caryn Ward and Dale Cusumano (2017) and the State Implementation and Scaling up of Evidence-based Programs Center

Implementation Team Look Fors*

*Look Fors* identify best practices teams and staff use to facilitate meetings, learning exercises, and coaching sessions. Items are recorded as observed or not observed during the session with an example of the behavior or permanent product observed. Observation data are used to guide feedback and support in order to improve facilitation of various implementation activities.

Ai Expert _____  Team Lead _____  Date: _____

Implementation Team Members: _____

Meeting Facilitator(s): _____  Observer: _____

Location: _____  Meeting Topic: _____

Enter Meeting Agenda:

**Directions:** Insert an "x" or "☐" in the box to indicate that the behavior was observed and/or notes are included. In the section below the item, include behaviors observed or permanent products that serve as examples of the item. As a reminder, indicators do not produce scores but instead serve as guides for coaching support from the Ai Expert team.

Basic Meeting Protocol/Technical Items

☐ Appropriate IT **members** and others as necessary are in **attendance** (sign in sheet):

Behaviors or Permanent Products Observed:

_____

☐ **Roles** assigned and used: Facilitators, Note Taker, Timekeeper, etc.

Behaviors or Permanent Products Observed:

_____

☐ Previous meeting notes reviewed:

Behaviors or Permanent Products Observed:

_____

☐ Meeting goals and objectives reviewed and agreed upon:

Behaviors or Permanent Products Observed:

_____

☐ Process to record items tabled for discussion in next or future meetings is used:

Behaviors or Permanent Products Observed:

_____

☐ Feedback on meeting effectiveness collected and discussed (e.g., helpful, respectful, solution-oriented; pre-post assessment of learning):

Behaviors or Permanent
Products Observed: _____

☐ Action plan to address items from meeting effectiveness questions developed or scheduled for next meeting:

Behaviors or Permanent
Products Observed: _____

Planning for Ongoing Improvement Cycles

☐ Current **Action Plan reviewed** and linked to current meeting goals and objectives (reviewed next):

Behaviors or Permanent
Products Observed: _____

☐ **Guiding questions** relevant to the activities used:

Behaviors or Permanent
Products Observed: _____

☐ Data were used to guide all decision making:

Behaviors or Permanent
Products Observed: _____

☐ **Specific descriptive** (behavior-based) **feedback** (positive and constructive) is provided on completed IT action items:

Behaviors or Permanent Products Observed:

_____

☐ Clear meeting summary of **identified next right steps** on part of the IT(s) (e.g., action items, sharing of resources) is reviewed.

Behaviors or Permanent Products Observed:

_____

☐ Time is scheduled to engage in **Study and Act** (e.g., debrief) for identification of implications for the specific team being met with and actions of the facilitators.

Behaviors or Permanent Products Observed:

_____

Implementation Instruction and Generalizing

☐ **Explicit teaching** (5-15 minutes mini-lesson) of Active Implementation best practices provided (e.g., Implementation Stage-based work, criteria for Usable Innovation, implementation plan drivers, teams, improvement cycles):

Behaviors or Permanent Products Observed:

_____

☐ **Best practices** in **adult learning** are used in mini-lesson (e.g., content linked to current work or experience, review previous prerequisite learning, modeling of skills, behavior rehearsals with feedback, explicit explanations of critical components and details of adaptations are provided):

Behaviors or Permanent
Products Observed:

_____

☐ **Rationales** for meeting objectives provided as objectives are introduced:

Behaviors or Permanent
Products Observed:

_____

☐ **Explicit connections** to other implementation practices, frameworks, and tools made when appropriate (e.g., assessing fit on heptagon tool–connect to initiative inventory work; assessing capacity and action planning–connect to implementation assessment data collection)

Behaviors or Permanent
Products Observed:

_____

☐ All activities include use of the following question to support generalization: *How is this related or could be used for other work/initiatives?*

Behaviors or Permanent
Products Observed:

_____

☐ Pre-post knowledge and/or skill assessment of objectives used with answers reviewed (if applicable):

Behaviors or Permanent
Products Observed:

_____

Managing Adaptive Challenges

253

☐ Facilitation activities used to **engage all voices** of IT (e.g., use of nominal group process, small group activities)

Behaviors or Permanent Products Observed:

_____

☐ Reminders provided as needed of the **"way of this work"**–learning together, creating systems, ambiguous at times, un-comfortableness OK at times, use of adaptive strategies when appropriate (e.g., protecting voices, identifying adaptive challenges)

Behaviors or Permanent Products Observed:

_____

☐ Review of **Information** (e.g., **Issues/Barriers/Facilitators**) to be **communicated** (up a level, down a level, and out five years):

Behaviors or Permanent Products Observed:

_____

Comments/Notes/Recommendations:

Operationalize and generalize: Use a few specific examples from the meeting related to a general concept, then use the concept to generalize the feedback to a range of examples likely to be encountered.

# Chapter 15: Systemic Change

To produce socially significant outcomes for whole populations, enabling systems must be established, sustained, and improved. The Systemic Change framework has evolved from extensive experience at the state and national levels and from the literature on organization and system development and change. The feedback loops are long: it takes several years to see patterns and outcomes. Since 2007 the Systemic Framework has come together and been tested as described in this chapter.

## Organizations and systems

Implementation requires changes in practices and organization supports for practices. And, there are factors that affect the opportunity for innovations to be used at all. For Active Implementation, the question is: in what environment does change need to occur? Practitioners, managers, and leaders always are employed in an entity. "Employed" (https://www.dictionary.com) means selected and "paid by" (e.g., staff; contractors) or "used by" (e.g., volunteers) an entity (organization, system, or community). Systems operate outside of organizations and influence a number of organizations via policies, procedures, regulations, funding formulae, and so on. Practitioners, organizations, and systems are embedded in communities that are collections of people with social norms, political views, religious affiliations, neighborhood and village routines, clan and family allegiances, and so on.

*Systemic Change is essential for producing population benefits. Effective implementation supports and the use of effective innovations are new ways of work that are not part of the status quo. Systems must change and new structures, roles, and functions must be established to sustain and improve outcomes over time. The goal is not just to change a system one time for a while. Instead, the goal is to establish and sustain an enabling context for implementation and innovations.*

# Focal entity

Implementation can be used to support innovations in any of these environments. This chapter's primary focus is on practitioners using innovations in organizations in a system to benefit recipients. The focus of behavior change could be managers and directors who are learning leadership-related innovations (Baron, Watson, Coughlin, Fixsen, & Phillips, 1979; Mosson, von Thiele Schwarz, Hasson, Lundmark, & Richter, 2018). Or, the focus may be on directors or units of government who are learning new ways to fund initiatives and implementation supports and to monitor fidelity at the point of delivery (Robbins & Collins, 2010; Voit, 1995). Or, the focus may be on citizens who are part of a neighborhood volunteer group using innovations to support others in the community (Hawkins et al., 2002; Jacobs et al., 2018; Salazar et al., 2016).

In each of these instances, the people who are learning an innovation are employed by an entity of some kind. The Active Implementation Frameworks apply equally in each instance to support those who are learning to use innovations, using those innovations with fidelity, and sustaining the use of innovations and their benefits. In each instance there also is the world beyond the entity. "Beyond the entity" means that the entity itself does not employ the individuals who live and work in the environment beyond the entity.

These are important distinctions. Whose behavior is the focus of implementation efforts and in what entity are they employed? It is important to keep the focus even in the midst of coping with the difficulties of change.

Systemic Change is essential for producing population benefits. Effective implementation supports and the use of effective innovations are new ways of work that are not part of the status quo. Systems must change, and new structures, roles, and functions must be established to sustain and improve outcomes over time. The goal is not just to change a system one time for a while. Instead, the goal is to establish and sustain an enabling context for implementation and innovations.

The benefits of a Systemic Change process are described by VanDeusen Lukas et al. (2007, p. 318):

"Alignment increased the likelihood that specific redesign would build momentum for further change as staff understood how their roles in achieving project objectives contributed to larger organizational goals. Integration facilitated redesign efforts by ensuring that all parts of the organization affected by redesign engaged in the redesign process, by fostering implementation through shared lines of communication and authority, and by resolving conflicting priorities and needs when multiple improvement projects affected common systems. This fundamentally changed how work was done throughout the organization, an important building block of sustainability."

Rycroft-Malone (2004) adds that a strong context is one where "there is clarity of roles, decentralized decision making, valuing of staff, transformational leaders, and a reliance on multiple sources of information on performance ... An additional component of the environment that seems to play a role in shaping its readiness for implementation is that of evaluation. Measurement generates evidence on which to base practice and is part of the evaluation or feedback process that demonstrates whether or not changes to practices are appropriate, effective, and/or efficient."

For example, in global health, Dohrn, Nzama, and Murrman (2009, p. S29) describe the need for systemic change:

"The profound impact of the HIV epidemic in South Africa has triggered a reappraisal of the role of nurses. With appropriate support, nurses can dramatically enhance access to health services, including those required for the care and treatment of complex and chronic diseases. Policy-level support is needed to establish the regulatory and professional frameworks to authorize expanded scopes of work. Training and credentialing systems need to be adapted, curricula standardized at basic and advanced levels, and access to continuing education supported. At the clinical level, support is needed for the redefinition of roles and job responsibilities within the health care team, including implementation of task shifting, mentoring, and community mobilization, and retention and support strategies."

Thus, the entire system for preparing and supporting nurses needed to change in substantive ways so that the HIV epidemic could be stemmed for the population in South Africa.

How to create alignment and a strong context is the work guided by the Systemic Change framework.

## Engaging executive leadership for change

Systemic Change begins with the Exploration Stage. National Implementation Teams or other external facilitators engage in Exploration Stage activities with leaders and staff to establish the need for system change. They also help to create the readiness, willingness, and ability of system leaders and others to engage in Systemic Change processes. The perceived need for change must be great enough, important enough, and documented well enough to merit engaging in purposeful Systemic Change. Needs are apparent when viewing racial and economic disparities in literacy, rates of maternal and child mortality, lack of access to food and clean water and sanitation, and so on. Willingness is created and expanded during the

Exploration process by assuring stakeholders and affected groups are informed and are informing the change process and are prepared to "do their part." Readiness is created by planning access to human and financial resources required to begin the process. Attempting system change in the absence of Exploration Stage activities is risky business and substantially reduces the chances for success (Maar et al., 2015; Panzano & Billings, 1994; Romney et al., 2014; Saldana et al., 2012).

Once executive leadership is well informed and is ready for Systemic Change, creating alignment and a strong enabling context is guided by the Systemic Change framework where bottom-up change is accomplished with top-down support (Darling-Hammond & McLaughlin, 1995).

## Systemic Change framework

The Systemic Change framework is the product of extensive reviews of the literatures across disciplines, examination of examples of attempted system change efforts, and learning from intensive and purposeful work to change large systems. Some examples of documented experience and data related to Systemic Change are accumulating (Fixsen et al., 2013; Foege, 2011; Folker & Lauridsen, 2017; Glennan Jr. et al., 2004; Huaynoca, Chandra-Mouli, Yaqub Jr, & Denno, 2013; Khatri & Frieden, 2002; J. A. Klein, 2004; Kotter, 1996; Morgan & Ramirez, 1983; Nord & Tucker, 1987; Omimo et al., 2018; J. M. Prochaska et al., 2001; Rossi & Wright, 1984; Schofield, 2004; Solberg, 2007; Solberg, Hroscikoski, Sperl-Hillen, O'Connor, & Crabtree, 2004; Tikkanen, Pyhältö, Soini, & Pietarinen, 2016; Vernez et al., 2006; Watkins, 1995).

The purposeful Active Implementation work in systems has led to the development of Systemic Change methods that are teachable, learnable, doable, and assessable in practice (Fixsen, Ward, Ryan Jackson, et al., 2018; Ryan Jackson et al., 2018). The goal is to assure that the structures, roles, and functions within a system are more enabling than hindering in their impact on the services provided and the degree to which socially significant outcomes can be achieved.

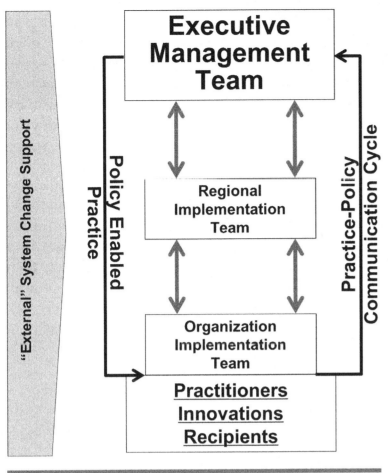

The approach to Systemic Change is illustrated in Figure 32. Executive Management Teams (national, state/ provincial, regional) establish policies and regulations intended to improve practices and improve outcomes for recipients of human services. This is a common component of almost every attempt to encourage improved outcomes. The task of accomplishing change requires an Implementation Team that has the expertise to make full and effective use of the Active Implementation Frameworks to support practitioners learning, using, and sustaining an innovation with fidelity that results in intended outcomes for recipients. Implementation Teams are not commonly available and must be developed to initiate and sustain system change. This is one of the first tasks for the Executive Management Team to initiate and support.

Figure 32. An implementation-informed approach to Systemic Change

## Developing Implementation Teams

The first step toward system change is to begin using an effective innovation with the support of effective implementation in the form of an expert and experienced Implementation Team. The development of expert Implementation Teams and the full and effective use of the Active Implementation Frameworks and innovations in practice disturb the status quo. This allows engagement with the system to discover how *this* unique system currently works and what *particular* aspects of *this* system need to change. General categories of facilitators and barriers are known, but what matters is how they impact change (if at all) in a unique legacy system.

259

When engaged in Systemic Change, positive and negative reactions from individuals and groups impacted by the change process are expected and encouraged. To cope with the often unpredictable content of these reactions, the Implementation Team has frequent Practice-Policy Communication with the Executive Management Team so the leaders can constructively intervene, clear barriers, and strengthen facilitators. Based on this recursive feedback cycle, legacy systems are changed in functional ways, and innovations are not crushed by the already established routines that sustain the status quo (Nord & Tucker, 1987).

The next step is to expand the number of Implementation Teams so that more organizations and practitioners are supported in their use of an innovation with fidelity and intended outcomes. Expertise (home-grown talent) that has developed at the Organization Implementation Team level is leveraged to develop the first Implementation Team in a different region (called a Regional Implementation Team in Figure 32). That team then establishes more Organization Implementation Teams and the process of scaling continues until the entire system has access to implementation support for all practitioners (Figure 33). At that point, the system will generate socially significant outcomes for the entire population.

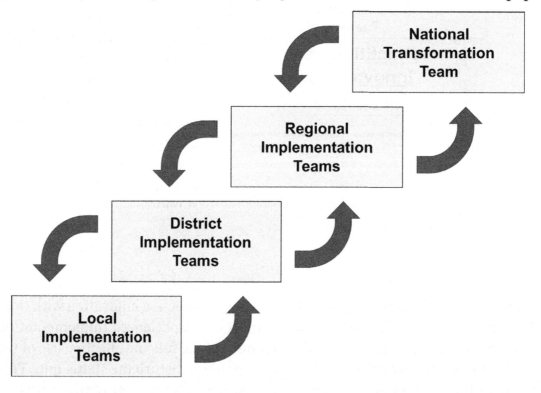

Figure 33. Linked Implementation Teams for implementation capacity development in support of Systemic Change

## Practice-Policy Communication Cycle

The Practice-Policy Communication Cycle (Figure 32) is the timely communication from the practice level to the policy level to inform policymakers of the intended and unintended consequences of their policies and guidelines. The "cycle" is completed as the policy makers create and improve policies and see the results that enable the use of Active Implementation to support the full and effective use of innovations. The cycle continues as those changes are further evaluated for impact and improvement or are deemed functional enough to be embedded in policies and guidelines. With the Practice-Policy Communication Cycle in place and Implementation Teams functioning as sensors of alignment and misalignment at the practice level, the Executive Management Team has the ability to continually "monitor and question the context in which it is operating and to question the rules that underlie its own operation" (Morgan & Ramirez, 1983, p. 15).

During Exploration and Installation, the Executive Management Team must be prepared for frequent (weekly, monthly) Practice-Policy Communication from the front line via the Implementation Team and be prepared to engage in constructive problem solving with stakeholders within and outside the system. As roles, functions, and structures are strengthened and barriers are eliminated, coherence is created as system components and resources are aligned with announced system goals and intended outcomes.

Practice-Policy Communication changes Executive Management Team members' views of problems and potential solutions. Monthly meetings with the Executive Management Team help to assure continual feedback on past decisions (before the knowledge becomes obsolete) and continual input into new decisions on how to proceed with Systemic Change (just in time to be useful). This is especially important because Implementation Science is not part of the typical education or preparation of system leaders. Practice-Policy Communication is a forum for teaching and learning about implementation and its importance and application in human service systems and organizations. Changing the views and understanding of executive leaders is an important outcome that must be earned continually with changes in leadership.

## External System Change Support

The purpose of the "External" System Change Support shown in Figure 32 is to facilitate the use of the Systemic Change processes. "External" is in quotes because there are ways to have individuals already within an organization perform the external facilitation role ("outsiders within;" Jalava, 2006; J. A. Klein, 2004).

National Implementation Teams, where they exist, can provide external facilitation in the Systemic Change context. The team members are experts in using the Active Implementation

Frameworks to initiate and develop more Implementation Teams, experts in the use of effective innovations to provoke system change, and experts in helping executive leaders manage the change process (Blase, Fixsen, et al., 2005; Fixsen et al., 2013; Fixsen, Ward, Ryan Jackson, et al., 2018). The external facilitation role is initiated in a Transformation Zone within an organization or a system.

## Transformation Zone

In human service systems, services cannot be shut down, reconfigured, re-skilled, and restarted in some new and hopefully more effective mode. The requirement to develop an enabling context in the midst of continuing to operate the legacy system adds yet another degree of complexity to any attempts to purposefully change systems. Consequently, attempts to change whole systems all at once rarely succeed. To the extent system change requires behavior change, the chances of whole-system change is virtually zero (Rossi & Wright, 1984).

> *The requirement to develop an enabling context in the midst of continuing to operate the legacy system adds yet another degree of complexity in attempts to purposefully change systems.*

To prevent change leaders and external facilitators from being overwhelmed by systemic issues that need to be resolved, system change is initiated in a Transformation Zone (Fixsen, Blase, & Van Dyke, 2012). A Transformation Zone is a vertical slice of an entire system from the practice level to the policy level and includes all major levels within the system. The slice is big enough to encounter nearly all the issues that likely will arise in system change, and small enough to keep issues at a manageable level until the beginnings of the "new system" are established and functioning well (see Figure 34).

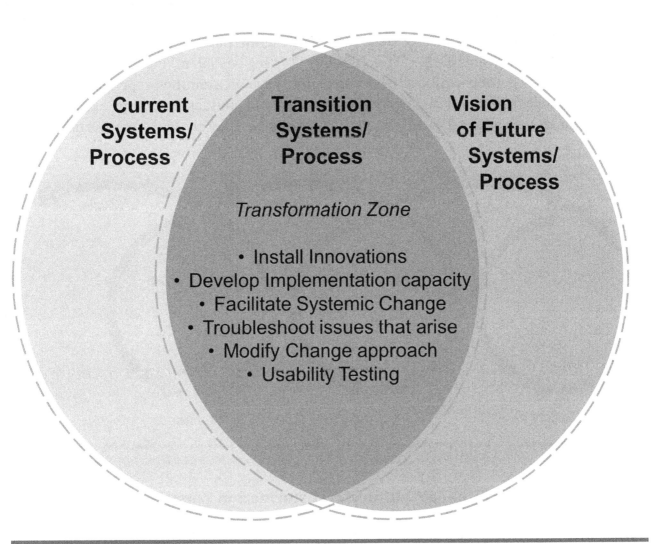

**Current Systems/ Process**

**Transition Systems/ Process**

**Vision of Future Systems/ Process**

*Transformation Zone*

- Install Innovations
- Develop Implementation capacity
- Facilitate Systemic Change
- Troubleshoot issues that arise
- Modify Change approach
- Usability Testing

Figure 34. A Transformation Zone to move from the status quo system to a system designed to support effective innovations and effective implementation

A Transformation Zone is the place to troubleshoot issues that arise and make modifications to develop the features of a "high reliability system" (Weick, 1987) where high fidelity performance leads to consistently high-quality outcomes. According to Weick, high reliability systems start with a centralized structure where a set of core values, decision premises, and assumptions are developed and operationalized so that people can understand, buy into, and engage in new ways of work with direction and support. Doing system-change work in a Transformation Zone has the advantages noted for "continuous delivery" (Humble & Farley, 2011) where enabling system components are established, used, and tested in real time allowing effective functions, roles, and structures to be established and errors to be quickly detected and corrected through use in daily practice. This also is called "reengineering in place" (Ulrich, 2002).

The ideas of continuous delivery and reengineering in place are encompassed in the Improvement Cycle framework. The Usability Testing visual in Figure 35 depicts the recurring cycles of getting started and getting better based on examined experience and data. The Active Implementation Frameworks provide the plan, and facilitation provides support for learning to deliver/implement the plan effectively, efficiently with improvement each time.

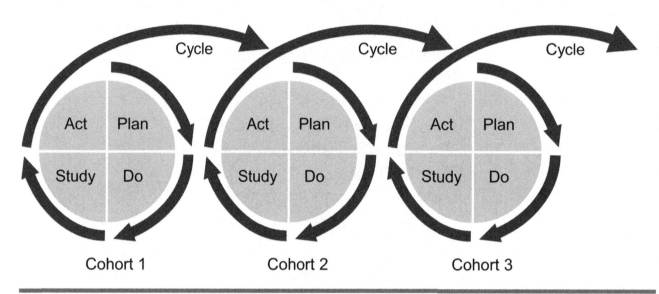

Figure 35. Usability Testing in a Transformation Zone to create an enabling context

**Example of Systemic Change within a Transformation Zone**

In a U.S. state education system with perhaps 2,000 schools and 1.5 million students, a Transformation Zone (the vertical slice) consists of the state superintendent of education and his or her cabinet (the state Executive Management Team), a State Implementation Team, leaders of key divisions of the state education system (the state design team), two or three regions of the state system (out of, perhaps, a dozen or more regions), three districts in each region, and three schools in each district where teachers and staff educate students (Fixsen et al., 2013). In this way, a State Implementation Team and a National Implementation Team (external facilitators) have access to all levels of the legacy system.

As shown in Figure 36, a National Implementation Team (external facilitators) simultaneously works at all levels of a system. As changes in one level impact other levels of the system, the Implementation Team is there to sense the impact and immediately respond. The immediate response typically is to add skills or communication patterns to staff in the affected area to begin to solve a problem. This is a reactive response. When the problem is more systemic, then the problem becomes part of the Practice-Policy Communication with the Executive Management Team. This is a proactive response. Attempting to make changes one level at a time is a losing proposition because changes at one level are met with standard (legacy; not helpful) responses from adjoining levels. Without some way to sense relevant issues and quickly respond to them, changes at one level produce unexpected impacts on other levels and soon overwhelm the change process and discourage making further changes in a resilient system.

# Simultaneous, Multi-Level Interventions

Implementation Team

- Teacher/Staff Competence
- School/District Supports
- Management (leadership, policy)
- Administration (HR, structure)
- Supervision (nature, content)
- Regional Supports
- State/Community Supports
- Federal and National Supports

Figure 36. Implementation Teams and Systemic (multi-level) Change in an education example

It is up to Implementation Teams to support required change at each level and to assure purposeful and productive linkages among levels (align, integrate, leverage).

Initiating and managing change in a Transformation Zone provides opportunities to detect which parts of the legacy system are working and which parts need to change. If the experience described by Ulrich (2002) holds up in human services, only 20% of the status quo may need to be changed to produce significant gains in effectiveness and efficiency. Detecting the 20% that needs to change to vastly improve effectiveness and efficiency is a product of engaging all levels of the system, making changes, and discovering what to keep and what to change based on experience and impact on fidelity. The initial changes occur in a Transformation Zone.

As work progresses in the Transformation Zone, a coherent, aligned, and integrated system is established as the Implementation Teams and the external facilitators develop supports for effective implementation of effective innovations. A purposefully designed system, as it is being established, creates a coherent and aligned set of system components that leverage existing resources and that routinely produce high levels of fidelity.

By developing Regional and Organization Teams that assure the availability of effective implementation supports in an aligned system, Executive Management Teams can delegate responsibility and accountability far down the hierarchy in a task-driven, process-sensitive, outcome-oriented organization. Organizations and systems can trust well-prepared Implementation Teams and practitioners to do the right thing without excessive supervision (Beer, Eisenstat, & Spector, 1990; Jalava, 2006) and can verify that trust with regular assessments of fidelity.

*Creating change in units within a system*

Units within a legacy system have their own legacy structures, roles, and functions. These units sometimes have assignments that are legislated (e.g., monitoring and evaluation) or must adhere to well-established industry professional standards (e.g., finance; human resources) or are governed by contracts within the system (e.g., support for an initiative) or have other reasons for being and doing. Yet, Systemic Change may be impeded by one or more of these operating units. These are adaptive challenges in the zone of complexity where uncertainty and lack of agreement create challenges for leaders and change agents; how to change a unit while it continues to operate in relation to other units within the system and how to carry out Systemic Change without losing the function of the unit or violating any mandated requirements.

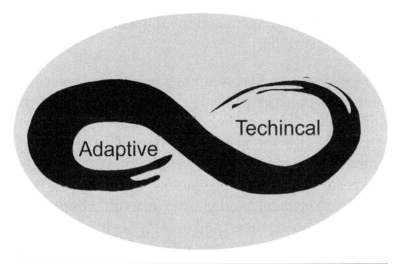

Figure 37. The flow of work in the Transformation Zone

Figure 37 shows the flow of adaptive and technical work in a Transformation Zone. Changing the ways of work within a unit may be more on the technical side where agreement and certainty are better established while the impact on other units may be more on the adaptive side where there is less certainty and agreement. In cases where the ways of work must change while continuing to perform key functions, the change strategy is to centralize and socialize, then decentralize (Dohrn et al., 2009; Unger, Macq, Bredo, & Boelaert, 2000; Useem & Chipande, 1991; Weick, 1987).

In cases where the ways of work must change while continuing to perform key functions, the change strategy is to centralize and socialize, then decentralize.

To **centralize** means that the external facilitators and the Executive Management Team focus their time and energy on changing one unit while sensing and dealing with any impacts on other units within the system. Technical changes to the ways of work (e.g., processes for selecting staff; inclusion of new measures and prompt reporting of useful data in monitoring and evaluation) are taught by the external facilitator and the Implementation Team. The teaching is explicit and based on the best available evidence relative to the functions in that unit. In this process staff in the unit are socialized to the philosophy, values, and methods required to carry out the new ways of work (e.g., meet fidelity requirements for performance of those functions).

To **socialize** means to use the Implementation Drivers so that those employed in the unit know what to do and how to do it and why it is important for those they interact with outside their unit. As the changes are being developed in the unit, the Implementation Team is alert to any impact on other operating units within the system so adjustments can be made quickly in communication or workflow issues. Issues that impact organization policies and procedures are lifted up to the Executive Management Team for prompt action.

Once the changed operating unit performs its functions in the new ways, it is **decentralized** and operates as part of the new culture within the system; it has moved from adaptive work to more standardized technical work.  Executive management and the Implementation Team then can shift their focus to the next unit to be changed.

The infinity image in Figure 37 denotes the expectation that system-change efforts will circle back to each unit in the system.  As other units in a system change and become part of the newly aligned and integrated ways of work, those changes affect all other units in the system in some way, including units recently changed.  It is the nature of systems that yesterday's good example may become today's impediment to progress.  If a given unit is not fully engaged in the process of adjusting its practice to create a more enabling context, then it will be time for the Implementation Team and executive management to once again focus attention on the unit to  better understand the unit's challenge, address them, and develop their competence to make use of the new ways of work that align with the vision and mission.

## Example of creating change in units within a system

Teaching-Parents in Teaching-Family group homes need to have a checking account to pay for groceries, clothing, and incidentals for the youths in their care.  This is an important part of family-style treatment and provides many opportunities for teaching youths how to interact with members of the community in socially appropriate ways.  Checking accounts for front-line practitioners are not part of the status quo, and the idea itself is frowned on by professional bookkeepers and accountants who initially refused to establish a checking account for each group home.

As a part of the external facilitation process, a member of the Implementation Team began working intensively (daily) with the finance unit, gave rationales for the new ways of work and the importance to youth treatment and outcomes, and worked with existing finance staff to develop new forms for Teaching-Parents to provide receipts for expenditures and request funds to replenish the checking account balance (up to $1,000 at that time) as often as needed.  This met an accounting requirement. With support from the Implementation Team member, new bookkeeping formats and categories were developed by finance staff to track expenditures for each Teaching-Family group home checking account.   This met a bookkeeping requirement.  The finance staff also were taught how to give constructive feedback to Teaching-Parents regarding expenses that did not exactly fit the guidelines (e.g., purchase a part to repair the van when, for insurance purposes, van repairs were to be done by a certified dealer).  Once this process was established and practiced, and ancillary issues were resolved (e.g., alerting the accounting firm to the changes in bookkeeping and reporting; reassuring the board regarding accountability), accounting best practices were met, the finance staff were comfortable with their new roles, and checking accounts were supportive of Teaching-Parents. This met the therapeutic requirement.

The director of finance and staff then continued their work in the new mode with normal oversight. This is an example of centralizing a unit, socializing the staff to new ways of work, then decentralizing the new roles and functions. This process is repeated as needed for every unit in the Transformation Zone to establish new ways of work that fully support the use of an innovation with fidelity in order to achieve the intended outcomes in organizations and systems.

## Expanding the Transformation Zone

As the work in the Transformation Zone progresses, fundamental changes in allocation of staff and resources, operating procedures, and communication patterns are established. Common language, common methods, and common measures become the norm and facilitate alignment, integration, and leveraging of existing resources. While this work is progressing, the external facilitators and executive management do Exploration and preparation work with other regions or operating units (e.g., hospitals, clinics, schools, neighborhoods) to create readiness to expand the Transformation Zone. Given the fundamental systemic changes in the first Transformation Zone, the external facilitator and central Implementation Team likely can expand into two or three additional Transformation Zones with the expectation that many of the major system issues have been encountered and dealt with in the first Transformation Zone. Thus, developing implementation capacity to support the use of an innovation likely will encounter fewer difficulties, and the goals of improved outcomes can be reached more quickly. As this work progresses, the remaining regions or units within a system can be prepared, and soon the entire system is within a Transformation Zone and the roles, functions, and structures worked out in the Transformation Zone become the new status quo.

Early experience in complex state education systems suggests that subsequent Transformation Zones begin producing positive outcomes in about half the time required in the first Transformation Zone (Ryan Jackson et al., 2018). Implementation capacity development in additional regions in a state occurs more quickly because many of the systemic issues have been resolved, and because expanded implementation capacity is based on existing implementation capacity already operating in the state.

## Enactment in practice

Systemic Change is initiated when an innovation is introduced to solve a serious problem; that is, Systemic Change is mission driven. In their study of system change, Svensson, Tomson, and Rindzeviciute (2017, p. abstract) conclude, "The resources needed to perform institutional work are created through the enactment of practice."

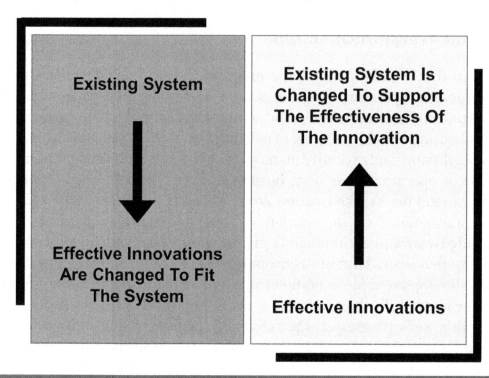

Figure 38. The status quo is powerful and the existing system typically changes (adapts) key features of effective innovations to fit the existing system. Enabling contexts are created when the existing system is changed to support high fidelity and sustained use

The "enactment of practice" is the essence of initiating Systemic Change. As shown on the left side of Figure 38, when effective innovations and effective implementation are introduced into a system, they disturb the status quo and disrupt existing ways of work. When the status quo is disturbed, "local change typically has to fight significant organizational inertia and seldom survives continual attacks from the organization at large" (J. A. Klein, 2004). In the absence of purposeful Systemic Change methods, resilient legacy systems sustain the status quo and adapt key features of innovations to fit the usual ways of work in the system (put new names to current ways of work). Effective innovations that are not used as intended (with fidelity) in practice have no chance to produce the intended outcomes.

As shown on the right side of Figure 38, if new (and improved) results are to be realized, the status quo (the existing system) needs to change to facilitate the work of innovation practitioners and Implementation Teams. The task is to align changes in the system so they support one another in coherent and purposeful ways that produce improved system performance and improved outcomes year after year. Thus, enabling contexts are the product of purposefully making changes in systems so that innovations are used as intended and their effectiveness is sustained over time.

In a series of studies regarding high reliability organizations, Weick (Weick, 1979, 1987, 1995; Weick et al., 1999) found that reliability (consistent high fidelity performance producing intended outcomes) is dynamic; it is a condition in which problems are temporarily under control due to ongoing compensating changes in the components. Given the fragility, it is very important to measure fidelity and celebrate the ongoing high level of fidelity to maintain high reliability (said to be "an ongoing accomplishment"). Without fidelity data, there is no yardstick against which change can be assessed. Fidelity data direct attention to relevant aspects of a system that need to be changed (barriers removed; facilitators strengthened) to improve the use of an innovation and recipient outcomes. Without fidelity data, there are no immediate and relevant problems to attend to and those in the system can become complacent.

For Weick, the sensors of high reliability must be as complex as the system that they intend to regulate. In interactive human services, the practitioners *are* the technology. They use themselves–their knowledge, skills, abilities, and support systems–to build a pattern of interactions with a recipient that reliably produces positive outcomes; they "enact their environments." Weick also makes the point that sustained high quality outcomes are the product of continually changing organization and system supports. For Active Implementation, Implementation Teams and measures such as the Implementation Quotient are the sensors, and the Active Implementation Frameworks are the guide for making continual change focused on sustaining and improving socially significant outcomes.

## Dissatisfaction

Systemic Change is mission driven. The mission can be an aspirational goal (e.g., assure that every child is a proficient reader by age nine) or related to a problem (e.g., reduce maternal and newborn mortality by 80% in the next ten years). The mission must be important enough to initiate and sustain system change efforts.

Systems are large and complex and are powered by inertia of legacy decisions and ghostly ways of work (Fixsen, Blase, & Van Dyke, 2012), where workarounds and informal communication patterns (aspects of ghost systems) keep things going in spite of (not because of) the formal system structures, policies, and procedures (Behrens, 2009; Fixsen et al., 2012; Koestler, 1967). In ghost systems, "everyone practices a little bit of ignorance … to maintain the status quo" (Von Krogh, Ichijo, & Nonaka, 2000, p. 212).

It takes courage to decide to change a system on purpose, to step out of the past, and to work toward an improved future. There has to be sufficient dissatisfaction with existing processes and outcomes to merit such a courageous decision. Sterman (2006, p. 509) states, "As we perceive discrepancies between desired and actual states, we take actions that (we believe) will cause the real world to move toward the desired state. New information about the state of the world [Practice-Policy Communication] causes us to revise our perceptions and the decisions we make in the future."

Beckhard and Harris (1987) include dissatisfaction in their formula for overcoming resistance to change:

Dissatisfaction x Vision x First Steps > Resistance to Change

With these factors in mind, they note that change is possible when the level of dissatisfaction with the status quo, the clarity of the vision for a better future, and a grasp of the first steps to be taken interact and combine to be greater than the existing resistance to change. For example, dissatisfaction with current health outcomes is apparent in the development of the Sustainable Development Goals by the United Nations (Kruk, Gage, Joseph, et al., 2018; World Health Organization, 2015). Mission-driven system change is apparent in Michigan's Top 10 in 10 Vision of being a top-ten state in education in ten years (Michigan Department of Education, 2015). Specific first steps are apparent in the State Capacity Development Plan for system change in state education systems (Ward, Ryan Jackson, Cusumano, & Fixsen, 2018).

Taking the first steps means engaging the system in the change process and responding rapidly to impediments *en route* to achieving the vision. To take the first steps successfully, Kalita, Zaidi, Prasad, and Raman (2009, p. 57) note, "there is a strong need for trained, motivated, empowered and networked health personnel. It is precisely at this level that a lack of technical knowledge and skills and the absence of a supportive network or adequate educational opportunities impede personnel from making improvements." Dissatisfaction in the absence of action (first steps) to solve problems and realize the vision leads to greater dissatisfaction, disengagement, and jaded views of the work to be done (Tucker & Singer, 2015).

It is important to keep in mind that reactions to attempts to change a system leave traces of satisfaction and dissatisfaction that cannot be "taken back." The system-change bell cannot be un-rung; it has echoes that last a generation or more. Attempts to change systems change the views of people in the system and make future change more or less difficult as a result.

## Faster, better, cheaper

Once the change process has begun, there must be a process already in place to manage Systemic Change. "Major restructuring efforts are politically challenging because the benefits of change often do not appear for several years, but the costs are immediate" (Rhim et al., 2007, p. 13). For large-scale change there always are three factors to consider: how quickly change must be accomplished, how effective the results of change must be, and how much the change effort will cost. These three factors are captured in Wexelblatt's Algorithm shown in Figure 39 (Liu & Layland, 1973). As the lead programmer for NASA in the 1950s and 1960s as the U. S. prepared to send people to the moon and back, Wexelblatt found that the initial efforts to quickly produce programs on a limited budget turned out software programs that did not work very well. Later, his group could quickly produce high-quality programs but that was very expensive.

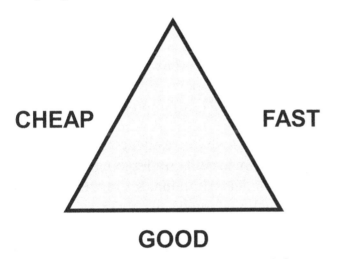

When developing a program you may pick any two.

Thus, Wexelblatt's Algorithm states that while funders and others want outcomes that are fast, cheap, and good, they can have any two of the factors but not all three. Cheap and fast products are not good. Good and fast products are not cheap. Good and cheap products are not fast. In computing, quality mattered most for a successful moon mission. In human services, we are not yet to the point where fidelity and intended outcomes are mission critical.

Figure 39. Wexelblatt's algorithm pertaining to accomplishing large scale goals

## Related research

Research studies related to legacy systems, resilient ghost systems, recursive feedback, facilitation, inner and outer settings, and Transformation Zones are illustrated in this section.

## Legacy systems

Systemic Change assumes the status quo is powerful, difficult to understand, and challenging to change.

It is a truism that all organizations and systems are perfectly designed to achieve exactly the results they obtain ("If you do what you've always done ..."). This statement does not impute intention to the design of human service systems (Barber & Fullan, 2005; Greenhalgh et al., 2009; Ulrich, 2002). Quite the contrary. Human service systems are legacy systems that are the product of "decades of quick fixes, functional enhancements, technology upgrades, and other maintenance activities [that] obscure application functionality to the point where no one can understand how a system functions" (Ulrich, 2002; p 41-42). Legacy systems represent a layered history of well-intentioned but fragmented change efforts. For example, Chao (2007, p. 1) states, "hospitals are houses of rituals. Often irrational institutional routines and inefficiencies can be viewed as barriers to care. These seemingly unnecessary routines are often remnants of long traditions that are deeply embedded in the culture of medicine."

## Resilient ghost systems

Active Implementation Systemic Change methods include intensive engagement with an existing system. The assumption is that the status quo is powerful and resists change in multiple ways that come to be understood only after change is attempted.

Legacy systems are resilient (Zimmerman et al., 1998) where resilience is defined as "the capacity of systems to absorb disturbance and reorganize while undergoing change so as to still retain essentially the same function" (Kroeze, Caniëls, Huitema, & Vranken, 2017, p. iv). As noted previously, resilient legacy systems function largely as "ghost systems" where workarounds and informal communication patterns keep things going in spite of (not because of) the formal system structures, policies, and procedures (Behrens, 2009; Fixsen et al., 2012; Koestler, 1967). In ghost systems, "everyone practices a little bit of ignorance ... to maintain the status quo" (Von Krogh et al., 2000, p. 212).

The status quo is dynamic. As explained by Weick (1987, p. 119), "People need to see that inertia is a complex state, that forcefield diagrams have multiple forces acting in opposed directions, and that reliability is an ongoing accomplishment." Weick (1987, p. 119) goes on to say that sustaining change requires vigilance because "Once situations are made reliable, they will unravel if they are left unattended." Because of the continuing "multiple forces acting in opposed directions," a goal is to develop and embed in systems the capacity for continual change (Zahra & George, 2002) so that future innovations can be incorporated and supported readily–"an ongoing accomplishment."

The cumulative unplanned nature of current (legacy) systems means that it is futile to objectively analyze "how they work" as a prelude to Systemic Change (Snowden & Boone, 2007; Ulrich, 2002). The best way to know a system is to engage in changing the system. It is only then that the complex and unplanned linkages, informal communication channels, and ghostly ways of work in a unique legacy system start to appear as identifiable facilitators and barriers to change. And, once the system is engaged in a change process, people in and out of the system respond and change in ways that could not be predicted in advance (Conklin, 2005; Rittel & Webber, 1973). Instead of trying to excavate the layers ahead of time in an attempt to discern how an existing legacy system works, the strategy is to use Systemic Change methods in real time to defragment silos, create alignment, leverage existing resources, and essentially develop a new system that reliably produces the desired outcomes (Conklin, 2005; Gilpin & Murphy, 2008; Morrissey et al., 2002).

Kurt Lewin described system change as unfreezing the existing system, changing it, and refreezing it in its new and more effective configuration (Lewin, 1951). Initiating change is designed to unfreeze a legacy system while engaging in a Systemic Change process to vastly improve fundamental structures, roles, and functions in the system. Importantly, refreezing includes embedding the capacity for constant adjustment into the system so that the ability to produce consistent and improved outcomes is the new norm (the new status quo). In this view, system change results in a new system that is specifically tailored and designed by the organization to fit their culture, staff, organizational norms, management style, vision, and stakeholders.

## Recursive feedback

Systemic Change relies on frequent (e.g., monthly) communication from the practice level to the executive leaders in a system. The Practice-Policy Communication Cycle brings real issues in real time to the attention of decision makers who promptly develop action plans to eliminate identified barriers and strengthen facilitators. The new system is established by using this process, and the new system continues to improve by continuing to use the Practice-Policy Communication Cycle.

Marzano, Waters, and McNulty (2005) note that system change is "emergent, unbounded, complex, nonlinear, [and] a disturbance of every element of a system." Disturbing the status quo creates a "chaotic context" (Snowden & Boone, 2007) that demands rapid responses to issues as they arise. Rapid responses are based on recursive feedback from experience to policy makers. A fundamental advantage of recursive feedback is that it helps leaders continually adjust their assumptions about the surrounding world and the relationships among its parts. This "mental model" (an intuitive perception about acts and their consequences) is dynamic. With access to recursive feedback, leaders can develop and use adjusted mental models to improve processes and outcomes.

"Deep change in mental models, or double loop learning, arises when evidence not only alters our decisions within the context of existing frames, but also feeds back to alter our mental models. As our mental models change, we change the structure of our systems, creating different decision rules and new strategies. The same information, interpreted by a different model, now yields a different decision ... and we must be able to cycle around the loops faster than changes in the real world render existing knowledge obsolete (Sterman, 2006, p. 506)."

Rapid recursive feedback is essential given the resilience of systems as they "absorb disturbance and reorganize" when attempts are made to change the system (Kroeze et al., 2017). The need to have executive management engaged in receiving and responding to recursive feedback was noted by Leonard-Barton and Kraus (1985, p. 104) who pointed out that "The higher the organizational level at which managers define a problem or a need, the greater the probability of successful implementation. At the same time, however, the closer the definition and solution of problems or needs are to end-users, the greater the probability of success." The solution to this paradox is contained in the Practice-Policy Communication Cycle that emphasizes the importance and interrelationship of executive management and the experience of end users.

**Facilitation**

Active Implementation Teams are external facilitators of Systemic Change. They are experts who can develop more Implementation Teams (i.e., implementation capacity) that use the Active Implementation Frameworks to initiate and manage change. Implementation Teams work closely with executive leaders and stakeholders to facilitate the change process and accomplish the goals established for the system.

"Outsiders within" (J. A. Klein, 2004) can function as "paradoxical managers" (Crom, 2007): they are excused from standard roles and functions and given authority to consider changes in standard organization structures, roles, and functions so that innovations can be incorporated and outcomes improved. The paradox is that current employees who are immersed in status quo ways of work are asked to imagine completely new ways of work so that improved outcomes can be realized.

Facilitation has been called a "mobile agent-based negotiation process" (Shin, Cha, Ryu, & Jung, 2006), "knowledge activation" done by "knowledge activists" (Von Krogh et al., 2000), the use of "meta-abilities" to support the use of innovations in organizations (Meldrum & Atkinson, 1998), "external coaches" (N. Donaldson, Rutledge, & Geiser, 2005), and so on.

Glisson et al. (2010) note how trained external specialists work with service providers and managers, government officials, leaders of related systems, and community leaders to identify and help resolve barriers to the use of an innovation. In the interest of establishing a common language for common concepts, the phrase "external facilitation" is used to describe this essential role (Berta et al., 2015; Harvey, 2002; Lessard et al., 2016; Stetler et al., 2006).

## Inner and outer settings

Systemic Change focuses on purposeful change at a human service system level. For Systemic Change, the system is the employer of those who are intended to use an innovation and is the focus of the use of Active Implementation. The national and global contexts then become the entities beyond the system.

In the implementation literature there is discussion about inner and outer settings and contexts (Aarons et al., 2011; Acosta et al., 2013; Allen et al., 2017; Damschroder et al., 2009; Fernandez et al., 2018; Greenhalgh et al., 2004; Watson et al., 2018). For example, Damschroder, et al. (2009), when defining the Consolidated Framework for Implementation Research (CFIR), state:

"The next two domains in the CFIR are inner and outer setting. Changes in the outer setting can influence implementation, often mediated through changes in the inner setting. Generally, the outer setting includes the economic, political, and social context within which an organization resides, and the inner setting includes features of structural, political, and cultural contexts through which the implementation process will proceed. However, the line between inner and outer setting is not always clear and the interface is dynamic and sometimes precarious. The specific factors considered 'in' or 'out' will depend on the context of the implementation effort. For example, outlying clinics may be part of the outer setting in one study, but part of the inner setting in another study. The inner setting may be composed of tightly or loosely coupled entities (e.g., a loosely affiliated medical center and outlying contracted clinics or tightly integrated service lines within a health system); tangible and intangible manifestation of structural characteristics, networks and communications, culture, climate, and readiness all interrelate and influence implementation."

To avoid any confusion, for Active Implementation the inner setting is the entity that employs those who are intended to use an innovation, and the outer setting is the world beyond that entity. For example, Active Implementation exerts the strongest influence on those in an organization (inner setting), and organization staff are accountable for influencing those beyond the organization (the System Intervention Driver to influence the outer setting) to improve alignment and integration of relevant factors with the use of an innovation.

The support of the broader community in which innovations are used is given attention by implementation experts. Glisson and Schoenwald (2005) discriminate organization and community strategies: "ARC uses intervention strategies at two levels, the organizational level and the interorganizational domain level, to cultivate social contexts that complement and support the implementation of effective mental health services. Strategies at the organizational level focus on specific organizations, while strategies at the interorganizational domain level focus on collections of organizations and stakeholders in a specific community." Glisson and Schoenwald note that community systems often are "unregulated, underorganized, and fragmented." These features pose challenges for any attempt to create coherence and alignment in support of the full and effective use of innovations.

## Transformation Zone

To increase the likelihood of success, Systemic Change includes the use of Transformation Zones to initiate just enough change and manage change just in time to produce needed change to support desired results.

Attempts to change whole systems all at once rarely succeed. The ambitious goals and massive investments in the Great Society Programs in the U.S. did not produce desired results (Rossi & Wright, 1984; Watkins, 1995), system reforms in child welfare have not produced positive outcomes (Annie E. Casey Foundation, 1995, 2003), and many of the Millennium Development Goals set by the United Nations were not met despite concerted and well-funded efforts by governments and foundations (World Health Organization, 2015). Human services are based on interactions among practitioners and recipients, and system change is synonymous with behavior change (Hawe, Shiell, & Riley, 2009; Michie et al., 2011). Behavior change is difficult to carry out all at once on any substantial scale (Vernez et al., 2006) because "The only thing that cannot be attained through law or money is the changing of people themselves" (Jalava, 2006, p. 159).

When changing a large organization, Nord and Tucker (1987, p. 18) describe the value of "parallel structures" where a formally sanctioned organization is developed side by side with the existing formal organization. The parallel organization has delegated "power, freedom from the normal written rules and procedures of the formal organization, and simplicity." The parallel structure (Transformation Zone) allows for "reengineering in place" where new methods are developed and improved outcomes are produced while still running the overall organization in the old way.

Initiating and managing change in a Transformation Zone provides opportunities to detect which parts of the legacy system are working and which parts need to change. Ulrich (2002, pp. 61-62) states, "Ultimately, [a] deployment project must know which functions to implement, which legacy functions to reuse, which ... functions should not be implemented, which legacy functions should not be deactivated, and how the data should be transformed." Based on this work, Ulrich found that about 80% of a legacy system remained after system transformation was complete. Only 20% of the status quo needed to be changed to produce significant gains in effectiveness and efficiency. The problem is in detecting the 20% that needs to change to vastly improve effectiveness and efficiency. This is a product of engaging the system in a Transformation Zone, making changes, and discovering what to keep and what to change based on experience and impact on fidelity.

Unger et al. (2000) studied system reform designed to grant a high degree of autonomy to regional health agencies. Based on their analyses across several countries, they noted that "Decentralization of power always increases the need for the coordination and training of peripheral staff" (p. 1007). In that regard, systems reform for complex and highly interdependent work depends upon "training of field staff, on-the-spot expert coaching, and promotion of a new organizational culture" (p. 1012). These observations fit well with the identified need for Implementation Team support for high fidelity change at the practice level coupled with recursive feedback in the Practice-Policy Communication Cycle. Developing the capacity to coordinate and train staff begins in a Transformation Zone.

Fixsen et al. (2012) describe a Transformation Zone as a slice of the overall system from front line practice to the national headquarters. The Transformation Zone (also known as a zone of proximal development (Moll, 1990) is large enough to encompass all levels: practice, organization, system, and community. And, the Transformation Zone is small enough to allow capacity to be developed and transformative changes to be made without too many negative outcomes (e.g., limit risk; reduce potential harm; concerns are not overwhelming). The changes are worked out simultaneously at all levels in the Transformation Zone before spreading to the rest of the regions, state, or country. A Transformation Zone differs from a demonstration project or pilot test in that a Transformation Zone is designed to produce the first working example of a new system and to use that capacity to rapidly spread that example to the entire system.

An instructive example is found in the work of Foege (2011) and colleagues who eradicated smallpox globally—a massive and successful scaling venture. What became a successful surveillance and containment strategy began in a Transformation Zone in one area of Nigeria in 1966. Foege (2011) recounted, "Serendipity provided a chance for us to rethink the eradication strategy" (p 54). Given the limited supply of high quality vaccine in a remote area of Nigeria, the decision was made to vaccinate the person who was found to have smallpox (surveillance) and inoculate the family members, neighbors, and others who had contact with the infected person and were susceptible to the disease (containment). The difficulty with this strategy is surveillance; how to find each person who has smallpox in a district, region, and country. Taking advantage of an existing network, the program leaders contacted missionaries in villages who then reported any cases of smallpox to the team. The person with smallpox was inoculated, and those who had contact with that person were located and inoculated to contain the spread. If any one of them already had smallpox, the containment strategy of locating and inoculating was repeated. This targeted approach conserved the supply of vaccine while effectively eliminating smallpox from a region of a country (p 59).

Given the early indications of success, the team began training other health workers from Nigeria. The Transformation Zone was expanded, teams were developed to replace the missionary networks, and the surveillance and containment strategy was replicated in another region of Nigeria that reported an outbreak of smallpox. In the new region, it was discovered that "there was a decided tendency to underreport cases if positive reports meant more work for the searcher" (p 110). The experience in Nigeria led to the development of separate specially trained teams for surveillance and for containment.

The success of the replication with newly trained staff provided sufficient confirmation that the targeted surveillance and containment strategy was more effective and efficient than the mass inoculation strategy that was favored by the global health community (p 59). Developed out of necessity and replicated on purpose, the surveillance and containment strategy was established and methods for developing the competencies of health workers was established in the Transformation Zones in Nigeria. Smallpox was eliminated in Nigeria and, by 1979, in the world.

# Chapter 16: Scaling Implementation Capacity and Innovation Outcomes

Scaling is essential to realizing socially significant benefits in human services. Scaling effective innovations requires scaling effective implementation supports. To accomplish the goals of scaling, systems must change to enable the development of implementation capacity to assure benefits for whole populations. The Active Implementation Frameworks are used to purposefully and effectively scale effective implementation supports for effective innovations in enabling system contexts.

For scaling to be successful, all the Active Implementation Frameworks are in use simultaneously in an integrated and compensatory fashion. The most flexible and adaptable people in a room are Implementation Team members who gently and relentlessly pursue the goals of scaling by engaging more and more people in the process to shore up support and overcome barriers. Drivers, Stages, Systemic Change, Usable Innovations, and Improvement Cycles are guides for Implementation Team action each day.

> *The quality of the innovation as delivered in practice (fidelity) relies on purposeful use of effective implementation methods. Scaled use of an effective innovation depends on expanded implementation capacity to support, sustain, and improve high quality replications of the innovation.*

The quality of the innovation as delivered in practice (fidelity) relies on purposeful use of effective implementation methods. Scaled use of an effective innovation depends on expanded implementation capacity to support, sustain, and improve high quality replications of the innovation. For example, there are about 60 million students attending 100,000 schools in the United States. When effective instructional innovations are developed, behavioral/educational impact is realized only when six million teachers, administrators, and staff use those innovations with fidelity every day to produce improved student outcomes this year and next year and thereafter. It is insufficient to impact some students in some schools and not reach all students in all schools. The same can be said of innovations in health and social services. Innovations cannot produce socially significant outcomes unless they are used as intended in practice with individuals in the population of intended beneficiaries.

## Ethical and moral considerations

Ethical and moral considerations arise in the context of scaling. Realizing the benefits of effective innovations supported by effective implementation and enabling contexts is the goal of scaling. Yet, realizing benefits of innovations at scale cannot be achieved all at once in any system. Scaling begins in a Transformation Zone and expands to the entire system over a period of years. Thus, for a time, until the whole population is reached, scaling creates disparity–some people are advantaged, and others are not (yet). Those who are planning scaling efforts need to be cautious that existing inequalities are not exacerbated in the process of scaling. It is tempting to go where we are most wanted and not where we are most needed. The tree with low-hanging fruit may not be the morally appropriate tree to choose when existing inequalities are considered.

Who will be the first to be inoculated with a new life-saving serum that is in short supply? Who will wait? While the United Nations Millennium Development Goals (MDGs) led to nearly a 50% reduction in maternal mortality globally after 15 years, the benefits were not evenly distributed. In 2015, the risk of a woman in a low-resource country dying from a maternal-related cause during her lifetime was about 33 times higher compared to a woman living in a high-resource country. Maternal mortality is a health indicator that shows very wide gaps between rich and poor families and between urban and rural areas, both between countries and within them (http://www.who.int/gho/maternal_health/en/). Ethically and morally, the initiation of scaling must include those who are most in need along with those who are most ready or convenient to access. This issue will be explored further in the section on the Transformation Zone.

## Related research

Good progress is being made in developing effective innovations in human services (Abrams et al., 2012; Chorpita et al., 2005; Elliott & Mihalic, 2004; Glasner-Edwards & Rawson, 2010; Patton et al., 2016; Stringer, Ekouevi, Coetzee, & et al., 2010). In addition, key factors related to the use of effective innovations and other innovations in typical practice settings are being operationalized and tested in Implementation Science (Adondiwo et al., 2013; Barker et al., 2016; Glisson et al., 2010; Omimo et al., 2018). While work continues on developing innovations and improving and extending the science of implementation, attention now includes scaling human service innovations in communities across the nation and the globe to produce social impact.

The conclusion from a review by Milat, Bauman, and Redman (2015) is that scaling is not defined well, and there is little agreement about what it means within and across disciplines. There is basic agreement that scaling means expanded use of an innovation. However, there is not agreement on what it takes to move beyond interesting demonstrations to purposeful scaling. For our purposes, *scaling refers to the extent to which an innovation is used with good effect in the entire population of interest.*

## The logic of scaling

By itself, knowing the number of individuals, organizations, or systems that are attempting to use of an innovation means little as a scaling metric. To call the use of an intervention in 26 schools (out of 100,000 in the U.S.) "scaling up" is a misnomer (Clements, Sarama, Wolfe, & Spitler, 2014). The denominator and the quality of the numerator each need to be operationalized to determine the extent to which scaling is achieved.

Some basics of scaling are outlined below and described further in ensuing sections.

1. The goal of scaling is to reach the entire population
   a. Entire populations cannot be reached all at once
   b. Transformation Zones are required to establish the first examples of scaling
   c. Usability Improvement Cycles are based on examined experience and data so that constant adjustments are made to reach the goals
2. Scaling innovations requires first scaling implementation capacity
   a. Establish an implementation infrastructure in the form of linked Implementation Teams
   b. Initiate implementation capacity to create more implementation capacity so that practitioners receive effective support for using multiple innovations
   c. Focus on alignment, integration, and leveraging existing structures, roles, and functions so that outcomes are improved with effective and efficient use of resources
3. Scaling requires Systemic Change
   a. Exploration Stage agreements are established for initiating and managing change processes to achieve goals at a provincial, state, or national level
   b. Establish Practice-Policy Communication loops (constant adjustment based on recursive feedback) occur with engaged leaders
   c. Top-down support for bottom-up change is present for practices and outcomes
4. Scaling requires relevant and regular action assessments
   a. Frequent assessments of implementation capacity functions to monitor progress (implementation fidelity)

b. Frequent assessments of fidelity at the practice level monitor implementation outcomes (intervention fidelity)

c. Action planning is based on data to meet, exceed, and expand implementation capacity requirements

## The denominator

The intent of scaling is to reach the entire population of intended beneficiaries. For example, in the 1950s the World Health Organization documented over 50 million cases of smallpox globally. The National Institute of Mental Health estimates there are over ten million adults with one or more forms of severe mental illness in the U.S. There are one million students enrolled in 2,370 schools in the state of Washington. The World Bank is concerned with alleviating extreme poverty for over one billion people in 188 countries living on $1.50 or less a day. There are about 250,000 people in the United States diagnosed with pulmonary hypertension, a rare and often fatal disease. As these examples illustrate, *the denominator for scaling varies greatly across domains, levels of systems, and specific interests and always includes the known population that could benefit.*

### Denominator moderators

For some innovations, the denominator may be influenced by local variables. For example, the denominator for scaling air conditioners depends on local weather. People who live in cooler climates do not need air conditioners. Consequently, those homes located in areas below a given climate cut-point should not be included in the denominator. Local variation also may be influenced by unique circumstances where, for example, trade winds, housing construction, and cultural factors combine to reduce the need for air conditioning in Hawaii (Sailor & Pavlova, 2003).

In human services, the denominator may be influenced by fluctuations in society that impact risk factors related to mental health problems (e.g., PTSD associated with wars), the local incidence of violence (e.g., urban crowding), or the degree to which protective factors ameliorate risks (e.g., changes in school climate that enhance belonging and connectedness). The population of pregnant women at risk of maternal mortality may be influenced by local variation in the availability adequate water, food, and sanitation.

## The numerator

While identifying and quantifying the population of intended beneficiaries (the denominator) is fairly straightforward (Last, 2001), determining the numerator in human service applications is complicated. The numerator is the number of members of the population who actually experience the innovation and have the opportunity to benefit. *The numerator for scaling reflects the quality of the innovation as it is delivered in practice.*

It makes little sense to expend resources in attempts to scale innovations that do not produce intended benefits. Attempts to scale ineffective or harmful innovations are a waste of time, money, and opportunity, and likely produce the jaded view of innovations and new initiatives often encountered in human service settings. Yet, this is the norm and not the exception as well-meaning policy makers and leaders press for quick solutions in human service systems that are ill equipped to respond in ways that actually produce intended outcomes. System administrators and managers, let alone practitioners, simply do not have the levers for meaningful change available to them. It is like asking a scholar who only knows Roman numerals to calculate the solution to a complex math problem. The means are not available to achieve the ends.

Fidelity, the extent to which an effective innovation is used as intended is an important determinant of the social benefit of innovations as they are scaled. Pronouncements ("you have completed the workshop and we now declare you are using our innovation"), claims ("our group read your manual and we are using your innovation"), or policy statements ("we passed a law and funded an agency to take care of that") are not the same as actually using an innovation as intended (i.e., with fidelity), producing promised outcomes, and sustaining the innovations and implementation supports that become the new standard practices in changed human service systems.

The importance of fidelity was apparent in the 1950s when some early batches of the newly developed Salk polio vaccine used to inoculate school children were substandard (low fidelity production). Those substandard batches of polio vaccine actually *increased* the chances of children contracting the disease (not something society wants to see scaled). Those children who suffered the low quality vaccine received an injection but did not receive a high fidelity inoculation for polio. Recipients of low fidelity vaccines would not count in the numerator related to scaling the Salk vaccine. Fortunately, medical personnel quickly detected and corrected the problem, and damage to children–while severe for infected children–was limited for the population of children (Bayly, 1956).

In another example, the developers of the widely used Positive Behavioral Interventions and Supports (PBIS) program in education explicitly state many, but not all, uses of PBIS met fidelity criteria in their study of scaling (Horner et al., 2014). Consequently, students in schools using PBIS with fidelity would count in the numerator. Students in other "PBIS schools" did not actually experience PBIS being used as intended and would not count in the numerator when calculating scaling of social impact (McIntosh et al., 2016).

## Numerator moderators

When attempting to scale interaction-based innovations, fidelity (quality) is difficult to achieve and more difficult to maintain as people come and go in a sea of change. In addition, implementation capacity is limited and, therefore, the ability of organizations and systems to achieve and sustain high fidelity performance and socially significant outcomes is limited. Fidelity, capacity, and sustainability are moderators of a scaling numerator and should be assessed in any analysis of scaling attempts.

As noted throughout descriptions of Active Implementation, the quality of an innovation as it is delivered in practice is at risk because human services are *interaction-based*–they involve a human provider and a human recipient, each with personal characteristics and changing emotional states in shifting contexts. In other fields, innovations are *atom-based*. For example, when developing highway bridges (McNichol, 2006) and new components of rockets (Boyle, 2003), the innovations are atom-based–meaning they stay put after they are developed and do not change from one engineer to the next, shift into new configurations overnight, or decide not to show up.

While they may be extremely complicated, developing and scaling atom-based innovations present "tame problems" while interaction-based innovations present "wicked problems" (Conklin, 2005; Rittel & Webber, 1973). Given the complexity of multiple human beings interacting and influencing one another, wicked problems are difficult to define, "fight back" when solutions are attempted, and require continual resolution (re-solution) to improve and maintain impact. Wicked problems associated with interaction-based innovations impact the numerator for scaling.

It is well established that the availability of (access to) services is not the same as the quality of services as delivered (Donald et al., 2018; Kruk, Gage, Arsenault, et al., 2018). Given the complexity of interaction-based innovations, the quality of the numerator is difficult to assess. A good *fidelity* measure assesses the extent to which the essential components of an interaction-based innovation are present and used as intended (with fidelity) in daily practice (Rahman et al., 2018; Sanetti & Kratochwill, 2014; Schoenwald & Garland, 2013). In addition, a good fidelity measure is highly related to outcomes–high fidelity use of the innovation in practice is associated with noticeable socially significant outcomes and low fidelity use of the innovation is associated with poor outcomes for users and recipients. With a strong relationship between the two, if fidelity is known, then outcomes are predictable (Bond & Salyers, 2004; Forgatch et al., 2005; Tiruneh et al., 2018).

The complexity of interaction-based innovations also requires purposeful and persistent *implementation capacity* to reliably produce high fidelity uses of innovations.

Implementation capacity is largely missing in human service systems (Schofield, 2004). The lack of fidelity measures and the near absence of implementation capacity stand in the way of generating and scaling a numerator that meets a standard for quality (e.g., high fidelity use of innovations that reliably produce intended outcomes).

Fidelity and implementation capacity are related to a final impediment to scaling. A numerator cannot continue to increase without attention to *sustaining* the quality of the innovation by those who already are using an innovation as intended (Tommeraas & Ogden, 2016). Out of necessity, initial attention is directed to expansion of the number of new users ("adoption" and Initial Implementation of innovations). Over time, as the number of users increases, increasing attention must be paid to de-adoption and re-adoption (Massatti et al., 2008; Panzano & Roth, 2006) in addition to developing new users. A container that is draining as fast as it is being filled simply maintains the same level. Likewise, if the number of users "de-adopting" an innovation equals the number of new users "adopting" an innovation, the numerator stays the same and scaling plateaus at that point. Sustaining those who already are using an innovation while continuing to develop new users is essential to any successful scaling attempt.

## Scaling the numerator

Given that the denominator (the population of interest) is relatively fixed, social impact depends on scaling the numerator. In atom-based business environments, the production methods (manufacturing processes) for an innovation are essential to scaling. In health, the biologically-based Salk vaccine was difficult to produce in large quantities and resulted in some low fidelity (and harmful) batches of the vaccine. Consequently, the innovation was changed and production methods were changed to reliably produce high fidelity supplies of the chemically-based Sabin vaccine (Bayly, 1956). In computer science, after silicon-based transistor circuits were invented, the production of usable silicon wafers was problematic with about one usable transistor circuit produced out of 100 attempts. When the engineers examined the low fidelity transistor circuits, they discovered that hair, dry skin, pesticides in the air (they were in the middle of citrus groves before Silicon Valley paved them over), and so on contaminated the manufacturing process. This led to the development of ultra-clean environments for producing silicon wafers and for assembling computer hardware and other electronics (Kaeslin, 2008). With improvements in production processes, atom-based manufacturing plants now send usable products out the door (expand the numerator) at an increasingly rapid pace (Ohno, 1988; Wilson et al., 1993).

Given certain constraints, atom-based products usually are reliable once they leave the production plant. Nevertheless, for high fidelity and sustained use, vaccines need to be stored properly, automobiles need to be serviced and repaired, computer software requires frequent

287

updating (automatically, to take users out of the process), and electronic parts are bound to fail under certain environmental conditions or after so many hours of use. Whole industries have been developed to maintain, repair, improve, and replace what has been produced (i.e., sustain the numerator).

For interaction-based innovations, the challenges involved in production and maintenance are compounded many times over. Given the difficulties in reliably producing human competencies and their sensitivity to many "contaminants" in service environments that are anything but "ultra-clean," the shelf life of many interaction-based innovations is short. In this sense, human interaction skills are "perishable." "Production" depends on the skill of an Implementation Team that does training, coaching, and fidelity assessments in hospitable organization and system environments. "Maintenance" requires ongoing support from coaches and Facilitative Administrators and repeated assessments of fidelity and outcomes to stay on track.

The introduction of Implementation Teams in human service organizations is tantamount to moving the production unit into the service environment (Fixsen et al., 2013; Higgins, Weiner, & Young, 2012; Metz et al., 2014; Schofield, 2004). Interaction-based innovations without the ongoing support of Implementation Teams stand little chance of high fidelity use or sustained use in turbulent human service environments (Brunk et al., 2014; Fixsen et al., 2001; McIntosh, Mercer, Nese, Strickland-Cohen, & Hoselton, 2015; Schoenwald et al., 2000).

## Active Implementation and scaling

While the goal of scaling is to assure benefits of innovations for whole populations, the focus of scaling is on developing implementation capacity and facilitating Systemic Change. All components of the Active Implementation Frameworks are at work in scaling. Indeed, some of the Active Implementation Frameworks were developed during previous attempts at scaling innovations in large systems. For example, an understanding of Systemic Change and improvement cycles has been established, refined, and broadened by scaling attempts. The previous versions of the Active Implementation Frameworks were expanded and refined, and the current versions of the Active Implementation Frameworks survived the test of experience and were found to be usable, beneficial, and replicable even in stressful scaling and system change environments.

The linkages among interventions, implementation, and capacity are depicted in Figure 40. Beneficial outcomes for recipients are produced by high fidelity use of effective innovations as practitioners interact with recipients. Practitioner and organization performance are produced by high fidelity use of implementation supports within organizations.

Implementation Teams represent the capacity within organizations and systems to develop, sustain, and improve the system of supports for practitioners.

The combination of factors shown in Figure 40 represents a scalable unit as defined by Barker et al. (2016): a scalable unit is "a microsystem or a mesosystem that can be replicated as the intervention is scaled up." Any one part of a scalable unit without the others will not produce and sustain population benefits.

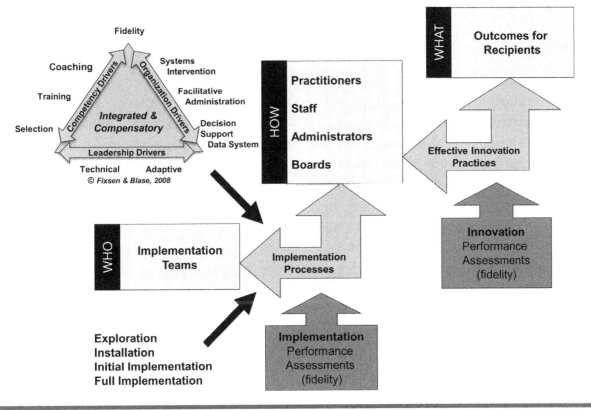

Figure 40. The logical components of a scalable unit with assessments of intervention fidelity, implementation fidelity, and overall capacity to assure quality and impact

## Assessing scaling outcomes

In human service contexts, the goal of scaling is to benefit populations of individuals and society. Therefore, scaling is measured in terms of socially significant outcomes. Given the complexities inherent in interaction-based innovations and implementation supports, reaching 100% of a population may be an aspirational goal (at least for this century). Yet, scaling innovations to benefit society still is the intention so that an innovation becomes a sustainable standard practice reliably producing social benefits.

289

Based on their experience in scaling within provider organizations, Fixsen et al. (2013) assert a criterion of 60% as a minimum for functional scaling (also see Scheirer, 2005). If 60% of the population of potential recipients are benefiting from an innovation used with fidelity, the innovation would meet a *minimum criterion* for being "scaled up." A minimum of 60% may be a stretch goal for human service innovations. For example, PBIS is being used to some extent in 25,000 (numerator) of the 100,000 (denominator) schools in the U.S.–25% of all schools. This is a remarkable achievement without equal in U.S. education systems but still short of 60%. As documented by Horner et al. (2014), even the states with 500 or more schools using PBIS continue to struggle to gain acceptance and funding as an integral part of the education system–a sure sign they are not yet standard practice.

The 60% criterion is an estimate of the tipping point where an innovation has a chance of becoming standard practice in a system and lose its status as an innovation. At the minimum 60% scaling criterion, an innovation might be said to move from the "acknowledgement phase" where an innovation is broadly used to the "invisibility stage" where an innovation is incorporated into the fabric of society–the new status quo (Faggin, 1985). For example, standardized financial accounting and auditing of public funds were innovations in 1900; desktop computer hardware, software, and internetworking were innovations in 1980. Within a couple of decades of their "acknowledgement," accounting departments and information technology departments were developed to support these innovations. As a result, the innovations and the supporting departments became part of "standard practice" (a new status quo) in nearly all public and private organizations. Viewed from this perspective, the 60% criterion is attainable and necessary to produce social impact over the long run. Perhaps in the next decade or two "departments of implementation and scaling" will become part of standard practice to support effective interaction-based innovations in human services so that the 60% criterion can be surpassed routinely.

## Approaches to scaling

There are two approaches to scaling innovations to reach the 60% minimum criterion to achieve social impact in human services. An *innovation-centric approach* focuses on one innovation, and social impact is assessed by the fidelity and outcomes of that one innovation. A *system-centric approach* is focused on the capacity to support the effective use of multiple innovations, and social impact is assessed by the fidelity and outcomes of Implementation Teams and the fidelity and outcomes of a range of innovations now and in the future. There are similarities and some significant differences in the two approaches.

# Innovation-centric scaling

The result of innovation-specific implementation capacity development is the ability to use one innovation on a larger scale. A great deal of the literature on attempts to scale the use of innovations is specific to a given innovation (Alexander, Pugh, Parsons, & Sexton, 2000; Bruns, Suter, Leverentz-Brady, & Burchard, 2004; Bryce et al., 2010; Chamberlain, 2003; Drake, Essock, ct al., 2001; Fixsen & Blase, 2018; Galavotti, Sebert Kuhlmann, Kraft, Harford, & Petraglia, 2008; Horner et al., 2014; W. R. Miller, 2000; Olds, Hill, O'Brien, Racine, & Moritz, 2003; Rubin et al., 2011; Schoenwald et al., 2000; Slavin & Madden, 2004; Spicer et al., 2014; Szapocznik & Williams, 2000).

The innovation-centric approach has not led to examples of benefits for whole populations (Green, 2008; Kessler & Glasgow, 2011; Wright, Wall, & Ritchey, 2018). Nevertheless, these efforts over the past several decades have offered opportunities to learn about innovations, implementation supports required for using and sustaining innovations with fidelity, and the aspects of organizations and systems that need to align to support expanded uses of innovations.

A dramatic example of successful innovation-specific scaling occurred in global health. Fenner et al. (1988) recount the 175-year history of the smallpox vaccine and the intensive global efforts that eventually led to the eradication of smallpox in 1979. They concluded, "health officials in most countries have recognized that traditional health care systems—comprising a network of medical practitioners, health centres, and hospitals—have been designed fundamentally to provide therapeutic services for those who seek help and are ill-equipped to deliver preventive and other services which must reach all or most persons in a community" (p 1352). Thus, one of the barriers to scaling effective innovations is the system itself (the status quo). Beyond the challenges posed by existing systems, the authors describe the need for prompt detection and rapid responses to each and every implementation difficulty encountered. Fenner et al. (1988) and Foege (2011) describe how the global health community had to overcome major impediments related to maintaining the quality and stability of the smallpox vaccine, supply of materials and qualified personnel in remote and low-resource areas, leadership and collaboration among nations, shifting populations due to war and migration, fragile political resolve, and advocates of alternative solutions.

The decades and millions of dollars invested in eradicating smallpox are an example of a "brute-force" approach (Christakos, 2011; Puska & Uutela, 2001) to implementation and scaling. Brute-force approaches may get the job done but they do not leave improved system capacity in their wake. Eradication of smallpox did not establish improved global or national health systems with the generalized capacity to help eradicate other diseases or health concerns in the ensuing decades (e.g., tuberculosis, AIDS epidemic). Innovation-centric approaches require overcoming systemic barriers one innovation at a time in a siloed approach. The status quo itself is not addressed systemically.

## Scale-up shifts

Innovation-centric scaling is limited by scale-up shifts. A scale-up shift is defined as the point at which implementation supports must be expanded in order to produce the next level of growth in the use of an innovation.

Initially, innovation developers and members of a research group (collectively called purveyors) can function as an Implementation Team for an innovation. "Purveyors" represent a program or practice and "actively work to implement the defined practice or program with fidelity and good effect at an implementation site" (Fixsen, Naoom, et al., 2005, p. 12). Purveyors know the innovation well, since they developed it, and they personally can interact with other groups to assure adequate use of the innovation. Depending on the complexity of an interaction-based innovation, a research group might be able to establish up to about 100 replications of the innovation with reasonable fidelity. A typical purveyor group does not have the capacity to expand beyond the 50-100 range. Dealing with the innovation and the problems associated with its uses by practitioners in a variety of settings becomes unmanageable as a mounting number of startup, implementation, and sustainability issues overwhelm the developer group.

To scale up further, the purveyor group must shift from producing more examples of the innovation to now producing more examples of itself. That is, producing more purveyor groups that know the innovation well and can support others who want to use the innovation. The shift is to producing Implementation Teams (by whatever name). For example, the Teaching-Family Model shifted its focus to site development (organized groups of group homes supported by an Implementation Team) in order to expand beyond 60 or so Teaching-Family group homes (Blase, Fixsen, Maloney, et al., 1984; Blase, Fixsen, & Phillips, 1984; Fixsen & Blase, 2018). Multisystemic treatment services (MSTS) shifted its focus to developing network partners (Implementation Teams) who could develop and support high fidelity use of MST (Brunk et al., 2014). For atom-based innovations this is the point where the purveyor group moves out of the garage and into a manufacturing facility (Isaacson, 2014). The shift to developing Implementation Teams brings larger organization and systemic issues into play.

The next scale-up shift occurs when the management of multiple Implementation Teams in a variety of settings consumes the available resources. Developing and managing the quality of many Teaching-Family Sites or MST partners requires considerable time and effort; the development of new data and quality control systems soon outstrip the knowledge and funding available to the innovation. In manufacturing, the atom-based innovation becomes a commodity that can be produced with high reliability in many factories all over the world. Factories become the unit of replication. There is no equivalent for interaction-based innovations where an innovation spawned a business that eventually served the needs of entire populations. For interaction-based innovations that reach this point, the expansion ends here with 500–1,000 examples of the innovation being used with fidelity and socially significant outcomes that benefit a segment of the population.

The scale-up shifts are depicted in Figure 41. Imagine a million community health workers on the right side of the figure. How many Implementation Teams will be required? How will they be developed and sustained and improved? Scaling innovations must focus on scaling implementation capacity with more and more teams on the left side without losing quality at the practitioner level on the right side.

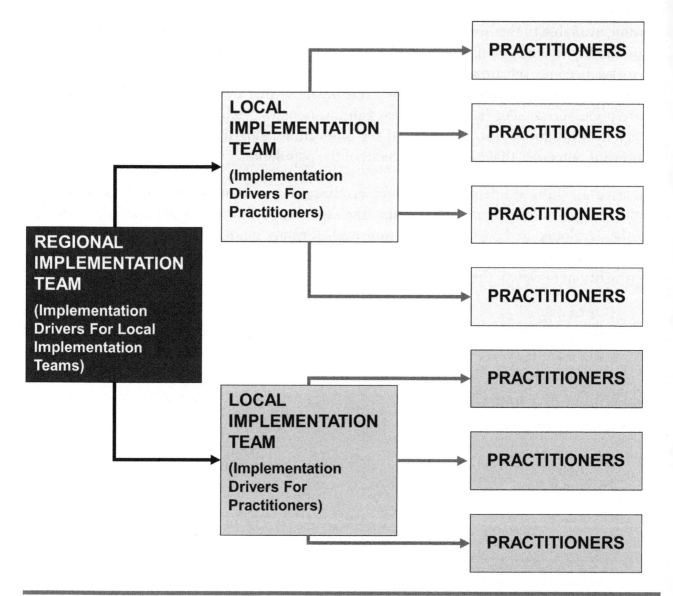

Figure 41. Scale up shifts from supporting high fidelity practitioners to developing linked Implementation Teams to continually add implementation capacity to eventually serve an entire population

## System-centric scaling

The limited success of innovation-centric approaches to scaling has put more attention on a system-centric view. This view focuses on developing implementation capacity in *whole systems* responsible for the use of multiple innovations in one or more domains of human services (e.g., education, child welfare, early childhood home visiting, maternal and child health, tuberculosis prevention and treatment).

In the scaling and system change literature, there is debate about the merits of top-down or bottom-up approaches (Klingner, Boardman, & McMaster, 2013; Pülzl & Treib, 2006), the wisdom of requiring fidelity or accepting adaptations in use of innovations (Aarons et al., 2012; Szulanski & Jensen, 2008), and the value of policy-first or outcome-first strategies (Haskins & Baron, 2011; Manna, 2008). There also is discussion of scaling strategies using more linear and planned approaches (Winter & Szulanski, 2001) or complexity theory that emphasizes emergent forms and comfort with "not knowing" (Lanham et al., 2013; Manna, 2008).

In general, there is no "or" in scaling work, there is only "and." That is, top-down *and* bottom-up capacity development involves policy-first *and* outcome-first strategies where fidelity *and* adaption are required. A planned approach helps to operationalize the work to be done *and* complexity theory helps to make sense of these apparent contradictions and anticipate the emergent nature of the work (Fixsen et al., 2017).

Like an innovation-centric approach, a system-centric approach still focuses on effective innovations and implementation supports. The difference is that a system-centric approach to scaling starts with population benefits as the end in mind (Khatri & Frieden, 2002; Perla, Bradbury, & Gunther-Murphy, 2013; Senge, 2006). Instead of developing implementation capacity by working through a progression of innovation-centric steps, the scaling process within a human service system can, from the beginning, focus on developing the implementation, organization, and system capacity essential to achieving and maintaining population benefits. In this approach, effective innovations are still important but are not the central focus of initial scaling activity. Instead, the focus is on transforming human service systems by developing implementation capacity in the form of linked Implementation Teams and establishing enabling contexts that can serve multiple innovations equally well. All of the Active Implementation Frameworks are in use in this process.

An example of system-centric scaling in education in the U.S. is shown in Figure 42.

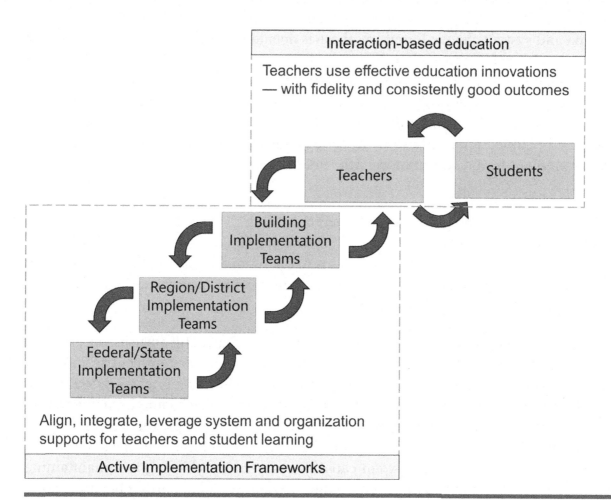

Figure 42. System-centric scaling in the form of linked Implementation Teams in large, complex state education systems. Based on the work of the State Implementation and Scaling up of Evidence-based Programs Center

In this example, State Implementation Teams create multiple Regional Implementation Teams that, in turn, create many more District Implementation Teams that establish a Building Implementation Team in each school so that every teacher will be supported by an Implementation Team with the expertise to assure full and effective uses of innovations to benefit students (Ryan Jackson et al., 2018). This is possible because each team uses the Active Implementation Frameworks. With common language, common methods, and common measures, linked Implementation Teams can communicate clearly and work independently and together to detect and correct problems *en route* to achieving mission-driven goals.

As shown in Figure 43, as system capacity increases in the form of District Implementation Teams functioning as assessed by the District Capacity Assessment (DCA), then the number of schools using an effective innovation with fidelity increases until the 60% scaling criterion is reached for that district at Time 6 (T6). Assessments were conducted every six months for T1 and T2 and annually thereafter. Thus, Time 6 is equivalent to five years to reach scale in the district with 27 schools.

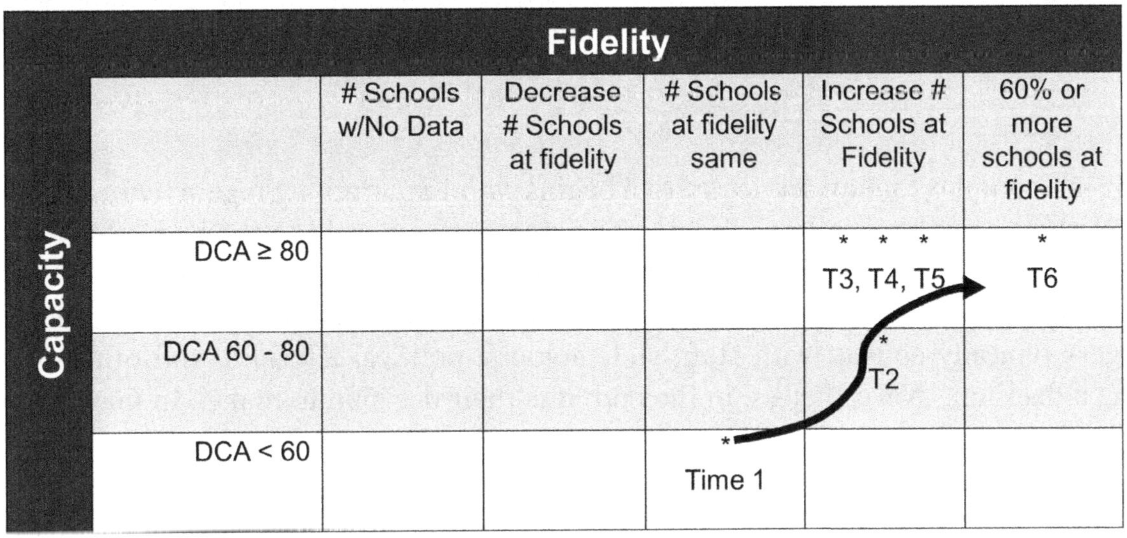

| Fidelity | | | | | |
|---|---|---|---|---|---|
| | # Schools w/No Data | Decrease # Schools at fidelity | # Schools at fidelity same | Increase # Schools at Fidelity | 60% or more schools at fidelity |
| **DCA ≥ 80** | | | | * * *<br>T3, T4, T5 | *<br>T6 |
| **DCA 60 - 80** | | | | *<br>T2 | |
| **DCA < 60** | | | *<br>Time 1 | | |

(left axis label: **Capacity**)

Figure 43. The interaction between organization implementation capacity (DCA) and fidelity of the use of an innovation. The District Capacity Assessment (DCA) measures the functioning of Implementation Teams in school district organizations and fidelity as measured in each school. Used with permission of Eric Kloos and the Minnesota Implementation Team.

In this example, the District Implementation Teams are the result of the work of Regional and State Implementation Teams. "Mobile agents" (Implementation Teams) with the ability to replicate themselves are a characteristic of "fractal organizations" (Gilpin & Murphy, 2008; Shin et al., 2006) and are used to great advantage in system-centric scaling. The linked Implementation Teams promote alignment and integration of system structures, roles, and functions so that resources can be leveraged to produce desired outcomes more efficiently, even in an "environment of turbulence, flux, fragmentation, disequilibrium and uncertainty" (Strongman, 2013).

A system-centric approach to scaling effective innovations necessarily is focused on Systemic Change. If a human service system already had skilled units that were integrated and aligned to support the full and effective use of innovations, social benefits already would be at a high level and improving every year. Unfortunately, that is not the case (National Center for Education Statistics, 2013; Starfield, 2000). Human service systems are legacy systems (Ulrich, 2002) made up of an accumulation of fragments of past mandates, good ideas, beliefs, and ways of work that evolved over many decades as leaders and staff came and went. They were not purposefully designed to produce and sustain high fidelity use of effective innovations. Given what is known about the power of the status quo, it is no surprise that organizations and systems need to change, often in dramatic and transformative ways (Osborne & Gaebler, 1992). With the end in mind, a system-centric approach plans to initiate and manage significant Systemic Change from the beginning.

## Scaling implementation capacity

Scaling in a complex human service system begins with Exploration Stage activities conducted by a National Implementation Team. The point of entry in systems is the Executive Management Team. This is the group that can go into a room and make a decision about the system without asking others for permission to make the change. Of course, Executive Managers typically consult with staff, stakeholders, political advisors, and others prior to making a decision. Nevertheless, in the end, it is their decision to make. In many cases the National Implementation Team begins discussions with others in a system before finally being granted access to the Executive Management Team. In any case, the Executive Leadership needs to agree with the goals of scaling; understand the rationales, processes, and timeframes for scaling linked Implementation Teams; and agree to participate in monthly meetings with the National Implementation Team to be apprised of progress and to solve problems that arise (Practice-Policy Communication Cycle).

Of those who initially express interest, not all leaders agree to participate in the exploration meetings and discussions. Of those who do participate, not all agree to engage in initial scaling action (Chamberlain et al., 2011; Robbins & Collins, 2010). Perhaps half of those who initially express interest may eventually agree to proceed with scaling once they learn how difficult the process is likely to be, and how long it will take to realize important outcomes on a useful scale. In every case, the goal is for the National Implementation Team and the Executive Team to have sufficient information and experience with one another to make a mutually agreeable decision to proceed (or not).

During a four-six month (sometimes longer) Exploration period, the National Implementation Team organizes discussion and activities with the Executive Team to:

- Establish shared vision, goals, methods
- Discuss who will give what and who will get what and when, where, why, and how things will happen (Give-Get agreements)
- Develop timelines for doing and expanding the scope of work
- Set expectations of proximal and distal measures and outcomes
- Decide on meeting schedules, attendance, and action plans

In these discussions (in person; in province; in country), readiness is assessed and readiness is created where possible by the National Implementation Team. Lack of readiness may be due to any number of combinations of factors in a system, many of which can be overcome during the Exploration Stage. A decision results in signing a memorandum of understanding with a bit of ceremony to memorialize the decision at the executive leadership level and publicly in the state.

Keep in mind that scaling begins with those who are ready, willing, and able to proceed with a reasonable expectation of success (Exploration Stage). While beginning work with those who are ready, the National Implementation Team continues to work with other states/ provinces to help create readiness. Ongoing legal or legislative disputes, lack of stakeholder support, leadership aversion to risk taking, lack of flexible funding, poor understanding of organic Systemic Change processes, and so on, individually or in combination, are good reasons to work on creating readiness. As a result of these efforts, the next cohort will be ready, willing, and able as the Transformation Zone expands to include more of the population. To insist on proceeding in the absence of readiness is folly unless an entirely new system is being established independently of the existing system. For example, an outside-the-system surveillance and containment approach to eradicating smallpox was designed to be one-and-done. Once the last cases of smallpox were treated, then the system to produce that result was dismantled (Fenner et al., 1988; Foege, 2011). The development of new systems rarely happens in human services where scaling must be done and results sustained in the context of current status quo systems.

Scaling implementation capacity requires developing Implementation Teams at multiple levels of a system. With pressures for "early wins" and funding deadlines and waning support for Systemic Change, it is difficult to keep the eye on the prize–consistent, scalable, and sustainable benefits to recipients. The use of the Active Implementation Frameworks at each level provides a consistent foundation for teaching and learning and data and benchmarks to make progress visible as implementation capacity is developed and expanded and the system begins to change. The development and operationalization of the Active Implementation Frameworks and the development of practical capacity assessments has substantially reduced the time required to establish scalable implementation capacity.

## Improving education: a scaling example

The approaches to scaling outlined in this chapter are being used and evaluated in a purposeful and proactive way in the context of state education systems in the U.S. The example is a system-centric approach to scaling that emphasizes, from the beginning, the need for Systemic Change to develop an implementation infrastructure that can support the full and effective use of innovations in classrooms across a state. Education systems are large, complex, fragmented, highly variable, and resourced very differently depending on unique state and local laws, regulations, and histories. A common phrase is "if you know one state you know one state"–a testament to the uniqueness of each state. Using a common approach to scaling in unique state education systems was seen as a severe test of the Active Implementation Frameworks and the system-centric approach to scaling. The National Implementation Team in this example is made up of 5.2 fulltime employees (FTE) in the State Implementation and Scaling up of Evidence-based Programs (SISEP) Center funded by the U.S. Department of Education Office of Special Education Programs and directed by Dr. Caryn Ward. All national team members working in states are experts in the use of the Active Implementation Frameworks.

## Exploration Stage

States were mutually selected for participation using an exploration process consisting of a series of informational conference calls and site visits to assess goodness of fit, readiness, and leadership commitment for systemic change.

The state selection criteria were:

1. The state has documented attempts to implement an evidence-based curriculum or instruction initiative or behavior support program
2. The state has demonstrated leadership commitment to system change at the state level
3. Within 12 months, the state is willing to allocate current funds and staff positions for two state Transformation Specialists
4. Within 12 months, the state is willing to allocate current funds and staff positions for Regional Implementation Team members
5. The state is willing to establish a data system that includes assessment of adult (teacher, staff, Implementation Team) behavior as well as student outcomes
6. The state is willing to participate in and contribute to a national community of practice.

Frequent email exchanges and telephone calls combined with two or more site visits were typical to create readiness by providing information about the Active Implementation Frameworks and their use in system change and scaling, and by securing the informed consent of the executive leadership regarding their participation in Systemic Change processes. The six selection criteria related to leadership commitment to system change and willingness to reallocate resources often discriminated states that were selected from those that were not. States that are selected are known as active scaling states.

## Transformation Zone

Once a decision is made to proceed, scaling work begins by developing implementation knowledge, skills, and abilities at the state level. Two or more individuals employed by the state are selected to lead the implementation capacity development and system change efforts in the state. In education, these people are called State Transformation Specialists (STSs) and they lead the State Implementation Team. An early decision by the National Implementation Team, Executive Management, STSs, and the State Implementation Team is to decide on a Transformation Zone.

Initial implementation capacity is developed in the Transformation Zone (Fixsen et al., 2012). In the transformation zone, changes are initiated, elements of the existing system are disturbed, and the process of *behaving* a path to system change is begun. A Transformation Zone is large enough to encompass nearly all the elements of the entire system and small enough not to be overwhelmed by the issues encountered as changes are initiated and managed. For SISEP, a Transformation Zone is a vertical slice of the entire education system, from the classroom to the capitol. As outlined in Figure 44, a Transformation Zone in education includes the state leaders and staff, two or three regions, three districts in each region, three schools in each district, and all the teachers, staff, and students in each school.

The Transformation Zone's purpose is to provide opportunities for purposeful training and coaching to establish the first examples of Implementation Teams at each level and have them begin to function independently and together. A related purpose is to disturb the existing system (Marzano et al., 2005), and evoke reactions that provide opportunities for the State Management Team to make changes in the system to accommodate and support implementation team development and functioning. The Practice-Policy Communication Cycle (Fixsen et al., 2013) provides bottom-up information to improve top-down support for implementation and scaling capacity development (recursive feedback). Over time, additional cohorts of regions, districts, and schools are added to the systems change effort as the STSs and colleagues develop an implementation team in each region of the state, and each RIT develops implementation teams in each district in their region and so on to reach every school (building) in a state.

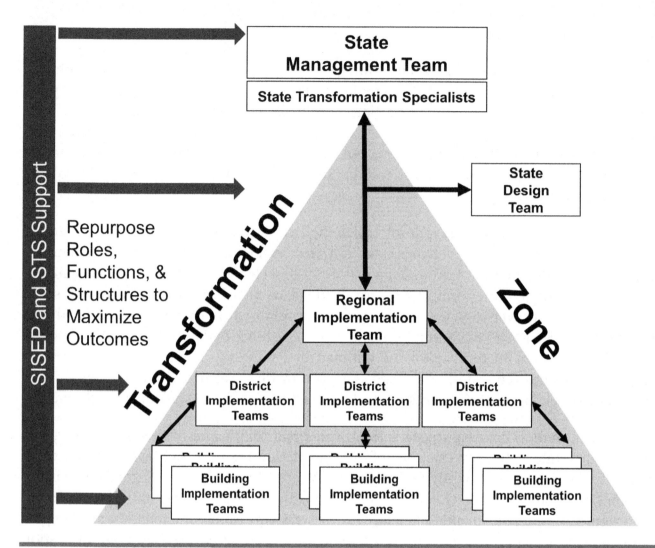

Figure 44. A Transformation Zone is a geographic section of a system that is large enough to encompass all aspects of the system, and small enough to manage the development of capacity and reactions to systemic changes. In education, two or three regions are selected using Exploration Stage activities. Within a region, three school districts and three schools within each district are selected using Exploration Stage activities to provide enough opportunities for teaching and learning the Active Implementation Frameworks, and for making systemic changes. Thanks to Wendy Iwaszuk and Andrea Cobb in Washington State for developing the graphic

As noted on the left side of Figure 44, it is the role of SISEP and the State Transformation Specialists (STSs) to help organize team members at each level and help them develop the required Active Implementation expertise. This is not a typical "train the trainer" approach where the original trainers bow out of the process after the first handoff. In Figure 44 and in practice, SISEP staff provide the original training and coaching and assessments at each level and persist with implementation-informed coaching until the Active Implementation

Frameworks are in use as intended by the Implementation Team at each level and at all levels simultaneously. From the first contacts with a state, the SISEP staff work with leaders and staff at every level to assure readiness for capacity development and engagement in the processes of change and managing change. In this way, SISEP and colleagues in state systems work together to assure a good fit between Implementation Team development and local readiness and resources.

## Attending to ethical and moral issues

With respect to the ethical and moral issues regarding creating disparity when working in a Transformation Zone, districts and schools that were in the lowest performing group in the state (i.e., bottom 5%) are over-selected for inclusion in the Transformation Zone. In addition, variability such as rural and urban, small and large schools, and different demographics of students add learning value in the first few Transformation Zones. In this case, while selection was done using typical Exploration Stage activities, more of the low-performing schools were included in the pool of possibles. There are not enough data as of today to describe potential educationally significant outcomes for teachers and students in the low-performing schools. However, teacher turnover was reduced dramatically, and the modest amount of student data collected so far are encouraging with significant gains made on end-of-term state testing.

## Linked Implementation Team development

The development of implementation capacity in the form of linked Implementation Teams is the focus in active scaling states (Fixsen et al., 2013). The linked Implementation Teams also are known as a cascading system of support. Any one level of capacity without the other levels is insufficient for effective and sustainable change at scale (Darling-Hammond & McLaughlin, 1995; Fixsen et al., 2017; Fullan, 2001).

> With advancements in implementation and scaling methods and measures, the time required to reach the teacher-student level has been cut in half –about 30 months instead of five years or more (when it could be done at all).

The task of the State Implementation Team shown in Table 29 is to develop Regional Implementation Teams to begin scaling in the Transformation Zone. Developing implementation capacity is nearly cost-neutral from a funding standpoint; the "cost" is the purposeful effort required on the part of everyone involved to initiate and manage processes to change hearts, minds, and behavior (Blase et al., 2015) . Every system already has staff assigned to improvement and monitoring activities that are mandated by state and national governments or initiated by local leaders. As these staff are selected to be members of Implementation Teams, their current work is repurposed, and their current roles are reassigned so that team members can learn the new ways of work and devote their time to accomplishing improvement goals. Stopping what is not working is accomplished as the new and more effective ways of work are learned and produce desired outcomes.

The process of teaching and learning and using the complex sets of knowledge, skills, and abilities involved in the Active Implementation Frameworks is outlined in Table 29. The ten time periods noted in the top row of Table 28 are not defined. A time period is complete when the knowledge, skills, and abilities required of participants named in that column are learned and used effectively.

Table 29. Developing an infrastructure of linked Implementation Teams in a state education system. The repeated structures and methods of development are an example of "fractal organization" development (Shin, Cha, Ryu, & Jung, 2006)

| Time Periods 1 – 10 | | | | | | | | | |
|---|---|---|---|---|---|---|---|---|---|
| 1 | 2 | 3 | 4 | 5 | 6 | 7 | 8 | 9 | 10 |
| SMT SISEP | SMT SISEP | SMT SISEP | SMT SISEP | SMT SISEP | SMT SISEP | SMT SISEP | SMT SISEP | SMT SISEP | SMT SISEP |
| STSs | STSs & SIT | STSs & SIT | STSs & SIT | STSs & SIT | STSs & SIT | STSs & SIT | STSs & SIT | STSs & SIT | STSs & SIT |
| | Active Model RIT | Co-Lead RIT | Co-Lead RIT | Coach RIT | Coach RIT | Coach RIT | Coach RIT | Coach RIT | Coach RIT |
| | | Active Model DIT | Active Model DIT | Co-Lead DIT | Co-Lead DIT | Coach DIT | Coach DIT | Coach DIT | Coach DIT |
| | | | | Active Model BIT | Active Model BIT | Co-Lead BIT | Co-Lead BIT | Coach BIT | Coach BIT |
| | | | | | | | | Teachers | |
| | | | | | | | | Students | |

With advancements in National Implementation Team methods and measures, the time required to reach the teacher-student level has been reduced substantially. In the attempts to develop implementation capacity in the first four states (starting in 2008), it could not be done at all. In the first "successful" state (starting in 2008), it took about five years. In current active scaling states (starting in 2013 or after), the teacher-student level is reached in about 30 months.

This is an example of usability testing improvement cycles with state systems as the unit of analysis. The SISEP National Implementation Team was, and continues to be, engaged in trial and learning. The result is greater success in less time as methods firmed up and scaling activities in states became more purposeful and assessable.

As indicated in Table 29, capacity development follows the active modeling "I do; we do; you do" approach to teaching complex skills in service settings. *Just enough, just in time preparation and coaching* are provided as needed to move from one time period to the next expeditiously. With linked Implementation Teams at the heart of the implementation infrastructure, the National Implementation Team provides active modeling (I do) of the new skills, then follows up with co-leading (we do) and coaching (you do) during subsequent events in order to develop in-state capacity to establish linked teams as part of a sustainable state implementation infrastructure. The ideas behind just-in-time methods are borrowed from management of inventory stocks and flow to reduce waste and improve production in manufacturing and business (Folinsa, Fotiadis, & Coudounaris, 2017; Wafa & Yasin, 1998). The same benefits of effectiveness and efficiency can be obtained in human services.

For example, educators generally are not aware of Exploration Stage activities that result in a mutually informed agreement to proceed with change; activities that make a big difference in eventual outcomes and costs (Romney et al., 2014). Thus, the National Implementation Team actively models Exploration skills for State Transformation Specialists (STSs) and members of the State Implementation Team (SIT), beginning the process (just-in-time) as regional agencies are approached to consider engaging in the development of Regional Implementation Teams (RITs). Then the National Implementation Team co-leads and coaches STSs as Exploration work is carried out by STSs and the SIT with additional regional agencies. When a RIT has developed sufficiently to begin work with districts, the National Implementation Team actively models Exploration activities in a district (just-in-time) since this is a new set of skills for RIT and SIT members and STSs. This process is repeated at each new level until the STSs and all the Implementation Team members have experience and have acquired initial skills to conduct the work effectively with coaching from the SIT, STSs, and National Implementation Team.

Knowing the Active Implementation Stages, it is not enough to do Exploration work with leaders, staff, and stakeholders at the state level. Just because the state level is ready, willing, and able to proceed does not mean that others in the system are equally prepared. Exploration must be repeated at each level.

Thus, at the point where the State Implementation Team members have learned the fundamentals of the Active Implementation Frameworks, they are ready to begin their work of developing Regional Implementation Teams. As shown in Table 30, the Initial Implementation work of the state team is to do Exploration with regional agencies to assess and create readiness in those groups in the state. When the first Regional Implementation Team is formed and the members have learned the fundamentals of the Active Implementation Frameworks, they are ready to begin their work of developing Regional Implementation Teams. This process is repeated to form local Implementation Teams. In each case, just enough modeling, training, and coaching is provided just in time to move each team from one stage to the next.

The Exploration Stage is just one of many components that define the Active Implementation Frameworks. All the Active Implementation Frameworks components must be taught, learned, and used as the new way of work to accomplish the aims of a system. Given the complexity of the Active Implementation Frameworks, each new way of work at each level is first done by experienced National Implementation Team staff so that staff embedded in the system can see what it looks like and sounds like in practice before the embedded staff are asked to try it on their own. The "first steps" needed to overcome resistance to change (Beckhard & Harris, 1987) must be clear and specific (rule-initiated) to instill confidence while developing competencies. The preparation and debrief time set aside for any event (e.g., an Exploration Stage meeting) provide opportunities for discussion of nuances and unusual events as well as continual review of the basic knowledge, skills, and abilities needed to achieve the goals. This is an example of the centralize, socialize, then decentralize process (Weick, 1987) discussed as a part of the Systemic Change framework.

# Table 30. Cascading stages of implementation where Initial Implementation at one level begins with Exploration activities at the next level

| | External Facilitation (Federal/National Implementation Team) | | | | | | | |
|---|---|---|---|---|---|---|---|---|
| **State** | Exploration | Installation | Initial Implementation | Full Implementation | | | | |
| **Region** | | | Exploration | Installation | Initial Implementation | Full Implementation | | |
| **Local** | | | | | Exploration | Installation | Initial Implementation | Full Implementation |
| **Service Delivery** | | | | | | | Recipients | Practitioners |

Attempting to skip ahead from one time period to another (Table 29) or skip Exploration at each level (Table 30) is counterproductive, leading to disconnects in the system and wasted resources. Fragmentation is endemic in human service systems; the goal is to align, integrate, and leverage resources by developing linked Implementation Teams that have the ability to make intended improvements purposefully, effectively, and efficiently.

## System Capacity Development Plan

A State Capacity Development Plan (Figure 45) has been created to guide the work of the National Implementation Team. The plan evolved as experience was gained in working with ten different state education systems, with little success in the beginning and with purposeful success after six years of trial and learning. The State Capacity Development Plan provides guidance for the intensive work done in state systems every month.

State Capacity Development Plan V2.2

State Implementation & Scaling-up of Evidence-based Practices

## Purpose

The State Capacity Development Plan (SCDP) provides a State Education Agency (SEA) with clear criteria to fully and effectively use innovations that are teachable, learnable, doable, and assessable in classrooms for the benefit of all students (Fixsen, Blase, Metz, & Van Dyke, 2013). The SCDP applies the USABLE INTERVENTION CRITERIA to identify the necessary roles, functions, and structures the SEA must put into practice within in the first 18-24 months of initiating change in a SEA. The plan operationalizes who will do what, by when, to achieve the desired outcomes in a SEA. SISEP's implementation informed support for a SEA uses the ACTIVE IMPLEMENTATION FRAMEWORKS. Putting in place each component of the SCDP ensures that organizational infrastructures are in place and that the roles and functions embedded in implementation teams are linked at the State, Regional, District, and Building level. This CASCADING SYSTEM OF SUPPORTS ensures that each team holds itself accountable for intervention and implementation outcomes through the use of structured COMMUNICATION PROTOCOLS. Hence, implementation capacity across all levels of the system is established and institutionalized so practice informs supportive policy development and policy in turn enables effective and sustainable practice in the classroom: the function of a PRACTICE-POLICY COMMUNICATION LOOP. The SCDP identifies the critical practices of successful implementation and scale-up in observable and measurable units, within a specified amount of time, to produce educationally significant outcomes for all of the students we serve.

**Figure 45. A State Capacity Development Plan for a State Education System**

The plan has 57 goals to be accomplished in the first 18-24 months of work in a state. An excerpt is provided in Table 31. The excerpt shows some of the goals for months 11-17. Each goal indicates who is involved (Roles), the Roles and Functions that are to be taught and learned, the National Implementation Team (i.e., SISEP) Activities related to accomplishing the goal, and Performance Assessment indicators related to accomplishing the goal. Operationalizing the scaling process has led to significant improvements in effectiveness and efficiency.

The work of the National Implementation Team expands as capacity is developed at each level. For example, by Time Period Five in Table 29, a SISEP team member in a given state is in direct personal contact with 110 to 150 state, regional, district, and school personnel during a three-day site visit in any given month. The focus of each site visit is the development of knowledge, skills, and abilities at each level and aligned relationships among levels. It is estimated that each of those individuals work throughout each month with another 10–20 staff in their units. Thus, perhaps 2,000 staff members in the system are learning, teaching, and doing their work in implementation-informed ways. As a result of working throughout the system, aligned and integrated structures and functions are developed, and collaborative interactions among them are established to leverage current resources in the system.

Table 31. Detail of a State Capacity Development Plan for a State Education System. The Plan has 57 goals to accomplish in the first 18-24 months in a state

| Time Line | Roles-Function-Structures SISEP & SEA | | Operational Definitions SISEP Activities | Performance Assessment SEA Outcome |
|---|---|---|---|---|
| | Roles | Essential Functions-Structures | | |
| | SDT RIT STS | Plan for the State's UI that includes a plan for continued selection and capacity development of coaches | Coaching Plan at each level of the system that develops capacity for sustainability | coaches selected; practice profile, fidelity measure, performance assessment system, and coaching evaluations in place; data is used to engage in on-going coaching (PDSA) |
| Month 11-17 | SMT RIT STS | 33. Identify 6 districts in the TZ that might be good candidates for implementation capacity building | Provide purpose and rationale for RIT to engage in district exploration, selection, and district entry processes; active modeling of district Exploration meetings and discussion by SISEP and STS underway | District entry and regional entity processes outlined (who, what, when, how); SMT informed and approval given to proceed; RIT members studying Independent Learning Plan to convey accurate information to the DITs |
| Month 11-17 | STS RIT | 34. Initial contact with 3 districts in the TZ | SISEP, STSs actively model initial RIT meetings with district staff; regional entities in attendance; introduce the district entry resources and model the use of the AiHub | STSs and RIT members learn to conduct district entry processes; regional entities and districts learn about implementation and developing capacity in their regions, districts, and schools |
| Month 11-17 | STS RIT | 35. Continue work with first 3 districts; initiate contact with new districts if a mutual decision to proceed is not reached in the first 3 districts | Provide coaching on district entry; information re: selecting and defining evidence-based education methods, formation and functions of DITs, and establishing supportive district and school policy and administrative contexts | First 3 districts engaged in Exploration processes as districts complete the mutual selection process and start process of identifying potential members of the DIT in each district; in each district at least 4 DIT members identified; districts agree to a once a month meeting with RIT team members |

## Usability testing of System Capacity Development Plans

The State Capacity Development Plan is continually revised as more experience is gained. With each group of two or three states, the actual work of the National Implementation Team members is compared to the work described in the plan. Based on an examination of experience (i.e., practice-based evidence), aspects of the plan are changed and time frames are adjusted. The new plan then guides the work of the National Implementation Team in the next cohort of two or three states. This *Usability Testing* approach to revising and refining the State Capacity Development Plan is shown in Figure 46. Having the plan as a guide allows new team members to be purposeful in how they do their work in state systems and allows accumulated knowledge to be recorded and used to make further improvements with each cohort of states. Deviations from the plan may lead to better outcomes or poorer outcomes. In either case, learning is occurring.

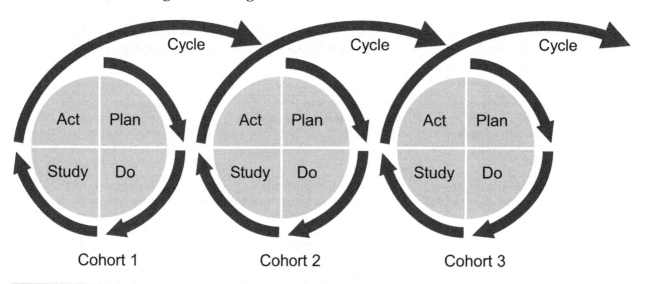

Figure 46. Usability testing applied to improving the State Capacity Development Plan

## Double-loop teaching and learning

Linked Implementation Teams are possible because all team members learn, use, and teach the Active Implementation Frameworks. This is an example of double-loop learning where team members are learning the content (first loop), and they are learning how to use the materials and methods (second loop) to teach the same content to others (Berta et al., 2015; Morgan & Ramirez, 1983; Sterman, 2006). Thus, each team has the capability of renewing itself as staff turnover occurs, and it has the ability to create more teams as the work expands, eventually, to create advantage for recipients in the entire population in a state.

An advantage of each team doing the work in a common and purposeful way is that new learning can occur at a steady pace and can be shared across teams. The use of the Active Implementation Frameworks by all teams promotes communication within and across teams. In this way, the benefits of new learning are magnified many times over in a state. The collective experiences add more practice-based evidence and knowledge to improve the Active Implementation Frameworks as well. Linked Implementation Teams contribute to the absorptive capacity of systems that are able to "recognize the value of new, external information, assimilate it, and apply it" (Cohen & Levinthal, 1990, p. 128). According to Zahra and George (2002), potential absorptive capacity consists of "knowledge acquisition and assimilation" capabilities, and realized capacity centers on "knowledge transformation and exploitation," the goal of Active Implementation.

## Recursive feedback loops: bottom-up change

The recursive practice to policy communication cycle is essential to Systemic Change. The benefits are realized in system changes that strengthen facilitators and remove barriers. Monthly in-person meetings with the Executive Leaders, State Transformation Specialists, and members of the National Implementation Team are necessary for sharing experience at the practice level (bottom-up) with the executives who decided (during Exploration and after) that changes to improve outcomes were a good idea. In every case, an engaged Executive Management Team has cleared barriers, changed structures and roles in the system, modified funding patterns, changed job descriptions, modified contracts, and so on (top-down) so that implementation capacity development and high fidelity use of selected innovations could flourish (bottom-up). The ways of work at the executive level are changed along with the system they direct as the conceptions (mental models) of "problems" and "solutions" change.

## Implementation capacity action assessments and results

The scaling work in states is reinforced by action assessments. These capacity assessments are designed to promote action planning while monitoring progress toward implementation capacity development. Progress toward developing linked Implementation Teams' capacity is assessed at each level. It should be pointed out that these are the first implementation capacity assessments to be created in any human service system. The capacity assessments are "action assessments" where each item asks about an important dimension of implementation capacity; each item is actionable; and the scores are sensitive to apparent improvements and setbacks. With each administration, action plans can be established; progress can be monitored; and gains can be documented and celebrated in the complex world of capacity development and system change. Corresponding with the levels in Tables 29 and 30, there is a:

1. State Capacity Assessment (SCA; Fixsen, Ward, Duda, et al., 2015)
2. Regional Capacity Assessment (RCA; St. Martin et al., 2015)
3. District Capacity Assessment (DCA; Russell et al., 2016; Ward et al., 2015)
4. School Assessment of Drivers Best Practices (ADBP; Fixsen, Ward, Blase, et al., 2018)
5. Classroom Observation Tool for Instructional Supports and Systems (OTISS; Fixsen, Ward, Ryan Jackson, & Chaparro, 2015).

The capacity assessments are a product of usability testing during the course of the intensive work in active scaling states where the usefulness of each assessment in the change process has been documented. The psychometric properties of the assessments are being established as experience is gained with the instruments (e.g., Cronbach's alpha of .89 for the DCA; 0.79 to 0.91 for ADBP subscales).

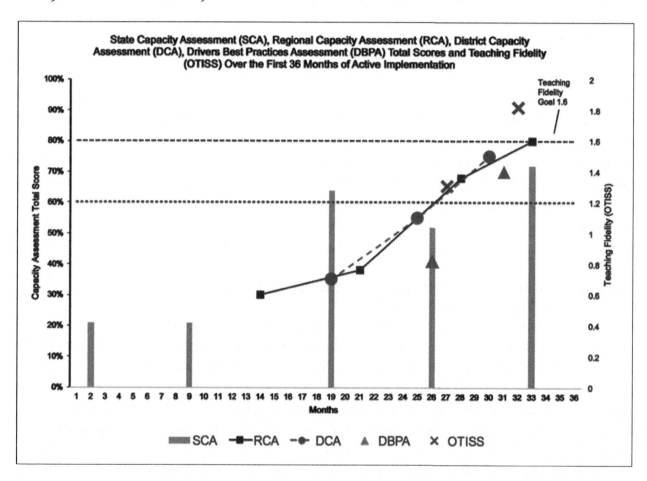

Figure 47. Capacity development for each level of the linked Implementation Teams with outcomes at the teacher level in schools (Ryan Jackson et al., 2018)

Figure 47 shows the results of the entire set of measures for one state related to the outcomes of the plan outlined in Table 29.

1) State capacity (SMT, STSs, SIT) begins to develop (SCA scores starting in Month 2)
2) Developing skills at the state level leads to development of regional capacity (RCA scores starting in Month 14)
3) State and regional work to develop district capacity is reflected in the DCA scores (starting in Month 19)
4) District capacity is used to develop school implementation capacity (DBPA scores starting in Month 26); and
5) School capacity improves teacher instruction in the classroom (OTISS scores starting in Month 27).

The data in Figures 47 and 48 are the first that show implementation capacity can be developed on purpose, measured consistently, and improved in complex state education systems. While capacity development occurs sequentially from one level to the next (see Table 28), the data in Figure 47 show that the Implementation Teams at all levels are learning and growing together within the first two years. The continued growth and integration of Implementation Teams is aided by this simultaneous and mutually interdependent process. Organizations (schools) and practitioners (teachers) are reached after only 26-28 months: by the 33rd month all capacity scores were approaching 80% (proficiency).

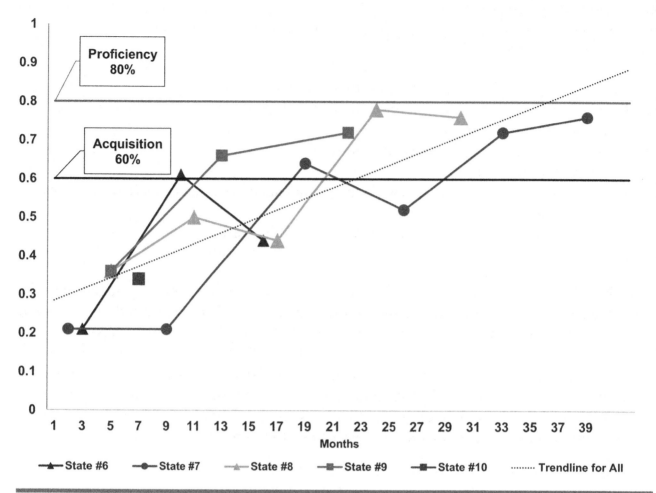

Figure 48. Study Two: State Capacity Assessment (SCA) scores over 39 months

As shown in Figure 48, these effects on state systems have been replicated in four states, demonstrating the universal applicability of the Active Implementation Frameworks within uniquely configured state systems. The relatively rapid development of implementation capacity is evident with each state moving from baseline scores in the 20–40% range and reaching the 60% acquisition goal within 24 months. Work in State #6 ended after 26 months with a state election and leadership change. Work began recently in State #10 where the baseline SCA has been administered.

The SCA subscale scores, shown in Table 32, provide more detailed information. Compared to the other subscale scores, the SMT Investment scores are higher at baseline. This is expected since, without evidence of leadership investment during the Exploration process, implementation and scaling capacity development work would not be happening in that state. Commitment to RIT development is 0% or nearly so in each state at baseline. Traditionally, Regional Education Agencies have not been included as a standard component of state education systems and lack identity and expected functions. Thus, regional capacity

314

development requires extra effort to include regions in thinking and planning at the state level and to negotiate agreements to reallocate regional staff time and resources required to initiate RITs. Over time, SMT System Alignment is the lowest subscale score in each state, and improvement is slow. System alignment requires embedding implementation and scaling best practices in official statements and documents. For example, to be fully in place, one SCA item requires that the "State Education Agency (SEA) has written and publicly available documents that describe methods for identifying and supporting effective innovations in education" and another requires, "The SEA has written guidance documents that describe or require providing implementation supports to districts as a primary purpose of regional educational agencies (e.g., ESDs, ECs, Service Co-ops, AEAs, ISDs)." Given the official nature of these requirements, they apply to all regions and districts in a state. SISEP begins working with two or three regions in a Transformation Zone and with a sample of districts and schools in each district. Thus, it is likely that the system alignment scores will improve more substantially as scaling expands to include more regions, districts, and schools.

Table 32. Subscale scores for each administration of the SCA in each active scaling state

| Month | SMT Investment | SMT System Alignment | Commitment to RIT Development | SCA Total |
|---|---|---|---|---|
| State #6 | | | | |
| 3 | 41% | 0% | 0% | 21% |
| 10 | 73% | 50% | 67% | 61% |
| 16 | 54% | 33% | 33% | 44% |
| State #7 | | | | |
| 2 | 42% | 0% | 17% | 21% |
| 9 | 41% | 0% | 50% | 21% |
| 19 | 79% | 30% | 63% | 64% |
| 26 | 63% | 30% | 50% | 52% |
| 33 | 88% | 40% | 69% | 72% |
| 39 | 83% | 30% | 94% | 76% |
| State #8 | | | | |
| 5 | 54% | 40% | 6% | 36% |
| 11 | 71% | 60% | 13% | 50% |
| 17 | 58% | 50% | 19% | 44% |
| State #9 | | | | |
| 5 | 46% | 20% | 0% | 26% |
| 13 | 100% | 50% | 25% | 66% |
| 22 | 88% | 40% | 69% | 72% |
| State # 10 | | | | |
| 7 | 67% | 10% | 0% | 34% |

## Summary

The data in Figures 47 and 48 are 1) the first repeated assessments of state capacity development in education, 2) the first to show that purposeful development of implementation capacity is possible in complex state education systems, and 3) the first to show purposeful capacity development can be replicated across state departments of education that are unique in terms of history, size, and operations. Each of these findings is significant for education and for scaling. While improving organization and system capacity for change is seen as critical in education and beyond (Barber & Fullan, 2005; Elmore,

316

Forman, Stosich, & Bocala, 2014; Flatten, Engelen, Zahra, & Brettel, 2011; Marzano, 2010; Padgett, Bekemeier, & Berkowitz, 2005), there are few measures of capacity (R. M. Goodman et al., 1993) and little evidence of change with repeated assessments of capacity (McGovern et al., 2007). In one study that employed repeated measures, McGovern et al. (2007) included a 35-item measure of capacity that was assessed three times over 18 months with scores that improved from slightly less to slightly greater than 3.0 on a five-point scale. In education systems that have been deemed "intractable" (Sarason, 1996), the data in Figures 47 and 48 are the first to reflect systematic change across state education systems and provide hope for a better future for students. The approach to developing capacity seems to meet the purpose of capacity to "accomplish something specific" while engaging in a process to "grow, progress, or improve." (http://edglossary.org/capacity).

The counterfactuals (Handley, Lyles, McCulloch, & Cattamanchi, 2018; U.S. Government Accounting Office, 2009) in education provide added credibility for the findings. It is not likely that the systemic changes reflected in the SCA scores in multiple state education systems occurred by chance, given the lack of improvement in education functioning and student outcomes documented since the 1970s.

The baseline data are in the 0-40% range for all ten states. This is an indicator of a large unmet need for implementation capacity development in education systems nationally. The development of capacity in states is informed by the Active Implementation Frameworks that provide a guide for action, methods to defragment and integrate system units, and a focus for improved system functioning.

Bryk (2016) and others (Akin et al., 2013; Harrison & Grantham, 2018; Sarason, 1996) advocate for using the trial and learning methods that are part of improvement science to vastly improve education-system functioning and student learning. The merits of this approach are apparent as the lessons learned from early failures and modest successes led to noticeably improved outcomes accomplished in less time for the most recent states.

## Eradicating smallpox: a scaling example

The approaches to scaling outlined in this chapter have been used to conduct a post hoc analysis of the eradication of smallpox as described by William Foege in the book *House on Fire* (Foege, 2011). Foege was a leader and innovator and fully engaged in practice as the global efforts to eradicate smallpox were planned, carried out, and adjusted in a mission-driven manner (Fenner et al., 1988). The quotes and page numbers below refer to the book *House on Fire*. We have selected this example because the book is available for further study by interested readers. In addition, it is the only example of a human service innovation that has been completely scaled globally. Thus, the example provides lessons for the field.

In the 1950s and 1960s mass inoculations were aimed at accomplishing "herd immunity" by protecting inoculated entire populations of people who might come into contact with an infected person. That is, the goal of herd immunity is to inoculate every person in a country so they will not contract the disease when traveling or when encountering visitors who may have the disease. For smallpox, mass vaccinations did not reach the last 20% of a population– the marginalized people, itinerants, beggars, drifters, migrants, and others who were more likely to have smallpox and to spread smallpox (p 52). Thus, outbreaks of smallpox continued.

The factors in the Formula for Success are used to outline the key components of the eradication efforts: effective innovation, effective implementation, and enabling context.

## Effective innovation

### Vaccine

After observing the apparent immunity of milkmaids and then purposefully injecting cowpox, then smallpox, in a young boy, in 1798 Edward Jenner published his findings that cowpox immunizes people against smallpox. Despite the long history of knowing what works, the production of the smallpox vaccine in the 1960s still was a "cottage industry" with inconsistent quality. As a first step toward reducing the incidence of smallpox, a World Health Organization (WHO) panel was convened to set standards for production and for preservation via freeze- drying to allow for reliable transport. Consultants then were sent out to help countries convert production to meet the new standards, and reference centers (fidelity assessors) were established to assure consistent high quality. By 1969 an effective process had been established, and by 1973 over 80% of the vaccine was being produced by the countries where the vaccine was being used (pp 48-49).

### Injection

The inoculation method initially involved manually injecting the vaccine via multiple needle pricks through a drop of vaccine on the skin, a method that required time and skill and was difficult to teach. "Take rates" (successful vaccination) varied within and across vaccinators (high or low fidelity practitioners). In the 1960s other methods were developed to consistently deliver measured doses of vaccine via a mechanical injector. With this method, one vaccinator could inject about 1,000 people per day with high take rates (pp 49-52).

As field experience accumulated, the injector was replaced by a bifurcated needle. Use of this method of injection "was easy to teach, provided take rates of 98% or higher, and required only about 20% of the vaccine" used with other techniques (p 101). The needles were inexpensive and could be cleaned and reused. Supplies were lightweight and suited to use by mobile teams. Vaccinators could vaccinate up to 500 people a day, fewer than the 1,000 people using the previous injector. But, the ease of training meant that more people could be deployed with the expectation of greater take rates in the population while conserving the supply of the vaccine (p 102).

## Surveillance

A search network was organized with reporting by "block" (roughly 100,000 population in a block). The block data were summed up by district, state, and nationally. "What exactly was a search?" (p 107). For six days each month, every available health worker employed in the system was mobilized to find cases of smallpox in their block. At the end of six days, they would go back to their regular jobs in malaria prevention and treatment, family planning, and other programs. If more workers were needed, day laborers were employed and taught to be searchers. A search protocol was developed with operational guides for each area. The team for each block searched 20–25 villages a day for six days and reported the results using standard protocols and forms.

## Containment

Separate teams were deployed for containment. In India each of the 386 districts had one vaccinator per 25,000 population, one supervisor for every four vaccinators, and one medical assistant per "block" of 100,000 people. In addition, each district had a mobile team of five vaccinators that could be sent anywhere at any time. Containment teams were taught to adhere to a protocol for vaccinations. "A single-page instruction sheet was developed on vaccination techniques, use of the bifurcated needle, the preferred site of vaccination, and the sterilization of bifurcated needles after use" (p 109).

## Effective implementation

"The objective may be global, but implementation is always local. The strategy for smallpox eradication did not change from country to country, but the local culture determined which tactics were most useful. Only the specific locality can provide information on who is sick, who is hiding from the vaccinators, when people are available for vaccination, how to hire watch guards, or how to secure the cooperation of the community. In all cultures, an approach of respect for local customs is needed" (p 192).

The targeted surveillance and containment strategy became the focus of implementation in each country. There were impediments to the new and effective strategy. First, the Center for Disease Control and Prevention (CDC) and WHO staff had been trained to do mass vaccinations. The surveillance and containment strategy was counter to their training and thinking. The CDC workers who were "too young to realize they couldn't do it" were most successful. Second, it was commonly accepted that smallpox spread rapidly with minimal contact with an infected person. The assumption of rapid transmission was not supported by evidence from practice that it often took multiple exposures to transmit the disease (p 73-74). Third, the WHO expert panel favored mass inoculations for herd immunity and was not prepared to support the new strategy. The evidence accumulated as the surveillance and containment strategy expanded into all 20 CDC-related countries with equal success as smallpox was eliminated in each of those countries after only a few years (e.g., 3.5 years from the beginning to the last case in Nigeria). Based on this practice-based evidence, WHO and CDC then supported surveillance and containment as the strategy for eradicating smallpox globally. The biggest test was in India where smallpox was endemic and accepted as part of life in a large and diverse population.

## Competency Drivers: selection, training, coaching, fidelity

In India, training was provided for staff at each level: state, district, and block. In one state, "preparations for the first search required over 60 training sessions simply to get down to the district level, and an additional 930 training sessions at the district and [block] levels" (p 108; linked Implementation Teams). Supervision (coaching) followed the same pattern with training for supervisors to follow quality control protocols (fidelity) to assure surveillance was carried out as intended in each block. The preparations paid off with searchers in the first month contacting 99% of the 140,000 villages in one state.

In India there are 29 states, 386 districts, and more than 25,000 blocks. Competency development had to be done well and be repeatable in several thousand training sessions provided at the block level across India where surveillance and containment was carried out each day (p 103; 108).

The incidence of smallpox discovered by the surveillance teams far exceeded expectations. The expectations were based on the existing passive reporting system where medical staff in a block reported the number of smallpox patients who came to them. The active surveillance method detected far more cases than imagined. For example, in one month the passive reporting system in one state reported 437 cases of smallpox while active surveillance found 5,989 new cases in that state (p 115). Given the overwhelming need that was detected, the first response by some was to end surveillance and devote all the resources to containment. However, the decision was: "Our first response should be to improve containment, not dumb down surveillance" (p 116). It is best to know the truth and deal with it, even when the truth is daunting.

Given the overwhelming need detected by surveillance teams in India, the number of teams was increased and the containment strategy was changed (Improvement Cycles). To use the teams more efficiently, only those living in adjacent houses were inoculated instead of the previously required 20-30 nearby houses. Experience from the first searches found that school children were the best informants so they became the initial focus of future searches (p 117; Improvement Cycles). The astounding number of cases detected each month led to difficult decisions. Was it more important to fully contain each outbreak or to reach as many outbreaks as possible? The optimism attached to the proponents of each option found their "optimism was trumped by reality" (p 118; fidelity). Either option left people unprotected and smallpox continued. And, given the shortage of high quality serum, "It was tempting to consider diluting the vaccine so we could vaccinate more people." (p 56; fidelity). A WHO study found that diluted vaccine resulted in ineffective prevention and treatment of smallpox. Thus, the focus was on assuring an adequate supply of high-quality serum when and where it was needed and to deploy enough teams to fully contain each outbreak by injecting the full dose of undiluted vaccine.

"Containment, as well as surveillance, improved when it was supervised and evaluated" (p 153; coaching and fidelity). In 1974 the program developed evaluation teams. The containment teams were asked to make a mark on the door of each house they visited. The mark changed each month. The evaluation team then could visit houses to record the number visited and ask a sample of households about what the containment team had done. The evaluation results along with key indicators in the data (e.g., percentage of outbreaks reported within 21 days of the first case in an outbreak) enabled program leaders to "quickly spot deficiencies in searching, investigating, and containing outbreaks; such weaknesses could be related to particular [blocks], districts, or even individuals" (p 155; improvement cycles; recursive practice-policy communication cycles). The evaluation program (Decision Support Data System) "became an indispensable management tool and the driver for quality improvement" (p 155; fidelity).

"Every new refinement in search and containment methods required training, new procedures for reporting, and new forms which had to distributed on an ongoing basis to thousands of [blocks] and districts" (p 155; Implementation Drivers; linked Implementation Teams).

In India where smallpox was endemic and the population was dense and mobile, the demand for vaccination far outstripped the ability to respond. "The marketplace took over, less careful operators proliferated, entire villages were no longer inoculated at the same time, and outbreaks of smallpox resulted." (p 91; fidelity). The advance of surveillance and containment methods threatened the livelihood of the operators and produced resistance to the strategy.

To the extent they were willing, local operators were hired to be vaccinators as part of the program (selection).

## Decision Support Data System

"Numbers consumed our days, became our compass, and guided our actions" (p 146). New outbreaks continued to be the key statistic. New data were developed to track contained outbreaks. A contained outbreak was defined as a previously infected area that went four weeks without a new case of smallpox. Despite the efforts of increasing numbers of containment teams, the number of new outbreaks continued to increase in part because surveillance techniques improved each month. Surveillance evolved from asking school children and other informants, to going house to house in high-risk parts of a village, to going to every house in a village. The quality of searches improved from some workers just "filling out a form" to nearly all workers taking pride in finding and reporting cases because every "missed case" provided an opportunity for an outbreak to continue.

The data from surveillance led to a conclusion that the number of outbreaks (not individual cases) was the best indicator of the containment work required. "The surveillance and containment strategy was a learning program" where the attempts at shortcuts provided evidence of what did not work. After three months of experience, it was clear that "the smallpox workers were learning and improving every month while the smallpox virus, for all of its evolutionary success, could not respond with the same agility" (p 121; improvement cycles).

Based on the location and density of missed cases, secondary searches were initiated to augment the standard monthly six-day search. Markets, fairs, religious ceremonies, and areas of high risk were searched by trained smallpox workers between the monthly searches. Protocols were developed for secondary searches. Smallpox workers would go through the crowds and use recognition cards to see if anyone had seen a person with smallpox, a highly visible disease. Additional searches were conducted among groups of itinerant workers, beggars, and others who were mobile and difficult to find in any given location. By January 1974 the monthly searches were occurring in all 100 million homes in the entire country. Quarterly data on new outbreaks helped to track the location of the disease and decide on the allocation of resources for surveillance and containment (p 149).

The soaring numbers of outbreaks, the labor-intensive work of containment, and the difficulty of continuing to train more teams meant the program constantly was behind in developing containment capacity. "The ideal was always ahead of the actual" (p 151). In addition, in 1974 the protocol was changed to have a supervisor visit each outbreak to evaluate the work of the containment team (coaching, fidelity). And, the program returned to the original plan of vaccinating 20 households around each house with smallpox (fidelity). Without enough containment teams, the next monthly search produced evidence of more outbreaks before the containment teams had visited all of the previous outbreak sites. "The amount of work, record keeping, and supervision for one outbreak was prodigious," and visits had to continue for four-six weeks (i.e., the incubation period) to be certain no new cases had developed before containment could be declared. Visits by supervisors monitored workers to be sure they followed the protocols for containment and to detect reasons for continued outbreaks in "contained" areas (coaching, fidelity).

"It was soon discovered that people from outside the immediate family and even outside the neighborhood were expected to visit a person who was sick with smallpox" (p 152). This led to the addition of watch guards at each patient's house with instructions to vaccinate every visitor day or night. "Hiring, training, and employing watch guards at each house was added to the work of the containment teams" (p 152). An additional problem was then discovered when outbreaks occurred in previously contained areas because some people had been missed. They had contact with an infected person but were working in the fields, or out shopping, or hidden when the containment team was vaccinating villagers. The containment teams countered this be asking an informant to list all the members of a household. Then the team and the watch guards spent extra time and effort to locate and vaccinate every person (improvement cycles).

"Effective evaluation allowed us to redeploy resources with confidence that the highest priority needs were being addressed" (p 174). Following a monthly search, ten villages in a district were randomly selected for evaluation (e.g., marks on doorways, interviews with household members; fidelity). With the evaluation teams in place, the key indicator of "outbreaks reported within 21 days of onset" reached 100% reporting and sustained at that level (fidelity). For any unexpected outbreaks, an "outbreak autopsy" (debrief session; improvement cycles) was performed to discover the reasons why. Delayed or incomplete containment actions (low fidelity) were the primary reason (p 175). As the number of new outbreaks declined, resources were freed up to devote more attention to each new outbreak.

## Enabling context

Given the scope of the problem, it was difficult to convince leaders that smallpox could be eliminated. "As more geographic areas became free of smallpox, it became easier to transmit this belief ... Once this [belief] was shared by a critical mass of people, no barrier was insurmountable" (p 53).

In one area of Nigeria in 1966, "Serendipity provided a chance for us to rethink the eradication strategy" (p 54) and move from a herd immunity approach to a surveillance and containment strategy. Given the limited supply of high quality vaccine in a remote area of Nigeria, the decision was made to vaccinate the person with smallpox and inoculate the family members, neighbors, and others who had contact with the infected person and were susceptible to the disease. The difficulty with this strategy is surveillance; how to find each person who has smallpox in a district, region, and country. Taking advantage of an existing network, the program leaders contacted missionaries in villages who then reported any cases of smallpox to the team. The person with smallpox was inoculated, and those who had contact with that person were located and inoculated to contain the spread. If any one of them already had smallpox, the containment strategy of locating and inoculating was repeated. This targeted approach conserved the supply of vaccine while effectively eliminating smallpox from a region of a country (p 59).

Given the early indications of success, the team began training other health workers from Nigeria. They used stopwatches to see how fast the trainees could set up an immunization site, attach ropes for crowd control, set up the supplies, clean the injectors, and so on until they provided the first injection. The surveillance and containment strategy then was replicated in another region of Nigeria that reported an outbreak of smallpox. The success of the replication with newly trained staff provided sufficient confirmation that the targeted surveillance and containment strategy was more effective and efficient than the herd immunity mass inoculation strategy (p 59).

The experience in Nigeria led to the development of separate teams for surveillance and for containment. It was discovered that "there was a decided tendency to underreport cases if positive reports meant more work for the searchers" (p 110).

Developed out of necessity and replicated on purpose, the surveillance and containment strategy was established, and methods for developing the competencies of health workers were established in other regions in Nigeria. Smallpox was eliminated in Nigeria. The strategy did not rely on local health systems or providers. It had its own structure of teams to create teams (capacity to develop capacity) to promptly engage villages to contain outbreaks that were detected by the surveillance system. The surveillance and containment strategy developed and operationalized in Nigeria became the goal of implementation and scaling globally.

## Systemic Change

India already had made a substantial commitment to eliminating smallpox with an intensive campaign to vaccinate at least 80% of the population in three years (pp 98-99). A central organization was developed at the national level and in each state. District operating units were developed and provided with vehicles, vaccine, and other supplies. District units supported mobile teams that each included 72 vaccinators, 12 sanitary inspectors, two health educators, a paramedical assistant, and a medical officer. There were 152 mobile teams that employed over 13,000 staff. Even as these teams reached 80% coverage in an area, smallpox outbreaks continued unabated as the remaining 20% continued to contract and spread the disease. "The euphoria of starting a new program already had run into the brick wall of reality" (p 99). The first policy response was to increase the goal from 80% to 100%, an impossible and demoralizing goal for mobile team members who knew how difficult it was to achieve the 80% goal. A government study found that, for a variety of reasons, the vaccination-take rates varied greatly by district, and perhaps only 50% of the population had been vaccinated effectively (fidelity). In 1967, 830,000 new cases of smallpox occurred. At the policy level, there was the growing realization that "the number of vaccinations given is a meaningless figure."

By 1973 "everything was falling into place: government commitment, increased national and international resources, increased vaccination staff, sufficient vaccine of good quality, and easy system for vaccinating using bifurcated needles, a timely reporting system, and cross-notification of cases between districts to provide a national approach. However, smallpox still was not disappearing." (p 104).

## Executive leadership and management

India's top health officials and over 600 high level leaders were deployed from federal and state governments as well as universities, hospitals, and private industry. The federal leaders set monthly goals, had monthly meetings with state leaders and teams that "provided a rapid exchange of information and obligated program directors at central and state levels to be involved in the field." (p 124). Their task was to identify and overcome any obstacles and to assure good working conditions for those doing the work of surveillance and containment (Practice-Policy Communication Cycle). Leadership teams were established to reach shared objectives that superseded competition for turf among represented units. Once the management structure was in place, it provided a platform for making adjustments to assure the work was done at all levels.

When the surveillance and containment strategy was fully functional in India, the Indian government employed over 150,000 surveillance and containment team members and nearly 100,000 watch guards (p 152).

The management system included special teams of epidemiologists who were highly mobile and could go to unusual or intensive outbreaks to provide additional expertise and support. The special teams provided a way to incorporate outside experts into a country sensitive to intrusion by outsiders. Eventually, 30 countries contributed 235 consultants who served on the special teams, each bringing "fresh energy and new eyes" to the work during their three months in India. (p 136). Before doing any work in India, each consultant had three days of training on the technical components of surveillance and containment, procedures they were expected to follow, forms required for reporting, and the role of the monthly meetings to review data and make adjustments. Not all consultants were able to adapt and contribute. Over time the leaders learned to look for qualities that "are not found in the usual résumé or recommendations by supervisors." The qualities they began to look for were integrity, cultural sensitivity, and optimism.

Recursive Practice-Policy feedback

The Executive Management Team in each state had a monthly meeting of 50 to 100 people for one day. The goal of each meeting was to review the work of the previous month and plan the goals and tactics for the next. Attendees included representatives of the federal government agencies, the state smallpox officer, state health and political leaders, district medical officers, special team members, urban health officers, and people from the blocks that were of special concern. The meetings were used to "get real-time feedback from field workers, pursue scientific inquiry, evaluate what was working and what was not, replenish funds and provide payment, and recharge the field-workers enthusiasm" (p 141). At the meetings, field workers shared innovations, and the effective innovations were quickly replicated and evaluated by others. Lessons from practice were identified and used to help meet targets that were set for the next month. The monthly meetings in each state and nationally kept leaders and others "looking for clues regarding what was working and what needed to be changed" (p 145).

In May 1974, for the first time, the number of contained outbreaks exceeded the number of new outbreaks in India. Even so, the number of new outbreaks was still large, over 800 new outbreaks per week. In that same month railway workers went on strike. This required planning for how supplies could be moved and distributed to outbreaks. The vaccinators in one state also declared their intention to strike for higher wages. Then India detonated its first nuclear device which led to global criticism and scrutiny of India, including criticism of the unacceptable incidence of smallpox. The political response was to abandon containment and surveillance and reinstate mass inoculation. "Whether effective or not, the known was preferred over the unknown" (p 169). On May 27 the decision to return to mass immunization was to be announced at the monthly meeting of the smallpox group. After the Minister announced his intentions to the group, a young physician stood up and pointed out that if a house is on fire, no one wastes water on the nearby houses, they pour water where it will do the most good—on the house that is burning! This, he said, is the difference between mass immunization and the surveillance and containment methods. The Minister thought about this and decided on the spot to give them one more month. On that same day the railway strike was settled and the other groups withdrew their threats to strike. The next month the data showed a decline in new outbreaks, and more dramatic declines occurred in new outbreaks in the following months—data that convinced the politicians and Minister to allow the program to continue beyond June 1974.

By May 1975 the last smallpox case was treated in India, 20 months after the surveillance and containment strategy was put in place. In late 1978 the last known case of smallpox in the world was treated. Smallpox was eliminated globally.

# Chapter 17: A Future for Implementation

It is time for change in human services. Research to develop innovations is improving, and the number of evidence-based innovations is growing. Increasingly, we know what to do. The log jam of innovations that are effective but not used in practice has focused attention on Implementation Science. With rapid advances in Implementation Science, we are learning how to make effective use of innovations in typical human service organizations and systems. Now the task is to scale implementation capacity in the form of skilled Implementation Teams to purposefully produce social impact for the effective innovations at hand as well as those yet to be developed. The people living in our global community deserve no less.

Implementation Science is a new science that continues to grow. Implementation frameworks provide guidance for implementation practice, and improved practice provides a better laboratory for studying implementation done well. This creates a virtuous cycle in which improvements in science and practice feed each other. The Active Implementation Frameworks continue to be used and evaluated in practice, and those data continue to guide the development of the next generation of improved frameworks.

What are the next steps? Advancing the science of implementation could be crowdsourced if we can establish common concepts, common language, and common measures so we can communicate clearly and precisely. Crowdsourcing science provided major breakthroughs and advancements in the past when communication about the position of stars could be expressed precisely by scientists in any part of the world and communicated clearly in a common language (Wootton, 2015). Major advancements in computer science occurred after hardware and software development groups were convened in the 1950s and established Common Business Oriented Language

> *By providing a common language, common concepts, and common measures, the Active Implementation Frameworks add value to the development of implementation science. If we can communicate clearly and consistently, then we can establish theory, test predictions based on theory, and advance the practice and science of implementation.*

(COBOL) and Formula Translator (FORTRAN). The idea of machine-independent software developed by "Amazing Grace" Hopper in the 1950s led to the development of many fragmented versions of software that only ran on specific machines (Appleman, 2000; Gertner, 2012). Establishing common software and approaches to development of new software opened the door for major changes that persist to this day. The benefits of crowdsourcing are such that software can be developed anywhere in the world; can be used and improved anywhere in the world; and can run on a wide variety of computers in almost any context.

Past research and practice development have helped to identify apparently potent variables. Practice and research-based knowledge has been summarized in frameworks that are a useful proxy for theory. As noted throughout this book, the Active Implementation Frameworks represent a step down the crowdsourcing path with major concepts identified, plain language used to describe the concepts, and practical measures of operations related to the concepts developed to assess their presence in practice. The Active Implementation Frameworks have been used prospectively to design organization and system interventions that have been tested in practice in a purposeful way. The Active Implementation Frameworks offer the beginnings of a theory with predictions of relationships among independent and dependent variables provided in each section. There are more than 130 "if-then" statements in this book, enough to keep researchers busy for years to come. It is our ambition to make the Active Implementation Frameworks obsolete in ten years as new practice and research "proceed from wonder to no wonder" and take the field to new levels beyond any current conception.

There are several challenges that need to be addressed to advance the science and practice of implementation. The long timeframes for implementation activities and outcomes present challenges for the process of discovery and improvement. Causes and effects often are separated by years, and linkages are difficult to detect without documented and repeated experience. In addition, "Context and 'confounders' lie at the very heart of the diffusion, dissemination, and implementation of complex innovations. They are not extraneous to the object of study; they are an integral part of it" (Greenhalgh et al., 2004, p. 615). These confounders present challenges related to measurement, research design, and theory development. Finally, the transdisciplinary involvement in implementation has contributed to the development of the field but also confuses language and conceptual thinking and frustrates efforts to find and summarize the literature(s).

Active Implementation benefits from frameworks that have been operationalized (i.e., made teachable, learnable, doable in practice) and can be applied in a variety of settings and systems. The presence and strength of the Active Implementation Frameworks can be assessed in practice using standard measures of capacity and practice that are practical and usable in research. The next steps involve establishing Active Implementation independent variables (e.g., expert Implementation Teams; Usability Testing) and evaluating the implementation and innovation outcomes in experimental designs. Multiple baseline designs (Caron & Dozier, 2019; Doussau & Grady, 2016; Handley et al., 2018; Speroff & O'Connor, 2004) are well suited to evaluating the frameworks in applied settings. For example, Implementation Teams can be introduced on a staggered timeframe in school districts or emergency maternal obstetric and newborn care clinics, and team functioning can be assessed with the Assessment of Drivers Best Practices (ADBP). The implementation independent variables then can be used to analyze impact on measures of practitioner performance (fidelity) and on student learning, maternal and newborn health, mortality or homelessness. The data will contribute to refining and extending the Active Implementation Frameworks so that they will continue to become more effective and efficient.

Science is based on theory and testable predictions (Wootton, 2015). The Active Implementation Frameworks provide the basis for theory and a source of predictions of outcomes in practice. These frameworks have proven useful for guiding changes in practices, organizations, and systems to achieve desired outcomes. By providing a common language, common concepts, and common measures, the Active Implementation Frameworks add value to the development of Implementation Science. If we can communicate clearly and consistently, then we can establish theory, test predictions based on theory, and advance the practice and science of implementation.

# References

Aarons, G. A., Green, A. E., Palinkas, L. A., Self-Brown, S., Whitaker, D. J., Lutzker, J. R., . . . Chaffin, M. J. (2012). Dynamic adaptation process to implement an evidence-based child maltreatment intervention. *Implementation Science, 7*. doi:10.1186/1748-5908-7-32

Aarons, G. A., Hurlburt, M., & Horwitz, S. M. (2011). Advancing a conceptual model of evidence-based practice implementation in public service sectors. *Administration and Policy in Mental Health, 38*(1), 4.

Aarons, G. A., Sommerfeld, D. H., Hecht, D. B., Silovsky, J. F., & Chaffin, M. J. (2009). The impact of evidence-based practice implementation and fidelity monitoring on staff turnover: Evidence for a protective effect. *Journal of Consulting & Clinical Psychology, 77*(2), 270-280. doi:10.1037/a0013223

Abrams, E. J., Simonds, R. J., Modi, S., Rivadeneira, E., Vaz, P., Kankasa, C., . . . Ruff, A. J. (2012). PEPFAR scale-up of pediatric HIV services: Innovations, achievements, and challenges. *Journal of Acquired Immune Deficiency Syndromes, 60*(3), 105-112. doi:10.1097/QAI.0b013e31825cf4f5

Acosta, J., Chinman, M., Ebener, P., Malone, P. S., Paddock, S., Phillips, A., . . . Slaughter, M. E. (2013). An Intervention to Improve Program Implementation: Findings from a Two-Year Cluster Trial of Assets-Getting to Outcomes. *Implementation Science, 8*(1). doi:10.1186/1748-5908-8-87

Adondiwo, A., Kubio, C., Kanyoke, E., Bagni, F., Dasoberi, I. N., Amenga-Etego, I. A., . . . Barker, P. M. (2013). Using quality improvement methods to test and scale up a new national policy on early post-natal care in Ghana. *Health Policy and Planning, 29*(5), 622-632. doi:10.1093/heapol/czt048

Akin, B. A., Bryson, S. A., Testa, M. F., Blase, K. A., McDonald, T., & Melz, H. (2013). Usability testing, initial implementation, and formative evaluation of an evidence-based intervention: Lessons from a demonstration project to reduce long-term foster care. *Evaluation and Program Planning, 41*(0), 19-30. doi:http://dx.doi.org/10.1016/j.evalprogplan.2013.06.003

Aladjem, D. K., & Borman, K. M. (Eds.). (2006). *Examining comprehensive school reform.* Washington, DC: Urban Institute Press.

Aldrich, R. M. (2008). From complexity theory to transactionalism: moving occupational science forward in theorising the complexities of behaviour. *Journal of Occupational Science, 15*(3), 147-156.

333

Alexander, J. F., & Parsons, B. (1973). Short-term Family Intervention: A Therapy Outcome Study. *Journal of Consulting & Clinical Psychology, 2*, 195-201.

Alexander, J. F., Pugh, C., Parsons, B., & Sexton, T. L. (2000). Functional family therapy. In D. S. Elliott (Ed.), *Book three: Blueprints for violence prevention (2nd ed.)*. Golden, CO: Venture.

Allanson, E. R., Tunçalp, Ö., Vogel, J. P., Khan, D. N., Oladapo, O. T., Long, Q., & Gülmezoglu, A. M. (2017). Implementation of effective practices in health facilities: a systematic review of cluster randomised trials. *BMJ Global Health, 2*(2). doi:10.1136/bmjgh-2016-000266

Allen, J. D., Towne, S. D., Maxwell, A. E., DiMartino, L., Leyva, B., Bowen, D. J., . . . Weiner, B. J. (2017). Measures of organizational characteristics associated with adoption and/or implementation of innovations: A systematic review. *BMC Health Services Research, 17*(1), 591. doi:10.1186/s12913-017-2459-x

Annie E. Casey Foundation. (1995). *The path of most resistance: Reflections on lessons learned from new futures*. Retrieved from Baltimore, MD: Annie E. Casey Foundation:

Annie E. Casey Foundation. (2003). The unsolved challenge of system reform. The condition of the frontline human services workforce. Retrieved from Baltimore, MD: Annie E. Casey Foundation:

Antman, E. M., Lau, J., Kupelnick, B., Mosteller, F., & Chalmers, T. C. (1992). A comparison of results of meta-analyses of randomized control trials and recommendations of clinical experts: Treatments for myocardial infarction. *JAMA, 268*(2), 240-248. doi:10.1001/jama.1992.03490020088036

Appleman, D. (2000). *How computer programming works*. Berkeley, CA: Apress.

Arrow, K. (1962). Economic welfare and the allocation of resources for invention. In R. Nelson (Ed.), *The rate and direction of inventive activity* (pp. 609-625). Princeton, NJ: Princeton University Press.

Ashby, W. R. (1956). *An introduction to cybernetics*. London: Chapman & Hall.

Baer, D. M., Wolf, M. M., & Risley, T. R. (1968). Some current dimensions of Applied Behavior Analysis. *Journal of Applied Behavior Analysis, 1*(1), 91-97. doi:10.1901/jaba.1968.1-91

Bailey, J. S., Wolf, M. M., & Phillips, E. L. (1970). Home-based reinforcement and the modification of pre-delinquents' classroom behavior. *Journal of Applied Behavior Analysis, 3*, 223-233.

Balas, E. A., & Boren, S. A. (2000). Managing clinical knowledge for health care improvement. In J. Bemmel & A. T. McCray (Eds.), *Yearbook of Medical Informatics 2000: Patient-Centered Systems*. (pp. 65-70). Stuttgart, Germany: Schattauer Verlagsgesellschaft.

Barber, M., & Fullan, M. (2005). Tri-level development: Putting systems thinking into action. *Education Weekly, 24*(25), 34-35.

Barker, P. M., Reid, A., & Schall, M. W. (2016). A framework for scaling up health interventions: lessons from large-scale improvement initiatives in Africa. *Implementation Science, 11*(1), 12. doi:10.1186/s13012-016-0374-x

Baron, R. L., Leavitt, S. E., Watson, D. M., Coughlin, D. D., Fixsen, D. L., & Phillips, E. L. (1984). Skill-based management training for child care program administrators: The Teaching-Family Model revisited. *Child Care Quarterly, 13*, 262-277.

Baron, R. L., Watson, D. M., Coughlin, D. D., Fixsen, D. L., & Phillips, E. L. (1979). *The Program Manager Training Manual*. Boys Town, NE: Father Flanagan's Boys' Home.

Bartley, L. H., Bright, C. L., & DePanfilis, D. (2017). Contributors to Fidelity of Child Welfare-Related Interventions: A Review. *Journal of Public Child Welfare, 11*(4-5), 433-463. doi:10.1080/15548732.2017.1340222

Bayly, M. B. (1956). The story of the Salk anti-poliomyelitis vaccine. Retrieved from http://www.whale.to/vaccine/bayly.html#THESALKVACCINEDISASTER

Beckhard, R., & Harris, R. (1987). *Organizational Transitions*. Reading, MA: Addison-Wesley.

Bedlington, M. M., Braukmann, C. J., Kirigin Ramp, K. A., & Wolf, M. M. (1988). A comparison of treatment environments in community-based group homes for adolescent offenders. *Criminal Justice and Behavior, 15*, 349-363.

Bedlington, M. M., Solnick, J. V., Schumaker, J. B., Braukmann, C. J., Kirigin, K. A., & Wolf, M. M. (1978). *Evaluating group homes: The relationship between parenting behaviors and delinquency*. Paper presented at the American Psychological Association Convention, Toronto, Canada.

Beer, M., Eisenstat, R. A., & Spector, B. (1990). Why change programs don't produce change. *Harvard Business Review, 68*(6), 158-166.

Behrens, S. (2009). Shadow systems: the good, the bad and the ugly. *Communications of the ACM, 52*(2), 124-129. doi:10.1145/1461928.1461960

Bernard, C. (1865). *An introduction to the study of experimental medicine*. Paris: First English translation by Henry Copley Greene, published by Macmillan & Co., Ltd., 1927; Dover edition 1957.

Berta, W., Cranley, L., Dearing, J. W., Dogherty, E. J., Squires, J. E., & Estabrooks, C. A. (2015). Why (we think) facilitation works: insights from organizational learning theory. *Implementation Science, 10*(1), 141. doi:10.1186/s13012-015-0323-0

Bertram, R. M., Suter, J. C., Bruns, E. J., & O'Rourke, K. E. (2012). Implementation research and wraparound literature: Building a research agenda. *Journal of Child and Family Studies, 20*(5). doi:10.1007/s10826-010-9430-3

Best, A., Greenhalgh, T., Lewis, S., Saul, J. E., Carroll, S., & Bitz, J. (2012). Large-System Transformation in Health Care: A Realist Review. *The Milbank Quarterly, 90*(3), 421-456.

Black, D. D., Downs, J. C., Phillips, E. L., & Fixsen, D. L. (1982). *Crisis Intervention: Administrative Procedures for Working with Disruptive Students.* Boys Town, NE: Father Flanagan's Boys' Home Education Program.

Blanchard, C., Livet, M., Ward, C., Sorge, L., Sorensen, T. D., & McClurg, M. R. (2017). The Active Implementation Frameworks: A roadmap for advancing implementation of Comprehensive Medication Management in Primary care. *Research in Social and Administrative Pharmacy, 13*(5), 922–929. doi:10.1016/j.sapharm.2017.05.006

Blase, K. A. (2006). *Developers, purveyors, and implementers of evidence-based programs.* Retrieved from National Implementation Research Network, University of South Florida:

Blase, K. A., & Fixsen, D. L. (2003). *Evidence-based programs and cultural competence.* Retrieved from National Implementation Research Network, University of South Florida: https://www.activeimplementation.org/resources/meeting-summary-evidence-based-programs-and-cultural-competence/

Blase, K. A., & Fixsen, D. L. (2013). *ImpleMap: Exploring the implementation landscape.* Retrieved from Chapel Hill, NC: National Implementation Research Network: https://www.activeimplementation.org/resources/implemap-exploring-the-implementation-landscape/

Blase, K. A., Fixsen, D. L., Maloney, D. M., & Phillips, E. L. (1984). Behavior technology in child-care: The Teaching-Parent and Teaching-Family Model. In J. Beker (Ed.), *The child-care worker in the United States: A comparative analysis of evolving role models.* New York: Human Sciences Press.

Blase, K. A., Fixsen, D. L., Naoom, S. F., & Wallace, F. (2005). *Operationalizing implementation: Strategies and methods.* Retrieved from National Implementation Research Network, University of South Florida:

Blase, K. A., Fixsen, D. L., & Phillips, E. L. (1984). Residential treatment for troubled children: Developing service delivery systems. In S. C. Paine, G. T. Bellamy, & B. Wilcox

(Eds.), *Human services that work: From innovation to standard practice* (pp. 149-165). Baltimore, MD: Paul H. Brookes Publishing.

Blase, K. A., Fixsen, D. L., Sims, B. J., & Ward, C. S. (2015). *Implementation science: Changing hearts, minds, behavior, and systems to improve educational outcomes.* Retrieved from National Implementation Research Network, University of North Carolina at Chapel Hill: http://www.winginstitute.org/News-And-Events/Summits/2014-Summit-Summary

Blase, K. A., Kiser, L., & Van Dyke, M. K. (2009). *The hexagon tool.* Retrieved from Chapel Hill, NC: Active Implementation Research Network: www.activeimplementation.org/resources

Blase, K. A., Maloney, D. M., & Timbers, G. D. (1974). *Teaching-Parent Training Manual.* Retrieved from Morganton, NC: Bringing It All Back Home Study Center:

Blase, K. A., Naoom, S., Wallace, F., & Fixsen, D. (2005a). *Concept mapping purveyor and implementer perceptions of using evidence-based programs in practice.* Retrieved from National Implementation Research Network, University of South Florida: https://www.activeimplementation.org/resources/understanding-purveyor-and-implementer-perceptions-of-implementing-evidence-based-programs/

Blase, K. A., Naoom, S., Wallace, F., & Fixsen, D. (2005b). *Understanding Purveyor and Implementer Perceptions of Implementing Evidence-Based Programs.* Retrieved from National Implementation Research Network, University of South Florida: https://www.activeimplementation.org/resources/understanding-purveyor-and-implementer-perceptions-of-implementing-evidence-based-programs/

Blase, K. A., Timbers, G. D., & Maloney, D. M. (1975). *An Administrative Policy Manual for Group Home Staff.* Retrieved from Morganton, NC: Bringing It All Back Home Study Center:

Blase, K. A., Van Dyke, M. K., Fixsen, D. L., & Bailey, F. W. (2012). Implementation science: Key concepts, themes, and evidence for practitioners in educational psychology. In B. Kelly & D. Perkins (Eds.), *Handbook of implementation science for psychology in education* (pp. 13-34). London: Cambridge University Press.

Bombard, Y., Baker, G. R., Orlando, E., Fancott, C., Bhatia, P., Casalino, S., . . . Pomey, M.-P. (2018). Engaging patients to improve quality of care: a systematic review. *Implementation Science, 13*(1), 98. doi:10.1186/s13012-018-0784-z

Bond, G. R., Becker, D. R., & Drake, R. E. (2011). Measurement of fidelity of implementation of evidence-based practices: Case example of the IPS Fidelity Scale. *Clinical Psychology: Science and Practice, 18*, 125-140.

Bond, G. R., Miller, L. D., Krumwied, R. D., & Ward, R. S. (1988). Assertive case management in three CMHCs: A controlled study. *Hospital and Community Psychiatry, 39*, 411-418.

Bond, G. R., & Salyers, M. P. (2004). Prediction of outcome from the Dartmouth assertive community treatment fidelity scale. *CNS Spectrums, 9*(12), 937-942.

Boyle, J. (2003). *Working "faster, better, cheaper": A federal research agency in transition.* Blacksberg, VA: Virginia Polytechnic Institute and State University,

Brachthauser, C. (2011). Explaining global governance – a complexity perspective. *Cambridge Review of International Affairs, 24*(2), 221-224.

Braukmann, C. J. (1979). Standards of ethical conduct for the National Teaching-Family Association. Boys Town, NE: Father Flanagan's Boys' Home.

Braukmann, C. J., Fixsen, D. L., Kirigin, K. A., Phillips, E. A., Phillips, E. L., & Wolf, M. M. (1975). Achievement Place: The training and certification of teaching-parents. In W. S. Wood (Ed.), *Issues in evaluating behavior modification* (pp. 131-152). Champaign, IL: Research Press.

Braukmann, C. J., Kirigin-Ramp, K. A., Tigner, D. M., & Wolf, M. M. (1984). The teaching family approach to training group home parents: Training procedures, validation research, and outcome findings. In R. Dangle & R. Polster (Eds.), *Behavioral parent training: Issues in research and practice* (pp. 144-161). New York: Guilford Press.

Braukmann, P. D., Kirigin Ramp, K. A., Braukmann, C. J., Willner, A. G., & Wolf, M. M. (1983). The analysis and training of rationales for child care workers. *Children and Youth Services Review, 5*(2), 177-194.

Brody, S. D., & Highfield, W. E. (2005). Does planning work? Testing the implementation of local environmental planning in Florida. *Journal of the American Planning Association, 71*(2), 159-176.

Brookings Institution. (2018). *Millions Learning Real-time Scaling Labs Overview.* Retrieved from Washington, DC: Center for Universal Education at Brookings:

Brown, C. H., Chamberlain, P., Saldana, L., Padgett, C., Wang, W., & Cruden, G. (2014). Evaluation of two implementation strategies in 51 child county public service systems in two states: results of a cluster randomized head-to-head implementation trial. *Implementation Science, 9*(1), 134. doi:10.1186/s13012-014-0134-8

Brownson, R. C., Colditz, G. A., & Proctor, E. K. (Eds.). (2012). *Dissemination and implementation research in health.* New York: Oxford University Press.

Brunk, M. A., Chapman, J. E., & Schoenwald, S. K. (2014). Defining and evaluating fidelity at the program level: A preliminary investigation. *Zeitschrift für Psychologie, 222*, 22-29. doi:10.1027/2151-2604/a000162

Bruns, E. J., Suter, J. C., Leverentz-Brady, K., & Burchard, J. D. (2004). A national portrait of wraparound implementation. In C. Newman, Liberton, C., Kutash, K. & R. Friedman (Ed.), *A System of Care for Children's Mental Health: Expanding the Research Base. Proceedings of the Sixteenth Annual Conference.* Tampa, FL: Florida Mental Health Institute Research & Training Center for Children's Mental Health.

Bruns, E. J., & Walker, J. S. (2010). Defining practice: Flexibility, legitimacy, and the nature of systems of care and wraparound. *Evaluation and Program Planning: Systems of Care, 33*(1), 45-48. doi:DOI: 10.1016/j.evalprogplan.2009.05.013

Bryce, J., Gilroy, K., Jones, G., Hazel, E., Black, R. E., & Victora, C. G. (2010). The accelerated child survival and development programme in west Africa: A retrospective evaluation. *The Lancet, 375*(9714), 572-582. doi:10.1016/S0140-6736(09)62060-2

Bryk, A. S. (2016). Accelerating How We Learn to Improve. *Educational Researcher, 44*(9), 467-477. doi:10.3102/0013189X15621543

Caron, E., & Dozier, M. (2019). Effects of Fidelity-Focused Consultation on Clinicians' Implementation: An Exploratory Multiple Baseline Design. *Administration and Policy in Mental Health and Mental Health Services Research.* doi:10.1007/s10488-019-00924-3

Carpiano, R. M., & Daley, D. M. (2006). A guide and glossary on postpositivist theory building for population health. *Journal of Epidemiology and Community Health, 60*, 564-570.

Carroll, C., Patterson, M., Wood, S., Booth, A., Rick, J., & Balain, S. (2007). A conceptual framework for implementation fidelity. *Implementation Science, 2*(1), 40. Retrieved from http://www.implementationscience.com/content/2/1/40.

Chamberlain, P. (2003). The Oregon Multidimensional Treatment Foster Care Model: Features, outcomes, and progress in dissemination. *Cognitive and Behavioral Practice, 10*, 303-312.

Chamberlain, P., Brown, C. H., & Saldana, L. (2011). Observational Measure of implementation progress in community based settings: The stages of Implementation Completion (SIC). *Implementation Science, 6*, 116. doi:10.1186/1748-5908-6-116

Chamberlain, P., Moreland, S., & Reid, K. (1992). Enhanced services and stipends for foster parents: Effects on retention rates and outcomes for children. *Child Welfare, 71*(5), 387-401.

Chao, S. (Ed.) (2007). *The state of quality improvement and implementation research: Expert views workshop summary*. Washington, D.C.: Institute of Medicine of the National Academies: The National Academies Press.

Chapin Hall Center for Children. (2002). *Evaluation of family preservation and reunification programs*. Retrieved from Chicago, IL: http://aspe.hhs.gov/hsp/evalfampres94/

Chaple, M., & Sacks, S. (2016). The Impact of Technical Assistance and Implementation Support on Program Capacity to Deliver Integrated Services. *The Journal of Behavioral Health Services & Research, 43*(1), 3-17. doi:10.1007/s11414-014-9419-6

Chase, G. (1979). Implementing a human services program: How hard will it be? *Public Policy, 27*, 385-434.

Chinman, M., Hunter, S. B., Ebener, P., Paddock, S. M., Stillman, L., Imm, P., & Wandersman, A. (2008). The getting to outcomes demonstration and evaluation: An illustration of the prevention support system. *American Journal of Community Psychology, 41*, 206-224.

Chinman, M., Imm, P., & Wandersman, A. (2004). Getting To Outcomes: Promoting accountability through methods and tools for planning, implementation, and evaluation. Retrieved from Santa Monica, CA: RAND Corporation:

Chorpita, B. F., Bernstein, A., & Daleiden, E. L. (2008). Driving with roadmaps and dashboards: Using information resources to structure the decision models in service organizations. *Adm Policy Ment Health, 35*, 114-123.

Chorpita, B. F., Daleiden, E. L., & Weisz, J. R. (2005). Identifying and selecting the common elements of evidence based interventions: A distillation and matching model. *Mental Health Services Research, 7*(1), 5-20.

Christakos, G. (2011). Implementation and Technology. In *Integrative Problem-Solving in a Time of Decadence* (pp. 427-456): Springer Netherlands.

Clements, D. H., Sarama, J., Wolfe, C. B., & Spitler, M. E. (2014). Sustainability of a Scale-Up Intervention in Early Mathematics: A Longitudinal Evaluation of Implementation Fidelity. *Early Education and Development*, 1-23. doi:10.1080/10409289.2015.968242

Cohen, W. M., & Levinthal, D. A. (1990). Absorptive Capacity: A New Perspective on Learning and Innovation. *Administrative Science Quarterly, 35*(1), 128-152. doi:10.2307/2393553

Collins, S. R., Brooks, L. E., Daly, D. L., Fixsen, D. L., Maloney, D. M., & Blase, K. A. (1976). *An Evaluation of the Teaching-Interaction Component of Family-Living Teacher Training Workshops at Boys Town*. Boys Town, Nebraska: Father Flanagan's Boys' Home.

Collins, S. R., Brooks, L. E., Fixsen, D. L., Maloney, D. M., & Blase, K. A. (1976). *Training Manual for Observers Scoring Pre/Post Teaching Interaction Sequences*. Boys Town, Nebraska: Father Flanagan's Boys' Home.

Committee on Quality of Health Care in America. (2001). *Crossing the quality chasm: a new health care system for the 21st century*: Washington, DC: National Academy Press.

Conklin, J. (2005). Wicked problems and social complexity. In J. Conklin (Ed.), *Dialogue mapping: Building shared understanding of wicked problems* (pp. 1-25). New York: Wiley.

Corrigan, P. W., Steiner, L., McCracken, S. G., Blaser, B., & Barr, M. (2001). Strategies for disseminating evidence-based practices to staff who treat people with serious mental illness. *Psychiatric Services, 52*(12), 1598-1606.

Crom, S. (2007). Dispelling several myths about leadership for change. Retrieved from http://europe.isixsigma.com/library/content/c060222b.asp

Cummings, M. J., Goldberg, E., Mwaka, S., Kabajaasi, O., Vittinghoff, E., Cattamanchi, A., . . . Lucian Davis, J. (2017). A complex intervention to improve implementation of World Health Organization guidelines for diagnosis of severe illness in low-income settings: a quasi-experimental study from Uganda. *Implementation Science, 12*(1), 126. doi:10.1186/s13012-017-0654-0

D'Andreamatteo, A., Ianni, L., Lega, F., & Sargiacomo, M. (2015). Lean in healthcare: A comprehensive review. *Health Policy, 119*(9), 1197-1209. doi:https://doi.org/10.1016/j.healthpol.2015.02.002

Damschroder, L. J., Aron, D. C., Keith, R. E., Kirsh, S. R., Alexander, J. A., & Lowery, J. C. (2009). Fostering implementation of health services research findings into practice: A consolidated framework for advancing implementation science. *Implementation Science, 4*(50). doi:10.1186/1748-5908-4-50

Dancer, D., Braukmann, C. J., Schumaker, J., Kirigin, K. A., Willner, A. G., & Wolf, M. M. (1978). The training and validation of behavior observation and description skills. *Behavior Modification, 2*(1), 113-134. doi:10.1177/014544557821007

Dane, A. V., & Schneider, B. H. (1998). Program integrity in primary and early secondary prevention: Are implementation effects out of control? *Clinical Psychology Review, 18*(1), 23-45.

Darling-Hammond, L., & McLaughlin, M. W. (1995). Policies that support professional development in an era of reform. *Phi Delta Kappan, 76*(8), 642-645.

Day, D. V. (2000). Leadership development: A review in context. *Leadership Quarterly, 11*(4), 581-613.

de Vries, K., & Manfred, F. R. (2005). Leadership group coaching in action: The Zen of creating high performance teams. *Academy of Management Review, 19*(1), 61-76.

Dearing, J. W., & Cox, J. G. (2018). Diffusion Of Innovations Theory, Principles, And Practice. *Health Affairs, 37*(2), 183-190. doi:10.1377/hlthaff.2017.1104

Delbecq, A. L., & VandeVen, A. H. (1971). A Group Process Model for Problem Identification and Program Planning. *Journal of Applied Behavioral Science, 7*, 466-491.

Dicht, B. (2009). The most hazardous and dangerous and greatest adventure on which man has ever embarked. *Mechanical Engineering, 131(7),* 28-35.

Dincin, J., & Witheridge, T. F. (1982). Psychiatric Rehabilitation as a Deterrent to Recidivism. *Psychiatric Services, 33*(8), 645-650. doi:10.1176/ps.33.8.645

Dobson, L., & Cook, T. (1980). Avoiding Type III error in program evaluation: results from a field experiment. *Evaluation and Program Planning, 3*, 269 - 276.

Dohrn, J., Nzama, B., & Murrman, M. (2009). The Impact of HIV Scale-Up on the Role of Nurses in South Africa: Time for a New Approach. *Journal of Acquired Immune Deficiency Syndromes, 52*(1), 27-29.

Donald, A., Maximillian, B., Peter, J., Eoin, K., David, M., Marianne, M., . . . Merete, N. (2018). Fidelity scales and performance measures to support implementation and quality assurance for first episode psychosis services. *Early Intervention in Psychiatry, 0*(0). doi:10.1111/eip.12684

Donaldson, A., Newton, J., McCrory, P., White, P., Davis, G., Makdissi, M., & Finch, C. F. (2014). Translating Guidelines for the Diagnosis and Management of Sports-Related Concussion into Practice. *American Journal of Lifestyle Medicine*, 1-16. doi:10.1177/1559827614538751

Donaldson, N., Rutledge, D., & Geiser, K. (2005). *Role of the external coach in advancing research translation in hospital-based performance improvement.* Retrieved from http://www.ahrq.gov/downloads/pub/advances2/vol2/Advances-Donaldson_87.pdf

Dooley, K. J. (1997). A complex adaptive systems model of organization change. *Nonlinear Dynamics, Psychology, and Life Sciences, 1*(1), 69-97.

Dorsey, S., Kerns, S. E. U., Lucid, L., Pullmann, M. D., Harrison, J. P., Berliner, L., . . . Deblinger, E. (2018). Objective coding of content and techniques in workplace-based supervision of an EBT in public mental health. *Implementation Science, 13*(1), 19. doi:10.1186/s13012-017-0708-3

Doussau, A., & Grady, C. (2016). Deciphering assumptions about stepped wedge designs: the case of Ebola vaccine research. *Journal of Medical Ethics, 42*(12), 797.

Drake, R. E., Essock, S. M., Shaner, A., Carey, K. B., Minkoff, K., Kola, L., . . . Rickards, L. (2001). Implementing dual diagnosis services for clients with severe mental illness. *Psychiatric Services, 52*(4), 469-476.

Drake, R. E., Goldman, H. E., Leff, H., Lehman, A. F., Dixon, L., Mueser, K. T., & Torrey, W. C. (2001). Implementing evidence-based practices in routine mental health service settings. *Psychiatric Services, 52*(2), 179-182.

Drake, R. E., Wilkniss, S. M., Frounfelker, R. L., Whitley, R., Zipple, A. M., McHugo, G. J., & Bond, G. R. (2009). Public-Academic Partnerships: The Thresholds-Dartmouth Partnership and Research on Shared Decision Making. *Psychiatric Services, 60*(2), 142-144. doi:10.1176/ps.2009.60.2.142

Dreisbach, L., Luger, R., Ritter, D., & Smart, D. J. (1979). *The confederate role workshop: Trainer's manual.* Boys Town, Nebraska: Father Flanagan's Boys' Home.

Driscoll, K. C., Wang, L., Mashburn, A. J., & Pianta, R. C. (2011). Fostering Supportive Teacher–Child Relationships: Intervention Implementation in a State-Funded Preschool Program. *Early Education and Development, 22*(4), 593-619. doi:10.1080/10409289.2010.502015

Drucker, P. F. (2004). What makes an effective executive? *Harvard Business Review, June,* 58-63.

Dunst, C. J., Bruder, M. B., & Hamby, D. W. (2015). Metasynthesis of inservice professional development research: Features associated with positive educator and student outcomes. *Educational Research and Reviews, 10*(12), 1731-1744. doi:10.5897/ERR2015.2306

Durlak, J. A., & DuPre, E. P. (2008). Implementation matters: A review of research on the influence of implementation on program outcomes and the factors affecting implementation. *American Journal of Community Psychology, 41*, 327-350. doi:10.1007/s10464-008-9165-0

Edmondson, A., & Moingeon, B. (1998). From Organizational Learning to the Learning Organization. *Management Learning, 29*(1), 5-20. doi:10.1177/1350507698291001

Elledge, C., Avworo, A., Cochetti, J., Carvalho, C., & Grota, P. (2018). Characteristics of facilitators in knowledge translation: An integrative review. *Collegian.* doi:10.1016/j.colegn.2018.03.002

Elliott, D. S., Ageton, S. S., & Canter, R. J. (1979). An Integrated Theoretical Perspective on Delinquent Behavior. *Journal of Research in Crime and Delinquency, 16*(1), 3-27. doi:10.1177/002242787901600102

Elliott, D. S., & Mihalic, S. (2004). Issues in disseminating and replicating effective prevention programs. *Prevention Science, 5*(1), 47 - 53.

343

Elmore, R. F., Forman, M. L., Stosich, E. L., & Bocala, C. (2014). The Internal Coherence Assessment Protocol & Developmental Framework: Building the Organizational Capacity for Instructional Improvement in Schools. Retrieved from Washington, DC: Strategic Education Research Partnership Institute:

Elwyn, G., Taubert, M., & Kowalczuk, J. (2007). Sticky knowledge: A possible model for investigating implementation in healthcare contexts. *Implementation Science, 2*(44). doi:10.1186/1748-5908-2-44

Faggin, F. (1985). The challenge of bringing new ideas to market. *High Technology*, 14-16.

Fairweather, G. W., Sanders, D. H., & Tornatzky, L. G. (1974a). *Creating change in mental health organizations.* Elmsford, NY: Pergamon Press.

Fairweather, G. W., Sanders, D. H., & Tornatzky, L. G. (1974b). Follow-up Diffusion of the Community Lodge. In G. W. Fairweather, Sanders, D., & Tornatzky, L. G. (Ed.), *Creating change in mental health organizations* (pp. 162-180). Elmsford, NY: Pergamon Press.

Feldstein, A. C., & Glasgow, R. E. (2008). A practical, robust implementation and sustainability model (PRISM) for integrating research findings into practice. *Joint Commission Journal on Quality and Patient Safety, 34*(4), 228-243.

Fenner, F., Henderson, D. A., Arita, I., JeZek, Z., & Ladnyi, I. D. (1988). *Smallpox and its eradication.* Geneva, Switzerland: World Health Organization.

Fernandez, M. E., Walker, T. J., Weiner, B. J., Calo, W. A., Liang, S., Risendal, B., . . . Kegler, M. C. (2018). Developing measures to assess constructs from the Inner Setting domain of the Consolidated Framework for Implementation Research. *Implementation Science, 13*(1), 52. doi:10.1186/s13012-018-0736-7

Fisher, D. (1983). The going gets tough when we descend from the ivory tower. *Analysis and Intervention in Developmental Disabilities, 3*(2-3 SU), 249-255.

Fixsen, D. L. (1978). *By-laws of the Teaching-Family Association.* Retrieved from https://www.teaching-family.org/

Fixsen, D. L., & Blase, K. (2009). *Implementation Tracker.* Retrieved from Chapel Hill: Active Implementation Research Network: https://www.activeimplementation.org/resources/implementation-tracker/

Fixsen, D. L., & Blase, K. A. (1993). Creating new realities: Program development and dissemination. *Journal of Applied Behavior Analysis, 26*, 597-615.

Fixsen, D. L., & Blase, K. A. (2018). The Teaching-Family Model: The First 50 Years. *Perspectives on Behavior Science.* doi:10.1007/s40614-018-0168-3

Fixsen, D. L., Blase, K. A., Duda, M., Naoom, S., & Van Dyke, M. K. (2010). Implementation of evidence-based treatments for children and adolescents: Research findings and their implications for the future. In J. Weisz & A. Kazdin (Eds.), *Implementation and dissemination: Extending treatments to new populations and new settings* (2nd ed., pp. 435-450). New York: Guilford Press.

Fixsen, D. L., Blase, K. A., & Fixsen, A. A. M. (2017). Scaling effective innovations. *Criminology & Public Policy, 16*(2), 487-499. doi:10.1111/1745-9133.12288

Fixsen, D. L., Blase, K. A., Metz, A., & Naoom, S. F. (2014). Producing high levels of treatment integrity in practice: A focus on preparing practitioners. In L. M. Hagermoser Sanetti & T. Kratochwill (Eds.), *Treatment Integrity: A foundation for evidence-based practice in applied psychology* (pp. 185-201). Washington, DC: American Psychological Association Press (Division 16).

Fixsen, D. L., Blase, K. A., Metz, A., & Van Dyke, M. K. (2013). Statewide implementation of evidence-based programs. *Exceptional Children (Special Issue), 79*(2), 213-230.

Fixsen, D. L., Blase, K. A., Metz, A., & Van Dyke, M. K. (2015). Implementation science. In J. D. Wright (Ed.), *International encyclopedia of the social and behavioral sciences* (2nd ed., Vol. 11, pp. 695-702). Oxford: Elsevier, Ltd.

Fixsen, D. L., Blase, K. A., Naoom, S. F., & Haines, M. (2005). *Implementation in the Real World: Purveyors' Craft Knowledge.* Retrieved from National Implementation Research Network, University of South Florida: https://www.activeimplementation.org/resources/implementation-in-the-real-world-purveyors-craft-knowledge/

Fixsen, D. L., Blase, K. A., Naoom, S. F., & Wallace, F. (2006a). *Researcher perspectives on implementation research.* Retrieved from National Implementation Research Network, University of South Florida: https://www.activeimplementation.org/resources/researcher-perspectives-on-implementation-research/

Fixsen, D. L., Blase, K. A., Naoom, S. F., & Wallace, F. (2006b). *Stages of implementation: Activities for taking programs and practices to scale.* Retrieved from National Implementation Research Network, University of South Florida: http://nirn.fpg.unc.edu/stages-implementation-activities-taking-programs-and-practices-scale

Fixsen, D. L., Blase, K. A., Timbers, G. D., & Wolf, M. M. (2001). In search of program implementation: 792 replications of the Teaching-Family Model. In G. A. Bernfeld, D. P. Farrington, & A. W. Leschied (Eds.), *Offender rehabilitation in practice: Implementing and evaluating effective programs* (pp. 149-166). London: Wiley.

Fixsen, D. L., Blase, K. A., Timbers, G. D., & Wolf, M. M. (2007). In search of program implementation: 792 replications of the Teaching-Family Model. *The Behavior Analyst Today, 8*(1), 96-110. doi:10.1037/h0100104

Fixsen, D. L., Blase, K. A., & Van Dyke, M. K. (2012). *From ghost systems to host systems via transformation zones.* Retrieved from Washington, DC: U.S. Department of Education Office of Vocational and Adult Education: http://www.lincs.ed.gov

Fixsen, D. L., Collins, L. B., Phillips, E. L., & Thomas, D. L. (1982). Institutional indicators in evaluation: An example from Boys Town. In A. J. McSweeney, W. J. Fremouw, & R. P. Hawkins (Eds.), *Practical Program Evaluation in Youth Treatment.* Springfield, IL: Charles C. Thomas.

Fixsen, D. L., Hassmiller Lich, K., & Schultes, M. T. (2018). Shifting systems of care to support school-based services. In A. Leschied, Saklofske, D., Flett, G. (Ed.), *Handbook of school-based mental health promotion: An evidence informed framework for implementation* (pp. 51-63). Toronto: Springer: Toronto: Springer.

Fixsen, D. L., Naoom, S. F., Blase, K., Friedman, R. M., & Wallace, F. (2008, July). *Understanding implementation.* Paper presented at the Professional Seminar, Tampa: University of South Florida.

Fixsen, D. L., Naoom, S. F., Blase, K. A., Friedman, R. M., & Wallace, F. (2005). *Implementation research: A synthesis of the literature*: National Implementation Research Network, University of South Florida, www.activeimplementation.org.

Fixsen, D. L., Phillips, E. L., Baron, R. L., Coughlin, D. D., Daly, D. L., & Daly, P. B. (1978). The Boys Town Revolution. *Human Nature, 1*, 54-61.

Fixsen, D. L., Phillips, E. L., & Wolf, M. M. (1973). Achievement Place: Experiments in Self-Government with Pre-Delinquents. *Journal of Applied Behavior Analysis, 6*(1), 31-47.

Fixsen, D. L., Phillips, E. L., & Wolf, M. M. (1978). Mission-oriented behavior research: The Teaching-Family Model. In A. C. Catania & T. A. Brigham (Eds.), *Handbook of applied behavior analysis: Social and instructional processes* (pp. 603-628). New York: Irvington Publishers, Inc.

Fixsen, D. L., Schultes, M.-T., & Blase, K. A. (2016). Bildung-Psychology and implementation science. *European Journal of Developmental Psychology, 13*(6), 666-680. doi:10.1080/17405629.2016.1204292

Fixsen, D. L., Ward, C., Blase, K., Naoom, S., Metz, A., & Louison, L. (2018). *Assessing Drivers Best Practices.* Retrieved from Chapel Hill, NC: Active Implementation Research Network https://www.activeimplementation.org/resources/assessing-drivers-best-practices/

Fixsen, D. L., Ward, C., Ryan Jackson, K., Blase, K., Green, J., Sims, B., . . . Preston, A. (2018). *Implementation and Scaling Evaluation Report: 2013-2017*. Retrieved from National Implementation Research Network, State Implementation and Scaling up of Evidence Based Practices Center, University of North Carolina at Chapel Hill:

Fixsen, D. L., Ward, C., Ryan Jackson, K., & Chaparro, E. (2015). *Observation tool for instructional supports and systems (OTISS)*. Retrieved from National Implementation Research Network, University of North Carolina:

Fixsen, D. L., Ward, C. S., Duda, M. A., Horner, R., & Blase, K. A. (2015). *State Capacity Assessment (SCA) for Scaling Up Evidence-based Practices (v. 25.2)*. Retrieved from National Implementation Research Network, State Implementation and Scaling up of Evidence Based Practices Center, University of North Carolina at Chapel Hill:

Flatten, T. C., Engelen, A., Zahra, S. A., & Brettel, M. (2011). A measure of absorptive capacity: Scale development and validation. *European Management Journal, 29*(2), 98-116. doi:https://doi.org/10.1016/j.emj.2010.11.002

Focge, W. H. (2011). *House on fire: The fight to eradicate smallpox*. Berkeley and Los Angeles, CA: University of California Press, Ltd.

Folinsa, D. K., Fotiadis, T. A., & Coudounaris, D. N. (2017). Just in time theory: the panacea to the business success? *International Journal of Value Chain Management, 8*(2), 171-190. doi:10.1504/IJVCM.2017.085485

Folker, A. P., & Lauridsen, S. M. (2017). Using action learning to reduce health inequity in Danish municipalities. *Leadership in Health Services*. doi:10.1108/LHS-11-2016-0060

Foote, S. B., & Town, R. J. (2007). Implementing evidence-based medicine through medicare coverage decisions. *Health Affairs, 26*(6), 1634-1642.

Ford, D. (1974). *Parent-child interaction in a token economy*. (Masters Thesis), University of Kansas, Lawrence, KS.

Forgatch, M. S., & DeGarmo, D. S. (2011). Sustaining Fidelity Following the Nationwide PMTO Implementation in Norway *Prevention Science, 12*(3). doi:10.1007/s11121-011-0225-6

Forgatch, M. S., Patterson, G. R., & DeGarmo, D. S. (2005). Evaluating Fidelity: Predictive Validity for a Measure of Competent Adherence to the Oregon Model of Parent Management Training. *Behavior Therapy, 36*(1), 3-13. Retrieved from http://www.pubmedcentral.nih.gov/articlerender.fcgi?artid=1464400.

Fraser, M. W., & Galinsky, M. J. (2010). Steps in Intervention Research: Designing and Developing Social Programs. *Research on Social Work Practice, 20*(5), 459-466. doi:10.1177/1049731509358424

Freemantle, N., & Watt, I. (1994). Dissemination: Implementing the findings of research. *Health Libraries Review, 11*, 133-137.

Fu, N., Flood, P. C., Rousseau, D. M., & Morris, T. (2018). Line Managers as Paradox Navigators in HRM Implementation: Balancing Consistency and Individual Responsiveness. *Journal of Management, 0*(0), 0149206318785241. doi:10.1177/0149206318785241

Fullan, M. (2001). *The new meaning of educational change* (3rd ed.). New York: Teachers College Press.

Galavotti, C., Sebert Kuhlmann, A. K., Kraft, J. M., Harford, N., & Petraglia, J. (2008). From innovation to implementation: The long and winding road. *American Journal of Community Psychology, 41*, 314-326.

Genov, A. (2005). Iterative usability testing as continuous feedback: A control systems perspective. *Journal of Usability Studies, 1*(1), 18-27. Retrieved from http://www.upassoc.org/upa_publications/jus/2005_november/iterative.html.

Gertner, J. (2012). The idea factory: Bell Labs and the great age of American innovation. NY: The Penguin Press.

Gifford, W. A., Squires, J. E., Angus, D. E., Ashley, L. A., Brosseau, L., Craik, J. M., . . . Graham, I. D. (2018). Managerial leadership for research use in nursing and allied health care professions: a systematic review. *Implementation Science, 13*(1), 127. doi:10.1186/s13012-018-0817-7

Gilpin, D. R., & Murphy, P. J. (2008). *Crisis management in a complex world.* New York: Oxford University Press.

Girard, N. J. (2013). Nurse Staffing Ratios. *AORN Journal, 97*(5), 604-538. doi:http://dx.doi.org/10.1016/j.aorn.2013.02.011

Glasner-Edwards, S., & Rawson, R. (2010). Evidence-Based Practices in Addiction Treatment: Review and Recommendations for Public Policy. *Health policy (Amsterdam, Netherlands), 97*(2-3), 93-104. doi:10.1016/j.healthpol.2010.05.013

Glennan Jr., T. K., Bodilly, S. J., Galegher, J. R., & Kerr, K. A. (2004). *Expanding the reach of education reforms.* Santa Monica, CA: RAND Corporation.

Glisson, C. (2007). Assessing and Changing Organizational Culture and Climate for Effective Services. *Research on Social Work Practice, 17*(6), 736-747. doi:10.1177/1049731507301659

Glisson, C., Green, P., & Williams, N. J. (2012). Assessing the Organizational Social Context (OSC) of child welfare systems: Implications for research and practice. *Child Abuse & Neglect, 36*(9), 621. doi:10.1016/j.chiabu.2012.06.002

Glisson, C., Landsverk, J., Schoenwald, S. K., Kelleher, K., Hoagwood, K., Mayberg, S., & Green, P. (2008). Assessing the organizational social context (OSC) of mental health services: Implications for research and practice. *Administration and Policy in Mental Health and Mental Health Services Research, 35*(1), 98-113. doi:10.1007/s10488-007-0148-5

Glisson, C., & Schoenwald, S. K. (2005). The ARC organizational and community intervention strategy for implementing evidence-based children's mental health treatments. *Mental Health Services Research, 7*(4), 243 - 259.

Glisson, C., Schoenwald, S. K., Hemmelgarn, A., Green, P., Dukes, D., Armstrong, K. S., & Chapman, J. E. (2010). Randomized trial of MST and ARC in a two-level evidence-based treatment implementation strategy. *Journal of Consulting & Clinical Psychology, 78*(4), 537-550.

Glisson, C., Schoenwald, S. K., Kelleher, K., Landsverk, J., Hoagwood, K. E., Mayberg, S., & Green, P. (2008). Therapist turnover and new program sustainability in mental health clinics as a function of organizational culture, climate, and service structure. *Adm Policy Ment Health, 35,* 124-133.

Golden, O. (1990). Innovation in public sector human services programs: The implications of innovation by "groping along.". *Journal of Policy Analysis and Management, 9,* 219-248.

Goodman, D. M., Srofenyoh, E. K., Ramaswamy, R., Bryce, F., Floyd, L., Olufolabi, A., . . . Owen, M. D. (2018). Addressing the third delay: implementing a novel obstetric triage system in Ghana. *BMJ Global Health, 3*(E). doi:10.1136/bmjgh-2017-000623

Goodman, R. M., McLeroy, K. R., Steckler, A. B., & Hoyle, R. H. (1993). Development of Level of Institutionalization Scales for Health Promotion Programs. *Health Education Quarterly, 20*(2), 161-178. doi:10.1177/109019819302000208

Graham, I., Logan, J., Harrison, M., Straus, S., Tetroe, J., Caswell, W., & Robinson, N. (2006). Lost in Translation: Time for a Map? *The Journal of Continuing Education in the Health Professions, 26*(1), 13 - 24.

Gray, M. P., Onyeador, O., & Wirth, J. A. (2018). Update on the PHA Pulmonary Hypertension Care Center Network: Early Experience With the National Accreditation Program. *Advances in Pulmonary Hypertension, 16*(4), 179-184. doi:10.21693/1933-088x-16.4.179

Green, L. W. (2008). Making research relevant: if it is an evidence-based practice, where's the practice-based evidence? *Family Practice, 25,* 20-24.

Greenberg, M. T., Domitrovich, C. E., Graczyk, P., & Zins, J. E. (2005). *The study of implementation in school-based preventive interventions: Theory, research and practice*

349

*(Volume 3)*. Retrieved from Rockville, MD: Center for Mental Health Services, Substance Abuse and Mental Health Services Administration:

Greenhalgh, T., Robert, G., MacFarlane, F., Bate, P., & Kyriakidou, O. (2004). Diffusion of innovations in service organizations: Systematic review and recommendations. *The Milbank Quarterly, 82*(4), 581-629.

Grigg, W. S., Daane, M. C., Jin, Y., & Campbell, J. R. (2003). *The nation's report card: Reading 2002*. Retrieved from Washington, DC: U.S. Department of Education, Institute of Education Sciences:

Grimshaw, J., & Eccles, M. (2004). Is evidence-based implementation of evidence-based care possible? *The Medical Journal of Australia, 180*(6), S50-S51.

Gustafson, D. H., Shukla, R., Delbecq, A. L., & Walster, W. (1973). Comparative study of differences in subjective likelihood estimates: Individuals, interacting, delphi, and nominal groups. *Organizational Behavior and Human Performance, 9*(2), 280-291.

Hall, G. (1974). The Concerns-Based Adoption Model: A Developmental Conceptualization of the Adoption Process Within Educational Institutions. Retrieved from University of Texas, Austin: Research and Development Center for Teacher Education:

Hall, G., & Hord, S. M. (1987). *Change in schools: Facilitating the process*. Albany, NY: SUNY Press.

Hall, G., & Hord, S. M. (2011). *Implementing change: Patterns, principles and potholes* (4th ed.). Boston: Allyn and Bacon.

Handley, M. A., Lyles, C. R., McCulloch, C., & Cattamanchi, A. (2018). Selecting and Improving Quasi-Experimental Designs in Effectiveness and Implementation Research. *Annual Review of Public Health, 39*(1), 5-25. doi:10.1146/annurev-publhealth-040617-014128

Hanney, S., Kuruvilla, S., Soper, B., & Mays, N. (2010). Who Needs What From a National Health Research System: Lessons From Reforms to the English Department of Health's R&D System. *Health Research Policy and Systems, 8*(1).

Harrison, M. I., & Grantham, S. (2018). Learning from implementation setbacks: Identifying and responding to contextual challenges. *Learning Health Systems, 0*(0), e10068. doi:10.1002/lrh2.10068

Harvey, G. (2002). Getting evidence into practice: the role and function of facilitation. *Journal of Advanced Nursing, 37*(6), 577-588.

Harvey, G., McCormack, B., Kitson, A., Lynch, E., & Titchen, A. (2018). Designing and implementing two facilitation interventions within the 'Facilitating Implementation of

Research Evidence (FIRE)' study: a qualitative analysis from an external facilitators' perspective. *Implementation Science, 13*(1), 141. doi:10.1186/s13012-018-0812-z

Haskins, R., & Baron, J. (2011). *Building the Connection between Policy and Evidence: The Obama evidence-based initiatives.* Retrieved from London: www.nesta.org.uk

Hattie, J. A. C. (2009). Visible learning: A synthesis of over 800 meta-analyses relating to achievement. London: Routledge.

Havclock, R. G. (1969). *Planning for innovation through dissemination and utilisation of knowledge.* Ann Arbor, MI: Center for Research on Utilisation of Scientific Knowledge.

Havelock, R. G., & Havelock, M. C. (1973). *Training for change agents.* Ann Arbor, MI: University of Michigan Institute for Social Research.

Hawe, P., Shiell, A., & Riley, T. (2009). Theorising Interventions as Events in Systems. *American Journal of Community Psychology, 43*(3), 267-276. doi:10.1007/s10464-009-9229-9

Hawkins, J. D., Catalano, R. F., & Arthur, M. W. (2002). Promoting science-based prevention in communities. *Addictive Behaviors, 27*, 951–976.

Heifetz, R. A., Grashow, A., & Linsky, M. (2009). *The practice of adaptive leadership.* Boston, MA: Harvard Business Press.

Henggeler, S. W., Pickrel, S. G., & Brondino, M. J. (1999). Multisystemic treatment of substance-abusing and -dependent delinquents: Outcomes, treatment fidelity, and transportability. *Mental Health Services Research, 1*(3), 171-184.

Henton, M., Rabin, B., Gaglio, B., Nekhlyudov, L., Dearing, J., Bull, S., & Marcus, A. (2014). A1-3: Small-scale Implementation Study of the Cancer Survival Query System. *Clinical Medicine & Research, 12*(1-2), 77. doi:10.3121/cmr.2014.1250.a1-3

Higgins, M., Weiner, J., & Young, L. (2012). Implementation teams: A new lever for organizational change. *Journal of Organizational Behavior.* doi:10.1002/job.1773

Hirschhorn, L. R., Semraul, K., Kodkany, B., Churchill, R., Kapoor, A., Spector, J., . . . Gawande, A. (2015). Learning before leaping: integration of an adaptive study design process prior to initiation of BetterBirth, a large-scale randomized controlled trial in Uttar Pradesh, India. *Implementation Science, 10*(117). doi:DOI 10.1186/s13012-015-0309-y

Horner, R. H., Kincaid, D., Sugai, G., Lewis, T., Eber, L., Barrett, S., . . . Johnson, N. (2014). Scaling up school-wide positive behavioral interventions and supports: Experiences of seven states with documented success. *Journal of Positive Behavior Interventions, 16.* doi:10.1177/1098300713503685

Horner, R. H., Todd, A. W., Lewis-Palmer, T., Irvin, L. K., Sugai, G., & Boland, J. B. (2004). The School-wide Evaluation Tool (SET): A Research Instrument for Assessing School-wide Positive Behavior Support. *Journal of Positive Behavior Interventions, 6*(1), 3-12.

Horsley, D. L., & Loucks-Horsley, S. (1998). CBAM brings order to the tornado of change. *Journal of Staff Development, 19*(4), 17-20.

Huaynoca, S., Chandra-Mouli, V., Yaqub Jr, N., & Denno, D. M. (2013). Scaling up comprehensive sexuality education in Nigeria: from national policy to nationwide application. *Sex Education, 14*(2), 191-209. doi:10.1080/14681811.2013.856292

Huaynoca, S., Chandra-Mouli, V., Yaqub Jr., N., & Denno, D. M. (2013). Scaling Up Comprehensive Sexuality Education in Nigeria: From National Policy to Nationwide Application. *Sex Education, 14*(2), 191-209.

Humble, J., & Farley, D. (2011). *Continuous delivery.* Boston: Pearson Education.

Hurley, J. J. (2012). Social Validity Assessment in Social Competence Interventions for Preschool Children: A Review. *Topics in Early Childhood Special Education, First published online April 6, 2012.*

Hurley, K. D., Lambert, M. C., Gross, T. J., Thompson, R. W., & Farmer, E. M. Z. (2017). The Role of Therapeutic Alliance and Fidelity in Predicting Youth Outcomes During Therapeutic Residential Care. *Journal of Emotional and Behavioral Disorders, 25*(1), 37-45. doi:10.1177/1063426616686756

Hysong, S., Best, R., & Pugh, J. (2006). Audit and feedback and clinical practice guideline adherence: Making feedback actionable. *Implementation Science, 1*(1), 9. Retrieved from http://www.implementationscience.com/content/1/1/9.

Improved Clinical Effectiveness through Behavioural Research Group. (2006). Designing theoretically-informed implementation interventions. *Implementation Science, 1*(4). Retrieved from http://auraserv.abdn.ac.uk:9080/aura/bitstream/2164/114/1/Iceberg2952.pdf.

Isaacson, W. (2014). *The innovators.* New York: Simon & Schuster.

Jacobs, C., Michelo, C., & Moshabela, M. (2018). Implementation of a community-based intervention in the most rural and remote districts of Zambia: a process evaluation of safe motherhood action groups. *Implementation Science, 13*(1), 74. doi:10.1186/s13012-018-0766-1

Jalava, J. (2006). *Trust as a decision.* Helsinki, Finland: University of Helsinki.

James, S. (2011). What works in group care? — A structured review of treatment models for group homes and residential care. *Children and Youth Services Review, 33*(2), 308-321. doi:https://doi.org/10.1016/j.childyouth.2010.09.014

Jensen, P. S., Weersing, R., Hoagwood, K. E., & Goldman, E. (2005). What is the evidence for evidence-based treatments? A hard look at our soft underbelly. *Mental Health Services Research, 7*(1), 53-74.

Jensen, R. J. (2007). Replication and Adaptation: The effect of adaptation degree and timing on the performance of replicated routines. Retrieved from Provo, UT: Brigham Young University:

Jiménez-Barrionuevo, Magdalena, M., García-Morales, Molina, V. J., & Miguel, L. (2011). Validation of an instrument to measure absorptive capacity. *Technovation, 31*(5), 190-202. doi:https://doi.org/10.1016/j.technovation.2010.12.002

Joyce, B., & Showers, B. (2002). *Student achievement through staff development* (3rd ed.). Alexandria, VA: Association for Supervision and Curriculum Development.

Kaeslin, H. (2008). Digital integrated circuit design, from VLSI architectures to CMOS fabrication. Cambridge: University Press.

Kaiser, R. B., Hogan, R., & Craig, S. B. (2008). Leadership and the fate of organizations. *American Psychologist, 63*(2), 96-110.

Kalita, A., Zaidi, S., Prasad, V., & Raman, V. R. (2009). Empowering health personnel for decentralized health planning in India: The Public Health Resource Network. *Human Resources in Health, 7*(1), 57.

Karlin, B. E., & Cross, G. (2013). From the Laboratory to the Therapy Room: National Dissemination and Implementation of Evidence-Based Psychotherapies in the U.S. Department of Veterans Affairs Health Care System. *American Psychologist, 69*(1), 19-33.

Kessler, R. C., & Glasgow, R. E. (2011). A proposal to speed translation of healthcare research into practice: Dramatic change is needed. *American Journal of Preventive Medicine, 40*(6), 637-644.

Khatri, G. R., & Frieden, T. R. (2002). Rapid DOTS expansion in India. *Bulletin of the World Health Organization, 80*(6), 457-463.

Khodyakov, D., Ridgely, M. S., Huang, C., DeBartolo, K. O., Sorbero, M. E., & Schneider, E. C. (2014). Project JOINTS: What factors affect bundle adoption in a voluntary quality improvement campaign? *BMJ Quality and Safety*, 1-11. doi:10.1136/bmjqs-2014-003169

Kifer, R. E., Lewis, M. A., Green, D. R., & Phillips, E. L. (1974). Training predelinquent youths and their parents to negotiate conflict situations. *Journal of Applied Behavior Analysis, 7*, 357-364.

Kilbourne, A. M., Neumann, M. S., Pincus, H. A., Bauer, M. S., & Stall, R. (2007). Implementing evidence-based interventions in health care: Application of the replicating effective programs framework. *Implementation Science, 2*(42). doi:10.1186/1748-5908-2-42

King-Sears, M. E., Walker, J. D., & Barry, C. (2018). Measuring Teachers' Intervention Fidelity. *Intervention in School and Clinic*, 1053451218765229. doi:10.1177/1053451218765229

Kirigin, K. A., Ayala, H. E., Braukmann, C. J., Brown, W. G., Minkin, N., Fixsen, D. L., . . . Wolf, M. M. (1975). Training Teaching-Parents: An evaluation of workshop training procedures. In E. Ramp & G. Semb (Eds.), *Behavior analysis: Areas of research and application* (pp. 161-174). Englewood Cliffs, N. J.: Prentice-Hall.

Klein, J. A. (2004). True change: How outsiders on the inside get things done in organizations. New York: Jossey-Bass.

Klein, K. J., Conn, B., & Sorra, J. (2001). Implementing computerized technology: An organizational analysis. *Journal of Applied Psychology, 86*(5), 811-824.

Klein, K. J., & Sorra, J. S. (1996). The challenge of innovation implementation. *Academy of Management Review, 21*(4), 1055-1080.

Klest, S. K. (2014). Clustering practitioners within service organizations may improve implementation outcomes for evidence-based programs. *Zeitschrift für Psychologie, 222*(1), 30-36. doi:10.1027/2151-2604/a000163

Klingner, J. K., Boardman, A. G., & McMaster, K. L. (2013). What Does It Take to Scale Up and Sustain Evidence-Based Practices? *Exceptional Children, 79*(2), 195-211.

Koestler, A. (1967). *The ghost in the machine.* NY: Penguin Group (1990 reprint edition).

Kontoghiorghes, C. (2004). Reconceptualizing the learning transfer conceptual framework: Empirical validation of a new systemic model. *International Journal of Training and Development, 8*(3), 210-221. doi:10.1111/j.1360-3736.2004.00209.x

Kotter, J. (1996). *Leading change.* Cambridge, MA: Harvard Business School Press.

Kraft, M. A., & Blazar, D. (2017). Individualized Coaching to Improve Teacher Practice Across Grades and Subjects: New Experimental Evidence. *Educational Policy, 31*(7), 1033-1068. doi:10.1177/0895904816631099

Kretlow, A. G., & Bartholomew, C. C. (2010). Using Coaching to Improve the Fidelity of Evidence-Based Practices: A Review of Studies. *Teacher Education and Special Education, 33*(4), 279-299. doi:10.1177/0888406410371643

Kroeze, C., Caniëls, M. C. J., Huitema, D., & Vranken, H. (2017). Editorial overview: Learning and Innovation in Resilient Systems. *Current Opinion in Environmental Sustainability, 28*, iv-vi. doi:https://doi.org/10.1016/j.cosust.2017.11.004

Kruk, M. E., Gage, A. D., Arsenault, C., Jordan, K., Leslie, H. H., Roder-DeWan, S., . . . Pate, M. (2018). High-quality health systems in the Sustainable Development Goals era: time for a revolution. *Lancet Global Health, 6*, e1196-1252. doi:http://dx.doi.org/10.1016/

Kruk, M. E., Gage, A. D., Joseph, N. T., Danaei, G., García-Saisó, S., & Salomon, P. J. A. (2018). Mortality due to low-quality health systems in the universal health coverage era: a systematic analysis of amenable deaths in 137 countries. *The Lancet, 392*(10160). doi:https://doi.org/10.1016/S0140-6736(18)31668-4

Kutner, M., Greenberg, E., Jin, Y., Boyle, B., Hsu, Y., & Dunleavy, E. (2007). *Literacy in everyday life: Results from the 2003 National Assessment of Adult Literacy (NCES 2007–480)*. Retrieved from Washington, DC: U.S. Department of Education, National Center for Education Statistics:

Kwak, Y. H., & Anbari, F. T. (2006). Benefits, obstacles, and future of six sigma approach. *Technovation, 26*(5), 708-715. doi:https://doi.org/10.1016/j.technovation.2004.10.003

Lanham, H. J., Leykum, L. K., Taylor, B. S., McCannon, C. J., Lindberg, C., & Lester, R. T. (2013). How complexity science can inform scale-up and spread in health care: Understanding the role of self-organization in variation across local contexts. *Social Science & Medicine, 93*(September), 194-202. doi:10.1016/j.socscimed.2012.05.040

Last, J. (2001). *A Dictionary of Epidemiology*: Oxford: University Press.

Leis, J. A., & Shojania, K. G. (2017). A primer on PDSA: executing plan–do–study–act cycles in practice, not just in name. *BMJ Quality and Safety, 26*(7), 572-577. doi:10.1136/bmjqs-2016-006245

LeMahieu, P. G., Grunow, A., Baker, L., Nordstrum, L. E., & Gomez, L. M. (2017). Networked improvement communities: The discipline of improvement science meets the power of networks. *Quality Assurance in Education, 25*(1), 5-25. doi:10.1108/QAE-12-2016-0084

Leonard-Barton, D., & Kraus, W. A. (1985). Implementing new technology. *Harvard Business Review, 6*, 102-110.

Lessard, S., Bareil, C., Lalonde, L., Duhamel, F., Hudon, E., Goudreau, J., & Lévesque, L. (2016). External facilitators and interprofessional facilitation teams: a qualitative study of their roles in supporting practice change. *Implementation Science, 11*(1), 1-12. doi:10.1186/s13012-016-0458-7

Lewin, K. (1951). *Field theory in social science.* New York: Harper and Row.

Lewis, C., Fischer, S., Weiner, B., Stanick, C., Kim, M., & Martinez, R. (2015). Outcomes for implementation science: an enhanced systematic review of instruments using evidence-based rating criteria. *Implementation Science, 10*(1), 155. doi:10.1186/s13012-015-0342-x

Lewis, G. (2014). Emerging lessons from the FIGO LOGIC initiative on maternal death and near-miss reviews. *International Journal of Gynecology & Obstetrics, 127*(S1), S17-S20. doi:10.1016/j.ijgo.2014.07.007

Liberman, R. P. (1979). Social and political challenges to the development of behavioral programs in organizations. In P. Sjoden, S. Bates, & W. Dockens III (Eds.), *Trends in behavior therapy* (pp. 369-398). New York: Academic Press, Inc.

Linehan, M. M. (1991). Cognitive-behavioral treatment of borderline personality disorder. New York: Guilford Press.

Linehan, M. M., Dimeff, L. A., Reynolds, S. K., Comtois, K., Welch, S. S., Heagerty, P., & Kivlahan, D. R. (2002). Dialectical Behavior Therapy Versus Comprehensive Validation Therapy Plus 12-Step for the Treatment of Opioid Dependent Women Meeting Criteria for Borderline Personality Disorder. *Drug and Alcohol Dependence, 67*(1), 13-26. doi:10.1016/S0376-8716(02)00011-X

Lipsey, M. W. (2009). The primary factors that characterize effective interventions with juvenile offenders: A metaanalytic overview. *Victims and Offenders, 4*, 124-147. doi:10.1080/15564880802612573

Lipsey, M. W., & Wilson, D. B. (1998). Effective intervention for serious juvenile offenders: synthesis of research. In R. Loeber & D. P. Farrington (Eds.), *Serious and violent juvenile offenders: Risk factors and successful interventions.* Thousand Oaks, CA: Sage Publications, Inc.

Liu, C. L., & Layland, J. W. (1973). Scheduling algorithms for multiprogramming in a hard real-time environment. *Journal of the Association for Computing Machinery, 20*(1), 46-61.

Lynch, E. A., Chesworth, B. M., & Connell, L. A. (2018). Implementation—The Missing Link in the Research Translation Pipeline: Is It Any Wonder No One Ever Implements Evidence-Based Practice? *Neurorehabilitation and Neural Repair, 0*(0), 1545968318777844. doi:10.1177/1545968318777844

Maar, M., Yeates, K., Barron, M., Hua, D., Liu, P., Lum-Kwong, M. M., . . . Tobe, S. W. (2015). I-RREACH: An Engagement and Assessment Tool for Improving Implementation

Readiness of Researchers, Organizations and Communities in Complex Interventions. *Implementation Science, 1*(1), 64. doi:10.1186/s13012-015-0257-6

Maloney, D. M., Harper, T. M., Braukmann, C. J., Fixsen, D. L., Phillips, E. L., & Wolf, M. M. (1976). Teaching conversation-related skills to pre-delinquent girls. *Journal of Applied Behavior Analysis, 9*, 371.

Maloney, D. M., Warfel, D. J., Blase, K. A., Timbers, G. D., Fixsen, D. L., & Phillips, E. L. (1983). A method for validating employment interviews for residential child care workers. *Residential Group Care and Treatment, 1*, 37-50.

Manna, P. (2008). *Federal aid to elementary and secondary education: Premises, effects, and major lessons learned.* Williamsburg, VA: College of William and Mary, Department of Government and the Thomas Jefferson Program in Public Policy.

Marshall, M., de Silva, D., Cruickshank, L., Shand, J., Wei, L., & Anderson, J. (2017). What we know about designing an effective improvement intervention (but too often fail to put into practice). *BMJ Quality and Safety, 26*(7), 578-582. doi:10.1136/bmjqs-2016-006143

Marsick, V. J., & Watkins, K. E. (2003). Demonstrating the Value of an Organization's Learning Culture: The Dimensions of the Learning Organization Questionnaire. *Advances in Developing Human Resources, 5*(2), 132-151. doi:10.1177/1523422303005002002

Martino, S., Ball, S. A., Nich, C., Frankforter, T. L., & Carroll, K. M. (2008). Community program therapist adherence and competence in motivational enhancement therapy. *Drug and Alcohol Dependence, 96*(1), 37-48. doi:https://doi.org/10.1016/j.drugalcdep.2008.01.020

Martino, S., Gallon, S., Ball, S. A., & Carroll, K. M. (2008). A Step Forward in Teaching Addiction Counselors How to Supervise Motivational Interviewing Using a Clinical Trials Training Approach. *Journal of Teaching in the Addictions, 6*(2), 39-67. doi:10.1080/15332700802127946

Marzano, R. (2010). *Teacher scales for reflective practice: Applying the art and science of teaching.* Englewood, Colorado: Marzano Research Laboratory: Englewood, Colorado: Marzano Research Laboratory.

Marzano, R., Waters, T., & McNulty, B. (2005). *School leadership that works: From research to results.* Alexandria, VA: Association for Supervision and Curriculum Development (ASCD).

Massatti, R., Sweeney, H., Panzano, P., & Roth, D. (2008). The de-adoption of innovative mental health practices (IMHP): Why organizations choose not to sustain an IMHP. *Administration and Policy in Mental Health and Mental Health Services Research, 35*(1-2), 50-65. doi:10.1007/s10488-007-0141-z

Masud Parvez, S., Azad, R., Rahman, M. M., Unicomb, L., Ram, P., Naser, A. M., . . . P. Luby, S. (2018). Achieving optimal technology and behavioral uptake of single and combined interventions of water, sanitation hygiene and nutrition, in an efficacy trial (WASH benefits) in rural Bangladesh. *Trials, 19*(358). doi:10.1186/s13063-018-2710-8

McDaniel, M. A., Whetzel, D. L., Schmidt, F. L., & Maurer, S. D. (1994). The validity of employment interviews: A comprehensive review and meta-analysis. *Journal of Applied Psychology, 79*(4), 599-616.

McGovern, M. P., Matzkin, A. L., & Giard, J. (2007). Assessing the Dual Diagnosis Capability of Addiction Treatment Services: The Dual Diagnosis Capability in Addiction Treatment (DDCAT) Index. *Journal of dual diagnosis, 3*(2), 111-123. doi:10.1300/J374v03n02_13

McGrew, J. H., Bond, G. R., Dietzen, L., & Salyers, M. P. (1994). Measuring the fidelity of implementation of a mental health program model. *Journal of Consulting & Clinical Psychology, 62*(4), 670-678.

McHugo, G. J., Drake, R. E., Teague, G. B., & Xie, H. (1999). Fidelity to assertive community treatment and client outcomes in the New Hampshire Dual Disorders Study. *Psychiatric Services, 50*(6), 818-824.

McIntosh, K., Mercer, S. H., Nese, R. N. T., & Ghemraoui, A. (2016). Identifying and Predicting Distinct Patterns of Implementation in a School-Wide Behavior Support Framework. *Prevention Science, 17*(8), 992-1001. doi:10.1007/s11121-016-0700-1

McIntosh, K., Mercer, S. H., Nese, R. N. T., Strickland-Cohen, M. K., & Hoselton, R. (2015). Predictors of sustained implementation of School-Wide Positive Behavioral Interventions and Supports. *Journal of Positive Behavior Interventions*, 1-10. doi:10.1177/1098300715599737

McNichol, D. (2006). *The roads that built America*. New York: Sterling Publishing Co.

Meldrum, M., & Atkinson, S. (1998). Meta-abilities and the implementation of strategy: Knowing what to do is simply not enough. *Journal of Management Development, 17*(8), 564-575. Retrieved from http://www.emeraldinsight.com/rpsv/~1120/v17n8/s3/p564.

Metz, A., & Albers, B. (2014). What Does It Take? How Federal Initiatives Can Support the Implementation of Evidence-Based Programs to Improve Outcomes for Adolescents. *Journal of Adolescent Health, 54*, S92-S96.

Metz, A., Bartley, L., Ball, H., Wilson, D., Naoom, S., & Redmond, P. (2014). Active Implementation Frameworks (AIF) for successful service delivery: Catawba County child wellbeing project. *Research on Social Work Practice, 25*(4), 415 - 422. doi:10.1177/1049731514543667

Meyers, D. C., Durlak, J. A., & Wandersman, A. (2012). The quality implementation framework: A synthesis of critical steps in the implementation process. *American Journal of Community Psychology, 50*(3-4), 462-480. doi:10.1007/s10464-012-9522-x

Michie, S., Fixsen, D., Grimshaw, J., & Eccles, M. (2009). Specifying and reporting complex behaviour change interventions: the need for a scientific method. *Implementation Science, 4*(1), 40. Retrieved from http://www.implementationscience.com/content/4/1/40.

Michie, S., Richardson, M., Johnston, M., Abraham, C., Francis, J., Hardeman, W., . . . Wood, C. E. (2013). The Behavior Change Technique Taxonomy (v1) of 93 Hierarchically Clustered Techniques: Building an International Consensus for the Reporting of Behavior Change Interventions. *Annals of Behavioral Medicine, 46*(1), 81-95. doi:10.1007/s12160-013-9486-6

Michie, S., van Stralen, M. M., & West, R. (2011). The behaviour change wheel: A new method for characterising and designing behaviour change interventions. *Implementation Science, 6*(1), 42. doi:10.1186/1748-5908-6-42

Michigan Department of Education. (2015). *Top 10 in 10 years: Goals and strategies.* Retrieved from Lansing, MI: Michigan Department of Education:

Milat, A. J., Bauman, A., & Redman, S. (2015). Narrative review of models and success factors for scaling up public health interventions. *Implementation Science, 10*(113). doi:10.1186/s13012-015-0301-6

Miller, J. G. (1991). Last One Over the Wall: The Massachusetts Experiment in Closing Reform Schools. Columbus: Ohio State University Press.

Miller, W. R. (2000, September 1). Guidelines from the International Motivational Interviewing Network of Trainers (MINT). *Motivational Interviewing Newsletter: Updates, Education, and Training*, pp. 2-3.

Miller, W. R., & Mount, K. A. (2001). A small study of training in motivational interviewing: Does one workshop change clinician and client behavior? . *Behavioural and Cognitive Psychotherapy, 29*, 457-471.

Miller, W. R., Yahne, C. E., Moyers, T. B., Martinez, J., & Pirritano, M. (2004). A Randomized Trial of Methods to Help Clinicians Learn Motivational Interviewing. *Journal of Consulting & Clinical Psychology, 72*(6), 1050-1062.

Minkin, N., Braukmann, C. J., Minkin, B. L., Timbers, G. D., Timbers, B. L., Fixsen, D. L., . . . Wolf, M. M. (1976). The social validation and training of conversation skills. *Journal of Applied Behavior Analysis, 9*, 127-139.

Modi, R. (2011). The magic lies in the magician, not in the wand. *Journal of Gynecological Endoscopy and Surgery, 2*(1). doi:10.4103/0974-1216.85270

Moll, L. C. (1990). Introduction to Vygotsky and Education: Instructional implications of sociohistorical psychology. In L. C. Moll (Ed.), *Vygotsky and education: Instructional implications of sociohistorical psychology* (pp. 1-30). Cambridge: Cambridge University Press.

Morgan, G. (1997). *Images of organization* (2nd ed.). Thousand Oaks, CA: Sage Publications.

Morgan, G., & Ramirez, R. (1983). Action learning: A holographic metaphor for guiding social change. *Human Relations, 37*(1), 1-28.

Morin, E. (2007). *On complexity.* Creskill, NJ: Hampton Press.

Morrissey, J. P., Calloway, M. O., Thakur, N., Cocozza, J., Steadman, H. J., & Dennis, D. (2002). Integration of service systems for homeless persons with serious mental illness through the ACCESS program. *Psychiatric Services, 53*(8), 949-957.

Mosson, R., von Thiele Schwarz, U., Hasson, H., Lundmark, R., & Richter, A. (2018). How do iLead? Validation of a scale measuring active and passive implementation leadership in Swedish healthcare. *BMJ Open, 8*(6). doi:10.1136/bmjopen-2018-021992

Murray, E., Treweek, S., Pope, C., MacFarlane, A., Ballini, L., Dowrick, C., . . . May, C. (2010). Normalisation process theory: A framework for developing, evaluating and implementing complex interventions. *BMC Medicine, 8*(63), 1-11. Retrieved from http://www.biomedcentral.com/1741-7015/8/63.

Mutamba, B. B., Kohrt, B. A., Okello, J., Nakigudde, J., Opar, B., Musisi, S., . . . de Jong, J. (2018). Contextualization of psychological treatments for government health systems in low-resource settings: group interpersonal psychotherapy for caregivers of children with nodding syndrome in Uganda. *Implementation Science, 13*(1), 90. doi:10.1186/s13012-018-0785-y

Naleppa, M. J., & Cagle, J. G. (2010). Treatment fidelity in social work intervention research: A review of published studies. *Research on Social Work Practice, 20*(6), 674-681. doi:10.1177/1049731509352088

Naoom, S. F., Blase, K. A., & Fixsen, D. L. (2006). *Lessons learned from 64 evidence-based program developers.* Retrieved from National Implementation Research Network, University of South Florida: https://www.activeimplementation.org/resources/lessons-learned-from-64-evidence-based-program-developers/

National Center for Education Statistics. (2013). *The Nation s Report Card: Trends in Academic Progress 2012.* Retrieved from Institute of Education Sciences, U.S. Department of Education: http://nces.ed.gov/nationsreportcard/subject/publications/main2012/pdf/2013456.pdf

National Commission on Excellence in Education. (1983). *A Nation at Risk: The Imperative for Educational Reform*. Retrieved from Washington, DC: U.S. Government Printing Office: http://nces.ed.gov/nationsreportcard/subject/publications/main2012/pdf/2013456.pdf

Navarro-Haro, M. V., Harned, M. S., Korslund, K. E., DuBose, A., Chen, T., Ivanoff, A., & Linehan, M. M. (2018). Predictors of Adoption and Reach Following Dialectical Behavior Therapy Intensive Training™. *Community Mental Health Journal*. doi:10.1007/s10597-018-0254-8

Nielsen, J. (2000). Why you only need to test with 5 users. Retrieved from http://www.useit.com/alertbox/20000319.html.

Nord, W. R., & Tucker, S. (1987). *Implementing routine and radical innovations*. Lexington, MA: D. C. Heath and Company.

Nutt, P. C. (2002). Why decisions fail: Avoiding the blunders and traps that lead to debacles. San Francisco: Berrett-Koehler Publishers Inc.

Ogden, T., Bjørnebekk, G., Kjøbli, J., Patras, J., Christiansen, T., Taraldsen, K., & Tollefsen, N. (2012). Measurement of implementation components ten years after a nationwide introduction of empirically supported programs – a pilot study. *Implementation Science, 7*, 49. Retrieved from http://www.implementationscience.com/content/pdf/1748-5908-7-49.pdf.

Ogden, T., Forgatch, M. S., Askeland, E., Patterson, G. R., & Bullock, B. M. (2005). Large scale implementation of Parent Management Training at the national level: The case of Norway. *Journal of Social Work Practice, 19*(3), 317-329.

Ohno, T. (1988). Toyota production system: Beyond large-scale production. New York: Productivity Press.

Olds, D. L., Hill, P. L., O'Brien, R., Racine, D., & Moritz, P. (2003). Taking preventive intervention to scale: The nurse-family partnership. *Cognitive and Behavioral Practice, 10*, 278-290.

Omimo, A., Taranta, D., Ghiron, L., Kabiswa, C., Aibe, S., Kodande, M., . . . Onduso, P. (2018). Applying ExpandNet's Systematic Approach to Scaling Up in an Integrated Population, Health and Environment Project in East Africa. *Social Sciences, 7*(1), 8. Retrieved from http://www.mdpi.com/2076-0760/7/1/8.

Osborne, D., & Gaebler, T. (1992). *Reinventing government*. NY: Addison-Wesley Publishing Co.

Oser, F. (2000). Self-efficacy and the school system. In W. J. Perrig & A. Grob (Eds.), *Control of human behavior, mental processes, and consciousness* (pp. 541-553). Mahwah, NJ: Lawrence Erlbaum Associates.

Øvretveit, J., Mittman, B., Rubenstein, L., & Ganz, D. A. (2017). Using Implementation Tools to Design and Conduct Quality Improvement Projects for Faster and More Effective Improvement. *International Journal of Health Care Quality Assurance, 30*(8), 755-768. doi:10.1108/IJHCQA-01-2017-0019

Oyeledun, B., Phillips, A., Oronsaye, F., Alo, O. D., Shaffer, N., Osibo, B., . . . Becquet, R. (2017). The Effect of a Continuous Quality Improvement Intervention on Retention-In-Care at 6 Months Postpartum in a PMTCT Program in Northern Nigeria: Results of a Cluster Randomized Controlled Study. *JAIDS Journal of Acquired Immune Deficiency Syndromes, 75*, S156-S164. doi:10.1097/qai.0000000000001363

Padgett, S. M., Bekemeier, B., & Berkowitz, B. (2005). Building sustainable public health: Systems change at the state level. *Journal of Public Health Management and Practice, 11*(2), 109-115.

Paneth, N. (2004). Assessing the Contributions of John Snow to Epidemiology: 150 Years After Removal of the Broad Street Pump Handle. *Epidemiology, 15*(5), 514-516. doi:10.1097/01.ede.0000135915.94799.00

Panzano, P. C., & Billings, R. S. (1994). The influence of issue frame and organizational slack on risky decision making: A field study. *Academy of Management Proceedings, 1994*(1), 377-381. doi:10.5465/ambpp.1994.10345891

Panzano, P. C., & Roth, D. (2006). The decision to adopt evidence-based and other innovative mental health practices: Risky business? *Psychiatric Services, 57*(8), 1153-1161.

Panzano, P. C., Seffrin, B., Chaney-Jones, S., Roth, D., Crane-Ross, D., Massatti, R., & Carstens, C. (2004). The innovation diffusion and adoption research project (IDARP). In D. Roth & W. Lutz (Eds.), *New Research in Mental Health* (Vol. 16, pp. 78-89). Columbus, OH: Ohio Department of Mental Health Office of Program Evaluation and Research.

Patton, G. C., Sawyer, S. M., Santelli, J. S., Ross, D. A., Afifi, R., Allen, N. B., . . . Viner, R. M. (2016). Our future: A Lancet commission on adolescent health and wellbeing. *The Lancet, 387*(10036), 2423-2478. doi:10.1016/S0140-6736(16)00579-1

Pérez, D., Van der Stuyft, P., Zabala, C. M., Castro, M., & Lefèvre, P. (2016). A modified theoretical framework to assess implementation fidelity of adaptive public health interventions. *Implementation Science, 11*(1), 1-11. doi:10.1186/s13012-016-0457-8

Perl, H. I. (2011). Addicted to discovery: Does the quest for new knowledge hinder practice improvement? *Addictive Behaviors, 36*(6), 590-596. doi:10.1016/j.addbeh.2011.01.027

Perla, R. J., Bradbury, E., & Gunther-Murphy, C. (2013). Large-Scale Improvement Initiatives in Healthcare: A Scan of the Literature. *Journal for Healthcare Quality, 35*(1), 30-40. doi:10.1111/j.1945-1474.2011.00164.x

Peters, T. J., & Waterman, R. H., Jr. (1982). *In Search of excellence: Lessons from America's best-run companies*. New York: Warner Books.

Phillips, E. L., Phillips, E. A., Fixsen, D. L., & Wolf, M. M. (1971). Achievement Place: Modification of Behaviors of Pre-Delinquent Boys within a Token Economy. *Journal of Applied Behavior Analysis, 4*(1), 45-54.

Phillips, E. L., Phillips, E. A., Fixsen, D. L., & Wolf, M. M. (1974). *The Teaching-Family handbook* (Second ed.). Lawrence. KS: University Press of Kansas.

Phillips, E. L., Phillips, E. A., Wolf, M. M., & Fixsen, D. L. (1973). Achievement Place: Development of the elected manager system. *Journal of Applied Behavior Analysis, 6*(4), 541-561.

Pinnock, H., Barwick, M., Carpenter, C. R., Eldridge, S., Grandes, G., Griffiths, C. J., . . . for the StaRI Group. (2017). Standards for Reporting Implementation Studies: (StaRI) Statement. *British Medical Journal, 356*(16795). doi:http://dx.doi.org/10.1136/bmj.i6795

Pirsig, R. M. (1974). Zen and the art of motorcycle maintenance: An inquiry into values. NY: William Morrow and Company, Inc.

Popper, K. (1963). Conjectures and refutations: The growth of scientific knowledge. New York: Harper Torchbooks.

Pressman, J. L., & Wildavsky, A. (1973). Implementation: How Great Expectations in Washington are Dashed in Oakland: or, Why It's Amazing that Federal Programs Work at All, This Being a Saga of the Economic Development Administration as Told by Two Sympathetic Observers Who Seek to Build Morals on a Foundation of Ruined Hopes. Berkeley, CA: University of California Press.

Prince, C. R., Hines, E. J., Chyou, P.-H., & Heegeman, D. J. (2014). Finding the Key to a Better Code: Code Team Restructure to Improve Performance and Outcomes. *Clinical Medicine & Research, 12*(1-2), 47-57. doi:10.3121/cmr.2014.1201

Prochaska, J. M., Prochaska, J. O., & Levesque, D. A. (2001). A transtheoretical approach to changing organizations. *Administration and Policy in Mental Health and Mental Health Services Research, 28*(4), 247-261. doi:10.1023/A:1011155212811

Prochaska, J. O., & DiClemente, C. C. (1984). *The transtheoretical approach: Towards a systematic eclectic framework*. Homewood, IL: Dow Jones Irwin.

Proctor, E. K., Landsverk, J., Aarons, G., Chambers, D., Glisson, C., & Mittman, B. (2009). Implementation research in mental health services: An emerging science with conceptual, methodological, and training challenges. *Administration and Policy in Mental Health and Mental Health Services Research, 36*(1), 24-34. doi:10.1007/s10488-008-0197-4

Proctor, E. K., Powell, B. J., & McMillen, C. J. (2013). Implementation strategies: Recommendations for specifying and reporting. *Implementation Science, 8*(1). doi:10.1186/1748-5908-8-139

Proctor, E. K., Silmere, H., Raghavan, R., Hovmand, P., Aarons, G., Bunger, A., . . . Hensley, M. (2011). Outcomes for Implementation Research: Conceptual Distinctions, Measurement Challenges, and Research Agenda. *Administration and Policy in Mental Health, 38*, 65-76. doi:10.1007/s10488-010-0319-7

Pronovost, P. J., Berenholtz, S. M., & Needham, D. M. (2008). Translating evidence into practice: A model for large scale knowledge translation. *British Medical Journal, 337*(7676), 963-965. Retrieved from http://www.jstor.org/stable/20511134.

Pülzl, H., & Treib, O. (2006). Implementing public policy. In F. Fischer, G. J. Miller, & M. S. Sidney (Eds.), *Handbook of public policy analysis* (pp. 89-108). New York: Dekker.

Puska, P., & Uutela, A. (2001). Community Intervention in Cardiovascular Health Promotion: North Karelia, 1972-1999. In N. Schneiderman, M. A. Speers, J. M. Silvia, J. H. Gentry, & G. H. Tomes (Eds.), *Integrating behavioral social sciences with public health.* Washington, DC: American Psychological Association.

Rahman, M., Ashraf, S., Unicomb, L., Mainuddin, A. K. M., Parvez, S. M., Begum, F., . . . Winch, P. J. (2018). WASH Benefits Bangladesh trial: system for monitoring coverage and quality in an efficacy trial. *Trials, 19*(1), 360. doi:10.1186/s13063-018-2708-2

Reger, R. K., Gustafson, L. T., DeMarie, S. M., & Mullane, J. V. (1994). Reframing the organization: Why implementing total quality is easier said than done. *Academy of Management Review, 19*, 565-584.

Reinke, W. M., Herman, K. C., Stormont, M., Newcomer, L., & David, K. (2013). Illustrating the Multiple Facets and Levels of Fidelity of Implementation to a Teacher Classroom Management Intervention. *Administration and Policy in Mental Health and Mental Health Services Research, 40*(6), 494-506. doi:10.1007/s10488-013-0496-2

Reiter-Lavery, L. (2004). *Finding great MST therapists: New and improved hiring guidelines.* Paper presented at the Third International MST Conference, MST Services, Charleston, SC.

Reppucci, N. D., & Saunders, J. T. (1974). Social psychology of behavior modification: Problems of implementation in natural settings. *American Psychologist, 29*(9), 649-660. doi:10.1037/h0037630

Rhim, L. M., Kowal, J. M., Hassel, B. C., & Hassel, E. A. (2007). *School turnarounds: A review of the cross-sector evidence on dramatic organizational improvement.* Retrieved from Lincoln, IL: http://www.centerii.org/restructuring/resources

Rittel, H. W. J., & Webber, M. M. (1973). Dilemmas in a general theory of planning. *Policy Sciences, 4*, 155-169.

Robbins, V., & Collins, K. (2010). *Implementation Drivers: An initial conversation when planning or reviewing a practice, program, or initiative.* Retrieved from Frankfort, KY: Kentucky Division of Mental Health and Substance Abuse:

Roberts, M. C. (Ed.) (1996). *Model programs in child and family mental health* Mahwah, NJ: Lawrence Erlbaum Associates.

Rogers, E. M. (1995). *Diffusion of Innovations* (4 ed.). New York: The Free Press.

Romney, S., Israel, N., & Zlatevski, D. (2014). Effect of exploration-stage implementation variation on the cost-effectiveness of an evidence-based parenting program. *Zeitschrift für Psychologie, 222*(1), 37-48. doi:10.1027/2151-2604/a000164

Rosenheck, R. A. (2001). Organizational process: A missing link between research and practice. *Psychiatric Services, 52*, 1607-1612.

Rossi, P. H., & Wright, J. D. (1984). Evaluation Research: An Assessment. *Annual Review of Sociology, 10*, 331-352.

Rubin, D. M., O'Reilly, A. L. R., Luan, X., Dai, D., Localio, A. R., & Christian, C. W. (2011). Variation in pregnancy outcomes following statewide implementation of a prenatal home visitation program. *Archives of Pediatric and Adolescent Medicine.*

Russell, C., Ward, C., Harms, A., St. Martin, K., Cusumano, D., Fixsen, D., . . . LeVesseur, C. (2016). *District Capacity Assessment Technical Manual.* Retrieved from National Implementation Research Network, University of North Carolina at Chapel Hill:

Ryan Jackson, K., Fixsen, D., Ward, C., Waldroup, A., Sullivan, V., Poquette, H., & Dodd, K. (2018). *Accomplishing effective and durable change to support improved student outcomes.* Retrieved from National Implementation Research Network, University of North Carolina at Chapel Hill:

Rycroft-Malone, J. (2004). The PARIHS framework: A framework for guiding the implementation of evidence-based practice. *Journal of Nursing Care Quality, 19*(4), 297-305.

Rycroft-Malone, J., Seers, K., Eldh, A. C., Cox, K., Crichton, N., Harvey, G., . . . Wallin, L. (2018). A realist process evaluation within the Facilitating Implementation of Research Evidence (FIRE) cluster randomised controlled international trial: an exemplar. *Implementation Science, 13*(1), 138. doi:10.1186/s13012-018-0811-0

Sabatier, P. A. (1986). Top-Down and Bottom-Up Approaches to Implementation Research: a Critical Analysis and Suggested Synthesis. *Journal of Public Policy, 6*(01), 21-48. doi:10.1017/S0143814X00003846

Saetren, H. (2005). Facts and myths about research on public policy implementation: Out-of-fashion, allegedly dead, but still very much alive and relevant. *The Policy Studies Journal, 33*(4), 559-582.

Saetren, H. (2014). Implementing the third generation research paradigm in policy implementation research: An empirical assessment. *Public Policy and Administration, 29*(2), 84-105. doi:10.1177/0952076713513487

Sailor, D. J., & Pavlova, A. A. (2003). Air conditioning market saturation and long-term response of residential cooling energy demand to climate change. *Energy, 28*(9), 941-951. doi:http://dx.doi.org/10.1016/S0360-5442(03)00033-1

Salazar, A. M., Haggerty, K. P., de Haan, B., Catalano, R. F., Vann, T., Vinson, J., & Lansing, M. (2016). Using communities that care for community child maltreatment prevention. *American Journal of Orthopsychiatry, 86*(2), 144-155. doi:10.1037/ort0000078

Saldana, L., & Chamberlain, P. (2012). Supporting Implementation: The Role of Community Development Teams to Build Infrastructure. *American Journal of Community Psychology, 50*(3-4), 334-346. doi:10.1007/s10464-012-9503-0

Saldana, L., Chamberlain, P., & Chapman, J. (2016). A Supervisor-Targeted Implementation Approach to Promote System Change: The R3 Model. *Administration and Policy in Mental Health and Mental Health Services Research.* doi:10.1007/s10488-016-0730-9

Saldana, L., Chamberlain, P., Wang, W., & Brown, H. C. (2012). Predicting program start-up using the stages of implementation measure. *Administration and Policy in Mental Health, 39*(6), 419-425. doi:10.1007/s10488-011-0363-y

Saldana, L., & Schaper, H. (personal communication, October 1, 2018). [Special analysis of SIC database].

Saliba, D., Rubenstein, L. V., Simon, B., Hickey, E., Ferrell, B., Czarnowski, E., & Berlowitz, D. (2003). Adherence to pressure ulcer prevention guidelines: Implications for nursing home quality. *Journal of the American Geriatrics Society, 51*(1), 56-62.

Salisbury, E. J., Sundt, J., & Boppre, B. (in press). Mapping the Implementation Landscape: Assessing the Systemic Capacity of Statewide Community Corrections Agencies to Deliver Evidence-Based Practices. *Corrections: Policy, Practice, and Research*(Special issue on Implementation and Effectiveness of Community Corrections).

Sandler, I., Ostrom, A., Bitner, M. J., Ayers, T. S., Wolchik, S., & Daniels, V. S. (2005). Developing effective prevention services for the real world: A prevention service development model. *American Journal of Community Psychology, 35*(3-4), 127-142.

Sanetti, L. M. H., & Kratochwill, T. (Eds.). (2014). *Treatment Integrity: A foundation for evidence-based practice in applied psychology* Washington, DC: American Psychological Association Press (Division 16).

Sarason, S. B. (1996). Revisiting "The culture of the school and the problem of change". New York: Teachers College Press.

Schein, E. (1992). *Organizational Culture and Leadership* (2 ed.): Jossey-Bass.

Scheirer, M. A. (2005). Is Sustainability Possible? A Review and Commentary on Empirical Studies of Program Sustainability. *American Journal of Evaluation, 26*(3), 320-347. doi:10.1177/1098214005278752

Schmidt, F. L., & Hunter, J. E. (1998). The validity and utility of selection methods in personnel psychology: Practical and theoretical implications of 85 years of research findings. *Psychological Bulletin, 124*(2), 262-274. doi:10.1037/0033-2909.124.2.262

Schoenwald, S. K., Brown, T. L., & Henggeler, S. W. (2000). Inside multisystemic therapy: Therapist, supervisory, and program practices. *Journal of Emotional and Behavioral Disorders, 8*(2), 113-127.

Schoenwald, S. K., Chapman, J. E., Kelleher, K., Hoagwood, K. E., Landsverk, J., Stevens, J., . . . Rolls-Reutz, J. (2008). A survey of the infrastructure for children's mental health services: Implications for the implementation of Empirically Supported Treatments (ESTs). *Adm Policy Ment Health, 35*, 84-97.

Schoenwald, S. K., & Garland, A. F. (2013). A review of treatment adherence measurement methods. *Psychological Assessment, 25*(1), 146-156. doi:10.1037/a0029715

Schoenwald, S. K., Halliday-Boykins, C. A., & Henggeler, S. W. (2003). Client-level predictors of adherence to MST in community service settings. *Family Process, 42*(3), 345-359.

Schoenwald, S. K., Sheidow, A. J., & Letourneau, E. J. (2004). Toward effective quality assurance in evidence-based practice: Links between expert consultation, therapist fidelity, and child outcomes. *Journal of Clinical Child & Adolescent Psychology, 33*(1), 94-104.

Schoenwald, S. K., Sheidow, A. J., Letourneau, E. J., & Liao, J. G. (2003). Transportability of Multisystemic Therapy: Evidence for Multilevel Influences. *Mental Health Services Research, 5*(4), 223-239.

Schofield, J. (2004). A model of learned implementation. *Public Administration, 82*(2), 283-308.

School Leaders Network. (2014). Churn: The high cost of principal turnover. Retrieved from https://connectleadsucceed.org

Schrenker, R., & Cooper, T. (2001). Building the Foundation for Medical Device Plug-and-Play Interoperability *Medical Electronics Manufacturing*(April), 10. Retrieved from http://www.24x7mag.com/2008/01/interoperability-is-just-around-the-corner8212right/.

Schrenker, R., & Cooper, T. (2018). Building the Foundation for Medical Device Plug-and-Play Interoperability Medical device communication standards are works in progress and hold the promise of universal communication among medical electronic devices and information systems.

Seers, K., Rycroft-Malone, J., Cox, K., Crichton, N., Edwards, R. T., Eldh, A. C., . . . Wallin, L. (2018). Facilitating Implementation of Research Evidence (FIRE): an international cluster randomised controlled trial to evaluate two models of facilitation informed by the Promoting Action on Research Implementation in Health Services (PARIHS) framework. *Implementation Science, 13*(1), 137. doi:10.1186/s13012-018-0831-9

Senge, P. M. (2006). The fifth discipline: The art and practice of the fifth discipline. New York: Doubleday.

Sexton, T. L., & Alexander, J. F. (2000). Functional family therapy. *Juvenile Justice Bulletin*, 1-7.

Sgaier, S. K., Ramakrishnan, A., Dhingra, N., Wadhwani, A., Alexander, A., Bennet, S., . . . Anthony, J. (2013). How the Avahan HIV Prevention Program Transitioned From the Gates Foundation to the Government of India. *Health Affairs, 32*(7), 1265-1273. doi:10.1377/hlthaff.2012.0646

Shelton, R. C., Lee, M., Brotzman, L. E., Crookes, D. M., Jandorf, L., Erwin, D., & Gage-Bouchard, E. (2018). Use of social network analysis in the development, dissemination, implementation, and sustainability of health behavior interventions for adults: A systematic review. *Social Science & Medicine*. doi:https://doi.org/10.1016/j.socscimed.2018.10.013

Shewhart, W. A. (1931). *Economic control of quality of manufactured product*. New York: D. Van Nostrand Co.

Shewhart, W. A. (1939). Statistical method from the viewpoint of quality control: Dover Publications.

Shin, M., Cha, Y., Ryu, K., & Jung, M. (2006). Conflict detection and resolution for goal formation in the fractal manufacturing system. *International Journal of Production Research, 44*(3), 447-465. doi:10.1080/00207540500142845

Shojania, K. G., & Grimshaw, J. M. (2005). Evidence-based quality improvement: the state of the science. *Health Affairs (Millwood), 24*(1), 138-150. doi:10.1377/hlthaff.24.1.138

Sigmarsdóttir, M., Forgatch, M., Vikar Guðmundsdóttir, E., Thorlacius, Ö., Thorn Svendsen, G., Tjaden, J., & Gewirtz, A. (2018). Implementing an Evidence-Based Intervention for Children in Europe: Evaluating the Full-Transfer Approach. *Journal of Clinical Child & Adolescent Psychology*, 1-14. doi:10.1080/15374416.2018.1466305

Skogøy, B. E., Sørgaard, K., Maybery, D., Ruud, T., Stavnes, K., Kufås, E., . . . Ogden, T. (2018). Hospitals implementing changes in law to protect children of ill parents: A cross-sectional study. *BMC Health Services Research, 18*. doi:http://dx.doi.org.libproxy.lib.unc.edu/10.1186/s12913-018-3393-2

Slavin, R. E., & Madden, N. A. (2004). Scaling up Success for All: Lessons for policy and practice. In T. K. Glennan Jr., S. J. Bodilly, J. R. Galegher, & K. A. Kerr (Eds.), *Expanding the reach of education reforms* (pp. 135-174). Santa Monica, CA: RAND Corporation.

Smith, S. N., Almirall, D., Prenovost, K., Goodrich, D. E., Abraham, K. M., Liebrecht, C., & Kilbourne, A. M. (2018). Organizational culture and climate as moderators of enhanced outreach for persons with serious mental illness: results from a cluster-randomized trial of adaptive implementation strategies. *Implementation Science, 13*(1), 93. doi:10.1186/s13012-018-0787-9

Snowden, D. J., & Boone, M. E. (2007). A leader's framework for decision making. *Harvard Business Review, 85*(11), 68-76.

Solberg, L. I. (2007). Improving medical practice: A conceptual framework. *Annals of Family Medicine, 5*, 251 - 256.

Solberg, L. I., Hroscikoski, M. C., Sperl-Hillen, J. M., O'Connor, P. J., & Crabtree, B. F. (2004). Key issues in transforming health care organizations for quality: the case of advanced access. *Joint Commission Journal on Quality and Patient Safety, 30*(1), 15-24.

Solnick, J. V., Braukmann, C. J., Bedlington, M. M., Kirigin, K. A., & Wolf, M. M. (1981). The relationship between parent-youth interaction and delinquency in group homes. *Journal of Abnormal Child Psychology, 9*(1), 107-119.

Speroff, T., & O'Connor, G. T. (2004). Study designs for PDSA quality improvement research. *Quality Management in Health Care, 13*(1), 17-32.

Spicer, N., Bhattacharya, D., Dimka, R., Fanta, F., Mangham-Jefferies, L., Schellenberg, J., . . . Wickremasinghe, D. (2014). Scaling-up is a craft not a science: Catalysing scale-up of health innovations in Ethiopia, India and Nigeria. *Social Science & Medicine, 121*, 30-38. doi:10.1016/j.socscimed.2014.09.046

Spoth, R., & Greenberg, M. (2011). Impact Challenges in Community Science-with-Practice: Lessons from PROSPER on Transformative Practitioner-Scientist Partnerships and Prevention Infrastructure Development. *American Journal of Community Psychology, 48*(1-2), 106-119. doi:10.1007/s10464-010-9417-7

Spoth, R., & Greenberg, M. T. (2005). Toward a comprehensive strategy for effective practitioner– scientist partnerships and larger-scale community health and well-being. *American Journal of Community Psychology, 35*(3-4), 107-126.

Spouse, J. (2001). Bridging theory and practice in the supervisory relationship: a sociocultural perspective. *Journal of Advanced Nursing, 33*(4), 512-522.

St. Martin, K., Ward, C., Harms, A., Russell, C., & Fixsen, D. L. (2015). *Regional capacity assessment (RCA) for scaling up implementation capacity*. Retrieved from National Implementation Research Network, University of North Carolina at Chapel Hill:

Stacey, R. D. (1996). *Complexity and creativity in organizations*. San Francisco: Berrett-Koehler Publishers.

Stacey, R. D. (2002). Strategic management and organisational dynamics: the challenge of complexity (3rd ed.): Harlow: Prentice Hall.

Stage, S. A., Jackson, H.G., Erickson M.J., Moscovitz, K.K., Bush, J.W., Violette, H. D., Ogier-Thurman, S., Olson, E., Bain, N., Jesse, W., & Pious, C. (2008). A validity study of functionally-based behavior consultation with students with emotional/behavioral disabilities. *School Psychology Quarterly, 23*(327-353).

Starfield, B. (2000). Is US health really the best in the world? *Journal of the American Medical Association, 284*(4), 483-485.

Stein, L. I., & Test, M. A. (1978). *Alternatives to mental hospital treatment*. New York: Plenum Press.

Sterman, J. D. (2006). Learning from evidence in a complex world. *American Journal of Public Health, 96*(3), 505-514. doi:10.2105/ajph.2005.066043

Stetler, C. B., Legro, M., Rycroft-Malone, J., Bowman, C., Curran, G., Guihan, M., . . . Wallace, C. (2006). Role of "external facilitation" in implementation of research findings: a qualitative evaluation of facilitation experiences in the Veterans Health Administration. *Implementation Science, 1*(1), 23. Retrieved from http://www.implementationscience.com/content/1/1/23.

Stetler, C. B., McQueen, L., Demakis, J., & Mittman, B. S. (2008). An organizational framework and strategic implementation for system-level change to enhance research-based practice: QUERI Series. *Implementation Science, 3*(30). doi:10.1186/1748-5908-3-30

Stith, S., Pruitt, I., Dees, J., Fronce, M., Green, N., Som, A., & Linkh, D. (2006). Implementing community-based prevention programming: A review of the literature. *The Journal of Primary Prevention, 27*(6). doi:10.1007/s10935-006-0062-8

Stolz, S. B. (1981). Adoption of innovations from applied behavioral research: "Does anybody care?". *Journal of Applied Behavioral Analysis, 14,* 491-505.

Stormont, M., Reinke, W. M., Newcomer, L., Marchese, D., & Lewis, C. (2014). Coaching teachers' use of social behavior interventions to improve children's outcomes: A review of the literature. *Journal of Positive Behavior Interventions.* doi:10.1177/1098300714550657

Stormont, M., Reinke, W. M., Newcomer, L., Marchese, D., & Lewis, C. (2015). Coaching Teachers' Use of Social Behavior Interventions to Improve Children 's Outcomes: A Review of the Literature. *Journal of Positive Behavior Interventions, 17*(2), 69-82. doi:10.1177/1098300714550657

Stringer, E. M., Ekouevi, D. K., Coetzee, D., & et al. (2010). Coverage of nevirapine-based services to prevent mother-to-child hiv transmission in 4 African countries. *JAMA, 304*(3), 293-302. doi:10.1001/jama.2010.990

Strongman, L. (2013). Complexity Theory—A Brief Introduction. *The General Science Journal,* 1-7.

Strouse, M. C., Carroll-Hernandez, T. A., Sherman, J. A., & Sheldon, J. B. (2004). Turning Over Turnover: The Evaluation of a Staff Scheduling System in a Community-Based Program for Adults with Developmental Disabilities. *Journal of Organizational Behavior Management, 23*(2), 45-63.

Sugai, G., Sprague, J., Horner, R., & Walker, H. (2000). Preventing school violence: The use of office discipline referrals to assess and monitor school-wide discipline interventions. *Journal of Emotional and Behavioral Disorders, 8*(2), 94-101.

Sutton, R. I., & Staw, B. M. (1995). What theory is not. *Administrative Science Quarterly, 40,* 371-384.

Svensson, J., Tomson, K., & Rindzeviciute, E. (2017). Policy change as institutional work: introducing cultural and creative industries into cultural policy. *Qualitative Research in Organizations and Management: An International Journal, 12*(2). doi:10.1108/QROM-05-2016-1380

Swales, M. A., Taylor, B., & Hibbs, R. A. (2012). Implementing Dialectical Behaviour Therapy: Programme survival in routine healthcare settings. *Journal of Mental Health, 21*(6), 548-555. doi:10.3109/09638237.2012.689435

Szapocznik, J., & Williams, R. A. (2000). Brief strategic family therapy: Twenty-five years of interplay among theory, research and practice in adolescent behavior problems and drug abuse. *Clinical Child and Famiy Psychology Review, 3*(2), 117-123.

Szulanski, G. (1996). Exploring internal stickiness: Impediments to the transfer of best practice within the firm. *Strategic Management Journal, 17*(Special Issue), 27-43.

Szulanski, G., & Jensen, R. J. (2006). Presumptive adaptation and the effectiveness of knowledge transfer. *Strategic Management Journal, 27*(10), 937-957. doi:10.1002/smj.551

Szulanski, G., & Jensen, R. J. (2008). Growing through copying: The negative consequences of innovation on franchise network growth. *Research Policy, 37*(10), 1732-1741.

Tabak, R. G., Khoong, E. C., Chambers, D. A., & Brownson, R. C. (2012). Bridging research and practice: Models for dissemination and implementation research. *American Journal of Preventive Medicine, 43*(3), 337-350.

Taylor, M. J., McNicholas, C., Nicolay, C., Darzi, A., Bel, D., & Reed, J. E. (2014). Systematic review of the application of the plan–do–study–act method to improve quality in healthcare. *British Medical Journal of Quality and Safety, 23*(290-298).

Teague, G. B., Bond, G. R., & Drake, R. E. (1998). Program fidelity in assertive community treatment: Development and use of a measure. *American Journal of Orthopsychiatry, 68*(2), 216-232.

Test, M. A. (2010). History of ACT. Retrieved from http://www.actassociation.org/origins/

Thomassen, O., Mann, C., Mbwana, J. S., & Brattebo, G. (2015). Emergency medicine in Zanzibar: the effect of system changes in the emergency department. *International Journal of Emergency Medicine, 8*(1), 22. doi:10.1186/s12245-015-0072-5

Thompson, R. W., Smith, G. L., Osgood, D. W., Dowd, T. P., Friman, P. C., & Daly, D. L. (1996). Residential care: A study of short- and long-term educational effects. *Children and Youth Services Review, 18*(3), 221-242. doi:https://doi.org/10.1016/0190-7409(96)00002-3

Tikkanen, L., Pyhältö, K., Soini, T., & Pietarinen, J. (2016). Primary determinants of a large-scale curriculum reform – National board administrators' perspectives. *Journal of Educational Administration, 0*(ja), 00-00. doi:10.1108/JEA-10-2016-0119

Tilly III, W. D. (2008). *How To Pin the Pendulum to the Wall: Practical Strategies to Create Lasting Change in Schools.* Paper presented at the ABAI Evidence-Based Education Conference, Reston, VA.

Tiruneh, G. T., Karim, A. M., Avan, B. I., Zemichael, N. F., Wereta, T. G., Wickremasinghe, D., . . . Betemariam, W. A. (2018). The effect of implementation strength of basic emergency obstetric and newborn care (BEmONC) on facility deliveries and the met need for BEmONC at the primary health care level in Ethiopia. *BMC Pregnancy and Childbirth, 18*(1), 123. doi:10.1186/s12884-018-1751-z

Titler, M. G., Kleiber, C., Steelman, V. J., Rakel, B. A., Budreau, G., Everett, L. Q., . . . Goode, C. J. (2001). The Iowa Model of Evidence-Based Practice to Promote Quality Care. In J. Rycroft-Malone & T. Bucknell (Eds.), *Models and Frameworks for Implementing Evidence-Based Practice: Linking Evidence to Action* (pp. 137-146). NY: John Wiley & Sons.

Tofail, F., Fernald, L. C., Das, K. K., Rahman, M., Ahmed, T., Jannat, K. K., . . . Luby, S. P. (2018). Effect of water quality, sanitation, hand washing, and nutritional interventions on child development in rural Bangladesh (WASH Benefits Bangladesh): a cluster-randomised controlled trial. *Lancet Child & Adolescent Health, 2*(4), 255-268. doi:10.1016/S2352-4642(18)30031-2

Tommeraas, T., & Ogden, T. (2016). Is There a Scale-up Penalty? Testing Behavioral Change in the Scaling up of Parent Management Training in Norway. *Administration and Policy in Mental Health and Mental Health Services Research, 44*, 203-216. doi:10.1007/s10488-015-0712-3

Tornatzky, L. G., Fergus, E. O., Avellar, J. W., Fairweather, G. W., & Fleischer, M. (1980). *Innovation and social process: A national experiment in implementing social technology.* New York: Pergamon Press.

Tucker, A. L., & Singer, S. J. (2015). The Effectiveness of Management-By-Walking-Around: A Randomized Field Study. *Production and Operations Management, 24*(2), 253-271. doi:10.1111/poms.12226

Tyack, D., & Cuban, C. (1995). *Tinkering toward utopia: A century of public school reform.* Cambridge, MA: Harvard University Press.

U.S. Department of Health and Human Services. (1999). *Mental health: A report of the Surgeon General.* Retrieved from Rockville, MD: U.S. Department of Health and Human Services:

U.S. Government Accounting Office. (2009). Program evaluation: A variety of rigorous methods can help identify effective interventions. Retrieved from http://gao.gov/products/GAO-10-30

Ulrich, W. M. (2002). *Legacy systems: Transformation strategies.* Upper Saddle River, NJ: Prentice Hall PTR.

Unger, J. P., Macq, J., Bredo, F., & Boelaert, M. (2000). Through Mintzberg's glasses: a fresh look at the organization of ministries of health. *Bulletin of the World Health Organization, 78*(8), 1005-1014.

Useem, M., & Chipande, G. (1991). Centralization and Experimentation in the Implementation of a National Monitoring and Evaluation System: The Experience of Malawi. *Evaluation Review, 15*(2), 233-253.

Van Dyke, M. K. (2015). *Active implementation practitioner: Practice profile.* Retrieved from Chapel Hill, NC: Active Implementation Research Network: https://www.activeimplementation.org/resources/active-implementation-practitioner-practice-profile/

Van Dyke, M. K., Kiser, L., & Blase, K. A. (2019). *The heptagon tool.* Retrieved from Chapel Hill, NC: Active Implementation Research Network: www.activeimplementation.org/resources

Van Meter, D. S., & Van Horn, C. E. (1975). The policy implementation process: A conceptual framework. *Administration & Society, 6,* 445-488.

VanDeusen Lukas, C., Holmes, S. K., Cohen, A. B., Restuccia, J., Cramer, I. E., Shwartz, M., & Charns, M. P. (2007). Transformational change in health care systems: An organizational model. *Health Care Management Review, 32*(4), 309-320.

Varella, J. A. (1977). Social technology. *American Psychologist, 32,* 914-923.

Vernez, G., Karam, R., Mariano, L. T., & DeMartini, C. (2006). *Evaluating comprehensive school reform models at scale: Focus on implementation.* Retrieved from Santa Monica, CA: http://www.rand.org/

Voit, E. S. (1995). Developing a Research Program: Saleem Shah's Leadership Role at the National Institute of Mental Health. *Law and Human Behavior, 19*(1), 5-14.

Von Krogh, G., Ichijo, K., & Nonaka, I. (2000). *Enabling knowledge creation.* New York, NY: Oxford University Press.

Voorberg, W. H., Bekkers, V. J., & Tummers, L. G. (2015). A systematic review of co-creation and co-production: Embarking on the social innovation journey. *Public Management Review, 17*(9), 1333-1357.

Vrakking, W. J. (1995). The implementation game. *Journal of Organizational Change Management, 8*(3), 31-46.

Wafa, M. A., & Yasin, M. M. (1998). A conceptual framework for effective implementation of JIT: An empirical investigation. *International Journal of Operations and Production Management, 18*(11), 1111-1124.

Walker, J., Koroloff, N., & Schutte, K. (2003). *Implementing high-quality collaborative Individualized Service/Support Planning: Necessary conditions.* Portland, OR: Portland

State University, Research and Training Center on Family Support and Children's Mental Health.

Walsh, C., Ryan, P., & Flynn, D. (2018). Exploring dialectical behaviour therapy clinicians' experiences of team consultation meetings. *Borderline Personality Disorder and Emotion Dysregulation, 5*(1), 3. doi:10.1186/s40479-018-0080-1

Wandersman, A. (2003). Community Science: Bridging the Gap between Science and Practice with Community-Centered Models. *American Journal of Community Psychology, 31*(3-4), 227-242.

Wandersman, A., Duffy, J., Flaspohler, P., Nonnan., R., Lubell, K., Stillman, L., . . . Saul, J. (2008). Bridging the gap between prevention research and practice: The interactive systems framework for dissemination and implementation. *American Journal of Community Psychology, 41*, 171-181.

Wang, W., Saldana, L., Brown, C. H., & Chamberlain, P. (2010). Factors that influenced county system leaders to implement an evidence-based program: a baseline survey within a randomized controlled trial. *Implementation Science, 5*(1), 72. doi:10.1186/1748-5908-5-72

Ward, C., Lenard, M., Tillery, D., Miller, A., Preston, A., & Cusumano, D. (2017). *Instructional Practice and Student Achievement: Validating a Contemporary Classroom Walkthrough Tool.* Retrieved from National Implementation Research Network, University of North Carolina at Chapel Hill:

Ward, C., Ryan Jackson, K., Cusumano, D., & Fixsen, D. (2018). *State Capacity Development Plan.* Retrieved from National Implementation Research Network, University of North Carolina at Chapel Hill:

Ward, C., St. Martin, K., Horner, R., Duda, M., Ingram-West, K., Tedesco, M., . . . Chaparro, E. (2015). *District Capacity Assessment.* Retrieved from National Implementation Research Network, University of North Carolina at Chapel Hill:

Washington State Institute for Public Policy. (2002). *Washington State's Implementation of Functional Family Therapy for Juvenile Offenders: Preliminary Findings* (02-08-1201). Retrieved from Olympia, WA: http://www.wsipp.wa.gov/pub.asp?docid=02-08-1201

Washington State Institute for Public Policy. (2016). Benefit-cost analysis: Juvenile justice. Retrieved from http://www.wsipp.wa.gov/benefitcost

Watkins, C. L. (1995). Follow Through: Why didn't we? *Effective School Practices, 15*(1), 57-66.

Watson, D. P., Adams, E. L., Shue, S., Coates, H., McGuire, A., Chesher, J., . . . Omenka, O. I. (2018). Defining the external implementation context: an integrative systematic literature review. *BMC Health Services Research, 18*(1), 209. doi:10.1186/s12913-018-3046-5

Webster-Stratton, C. H., Reid, J. M., & Marsenich, L. (2014). Improving Therapist Fidelity During Implementation of Evidence-Based Practices: Incredible Years Program. *Psychiatric Services, 65*(6), 789-795. doi:10.1176/ appi.ps.201200177

Weick, K. E. (1979). *The Social Psychology of Organizing*. Reading, MA: Addison-Wesley.

Weick, K. E. (1987). Organizational culture as a source of high reliability. *California Management Review, 29*(2), 112-128.

Weick, K. E. (1995). *Sensemaking in Organizations*. Thousand Oaks, CA: Sage Publications.

Weick, K. E., Sutcliffe, K. M., & Obstfeld, D. (1999). Organizing for high reliability: Processes of collective mindfulness. In R. S. Sutton & B. M. Staw (Eds.), *Research in Organizational Behavior* (pp. 81-123). Stanford, CA: Jai Press.

Weiner, B. (2009). A theory of organizational readiness for change. *Implementation Science, 4*(1), 67. Retrieved from http://www.implementationscience.com/content/4/1/67.

Weiner, B., Lewis, C. C., Stanick, C., Powell, B. J., Dorsey, C. N., Clary, A. S., . . . Halko, H. (2017). Psychometric assessment of three newly developed implementation outcome measures. *Implementation Science, 12*(1), 108. doi:10.1186/s13012-017-0635-3

Weinrott, M. R., Jones, R. R., & Howard, J. R. (1982). Cost-effectiveness of teaching family programs for delinquents: Results of a national evaluation. *Evaluation Review, 6*(2), 173-201.

Werner, J. S., Minkin, N., Minkin, B. L., Fixsen, K. L., Phillips, E. L., & Wolf, M. M. (1975). Intervention Package: An analysis to prepare juvenile delinquents for encounters with police officers. *Criminal Justice and Behavior, 2*, 55-83.

Westphal, J. D., Gulati, R., & Shortell, S. M. (1997). Customization or conformity? An institutional and network perspective on the content and consequences of TQM adoption. *Administrative Science Quarterly, 42*(2), 366-394.

Whyte, L. L. (1944). *Next development in man*. London: Cresset Press.

Williams, N. J., Ehrhart, M. G., Aarons, G. A., Marcus, S. C., & Beidas, R. S. (2018). Linking molar organizational climate and strategic implementation climate to clinicians' use of evidence-based psychotherapy techniques: cross-sectional and lagged analyses from a 2-year observational study. *Implementation Science, 13*(1), 85. doi:10.1186/s13012-018-0781-2

Williams, W. (1975). Implementation analysis and assessment. *Policy Analysis, 1*, 531-566.

Willner, A. G., Braukmann, C. J., Kirigin, K. A., Fixsen, D. L., Phillips, E. L., & Wolf, M. M. (1977). The training and validation of youth-preferred social behaviors of child-care personnel. *Journal of Applied Behavior Analysis, 10*, 219-230.

Wilson, P. F., Dell, L. D., & Anderson, G. F. (1993). *Root Cause Analysis: A Tool for Total Quality Management*. Milwaukee, WI: ASQ Quality Press.

Winter, S. G., & Szulanski, G. (2001). Replication as Strategy. *Organization Science, 12*(6), 730-743.

Wolf, M. M. (1978). Social Validity: The case for subjective measurement or how applied analysis is finding its heart. *Journal of Applied Behavior Analysis, 11*, 203-214.

Wolf, M. M. (2001). Application of operant conditioning procedures to the behavior problems of an autistic child: A 25-year follow-up and the development of the Teaching-Family Model. In W. T. O'Donohue, D. A. Henderson, S. C. Hayes, J. E. Fisher, & L. J. Hayes (Eds.), *A history of the behavioral therapies: Founders' personal histories* (pp. 289-294). Reno, Nevada: Context Press.

Wolf, M. M., Kirigin, K. A., Fixsen, D. L., Blase, K. A., & Braukmann, C. J. (1995). The Teaching-Family Model: A case study in data-based program development and refinement (and dragon wrestling). *Journal of Organizational Behavior Management, 15*, 11-68.

Wootton, D. (2015). The invention of science: A new history of the scientific revolution. New York: Harper Collins.

World Health Organization. (2015). *Health in 2015: from MDGs, Millennium Development Goals to SDGs, Sustainable Development Goals*. Retrieved from Geneva, Switzerland: World Health Organization: www.who.int

Wright, J. S., Wall, H. K., & Ritchey, M. D. (2018). Million hearts 2022: Small steps are needed for cardiovascular disease prevention. *JAMA*. doi:10.1001/jama.2018.13326

Wroe, E. B., McBain, R. K., Michaelis, A., Dunbar, E. L., Hirschhorn, L. R., & Cancedda, C. (2017). A Novel Scenario-Based Interview Tool to Evaluate Nontechnical Skills and Competencies in Global Health Delivery. *Journal of Graduate Medical Education, 9*(4), 467-472. doi:10.4300/jgme-d-16-00848.1

Yapa, H. M., & Bärnighausen, T. (2018). Implementation science in resource-poor countries and communities. *Implementation Science, 13*(1), 154. doi:10.1186/s13012-018-0847-1

Yeaton, W. H., & Sechrest, L. (1981). Critical dimensions in the choice and maintenance of successful treatments: Strength, integrity, and effectiveness. *Journal of Consulting & Clinical Psychology, 49*, 156-167.

Zaccaro, S. J., Blair, V., Peterson, C., & Zazanis, M. (1995). Collective Efficacy. In J. E. Maddux (Ed.), *Self-efficacy, adaptation, and adjustment: theory, research, and application* (pp. 305-328). Boston, MA: Springer US.

Zahra, S. A., & George, G. (2002). Absorptive capacity: A review, reconceptualization, and extension. *Academy of Management Review, 27*(2), 185-203.

Zimmerman, B., Lindberg, C., & Plsek, P. (1998). *Edgeware: Insights from complexity science for health care leaders.* Retrieved from Irving, TX: VHA Publishing:

Zucker, L. G. (1987). Institutional theories of organizations. *Annual Review of Sociology, 13,* 443-464.

Made in the USA
Las Vegas, NV
27 May 2021